Malaysia

Recent Trends and Challenges

The **Institute of Southeast Asian Studies (ISEAS)** was established as an autonomous organisation in 1968. It is a regional research centre for scholars and other specialists concerned with modern Southeast Asia, particularly the many-faceted issues and challenges of stability and security, economic development, and political and social change.

The Institute's research programmes are Regional Economic Studies (RES, including ASEAN and APEC), Regional Strategic and Political Studies (RSPS), and Regional Social and Cultural Studies (RSCS).

ISEAS Publications, an established academic press, has issued more than 1,000 books and journals. It is the largest scholarly publisher of research about Southeast Asia from within the region. ISEAS Publications works with many other academic and trade publishers and distributors to disseminate important research and analyses from and about Southeast Asia to the rest of the world.

Malaysia

Recent Trends and Challenges

EDITED BY

SAW SWEE-HOCK

K. KESAVAPANY

INSTITUTE OF SOUTHEAST ASIAN STUDIES
Singapore

First published in Singapore in 2006 by
Institute of Southeast Asian Studies
30 Heng Mui Keng Terrace
Pasir Panjang
Singapore 119614

Internet e-mail: publish@iseas.edu.sg
World Wide Web: http://bookshop.iseas.edu.sg

This book is published under the Malaysia Study Programme
funded by Professor Saw Swee-Hock.

ISEAS Library Cataloguing-in-Publication Data

Malaysia : recent trends and challenges / edited by Saw Swee-Hock and
K. Kesavapany.
1. Malaysia—Politics and government.
2. Islam and politics—Malaysia.
3. Malaysia—Population.
4. Elections—Malaysia.
5. Malaysia—Economic conditions.
6. Corporate governance—Malaysia.
7. Malaysia—Foreign relations—Singapore.
8. Singapore—Foreign relations—Malaysia.
I.   Saw, Swee-Hock, 1931-
II. Kesavapany, K.
DS597.2 M232   2006

ISBN 981-230-336-7 (soft cover)
ISBN 981-230-339-1 (hard cover)

Typeset by International Typesetters Pte. Ltd.
Printed in Singapore by Utopia Press Pte. Ltd.

Contents

Preface   vii

Foreword by Wang Gungwu   viii

Contributors   xi

1   Population Trends and Patterns in Multiracial Malaysia   1
Saw Swee-Hock

2   The Emerging Politics of *Islam Hadhari*   26
Terence Chong

3   Bangsa Malaysia: Vision or Spin?   47
Ooi Kee Beng

4   The 2004 Malaysian General Elections: Economic   73
Development, Electoral Trends, and the Decline of the
Opposition
Edmund Terence Gomez

5   The UMNO-PAS Struggle: Analysis of PAS's Defeat   100
in 2004
Ahmad Fauzi Abdul Hamid

6   The Malay Electorate in 2004: Reversing the 1999 Result?   132
    John Funston

7   UMNO and BN in the 2004 Election: The Political   157
    Culture of Complex Identities
    Zainal Kling

8   Malaysia's Civil Service Reform: Mahathir's Legacies and   195
    Abdullah's Challenges
    Ho Khai Leong

9   Reinventing Governance in Corporate Malaysia: 210
    The Challenges Ahead
    Michael Yeoh and Farizal Hj. Mohd. Razalli

10 Globalisation and Ethnic Integration in Malaysian   230
    Education
    Lee Hock Guan

11 Globalisation and the Challenges Facing Malaysia's   260
    Economy
    Denis Hew

12 Promising Start to Malaysia-Singapore Relations   275
    K. Kesavapany

Bibliography   287

Index   305

Preface

The chapters in this book are derived from commissioned papers and those presented at an ISEAS Workshop entitled "The Political Economy of Malaysia: Current Trends and Future Challenges" held in September 2004. Chapters 1, 2, 10, and 12 are specially commissioned from ISEAS scholars who are experts in their own field of interest. The other eight chapters are extensively revised versions of the papers presented at the Workshop. Both the Workshop and this book are the products of the Institute's Malaysia Study Programme.

We would like to thank Professor Wang Gungwu, Chairman of the ISEAS Board of Trustees, for contributing the Foreword, ISEAS scholars for preparing the commissioned essays, and the Workshop speakers for revising their papers for publication.

Saw Swee-Hock and K. Kesavapany

Foreword

I am very pleased to have been invited to take part in the one-day workshop on "The Political Economy of Malaysia: Current Trends and Future Challenges" held at the Institute of Southeast Asian Studies, Singapore, in September 2004. Most of the papers were by scholars from Malaysia and Singapore who were still very young at the time when Singapore was separated from the Federation of Malaysia. They would not have had the searing experience of the tensions that led the two to separate in 1965, but both have lived through some of the consequences of that separation and are now able to examine coolly the most recent manifestations of what I see as the "one plural society, two countries, two systems" syndrome. There have certainly been many ups and downs in that bifocal effect for the past 40 years.

After an absence of 28 years, I returned in 1996 to the plural society in which I had grown up, from where I had received my education and where I had taught for ten exhilarating years. This was on the eve of the financial crisis that badly hurt the region. That crisis contributed to the tense relationship between Malaysia and Singapore for the next seven years, although among observers, some of the issues seemed unnecessarily discordant. Only on the rare occasions when scholars of both countries came together to discuss the issues in dispute, often at the Institute of

Southeast Asian Studies (ISEAS), was I reminded of the underlying oneness of all the protagonists concerned. The workshop in 2004 that led to this volume of essays was an exceptionally warm gathering of like-minded authors who rejoiced at the restored friendliness between the two countries. It had, of course, as everyone commented, much to do with the fresh tone of the administration under the new prime minister, Datuk Seri Abdullah Badawi. The 11 months before the workshop had seen a marked improvement in the way various leaders of the two countries had begun to conduct diplomacy with one another. The changes are outlined in the last chapter in this volume by the Director of ISEAS, K. Kesavapany, who also recalls for us what he knows only too well: how it felt during those difficult years before he joined ISEAS, when he served as Singapore's High Commissioner to Malaysia.

The chapters here contain detailed information about the changes that are taking place in Malaysia, much of it of great importance to all Singaporeans who have business or family in Malaysia, those who have to deal with Malaysian officials at all levels, and not least, those whose job it is to analyse the longer-term trends in development that are likely to have profound bearing on both countries. Of immediate interest are the chapters examining the Malaysian general elections of 2004. The many facets of Malaysian society reflected in the way opposition political parties and their allies have sought to challenge the new leadership of the dominant member of the Barisan Nasional, the United Malays' National Organisation (UMNO), are particularly revealing. Understanding the changes occurring in that arena leads one to better appreciate the broader issues of governance and adaptation to global economic challenges that Malaysia still has to confront. At an even deeper level, we are shown some of the longer demographic trends, the undercurrents in the shaping of *Islam Hadhari* as a new marker for social harmony, and the re-examination of educational goals for nation-building, all key factors that will surround the future of *Bangsa Malaysia* for a long time to come. How these are eventually resolved would be of special importance to those tasked with determining how Singapore itself moulds its own national identity. Although such subterranean currents are difficult to observe from year to year, they should always be kept in mind as new generations in Malaysia and Singapore contemplate the darker aspects of their heritage, those earlier acts of truculence, and displays of distrust that had prevented greater cooperation in areas of mutual interest.

I am encouraged to see so much fraternal feelings among Malaysians and Singaporeans coming through in the 12 chapters here. It reminds me how strong that had been when I was young and how carefully nurtured it was in ISEAS right from the day it was founded. ISEAS was established in part to help ameliorate the painful feelings that accompanied the separation and to put in place a cross-border institution that would regularly bring scholars to re-examine and keep alive the positive relations that the peoples on both sides of the Straits of Johore have long enjoyed. I am delighted that ISEAS has sustained this role in the way that it has. This volume is a fine example of the efforts made by scholars on both sides to cement a feeling of trust.

Wang Gungwu
Director
East Asia Institute, Singapore

Contributors

Ahmad Fauzi Abdul Hamid is Senior Lecturer in Political Science at the School of Distance Education, Universiti Sains Malaysia, Penang. He holds a Ph.D. from the University of Newcastle-upon-Tyne and has published widely in recent years. He has also been an active contributor to the discourse on political Islam in Malaysia. In July 2005, he delivered the findings of his research entitled "The Education Strategy of Islamic Movements in Malaysia" at a regional workshop in Solo, Indonesia.

Terence Chong is a Fellow at the Institute of Southeast Asian Studies (ISEAS), Singapore, co-editor of *SOJOURN*, and editor of *TRENDS in Southeast Asia*. He received his Ph.D. in Sociology from the University of Warwick. As a sociologist, his research interests include the Southeast Asian middle-class and globalisation, political Islam in Malaysia, civil society in Southeast Asia, and the sociology of culture. He is currently the editor of a book on cultural globalisation in Southeast Asia and is the author of a forthcoming book on the sociology of Singapore theatre.

John Funston is Executive Director of the National Thai Studies Centre and a Visiting Fellow in the Faculty of Asian Studies, Australian National University. He holds a Ph.D. from the Australian National University. His major publications include the edited volume *Government and Politics in Southeast Asia* in which he contributed chapters on Malaysia and Thailand, and *Malay Politics in Malaysia: A Study of UMNO and PAS*.

Edmund Terence Gomez is Research Coordinator at the United Nations Research Institute for Social Development. He was formerly Associate Professor in the Faculty of Economics and Administration, University of Malaya. He received his Ph.D. in Development Studies from the University of Malaya. Among the books he has published are *Malaysia's Political Economy: Politics, Patronage and Profits*; *Chinese Business in Malaysia: Accumulation, Accommodation, Ascendance*; *Ethnic Futures: The State and Identity Politics in Asia*; *Chinese Business in Southeast Asia*; *Political Business in East Asia*; *Chinese Enterprise, Transnationalism and Identity*; and *The State of Malaysia: Ethnicity, Equity and Reform*.

Denis Hew is a Fellow and Coordinator of the Regional Economic Studies Programme at the Institute of Southeast Asian Studies, Singapore. He is also co-editor of the *ASEAN Economic Bulletin*, a leading academic journal that focuses on economic issues in Southeast Asia. Before joining ISEAS, he was Senior Analyst at the Institute of Strategic and International Studies, Malaysia. He holds a Ph.D. in Finance from the University of Manchester. His research interests include economic and financial development in Malaysia and ASEAN economic integration. His major publications are the edited volumes *Capital Markets in Asia: Changing Roles for Economic Development*; *APEC in the 21st Century*; and *Entrepreneurship and SMEs in Southeast Asia*.

Ho Khai Leong is a Research Fellow at the Institute of Southeast Asian Studies, Singapore. He received his Ph.D. from Ohio State University, USA. His current research interests include Malaysia and Singapore politics, political economy of Southeast Asia, China-ASEAN relations, corporate governance, and administrative reforms. He is the author of

Shared Responsibilities, Unshared Power: The Politics of Policy-making in Singapore and his latest publication is *Reforming Corporate Governance in Southeast Asia: Economics, Politics and Regulations,* in which he is both editor and contributor.

K. Kesavapany is Director of the Institute of Southeast Asian Studies, Singapore. He was Singapore's High Commissioner to Malaysia from 1997 to 2002. He also served as Singapore's Permanent Representative to the UN in Geneva and was concurrently accredited as Ambassador to Italy and Turkey. He was elected as the first Chairman of the General Council of the WTO when it was established in January 1995. He also led the Singapore team in the Korea-Singapore Free Trade Agreement (FTA) negotiations. Mr Kesavapany was awarded the Singapore Government Public Administration Medal (Gold) and the Long Service Medal. He was also awarded Order of Independence (first class) by the Hashemite Kingdom of Jordan and the Chilean Presidential Medal of the Centennial of Pablo Neruda in July 2004.

Zainal Kling is Professor in Anthropology and Sociology at the University of Malaya. He received his Ph.D. from the University of Hull. His interests are in the areas of social sciences in Southeast Asia with particular emphasis on family and kinship, social policy, social problems, and culture and socialisation. He has written several books as well as numerous journal articles.

Lee Hock Guan is a Fellow and Coordinator of the Regional, Social, and Cultural Studies Programme at the Institute of Southeast Asian Studies, Singapore. He received his Ph.D. in Sociology from Brandies University and his current research interests are civil society and democratisation, and ethnicity, nationalism, and citizenship in Southeast Asia, with special focus on Malaysia. His major publications include an edited volume on *Civil Society in Southeast Asia.*

Farizal Hj. Mohd. Razalli was formerly Head of the Policy and Research Unit at the Asian Strategy and Leadership Institute, Kuala Lumpur, and is currently undertaking an Erasmus Mundus scholarship under the European Union in Germany and Austria. His research interests are international political economics, international organisations, and trade arrangements. Among his recent publications are *ASLI's Business Outlook Survey Report 2004/2005* and *2005/2006* and *ASLI's Economic Forecast 2005*. His most recent paper, "The Impacts of Foreign Workers on Malaysian Society", was presented at the National Seminar on Unity.

Ooi Kee Beng is a Fellow and Coordinator of the Malaysia Study Programme at the Institute of Southeast Asian Studies, Singapore. He received his Ph.D. in Sinology from Stockholm University, Sweden. He is presently working on a biography of Malaysia's Tun Dr Ismail. His publications include reviews, articles, and books on Malaysian ethnography, politics, history and current affairs, the Chinese diaspora, language philosophy, political theory, Asian regionalism, and Chinese philosophy. Between 1996 and 2004, he lectured on Chinese history, history of Chinese ideas, and general knowledge of China at Stockholm University. Between 1997 and 2002, he translated Chinese classics on war strategy into Swedish for the Stockholm Military College.

Saw Swee-Hock is Professorial Fellow and Adviser to the Malaysia Study Programme at the Institute of Southeast Asian Studies, Singapore. He received his Ph.D. in Statistics from the London School of Economics. He was formerly Senior Lecturer in Statistics at the University of Malaya, Kuala Lumpur, and Professor of Statistics at the University of Hong Kong and the National University of Singapore. He is currently Council Member of the National University of Singapore and a recipient of its Distinguished Alumni Service Award. Among his major publications are *A Guide to Conducting Surveys*; *Malayan Economic Statistics*; *Changing Labour Force of Malaysia*; *The Population of Peninsular Malaysia*; *The Population of Singapore*; *Population Policies and Programmes in Singapore*; *ASEAN Economies in Transition* (editor); and *Investment Management*.

Michael Yeoh is Co-Founder and Chief Executive Officer of the Asian Strategy and Leadership Institute, Kuala Lumpur. He received his Ph.D.

in Organisational Development from the Irish International University. He is Secretary-General of the Corporate Malaysia Roundtable, the Non-Aligned Movement Business Council, and the Malaysia-China Business Council. He served on the Royal Commission on Police and the National Economic Consultative Council. He is the author of several books including *Vision and Leadership: Strategies for Vision 2020, Management Strategies for Vision 2020,* and *Globalization and the New South.* He also edited the book *Bridging the Divide.*

1

Population Trends and Patterns in Multiracial Malaysia

SAW SWEE-HOCK

Introduction

The demographic data upon which this chapter is based are extracted from the four pan-Malaysia Censuses of Population conducted after the formation of the Federation of Malaysia on 31 August 1963. There are some differences in the definitions, classifications, and tabulations of the results in these population censuses, and hence certain problems will be encountered in our analysis of the information selected for inclusion here. The manner in which the differences emerged in the census results and how they are dealt with in our presentation will be discussed in the respective sections of this chapter.

Population Growth

In interpreting the figures in respect of population size and growth, we should be mindful of the population censuses not being conducted at a uniform time interval of ten years as practised in most countries. The holding of the third pan-Malaysia Census in 1991 has resulted in a break in the intercensal time interval: ten years for the 1970–80 period, 11 years for the 1980–91 period, and nine years for the 1991–2000 period. What this implies is that we should pay more attention to the figures for annual rate of growth rather than intercensal rate of growth presented in Table 1.1, and also in other tables when time-series data are included.

It is also necessary to explain the presentation of the figures according to geographic areas. The practice of examining some of the census results in terms of these broad geographic regions in the census reports, has been adopted in our analysis. West Malaysia, also known as Peninsula Malaysia, consists of 11 states and the Federal Territory of Kuala Lumpur with common land boundaries and shared historical, political, and economic backgrounds. The two states of Sabah and Sarawak, collectively known as East Malaysia, are separated by the vast expanse of the South China Sea, apart from their separate history, economy and population.

The figures for 1960 are obtained from the pre-Malaysia Censuses conducted in this year in Sabah and Sarawak and from intercensal population estimates for West Malaysia when the census was held in 1957 instead of 1960. The changes in the size of the population over time are caused by natural increase and net international migration. The population of Malaysia prior to its establishment was estimated to total about 8,035,600 in the pre-merger year of 1960. By the next census held in 1970, the population had grown to above the ten-million mark of 10,439,400, an increase of 2,405,800 or an annual growth rate of 2.7 per cent during this ten-year period.[1]

In the second pan-Malaysia Census conducted in 1980, the population was enumerated as 13,136,100, an increase of 2,696,700 since 1970 or an annual growth rate of 2.3 per cent.[2] The race riots that flared up on 13 May 1969 in Kuala Lumpur started a fresh movement of non-Bumiputera persons to Singapore and other countries. Thereafter, the population increase recovered during the 11-year period to bring it to 17,563,400 in 1991, giving an annual growth rate of 2.7 per cent.[3] The latest Census held in 2000 reveals that the population had passed the 20-million mark with a figure of 23,274,700. This represents a large increase of 5,711,300 over that enumerated nine years ago in 1991, with the annual growth rate accelerated further to 3.1 per cent. This high growth rate can only come about with the substained large inflow of international migration, consisting primarily of migrant labour to alleviate labour shortage in certain sectors of the economy.[4]

Some interesting differences in the pattern of population growth in the three regions are underlined in Table 1.1. Between 1960 and 2000, the population of Sarawak grew steadily at the moderate level of 2.3 to 2.8 per cent per annum. This fairly uniform growth rate may be attributed to natural increase, not subjected to violent fluctuations, constituting

Table 1.1
Population Growth by Region, 1960–2000

Year	Population ('000)	Intercensal Increase	Annual Growth Rate
	Malaysia		
1960	8,035.6	—	—
1970	10,439.4	2,403.8	2.7
1980	13,136.1	2,696.7	2.3
1991	17,563.4	4,427.3	2.7
2000	23,274.7	5,711.3	3.1
	West Malaysia		
1960	6,836.7	—	—
1970	8,809.6	1,972.9	2.6
1980	11,426.6	2,617.0	2.7
1991	14,131.7	2,705.1	2.0
2000	18,523.6	5,880.6	4.3
	Sabah		
1960	454.4	—	—
1970	653.6	199.2	3.7
1980	955.7	302.1	3.9
1991	1,788.9	833.2	5.9
2000	2,679.6	890.7	4.5
	Sarawak		
1960	744.5	—	—
1970	976.3	231.8	2.8
1980	1,235.6	259.3	2.4
1991	1,642.8	407.2	2.7
2000	2,071.5	428.7	2.3

the primary factor of population growth in the state. The inward flow of international migration has continued to be rather insignificant as compared to the other two regions. During the whole 40-year period, the population was enlarged by about 2.8 times, rising from 744,500 to 2,071,500 since 1960.

A completely different pattern of population growth was experienced in Sabah, which includes the Federal Territory of Labuan in all the tables included in our discussion. It is more convenient for us to adopt this procedure in our discussion, more so when the merging of this tiny population with the far larger population of Sabah would not affect the salient features of the various aspects of the latter's population. In 2000, the population of Labuan was only 76,067 as against the huge population of 2,603,485 in Sabah.

A consistently higher rate of population growth was recorded in Sabah. The population increased by a higher rate of 3.7 per cent during the intercensal period 1960–70, and accelerated to 3.9 per cent and 5.9 per cent during the next two periods. A slight slackening to 4.5 per cent was recorded during the latest period 1991–2000. This exceptionally rapid rate of population was due to the fairly high volume of natural increase and, more importantly, the sustained large inflow of labour migrants from Indonesia and the Philippines. The population of Sabah was enlarged by about 4.5 times, from a low of only 454,400 in 1960 to 2,679,600 in 2000.

In the larger region of West Malaysia, the population was estimated to total 6,836,700 in 1960. By the first pan-Malaysia Census held in 1970, the population had reached 8,809,600 representing an annual growth rate of 2.6 per cent. This rate of population increase was raised slightly to 2.7 per cent in the next intercensal period 1970–80, followed by a downturn to 2.0 per cent during the period 1970–80. Subsequently, this rate of population increase accelerated to 4.3 per cent, bringing the total population to 18,523,600, 2.7 times larger than the figure of 6,836,700 in 1960. The inward flow of international migration, particularly from Indonesia, was responsible for the high rate of population increase in West Malaysia. Many of the newcomers were illegal migrant labourers, and some attempts were made in recent years to repatriate them to their country.

It is useful to examine the growth of the population separately in the urban and rural areas in Malaysia with a very large rural sector. The definition of an urban area varies from one country to another, and even within a particular country, changes in the definition may be introduced in the population censuses. In the early censuses conducted in Malaysia, urban areas have been equated to gazetted administrative districts with a population of 1,000 or more inhabitants. The process of gazetting an area is an essential part of government administration involving the careful mapping of the area to establish boundaries which are then notified in the government gazette for public information. The old definition is now considered as too restrictive, and the more realistic definition of an urban area with 10,000 or more inhabitants is now used. It is more important to note that this definition has also been employed in the other sections of this chapter dealing with urban-rural classification.

The growth of the population in the urban or rural area is determined by not only natural increase and international migration, but by internal movement of people within the country (see Table 1.2). The first intercensal period of 1970–80 witnessed a sharp jump in the urban population from 2,780,300 to 5,098,100, representing a spectacular annual growth rate of 6.3 per cent. This growth rate was reduced to

Table 1.2
Population Growth by Urban and Rural Areas,
1970–2000

Year	Population ('000)	Intercensal Increase	Annual Growth Rate
	Urban		
1970	2,780.3	—	—
1980	5,098.1	2,317.8	6.3
1991	8,898.6	3,800.5	5.2
2000	14,426.9	5,528.3	5.5
	Rural		
1970	7,659.1	—	—
1980	8,038.0	378.9	0.5
1991	8,664.8	626.8	0.7
2000	8,847.8	183.0	0.2

5.2 per cent during 1980–91, but picked up again to reach 5.5 per cent during the most recent period. In sharp contrast, the annual growth rate recorded in the rural area managed to reach only 0.5 per cent, 0.7 per cent, and 0.2 per cent during these respective intercensal periods. The extremely rapid increase in the urban population in all these years can be traced to the concentration of immigrant labour in the urban centres and, more importantly, the sustained movement of people from the rural sector to the urban conurbation.

The impact of the marked differential growth rate between rural and urban areas is reflected in the pronounced shift in the size of the population between these two areas. During the whole 30-year period, the urban population balooned from 2,780,300 to 14,426,900, slightly more than a five-fold increase. The rural population, on the other hand, was enlarged from 7,659,100 to only 8,847,800 during the same period. The obvious consequence of this differential growth rate is the remarkable rise in the proportion of the urban population from the original 26.6 per cent to 62 per cent at the end of the period. This trend towards rapid urbanisation has engendered serious problems in housing and employment.

Population Distribution

The distribution of the population over the various parts of Malaysia can be traced to the historical and economic development of the country. In the early days, prior to the incursion of Western influence, the people lived in settlements that sprang along the coasts and riverine banks where they engaged in fishing and farming. Except for Sabah and Sarawak, the densely-forested interior was almost devoid of inhabitants. Towards the middle of the 19th century, the distribution of the population began to undergo some changes consequent to the development of tin mining in Perak, Selangor, and Negri Sembilan by Chinese immigrant settlers. At that time, there was also a clustering of the population in gambier, pepper, tapioca, sugar, and coffee plantations.

At the end of the 19th century, another important event affecting population distribution was the introduction of rubber as a plantation crop with the help of cheap immigrant labour from south India. Rubber plantations sprang up in the western foothills of the Peninsula with well-drained terrain and accessible existing railway lines to transport the rubber to the seaports for export to industrialised countries. The deep-water harbours are sheltered from the southwest monsoon by Sumatra and from the northeast monsoon by the central mountain range.[5] In the more recent years, the population was drawn towards industrial estates located near or in the urban centres, usually in the western part of the country. As mentioned earlier, there was also the movement of people in the urban centres where economic activities was most vibrant.

The continuous development of the country along its western part would naturally be reflected in the geographic distribution of the population. Obviously, each of the 13 states has never been populated in proportion to the size of the land area since land size is only one of the many factors determining population distribution. The distribution of land area and population according to the 2000 Census is presented in Table 1.3. Malaysia has a total land area of 329,847 square kilometres,

Table 1.3
Population Distribution and Density by Region and State, 2000

Region/State	Area in Square Kilometre	Population ('000)	Population per Square Kilometre	Population (Percentage)
Region				
Malaysia	329,847	23,274.7	71	100.0
West Malaysia	131,598	18,523.6	141	78.8
Sabah	73,711	2,679.6	36	11.3
Sarawak	124,450	2,071.5	17	9.9
West Malaysian state				
Johore	18,987	2,740.6	144	11.8
Kedah	9,425	1,649.8	175	7.1
Kelantan	15,024	1,313.0	87	5.6
Malacca	1,652	635.8	387	2.7
Negri Sembilan	6,644	859.9	129	3.7
Pahang	35,965	1,288.4	36	5.5
Perak	21,005	2,051.2	98	8.8
Perlis	795	204.5	257	0.9
Penang	1,031	1,313.4	1,274	5.6
Selangor	7,960	4,188.9	526	18.0
Terengganu	12,955	898.8	69	3.9
Kuala Lumpur	243	1,379.3	5,676	5.9

with 39.9 per cent in West Malaysia, 37.7 per cent in Sarawak, and 22.4 per cent in Sabah. However, almost 86.5 per cent of the total population of 23,214,700 in 2000 was to be found in West Malaysia, while only 10.2 per cent and 9.3 per cent were residing in Sabah and Sarawak respectively. Sarawak stands out as a typical example of the lack of a relationship between land size and population since it has the largest land area but the lowest population density of only 17 persons per square kilometre. The figures seem to suggest that there is an inverse relationship between land area and population.

The Federal Territory of Kuala Lumpur with the smallest land area has the highest population density of 5,676 persons per square kilometre. This high density is to be expected since Kuala Lumpur is the capital city with almost no rural area to speak of. Among the 13 states, Penang, with the second largest city, has the highest density of 1,274 persons per square kilometre, followed by Selangor with a much lower figure of 526 persons. A fairly high density can be observed in Malacca with 387 persons and Perlis with 257 persons. At a slightly lower level are Kedah with 175 persons, Johor with 144 persons and Negri Sembilan with 129 persons. The lowest population density is situated in the eastern states of Kelantan with 87 persons, Terengganu with 69 persons, and Pahang with only 36 persons.

Another way of examining the figures given in Table 1.3 is to look at the distribution of the total population among the 13 states and Kuala Lumpur. The largest clustering of population is situated in Selangor with 18 per cent, not forgetting the 5.9 per cent in Kuala Lumpur. The share of the total population among the other states amounted to 11.8 per cent in Johor, 9.9 per cent in Sarawak, 8.8 per cent in Perak, and 7.1 per cent in Kedah. This is followed by three states with almost the same proportion of population: 5.6 per cent in Penang and Sarawak, and 5.5 per cent in Pahang. A much lower population is to be found in the remaining four states. The different sizes of population would be reflected in the relative political importance of the states expressed in terms of representation in the Federal Parliament.

Another interesting aspect of population distribution refers to the changes in the population according to urban-rural classification consequent to the rapid urbanisation mentioned earlier. In 1970, the population residing in the urban centres numbered some 2,780,300 or 26.6 per cent as against the 7,659,100 or 73.4 per cent in the rural area. Over the years, there occurred a pronounced shift in the population between the two areas, with the respective proportions moving towards 38.8 per cent and 61.2 per cent in 1980 and 50.7 per cent and 49.3 per cent in 1990. By the latest Census conducted in 2000, the population living in the urban area swelled to 14,426,900 or 62 per cent, while the number in the rural area shrank to 8,847,800 or 38 per cent. This trend had exerted intense pressures in the urban centres with regard to meeting the essential needs of the people, particularly jobs and housing.

Citizenship Pattern

The extent to which the population has a more settled character can be viewed in terms of citizenship information compiled in the population census. The item on citizenship was not included in the Censuses until the post-independence era after 1963 when great concern for citizenship issues and political enfranchisement became part of the process of nation-building. However, the procedure employed to collect the citizenship statistics in past-Malaysia Censuses has not been uniform.

In the first two Censuses, the item on citizenship was only applicable to respondents aged 12 and over. This particular cut-off point was linked to the compilation of information on the colour of identity cards, which was compulsory for all residents aged 12 and over. The procedure was altered in the last two Censuses when the collection of citizenship statistics was applied to all respondents regardless of age. The time series statistics has, therefore, been truncated into two incomparable periods.

The item on citizenship has assumed greater importance in recent years when the Census reports present many items of information for the citizen population only but not for the total population. For example, statistics for ethnicity are made available for the citizen population but not for the non-citizen population. We are, therefore, forced to study the affected statistics in terms of the citizen population only, though it might be more desirable in many instances to look at such statistics from the viewpoint of the overall population.

The first pan-Malaysia Census showed that out of the total population of 6,561,300 aged 12 and over in 1970, some 6,074,834 or 92.6 per cent were enumerated as Malaysian citizens. The position improved somewhat by the time the next Census was held in 1980 when 7,204,891 or 97.8 per cent aged 12 and over were Malaysian citizens. Similar figures for the total population of all ages are not available, and hence comparison with subsequent Censuses cannot be made.

In 1991, the number of Malaysian citizens out of the total population amounted to 16,812,300, and increased by 30.2 per cent to reach 21,889,900 in 2000. This is in sharp contrast to the non-citizen population which grew by 84.4 per cent, boosting the figure from 751,100 to 1,384,800 at the end of the period. The large inflow of migrant labour from Indonesia and the Philippines in recent years has been responsible for the spectacular growth of the non-citizen population. Natural increase — the excess of births over deaths — has always been a negligible factor of population growth of the non-citizen population. Table 1.4 shows the distribution of the population by citizenship, region, and state.

An idea of the migrant labour character of the non-citizen population can be inferred from a scrutiny of the age structure. The 2000 Census shows that out of a total of 1,384,800 non-citizens, 26.1 per cent were in the age group under 19, 57.7 per cent in the 20 to 39 age group, 13.3 per cent in the 40 to 59 age group, and 2.9 per cent in the age group 60 and over. The four corresponding proportions for the citizen population are 44.6 per cent, 30.7 per cent, 18.3 per cent, and 6.4 per cent. The huge clustering of foreigners in the prime working age group of 20 to 39 points to the predominance of migrant labour. The favourite states of the foreign labourers are Sabah, Selangor, and Johore.

The regional distribution of the non-citizen population can be examined in Table 1.4. Out of a total of 1,384,800 non-citizens enumerated in 2000, there were 691,000 or 49.9 per cent in West Malaysia, 630,900 or 45.6 per cent in Sabah, and 62,700 or 4.5 per cent in Sarawak. With a relatively settled population, Sarawak has fewer immigrant labourers. Within West Malaysia, the biggest concentration of non-citizens is located in Selangor with 186,400 or 13.5 per cent, and the second largest is in Johore with 150,500 or 10.9 per cent. The Federal Territory of Kuala Lumpur, the abode of most foreign professionals and businessmen, is occupied by some 92,400 non-citizens or 6.7 per

Table 1.4

Distribution of Population by Citizenship, Region, and State, 2000

Region/State	Number ('000)			Percentage		
	Citizen	Non-citizen	Total	Citizen	Non-citizen	Total
			Region			
Malaysia	21,889.9	1,384.8	23,274.7	94.1	5.9	100.0
West Malaysia	17,832.6	691.0	18,523.6	96.1	3.9	100.0
Sabah	2,048.5	630.9	2,679.6	76.5	23.5	100.0
Sarawak	2,008.8	62.7	2,071.5	97.0	3.0	100.0
			West Malaysian state			
Johore	2,590.1	150.5	2,740.6	94.5	5.5	100.0
Kedah	1,624.2	25.3	1,649.5	98.4	1.6	100.0
Kelantan	1,292.2	20.8	1,313.0	98.4	1.6	100.0
Malacca	612.8	22.9	625.7	96.4	3.6	100.0
Negri Sembilan	828.1	31.8	859.9	96.3	3.7	100.0
Pahang	1,233.6	54.8	1,288.4	95.7	4.3	100.0
Perak	2,012.9	38.3	2,051.2	98.1	1.9	100.0
Perlis	201.3	3.6	204.9	98.5	1.5	100.0
Penang	1,265.0	48.4	1,313.4	96.3	3.7	100.0
Selangor	4,002.4	186.4	4,188.8	95.6	4.4	100.0
Terengganu	883.0	15.8	898.8	98.2	1.8	100.0
Kuala Lumpur	1,286.9	92.4	1,379.3	93.3	6.7	100.0

cent. This proportion is in fact larger than that prevailing in the other 11 states.

We will proceed to examine the data given in Table 1.4 in terms of the two components of citizenship within the population in each state. The most unique position can be observed in Sabah where the proportion of citizens reached only 76.5 per cent, with the non-citizens occupying the other 23.5 per cent. In all the other states and Kuala Lumpur, the proportion of the population enumerated as citizens was well above 90 per cent. By and large, a higher proportion of citizens persists in the northern and eastern parts of the Peninsula. The proportion reached a high of 98.5 per cent in Perlis, 98.4 per cent in Kedah and Kelantan, and 98.2 in Terengganu.

Apart from the geographical remoteness of these states from main stream migration from mainly Indonesia, there are fewer employment opportunities for the foreigners due to slower economic development. A comparatively lower proportion of citizens exists in Kuala Lumpur with 93.3 per cent, Johore with 94.5 per cent, and Selangor with 95.6 per cent.

Ethnic Composition

The collection of information on ethnicity has assumed greater significance in recent years since it has a major impact on the formulation and monitoring of government policies and programmes designed to eliminate the identification of race with economic activities. Undoubtedly, ethnic data compiled from the Census would be essential for a fuller understanding of the country's demographics in view of the influence of ethnicity on the various population characteristics. The item pertaining to race has always been included in the population censuses conducted in Malaysia, though some changes in the definition and presentation of the statistics have been introduced over the years.

A better appreciation of ethnic information requires an explanation of the definition of the different ethnic terminologies used in the population censuses. The definition of "Chinese" has always been quite clear-cut: people of Chinese descent regardless of their country of birth or citizenship. The term "Indians" has not been consistently defined in past Censuses, but it is now employed to refer to persons from the

Indian subcontinent such as Indians, Pakistanis, Bangladeshis, and Sri Lankans. This definition, also disregarding citizenship or birthplace, makes sense because these people display common social and cultural traits, and hence similar demographic characteristics.

The term "Bumiputera" was introduced in the pan-Malaysia Censuses to accommodate the emergence of a large variety of indigenous communities after the creation of Malaysia in 1963. The Bumiputera group is now divided into "Malays" and "Other Bumiputeras" in most of the tables presented in the Census reports. The latter refers mainly to the *orang asli* in West Malaysia and the numerous small indigenous tribes in Sabah and Sarawak. The definition of "Malay" is enshrined in Article 160(2) of the Constitution of Malaysia, which specifies that a Malay is a "person who professed the Muslim religion, habitually speaks the Malay language and conforms to the Malay custom".

As indicated earlier, the presentation of statistics on ethnic groups in the two latest Censuses held in 1991 and 2000 is given in terms of Malaysian citizens rather than the combined total for citizens and non-citizens as provided in the earlier Censuses. This departure from the previous practice was meant to avoid distortion or misappropriation arising from the huge inflow of migrants in recent years. Restricting ethnic information to citizen population only would hopefully yield more meaningful statistics viewed in terms of government policies and electoral dynamics. It is important to bear in mind that ethnicity can only be studied in the two Censuses in terms of the citizen population. In fact, the statistics for non-citizen population released in the Census reports have not been made available according to quite a number of other variables, certainly not according to ethnicity.

A summary of the ethnic classification of the citizen population in the two latest population Censuses is presented in Table 1.5. During the nine-year intercensal period 1991–2000, the number of Malays among the citizen population was raised from 8,521,900 to 11,680,400, an increase of some 3,158,500 or 37.1 per cent. The same period witnessed a larger increase of 44.4 per cent by other Bumiputeras which saw their number grew from 1,778,000 to 2,567,800. In sharp contrast, the Chinese grew by a smaller rate of 23.1 per cent and the Indians by 27.7 per cent. The lower level of fertility and the negligible inflow of

14   *Saw Swee-Hock*

Table 1.5
Distribution of Citizen Population by Ethnic Group, 1991 and 2000

Ethnic Group	1991 ('000)	2000 ('000)	Increase No.	Increase %	Percentage 1991	Percentage 2000
Malays	8,521.9	11,680.4	3,158.5	37.1	50.7	53.4
Other Bumiputeras	1,778.0	2,567.8	789.8	44.4	10.6	11.7
Chinese	4,623.9	5,691.9	1,068.0	23.1	27.5	26.0
Indians	1,316.1	1,680.1	364.0	27.7	7.8	7.7
Others	572.4	269.7	−302.7	−52.9	3.4	1.2
Total	16,812.3	21,889.9	5,077.6	30.2	100.0	100.0

migrants were the principal contributory factors for the slow growth rate among these two communities. Inflow of people from China and the Indian subcontinent has ceased since the end of the Second World War.

One of the consequences of the differences in the rate of increase among the ethnic groups is the marked shift in the ethnic composition of the citizen population. The share of the Malays was enlarged from 50.7 per cent to 53.4 per cent between 1991 and 2000, and the other Bumiputeras also saw their share rose from 10.6 per cent to 11.7 per cent. During the same period, the share of the Chinese fell from 27.5 per cent to 26 per cent and that of the Indians from 7.8 per cent and to 7.7 per cent. Doubtless to say, these changes in the ethnic composition of the citizen population would have considerable political and economic implications in such a plural society like Malaysia. The same segments of the ethnic community have expressed their apprehension about their diminishing share of the population. The Malaysian Chinese Association (MCA) has even issued sparodic exhortations to Chinese couples to produce more babies.

It would be useful to look at the distribution of the citizen population according to the urban-rural classification within each ethnic community. Out of a total of 11,680,400 Malays enumerated among the citizen population in 2000, some 6,336,000 or 56.7 per cent were residing in the urban area, while the other 5,344,400 or 43.3 per cent in the rural area. Among the 2,567,800 other Bumiputeras, a smaller proportion of

Table 1.6
Distribution of Citizen Population by Ethnic Group, Region, and State, 2000 (in Percentages)

Region/State	Malays	Other Bumiputeras	Chinese	Indians	Others	Total
			Region			
Malaysia	53.4	11.7	26.0	7.7	1.2	100.0
West Malaysia	61.0	1.4	27.4	9.5	0.7	100.0
Sabah	15.3	65.3	13.2	0.5	5.8	100.0
Sarawak	23.0	49.8	26.7	0.2	0.2	100.0
			West Malaysian state			
Johore	55.7	1.4	35.4	6.9	0.6	100.0
Kedah	76.4	0.2	14.9	7.1	1.4	100.0
Kelantan	94.2	0.8	3.8	0.3	0.9	100.0
Malacca	62.7	1.1	29.1	6.5	0.6	100.0
Negri Sembilan	56.6	1.3	25.6	16.0	0.5	100.0
Pahang	71.8	5.0	17.7	5.0	0.5	100.0
Perak	52.4	2.3	32.0	13.0	0.3	100.0
Perlis	85.2	0.3	10.3	1.3	2.9	100.0
Penang	42.1	0.3	46.5	10.6	0.4	100.0
Selangor	52.1	1.4	30.7	14.6	1.1	100.0
Terengganu	96.5	0.3	2.8	0.2	0.2	100.0
Kuala Lumpur	42.7	0.9	43.5	11.4	1.5	100.0

34 per cent stayed in the urban area as against 66 per cent in the rural area. Most of them are indigenous peoples located in the remote interior regions of Sabah and Sarawak. The Chinese and Indians continued to be found mainly in the towns, their respective proportions of urban dwellers reaching 85.9 per cent and 79.7 per cent respectively.

The data in respect of the ethnic composition of the citizen population as compiled in the 2000 Census are presented in Table 1.6. The combined Bumiputera group constituted the majority in all states, except Penang and Kuala Lumpur. The majority position reached its highest level in Terengganu with 96.8 per cent and in Kelantan with 95 per cent. Within the Bumiputera group, the Malays dominate in all the states in West Malaysia, but not in Sabah and Sarawak. In these two states, the Malays comprised 15.3 per cent and 23 per cent respectively. The various indigenous peoples classified as "Other Bumiputeras" were in fact the majority, with 65.3 per cent in Sabah and 49.5 per cent in Sarawak.

The Chinese have always formed the majority in Penang, but this dominant position has been diminishing over the years. In 2000, the Chinese amounted to 46.5 per cent, just a shade higher than the 42.4 per cent for the Bumiputeras. In Kuala Lumpur, the share of the citizen population taken up by each of these two ethnic groups is almost equal, 43.5 per cent for the Chinese and 43.6 per cent for the Bumiputeras. The other states with a sizeable proportion of Chinese are also found along the western coast of Peninsula Malaysia: 35.9 per cent in Johore, 32 per cent in Perak, and 30.7 per cent in Selangor. A somewhat similar pattern of higher proportion in the states that sprang along the western part of the Peninsula is exhibited by the Indians: 16 per cent in Negri Sembilan, 14.6 per cent in Selangor, 13 per cent in Perak, 11.4 per cent in Kuala Lumpur, and 10.3 per cent in Penang. As mentioned earlier, the penetration of these two immigrant communities has been in these western states.

Unlike the pre-eminence of Malays among the Bumiputeras in all the states in West Malaysia, there is a greater variety of sub-groups in Sabah and Sarawak as can be observed in Table 1.7. In 2000, the largest indigenous community in Sabah are the Kadazans Dusuns whose share of the total citizen population approached 489,800 or 30.3 per cent.

Table 1.7
Distribution of Bumiputera Citizen Population
in Sabah and Sarawak by Sub–ethnic Group, 2000

Sub–ethnic Group	Number	Percentage
Sabah		
Malays	332,471	20.2
Kadazans/Dusuns	484,828	30.3
Bajans	347,193	21.1
Muruts	85,094	5.2
Other Bumiputeras	394,464	24.2
Total	1,601,356	100.0
Sarawak		
Malays	462,270	31.6
Ibans	603,735	41.3
Bidayuhs	166,756	11.4
Melanaus	112,984	7.7
Other Bumiputeras	117,690	8.0
Total	1,463,435	100.0

Incidentally, in the 1991 Census, the statistics for this group were presented separately in two categories, 217,600 for the Dusuns and 107,500 for the Kadazans. The second- and third-largest tribes are the Bajans accounting for 21.1 per cent, followed closely by the Malays with 20.2 per cent. The Muruts managed to make up only 5.2 per cent share of the citizen population.

An entirely different composition of the Bumiputera citizen population is displayed in Sarawak. The Ibans, also known as Sea Dayaks, constituted the biggest tribe totalling some 603,700 or 41.3 per cent. The Malays, living mainly in towns and coastal areas, form the second-largest community with a share of 31.6 per cent. The less important tribes are the Bidayahs with 11.4 per cent and the Melanaus with only 7.7 per cent. In the past, these two tribes resided in the riverine and coastal villages but some of them were later re-settled in the interior.

The figures given in Table 1.7 has not given justice to the much greater number of tribes existing in the two states. The other unmentioned indigenous tribes are rather small in number and for practical purposes have been lumped together as "Others". In Sabah, the minority tribes are the Kwijaus, Illanuns, Totuds, Rungus, Tambanuos, Dumpas, Paitans, Idahans, Minokoks, Kedayans, Bisayas, etc., numbering some 390,100 or 24.2 per cent of the Sabah population.[6] The corresponding figures for the "Other Bumiputeras" in Sarawak are not large, only 117,700 or 8 per cent. This small group consisted of Bisayahs, Kedayans, Kayans, Kenyahs, Kelabits, and Punans. The colourful variety of the indigenous peoples in the two Eastern Malayan states has indeed enhanced the greater ethnic diversity in the overall population of Malaysia.

Religious Pattern

Religious differences in Malaysia have a strong tendency to follow ethnic and cultural identities of the people, and have reinforced the great divide among them in almost every aspect of their daily life. The recent resurgence of religious fervour has propelled religion into the forefront as the key parameter determining the political and racial harmony of the nation. An evaluation of the religious affiliations of the people is somewhat handicapped by the traditional difficulties encountered in the collection of information on religion, a process involving a wide range of personal beliefs and practices. This should be taken into consideration when attempting to interpret the Census statistics concerning religion.

The different religions professed by the people in the country have been quite established, particularly among the Muslims who are prohibited by Islamic laws to convert to another religion or to renounce Islam. Whatever changes in religious affiliations that occurred in the past would in the main be a reflection of the changing ethnic composition discussed earlier. In looking at this linkage, we should be mindful of the difference in the Census statistics for religion and ethnicity. Whilst the ethnic statistics refer to the citizen population only, the statistics for religion are made available for the total population as well as for the two sub-components, citizens and non-citizens. In Table 1.8, the data refers to the religious affiliations of the total population in the last three Censuses. Similar figures for 1970 are not available because the item on religion was not included in the Census conducted that year.

It is clear that the predominant religion in the country is Islam which has enhanced in importance from around 52.9 per cent in 1980 to

Table 1.8
Distribution of Population by Religion, 1980–2000

Religion	1980	1990	2000
	Number ('000)		
Islam	6,918.3	10,257.2	14,049.4
Buddhism	2,265.5	3,222.1	4,467.5
Confucianism/Taoism/Others	1,518.7	928.0	615.1
Hinduism	920.4	1,112.3	1,457.9
Christianity	843.0	1,412.3	2,126.2
Tribal/Folk religion	259.5	206.0	195.8
Others	69.8	82.6	88.4
No religion	275.3	253.5	194.4
Unknown	—	24.2	80.0
Total	13,070.4	17,498.1	23,274.7
	Percentage		
Islam	52.9	58.6	60.4
Buddhism	17.3	18.4	19.2
Confucianism/Taoism/Others	11.6	5.3	2.6
Hinduism	7.0	6.4	6.3
Christianity	6.4	8.1	9.1
Tribal/Folk religion	2.0	1.2	0.8
Others	0.5	0.5	0.4
No religion	2.1	1.4	0.8
Unknown	—	0.1	0.3
Total	100.0	100.0	100.0

60.4 per cent in 2000 following the rise in the Malay population. Except for Buddhism and Christianity, the relative importance of other religions has been declining over the years. A slight rise in the proportion from 17.3 per cent to 19.2 per cent was recorded by Buddhism, but the most recent proportion is still a very poor second as compared to the Muslim proportion. One notable feature refers to the steep rise in the number of Christians from 843,000 to 2,126,200 between 1980 and 2000, resulting in their share moving up from 6.4 per cent to 9.1 per cent. Since Muslims almost never convert to Christianity, the rising importance of Christianity can only be brought about by Chinese, Indians, and other minority communities converting to this religion.

Christianity has even overtaken Hinduism as the third-largest religion professed by the peoples of Malaysia.

The overall rise in the proportion of persons declaring Buddhism as their religion should perhaps be examined further in relation to the sharp drop in the proportion of persons following Confucianism, Taoism, and other traditional Chinese religions. The statistics on this mixture of ill-defined Chinese religions are always difficult to collect in the population censuses because the loose character of these traditional religions is not amenable to precise identification in the field enumeration. We know that the Chinese population has continued to increase in the last two decades, and yet the number professing this mixture of traditional religions has fallen steeply from 1,518,700 in 1980 to 615,100 in 2000, with the corresponding proportion tumbling from 11.6 per cent to 2.6 per cent. This strongly suggests that there was a shift from this group of traditional religions to Buddhism among the Chinese respondents. In fact, the combined proportion for these two religious groups in Table 1.8 has been reduced from 29 per cent to 21.8 per cent, a trend quite consonant with the fall in the share of the Chinese in the total population of Malaysia.

A greater insight into the religious character of the plural society can be derived by studying the cross-classification of religion with ethnicity. However, this can only be accomplished in terms of the citizen population since the non-citizen population has not been tabulated according to ethnicity in the 2000 Census report. The data presented in Table 1.9 refer to the citizen population only. Despite this limitation, the close association of ethnicity along religious affiliations is quite apparent. The best example is of course the Malays, all of whom profess the Islamic faith as required by law. They are primarily Suni Muslims practising the Islam Shafe school of thought.

The above link is also perceptible among the Chinese and Indians, though not as rigid as in the case of the Malays. The dominant religion among the Indians in the citizen population has always been Hinduism, accounting for 84.1 per cent in 2000. The second most important religion professed by them is Christianity (7.8 per cent) and the third is Islam (4.1 per cent). Most of the Indian Muslims are Pakistanis and Bangladeshis. Though not prohibited by law, very few Chinese care to

Table 1.9
Distribution of Citizen Population by Religion and Ethnic Group, 2000

Religion	Malays	Other Bumiputeras	Chinese	Indians	Others	Total	Non-citizens
				Number ('000)			
Islam	11,680.4	932.0	57.2	69.0	174.8	12,913.4	1,136.0
Buddhism	—	21.6	4,325.0	20.1	52.4	4,419.0	48.5
Confucianism/Taoism/Others	—	3.1	605.6	1.2	0.7	610.7	4.4
Hinduism	—	2.2	16.1	1,412.7	2.3	1,433.3	24.6
Christianity	—	1,275.0	539.6	130.4	35.5	1,980.4	145.8
Tribal/Folk religion	—	186.4	7.9	0.9	0.7	195.3	0.6
Others	—	35.6	12.2	35.6	1.0	84.5	4.0
No religion	—	93.8	88.9	0.8	1.3	184.7	9.6
Unknown	—	18.2	39.5	9.3	1.7	68.6	11.4
Total	11,680.4	2,567.8	5,691.9	1,680.1	269.7	21,889.9	1,384.9
				Percentage			
Islam	100.0	40.8	1.0	4.1	64.8	60.4	82.0
Buddhism	—	0.8	76.0	1.2	19.4	19.2	3.5
Confucianism/Taoism/Others	—	0.1	10.6	0.7	0.2	2.6	0.3
Hinduism	—	0.1	0.3	84.1	2.6	6.3	1.8
Christianity	—	49.7	9.5	7.8	13.2	9.1	10.5
Tribal/Folk religion	—	7.2	0.1	0.1	0.2	0.8	0.0
Others	—	1.4	0.2	2.1	0.4	0.4	0.3
No religion	—	3.7	1.6	0.1	0.5	0.8	0.7
Unknown	—	0.7	0.7	0.6	0.6	0.3	0.8
Total	100.0	100.0	100.0	100.0	100.0	100.0	100.0

convert to the Islamic faith. They practise mainly Buddhism (76 per cent), Confucianism, Taoism and other traditional religions (10.6 per cent), and Christianity (9.5 per cent).

The other Bumiputera community has contributed not only a greater variety to the ethnic structure of the country, but also a wide range of religious affiliations. As compared to the above three ethnic groups, the other Bumiputera communities are the only people with the majority professing to be Christians (49.7 per cent). Muslims (40.8 per cent) occupy second position. The other interesting feature is that they have a sizeable proportion practising some form of tribal and folk religion.

It may be recalled that the non-citizen population has not been tabulated according to ethnicity in the 2000 Census report, but the report has made available statistics on religion classified according to the ethnicity of the population. A scrutiny of the statistics may give us some insight into the ethnic composition of this group of mainly foreigners. Out of the total non-citizen population of 1,384,880 in 2000, the number professing to follow the Islamic faith amounted to 1,136,000 or 82 per cent. This may be taken to confirm the commonly-held knowledge that the foreigners who entered Malaysia, whether legally or not, come principally from Indonesia. The extremely low number of Buddhists (3.5 per cent) and Hindus (1.8 per cent) surely point to the negligible inflow of Chinese and Indian immigrants.

The dominant role exerted by religion in the regional politics of the country has been shaped by the religious affiliations of the people in different states. In analysing the information provided in Table 1.10, we should bear in mind that the ethnic composition discussed earlier has a close association with the data given in the table. The dominance of Islam is obvious in Terengganu (96.9 per cent), Kelantan (94.5 per cent), Perlis (85.4 per cent), and Kedah (76.9 per cent). In these states, the battle for the Muslim vote during elections has always been very intense between the Pan-Malaysia Islamic Party (PAS) and the United Malays' National Organization (UMNO), the main party in Barisan Nasional.

Buddhism, practised mainly by the Chinese and to some extent by other minority communities, does not appear to assume such an important role in the various states. The highest proportion of Buddhism practised in these states managed to attain only 33.7 per cent in Penang

Table 1.10
Distribution of Population by Religion and State, 2000 (in Percentages)

Region/State	Islam	Buddhism	Confusion/ Taoism/ Others	Hinduism	Christianity	Tribal/ Folk Religion	Others	No Religion	Unknown	Total
East Malaysian state										
Sabah	64.1	6.5	0.4	0.1	27.4	0.0	0.2	1.0	0.2	100.0
Sarawak	31.3	12.0	2.6	0.1	42.6	5.2	1.3	3.9	0.9	100.0
West Malaysian state										
Johore	58.8	28.7	3.2	5.9	2.2	0.2	0.2	0.4	0.3	100.0
Kedah	76.9	13.5	2.0	6.5	0.8	0.0	0.1	0.1	0.0	100.0
Kelantan	94.5	4.4	0.1	0.2	0.2	0.5	0.0	0.0	0.0	100.0
Malacca	64.2	24.1	1.5	5.6	3.9	0.0	0.2	0.4	0.1	100.0
Negri Sembilan	58.6	20.3	3.0	13.9	2.7	0.6	0.3	0.5	0.1	100.0
Pahang	73.8	13.7	2.5	4.4	1.2	3.4	0.2	0.8	0.1	100.0
Perak	53.9	24.0	5.9	11.0	3.1	0.6	0.6	0.8	0.1	100.0
Perlis	85.4	11.4	1.4	1.0	0.5	0.0	0.1	0.1	0.0	100.0
Penang	44.2	33.7	8.8	8.7	3.6	0.0	0.3	0.4	0.2	100.0
Selangor	55.7	24.4	2.0	12.1	4.3	0.3	0.4	0.5	0.4	100.0
Terengganu	96.9	2.4	0.1	0.2	0.3	0.0	0.0	0.1	0.0	100.0
Federal Territory	46.2	34.2	2.7	8.4	5.6	0.0	0.7	0.9	1.4	100.0

and a high of 34.2 per cent in Kuala Lumpur. This is clearly related to the presence of a sizeable Chinese population in these two areas. The other states where a fair proportion of their population professed to practise Buddhism are Johore (28.7 per cent), Selangor (24.4 per cent), Malacca (24.1 per cent), and Perak (24 per cent). These are the states along the west coast of the Peninsula where a substantial number of Chinese reside.

The other religions are professed to a much smaller extent by the population in the various states except Sabah and Sarawak. Hinduism, the principal religion of Indians, was adhered by 13.9 per cent of the population in Negri Sembilan, 12.1 per cent in Selangor, and 11 per cent in Perak. More interesting is Christianity being practised by the majority of the people in Sarawak, 42.6 per cent as against 31.8 per cent for Islam. Even in Sarawak a fair proportion of the people practised Christianity, about one-fourth as compared to the two-thirds for Islam. Christianity is practised by a negligible proportion of the population in each of the West Malaysian states. In reality, the multi-religious character of the population does not prevail in every part of the country, certainly not in the northern and eastern states of the Peninsula.

Conclusion

The complex diversity of the population has not only added enduring richness to the social and cultural mosaic of the nation, but has engendered some difficulties and challenges in the political and economic life of the people. Race and religion have always been linked in Malaysian politics as reflected in times of election and the subsequent formation of governments at the state and Federal levels. The paramount consideration is underlined by the usual practice of accommodating the competing interests of the various component parties in Barisan Nasional while maintaining Malay dominance. Islam has recently become a major factor in Malaysian politics since the emergence of the PAS, propagating its brand of radical Islamic teachings and practices that appeal to certain segments of the Malay electorate.

The entrenched ethnicity of the population has been the central focus in the formulation of government policies in implementing the

New Economic Policy (NEP) up to 1991 and thereafter the National Development Policy (NDP). The underlying influence of ethnicity is quite pervasive in almost every aspect of government programmes and action, especially in the fields of education, labour, business, land ownership, and rural development. The overriding objective of government policies is the creation of national unity through the eradication of racial equality in the social and economic advancement of the people. The ramifications of this cardinal philosophy adhered rigidly by the government will be discussed in certain sections of the chapters that follow.

NOTES

1. R. Chander, *General Report of the Population Census of Malaysia, 1970*, Vols. 1 and 2 (Kuala Lumpur: Department of Statistics, 1977).

2. Khoo Teik Huat, *General Report of the Population Census of Malaysia, 1980*, Vols. 1 and 2 (Kuala Lumpur: Department of Statistics, 1983).

3. Khoo Soo Gim, *General Report of the Population Census of Malaysia, 1991*, Vols. 1 and 2 (Kuala Lumpur: Department of Statistics, 1995).

4. Shaari Bin Abdul Rahman, *Population and Housing Census of Malaysia, 2000*, Vol. 2. *Population Distribution and Basic Demographic Characteristics* (Kuala Lumpur: Department of Statistics, 2001).

5. Saw Swee-Hock, *The Population of Peninsular Malaysia* (Singapore: Singapore University Press, 1988).

6. L.W. Jones, *The Population of Borneo* (Athlone Press, 1966).

The Emerging Politics of *Islam Hadhari*

TERENCE CHONG

Introduction

Islam Hadhari was a key campaign issue during the 2004 general elections in Malaysia. Its message of a "progressive" Islam was popular with the electorate, resulting in a ringing endorsement of Prime Minister Abdullah Badawi at the polls on 21 March. The idea of a "progressive" Islam, however, is not new and has been a recurring feature of the Malaysian political landscape since the early 1970s. "Progressive" Islam is part of a long history of contested interpretations of Islam between the United Malays' National Organisation (UMNO), Pan-Malaysia Islamic Party (PAS) and Malaysian Muslim Youth Organisation (ABIM) for their respective interests. The ways in which "progressive" Islam is interpreted and contested can be analytically captured as the struggle for legitimacy within the modern nation-state.

The modern nation-state is a relatively recent project in Southeast Asia that frames the multiple religious, ethnic and linguistic fissures in the region. The way in which "progressive" interpretations of Islam are emphasised and de-emphasised by different groups at different times reflects the on-going dispute over the character of the nation-state and its accoutring principles of democracy, notions of citizenship, and constitution. The nation-state, in turn, has also issued challenges to Islamic interests and powers in the region. According to Hefner and Horvatich,

> Its capacity to shape public affairs and intervene in the most intimate domains of private life has presented Southeast Asian Muslims with a historically unprecedented challenge. It has reduced the territorial fragmentation long characteristic of this region, undercut the autonomy of Muslim social organisations, and, at times, deployed forces to hunt down and eliminate Muslim rebels.[1]

Increased religiosity and demands for an Islamic state are thus, on the one hand, a result of the rejection of the modern nation-state and on the other, invariably shaped by its existing institutes and practices.

Beginning from the *dakwah* movement in the early 1970s, this chapter looks at how different organisations, specifically ABIM and PAS, have espoused the message of a "progressive" Islam for their own interests. The concept of "progressive" Islam in Malaysia has been constantly shifting, to include a variety of characteristics such as social justice, human rights, civil empowerment, democracy, humanism, modernity, and modernisation. This ambiguity of meaning has allowed different organisations to co-opt it and is the very reason for its constant revival. The message of a "progressive" Islam has also been emphasised and de-emphasised according to the prevailing political conditions. All this will demonstrate that the "progressive" spirit of *Islam Hadhari* is not new but a variant of political Islamic discourse in Malaysia. However, it is argued that global political shifts since 11 September 2001 have created an important role for *Islam Hadhari* as a political discourse. The politics of *Islam Hadhari*, it is suggested, is playing out on four different fronts, namely, as a counterfoil to PAS's brand of Islam; as a struggle with "*Islam Madani*" for the "progressive" mantle; as a set of morals and ethics to accompany a "global mindset"; and, lastly, on a global level, as a means to construct Malaysia as a model Muslim society.

Dakwah Movement of the 1970s

The beginning of the *dakwah* (Islamic revivalism) movement is popularly traced to disenfranchised university students in the early 1970s.[2] This student-based revival was institutionalised by the establishment of ABIM in the University of Malaya, formed in 1969 and officially registered in 1971. Comprising a mixture of students from local and overseas universities with both religious and secular educations, ABIM's anti-establishment Islam was perhaps informed by the progressive politics of social and civil rights movements in Western democracies of that period. ABIM's wide-ranging, largely left-wing rhetoric and its shifting alliances, initially with PAS and later with UMNO upon Anwar's co-option, allowed it to endow Islam with a variety of political meanings. Linked with PAS — both Fadzil Noor and Abdul Hadi Awang, former and present presidents respectively, were from ABIM — ABIM initially criticised UMNO for the latter's superficial implementation of Islamic policies and openly questioned the ruling party's Islamic credentials. ABIM's challenge to UMNO also included demands for the cultivation of religious leadership, more Islamised foreign policies, an Islamic banking system, and an Islamic university, with UMNO later acquiescing to the latter two. ABIM's discourse was unmistakenly revivalist in nature and "although it has not declared its aim for the establishment of an Islamic state in Malaysia as openly as PAS does, it is assumed that that is its preference and final aim".[3]

ABIM's undeclared desires did not prevent it from pushing its progressive politics of social welfare. In 1974, ABIM attacked the ruling party by mobilising thousands of students to protest against rural Malay poverty and uneven wealth distribution in the streets of Kuala Lumpur. It was "the single most important event that gave the *dakwah* movement, particularly ABIM, its much needed political credentials in the eyes of Malaysian public".[4] As a champion of Malay privileges and political symbol of the *ethnie* of nationhood, UMNO's early legitimacy lay in its ability to manage inter-ethnic contention while protecting and furthering the interests of Malays. ABIM's protests, in combining religious fervour and socio-economic discontent, struck at the ruling party's *raison d'être*, thus challenging its legitimacy. The state made 1,200 arrests, including that of ABIM leader and former deputy prime minister, Anwar Ibrahim; and though the protests were organised by *dakwah* leaders in ABIM, UMNO treated the unrest "as a student problem rather than an Islamic challenge to its legitimacy and authority".[5] In seeing the protests as an act of civil rather than religious unrest, UMNO was better able to respond decisively to the problem and, at the same time, circumvent serious consequences of a religious backlash.

Like ABIM, PAS's political agendum included Islamic state reform. Its early political ideology, however, was a "synthesis of reformist Islam, democracy, nationalism and socialism", the emphasis of each depending on contemporary political conditions.[6] PAS was born in 1951 as a result of a defection of UMNO members who disagreed with the secular character of Malaysia's post-colonial state and for a time, PAS members enjoyed dual membership with UMNO. PAS's early brand of "progressive" Islam was starkly different from its resolutely dogmatic image of today. According to *The Sunday Times*, one of PAS's objectives was to "co-operate with other political organisations whose principles and objectives were not opposed to Islamic teaching. This was for attaining democracy, social justice and humanity".[7] Indeed, PAS, under the "progressive" leadership of Dr Burhanuddin from 1956, succeeded in grafting "together the streams of Islamist and nationalist thought with the intention of promoting a broad and universalist understanding of nationalism that went beyond the narrow confines of ethnocentricism and race-centred politics",[8] to articulate a discourse of "civilisational" Islam that predated *Islam Hadhari*. Unfortunately, with its early preoccupation with shoring legitimacy as protector of Malay rights and privileges, UMNO was ensconced in ethnic-based politics and was slow in responding to PAS's brand of Islamic synthesis.

PAS's early ability to accentuate the secular principles of nationalism, democracy, and socialism under the banner of Islamic reform provided it with a broad ideological space to manoeuvre according to its interests, as evident in its 1974 alliance, albeit short-lived, with Barisan Nasional (BN). PAS's acumen in accentuating progressive politics was again on show in the run-up to the 1999 election. With Anwar's sacking and UMNO's alleged corruption dominating the political imagination, PAS took advantage of the anti-establishment atmosphere to talk about Islam "through the language of democracy and human rights, respect for the rule of law, freedom of speech and expression, the right to live free from fear and threat".[9]

As we have seen, strands of "progressive" Islam were evident during the *dakwah* movement in the early 1970s, and were emphasised and de-emphasised according to contemporary political conditions. UMNO was caught in ideological impasse because of its dual commitment to the safeguarding of Islam, as guaranteed by the constitution, and to protect the special privileges of the Malays. In effect, this meant that UMNO could not afford to denounce Islamic challenges for fear of being seen to be unconstitutional, while any meaningful engagement with the progressive politics of PAS or ABIM would be an implicit acknowledgement that it had failed in its protection of Bumiputeras. Consequently, its response took the path of least resistance. UMNO embarked on a project of raising the public profile of Islam. "Government actions — such as sponsoring the annual Quran-reading competitions, building still more mosques, and instructing Malay ministers to wear their songkoks [Malay-Muslim hats] and attend mosque services — were largely symbolic (though still important)".[10]

By the mid- to late 1970s, geopolitical shifts around the world began to reverberate in Malaysia. The ideological impact of the Arab-Israeli war and its triggering of the oil crisis in 1973; the rise of Middle East countries as economic powerhouses; Muslim disenchantment with secular nationalism; and most crucially, the Iranian Revolution of 1979, began to alter the contours of Malaysia's political landscape. External politics and ideologies were internalised by local identities to, in turn, alter the mode and mood of the dialogue between such identities and the state. PAS's discourse of a "progressive" and "civilisational" Islam faded, to be replaced by a more dogmatic and less tolerant stance. The absorption and adaptation of external ideologies "was evident by the increasing mobilisation of the Muslim community [in Malaysia] by various organisations pursuing the fundamentals of Islam. They posed both a threat and challenge to the government. The demands and initiatives made by these organisations implied that the government seemed not to be pursuing enough of these fundamentals".[11] One local consequence of these global shifts, together with the rise of the *ulama* to leadership positions in PAS, was that they legitimised the political pursuit of a more dogmatic and narrowly-defined Islam. UMNO, or at least the in-coming Mahathir, realised that the world was changing and that local legitimacy now demanded greater institutional initiatives.

The Islamisation of UMNO: The 1980s

UMNO's co-option of Anwar in 1982, a year after Mahathir became prime minister, signalled the increasing Islamisation of UMNO's public profile as well as the halt of criticisms from ABIM. More importantly, Anwar's inclusion indicated Mahathir's intention to bring anti-establishment Islam under UMNO's wing and to broaden the ruling party's Islamic appeal.

> As a party representing Muslims but also constituting a comparatively secular, Malay-nationalist linchpin of the ruling BN coalition, UMNO could not deny the primacy of Islam as a basis for political organisation and *ad-deen* (way of life). Instead, UMNO struggled to shape, control, and tame the forces of Islamisation to serve its political goal of building a moderately Islamic polity.[12]

UMNO's institutionalisation of Islam began with *Penerapan Nilai-nilai Islam*, a policy guideline for the incorporation of Islamic ethics in governance. Though the policy guideline did not formally constitute an Islamic state, it was "the most purposeful expression of Islamisation process that UMNO had ever made".[13] The Islamisation process also included the setting up of the International Islamic University in 1983, the Islamic Development Foundation in 1985, the Islamic Insurance Company also in 1985, and most crucially, the Islamic Bank in 1984. Another important development was the establishment of *Pusat Islam* in 1980, "which was in effect a government-sponsored *dakwah* group intended to compete with other *dakwah* groups and to report on their activities. It was fully funded by the government, and was placed under a cabinet minister inside the Prime Minister's Department".[14]

Anwar Ibrahim's brand of progressive and socially-oriented Islam from his ABIM days was not completely sidelined. Institut Kajian Dasar (IKD, or Institute of Policy Development), founded by Anwar in 1985, was one of the first government institutes to seriously infuse "spiritual, moral and ethical relevance of religious beliefs and principle in the development of strategic policies and goals".[15] IKD's relatively liberal and progressive spirit of UMNO's interpretation of Islam, perhaps even reflecting the social consciousness of ABIM, predates the more conservative yet inclusive rhetoric of the Institute of Islamic Understanding Malaysia (IKIM). This "progressive" element in UMNO, however, caught less public attention compared to other highly visible structural changes that included Islamic administration reforms as well as the legal and constitutional amendments that empowered Islamic legal authorities. It has been observed that "nowhere in Asia has the Islamisation of law proceeded more methodically than in Malaysia. Dozens of new statutes and judicial decisions have clarified, expanded, and reformulated the law applicable to Muslims".[16] Whatever little evidence of progressive discourse from UMNO was muted by highly symbolic and public gestures such as the deployment of Islamic jargon and salutations, accelerated building of mosques and religious institutes, Islamic programmes on radio and television, and religious courses for the public.

UMNO's Islamisation process, aimed at pre-empting alternate Islamic agenda, had an effect on the position of PAS and its brand of Islam. PAS's direction, post-Asri, was an Islamic "discourse of resistance and delegitimation. Islamism became the vehicle for a counter-hegemonic and anti-systemic project that was aimed at bringing about a new social, moral and political order embodied by the Islamic state".[17] PAS's response to UMNO's institutionalisation of Islam was the increased emphasis of a religion-centred vision of a utopian state that drew its cultural and moral ethos from the Islamic text. This emphasis began around 1982 as party dissent against Asri eventually culminated with a deeply "fundamentalist" leadership. Party unhappiness with Asri stemmed from his unpopular decision to join the ruling coalition and his tendency to favour friends from his inner circle.

> But, these men failed to fit into the "fundamentalist" mould that the new PAS members desired. They were too secular for an Iranian model of leadership which was becoming a fad within PAS. They were too materialistic, too compromising and sympathetic towards the UMNO brand of Malay nationalism".[18]

UMNO's Islamisation process, together with PAS's new "fundamentalist" leaders, spurred the Islamic party to heighten its discourse of religious fundamentals and moral purity, both as a source of self-legitimacy and struggle for relevance, and as a mode of resistance against UMNO's own Islamic efforts. In other words, PAS could not compete with UMNO's vast economic resources and superior infrastructure in their race to out-Islamise each other, and thus reverted to Islam "not simply [as] a source of solace in a precarious life, [or as] an escape ... [but as] an alternative moral universe in embryo — a dissident subculture, an existentially true and just one, which helps to unite its members as a human community and a community of values".[19] PAS's interpretation of Islam as a "moral universe" legitimised its own existence as an *ulama*-led organisation with expert knowledge of the Quran and with authority over exegeses.

Consequentially, through the 1980s, UMNO and PAS competed with each other for legitimacy from the *ummah* on different levels: the former paraded its Islamic credentials by pointing to structural and institutional implementations while the latter appealed to moral and religious "purity" to outmanoeuvre UMNO. Such contestations came to a temporary halt after UMNO's 1987 schism. UMNO "dissidents", in contesting the by-elections in the Malay-dominated north-eastern states, found it expedient to "reach an understanding with PAS".[20] The unusual circumstance of the UMNO schism allowed PAS to work with UMNO "dissidents" without having to soften its ideological stance. Nonetheless, interpretations and contestations of Islam had generally "led to the 'holier-than-thou' contest of Islamic correctness and credibility between UMNO and PAS, with the former goaded to show its Islamic character, yet without being snared by attributions of 'fundamentalism' or 'fanaticism' intimidating to investors, developers or non-Muslims".[21] The 1980s came to a close with the shock resignation of Vice President Nakhaie "citing the party's poor management, organisation and decisiveness — and subsequent defection to UMNO in April 1989"[22] while Fadzil Noor took over as PAS president in 1989.

Vision 2020 and "Vision Islam": The 1990s

By the early 1990s, Malaysia's economic progress was winning UMNO international praise, from both scholars and *ulama*, for its brand of Islam. The government's efforts "to become Islamic without becoming an Islamic state" won it kudos for its "adequate simultaneous grasp of Islam and modernity, and initiatives taken in that light".[23] Indeed, at the close of the New Economic Policy (NEP), ideas of modernity, visions of Malaysia's industrial future, and the role of the Malays in this future became the dominant national discourse. This discourse emerged with, and was in many ways encapsulated by, Mahathir's *The Way Forward* speech, later known as *Vision 2020*, given on 28 February 1991. In identifying the deficiencies of the Malay community, the speech played a crucial role in circumscribing notions of "progress" with ethnic interests. The prime minister spoke of the "need for a mental revolution and cultural transformation" of the "Bumiputera community". He went on to note that "[i]f [Bumiputeras] are not brought into the mainstream, if their potentials are not fully developed, if they are allowed to be a millstone around the national neck, then our progress is going to be retarded by that much. No nation can achieve full progress with only half its human resources harnessed. What may be considered a burden now can, with the correct attitude and management, be the force that lightens our burden and hastens our progress. The Bumiputeras must play their part fully in the achievement of the national goal".[24]

In highlighting the Malay community and visions of modernity, it became important to make one compatible with the other and Islam provided the grounds for this. The IKIM, was established in February 1992 to follow up and complement *Vision 2020*. IKIM is staffed by personnel from local universities and private *ulama* whose "task is to find some common ground between Muslims and non-Muslims, academics and businessmen, Malays, Chinese and foreign investors, and to persuade all of the merits of the government's brand of economics" as well as the "painlessness of the government's Islamisation policies".[25] In its booklet, *An Inspiration for the Future of Islam*, IKIM states that its objectives were to

> provide a clearer picture of Islam in line with the demands and needs of the modern times. Islam is never a hinderance or millstone to development. It is not Islam that leads mankind towards underdevelopment. Islam should not be viewed as a religion that befits only the needs and demands of ancient societies. It is the Muslims who have not actually lived up to the standards Islam prescribes. There are many interpretations of the Islamic concepts and principles that are not appropriate to the modern way of life.[26]

Mahathir's "progressive" Islam in the early 1990s was nationalistic in tone and designed to usher elements of modernity into Islam by way of protecting or defending the faith as the quotes from his various speeches demonstrate.

> Knowing the contents of the Quran alone would not, for example, make a man a capable defender of the faith. To defend the faith, he must know the art of war, the weapons, the skills, the technology, etc., which he must learn elsewhere. The Quran directs him to equip himself with swords, horses, i.e. the weapons of defence at the time. Clearly it would be futile in this day and age to depend on swords and horses.[27]

> Muslims should regard industry as a means to strengthen the Muslim states and the Muslims so that they are better respected and capable of defending themselves. Ignorant Muslims cannot contribute towards the greatness of Islam. On the other hand, industrial capability, as well as the extensive command of all kinds of knowledge necessary for industrialisation, will make Islam and Muslims more respected.[28]

> Failure to learn and master these subjects, which are not specifically religious, will expose the Muslims to the danger of losing their religion .... Their acquisition of knowledge and skills, intellectual and material wealth is therefore a part of their means to preserve their faith — a part of the practices of their religion and their way of life.[29]

In holding up science and technology as the means with which to "defend the faith", Mahathir attempted to articulate an Islam for modernity. This brand of Islam — what Hilley calls "Vision Islam"[30] — was undoubtedly industrial and scientifically inclined, designed to be contrasted against what Hilley terms "PAS Islam".[31] This binary succeeded in creating within Malaysia the dialectic politics of a "modern" and "traditional" society, echoing the arguments of the Western modernisation theory that asserts that religion should recede from the public sphere in a modernising society.[32] In addition to out "Islamising" PAS, as was the *modus operandi* in the 1980s, UMNO, no doubt prompted by the very real challenges of globalisation and competition for global capital, synthesised notions of modernisation with its interpretation of a "progressive" Islam.

The "progressiveness" of "Vision Islam", however, had less to do with ideas of social justice or equitable wealth distribution, as in the 1970s, but was increasingly linked to its accommodation of modernity, western science and capitalism. These links made it possible for UMNO to deploy "Vision Islam" as an ideological pathway for the "imagined community" of Malays towards the fulfilment of *Vision 2020*. Not surprisingly, as a state-sanctioned Islam, "Vision Islam" invariably privileged state interests such as economic growth, the development and education of the domestic workforce, respect for secular laws, industrialisation, and the pursuit of knowledge for economic ends in the fields of science and technology (read: as oppose to religious knowledge), with little to say about human rights, freedom of speech, or social justice.

This state-sanctioned and conservative "progressive" Islam was, however, not completely homogenous. Anwar, from the upper echelons of UMNO, was also articulating a "progressive" Islam that was more liberal and individual-centred. "By being moderate and pragmatic", acccording to the then deputy prime minister in *The Asian Renaissance*, "Southeast Asian Muslims are neither compromising the teachings and ideals of Islam nor pandering the whims and fancies of the times. On the contrary, such an approach is necessary to realise the societal ideals of Islam such as justice, equitable distribution of wealth, fundamental rights and liberties".[33] Despite the profound dissimilarity between Anwar's "liberal" Islam and "Vision Islam", the former remained dormant for the time being while the latter took centre-stage.

"Vision Islam" was, of course, not uncontested.

> Despite spurious talk of so-called "Asian values" and Malaysia being a "model Islamic state" (or so says Washington), it quickly dawns on the newcomer that the real national ethos is consumerism in its crudest, crassest form. Malaysians may not be able to agree on much, but they can at least shop together till they drop — even if that is the only national achievement to note thus far.[34]

"Vision Islam", however, faced a more crucial challenge in 1999. The run up to the 1999 general election saw the 1997 Asian crisis, the expulsion and conviction of Anwar, alledged UMNO cronyism and corruption, and the consequent rise of the *reformasi* movement and its political manifestation as the National Justice Party (Keadilan). These series of events thrusted issues of democracy, good governance, and human rights to the forefront of Malaysian politics.[35] This period also coincided with a time when the global mainstream Islamic movement displayed signs of an ideological shift from its earlier "radical literalist" phase obsessed with the legalism of an Islamic state to a more "participatory" phase emphasising issues of democracy and good governance.[36] With the 1999 Malaysian general election dominated by such issues, PAS once again demonstrated its ability to articulate secular principles by talking about Islam in a language of democracy, human rights, and freedom of speech. PAS Islam, once again, turned "progressive" to take advantage of the prevailing anti-establishment sentiments to win broader legitimacy from those disenchanted by Anwar's sacking, and the alleged corruption and nepotism of UMNO.

Armed with "Vision Islam" and the tangible rewards of modernisation, UMNO responded by abandoning its defensive position and confronted the polity with the confidence from having synthesised Islam with the demands of economic growth. Mahathir's "Vision Islam" discourse culminated in his famous declaration that Malaysia was an "Islamic state". Made on 29 September 2001, the prime minister's remark quickly became known as the "929 declaration". To assuage non-Muslim fears, it was made clear that Mahathir meant that the Malaysian state, unlike PAS, observed the substance and spirit of Islam, instead of mechanically emulating its forms.

By the end of the 1990s, in the aftermath of the 1999 election, two interpretations of "progressive" Islam hung in the air — *Vision 2020* and the Anwar-linked, individual-centred Islam with an emphasis on human rights and freedoms, later précised as *Islam Madani* (modern). Anwar's *Islam Madani* draws its intellectual impetus from the humanist post-classical Muslim scholar, Muhammad Iqbal (1877–1938), who formulated his notion of *khudi*, or self, by drawing from western philosophers like Nietzsche and Islamic teachings to empower the Muslim individual.[37] The strong humanist elements in *Islam Madani* asserts that "individuals and civil society must be empowered with the necessary freedoms, before meaningful reforms can take place; nor can the draconian ISA [Internal Security Act] exist as the perpetual counterfoil to the individual's right to reform society".[38] With *Islam Madani*, it is possible to see the trajectory of a left-wing brand of "progressive" Islam in Malaysia. Beginning with the student-led ABIM, this brand of "progressive" Islam arose in the 1970s, in part inspired by social and civil movements elsewhere, taking to the streets in its criticism of the state. Always sharing close ties with "PAS Islam", the spirit of *Islam Madani* saw little contradiction between its more social and individual-centred outlook and the dogmatic teachings of "PAS Islam", with both synthesised for political effect whenever the opportunity presented itself. Left-wing Islam was co-opted by the state with Anwar's entry into UMNO and remained latent, while "Vision Islam" — the state's version of "progressive" Islam — took centre-stage, no doubt buoyed by the industrialisation of Malaysia. Left-wing Islam came full circle with Anwar's incarceration where, once again, it took to the streets, this time embodied by the *reformasi* movement in 1998.

The Emerging Politics of *Islam Hadhari*

One reason for the recurring politics of a "progressive" Islam is its ambiguity and malleability, thus imbuing it with a flexibility for different, often conflicting, interests. *Islam Hadhari* was a *cause célèbre* in the run-up to the March 2004 general election. In seeking the people's mandate, Prime Minister Abdullah Badawi presented his vision of "progressive Islam" because he did not want the country's Muslims "to fall into PAS' trap".[39] *Islam Hadhari*'s content, however, continues to be heavy on rhetoric and light on meaning, even with the Minister of Religious Affairs Dr Abdullah Md Zin's offering of "*wasatiyah* or a balanced approach to life".[40]

Nonetheless, *Islam Hadhari* was a politically astute strategy that succeeded in Islamising UMNO with the result of nullifying the attraction of "PAS Islam", so much so that commentators found it hard to distinguish UMNO from PAS.[41] The prime minister won by a landside and *Islam Hadhari* was proclaimed a triumph by the onlooking media.[42] Abdullah proceeded to identify the ten principles at the UMNO general assembly on 23 September 2004. They are:

1. Faith and piety in Allah
2. A just and trustworthy government
3. A free and independent people
4. Mastery of knowledge
5. Balanced and comprehensive economic development
6. A good quality of life

7. Protection of the rights of minority groups and women
8. Cultural and moral integrity
9. Safeguarding the environment
10. Strong defences

While the details of *Islam Hadhari* remain vague, it is traced to the teachings of Islamic philosopher Ibn Khaldun (1332–1406). Its notion of "progressiveness" is drawn from the adaptive mindset and practices whereby "nomadic societies moved in a law-like manner from their tribal and primitive origins to a progressive civilisation".[43] Given the importance that Ibn Khaldun places on laws, social order, and its enforcement, it is not surprising that the state finds *Islam Hadhari* attractive. According to Antony Black, Khaldun believed that men "instinctively desire comradeship (*suhba*). But the resulting ijtima' al-'umran (association of culture) requires 'a Restraining influence' (*wazi'*), that is Kingship (*mulk*). Indeed, cooperation itself requires the use of force. Wazi' or mulk is, therefore, 'a natural (*tabi'i*) quality of man which is absolutely necessary (*daruri*) to mankind'".[44] This emphasis on social restraint and order, as well as the legitimisation of the use of force, privileges state interest, and is in contrast to the more humanist and individual-centred philosophy of the Muhammad Iqbal-inspired *Islam Madani*.

Another characteristic of *Islam Hadhari* is its close association with the personality of Abdullah Badawi. Popularly known "Mr Clean", Abdullah's religious pedigree — his family is deeply religious; his father a *ulama* and was himself a graduate of Islamic studies from the University of Malaya — was effectively used as a counterfoil to PAS. Confronted with Abdullah's Islamic background, PAS found it difficult to criticise UMNO's lack of religious credentials during the 2004 election, as was previously de rigueur, and thus resorted to attacking his intentions. PAS President Abdul Hawi Awang accused the prime minister of being "inauthentic".[45]

The politics of *Islam Hadhari* is thus emerging on four fronts. Firstly, it is emerging as a struggle with the more civil society-based *Islam Madani* to claim the "progressive" Islam mantle in Malaysia. The increasing modernisation, rising levels of secular education, and cosmopolitanism of Malaysian society will place a high political premium on a secular-friendly "progressive" Islam. By virtue of his political isolation, Anwar's

Islam Madani may be the Islamic banner under which the opposition or civil society groups will gather for religious *imprimatur* or to mobilise Islamic anti-establishment sentiments.[46] The contestation between *Islam Hadhari* and *Islam Madani* is likely to centre on issues such as democracy, human rights, civil liberties, and empowerment. Should this happen, UMNO's, but more interestingly, *Islam Hadhari*'s, response could set the tone for future Islamic contestations in Malaysia. As it stands, *Islam Hadhari* ensures "interpretations [of Islam] are suited to the developmental needs of the prevailing time and conditions".[47] Anwar's release and gradual re-entry into politics may vitalise the ideology of *Islam Madani*. It is possible that *Islam Madani* will challenge the definition of Malaysia's "developmental needs" and the government's right to determine if "the prevailing time and conditions" are suitable for power decentralisation.

Secondly, as an extension of UMNO's long-standing battle with PAS, *Islam Hadhari* will continue to be used to counter "PAS Islam". In this sense, there will be no change in UMNO's drive to institutionalise Islam. According to the religious affairs minister, *Islam Hadhari* will be taught to Syariah court officers. He notes that "[u]nfortunately, we have some trainers saying that *Islam Hadhari* does not follow any school of thought. So intensive training must take place."[48] The government has also announced plans to set up a unit to impart the values of *Islam Hadhari* in the former PAS state of Terengganu. Called the Terengganu Bestari, this unit is deemed "necessary as we do not want certain groups to use Islam for the purpose of spreading hatred".[49] The institutionalisation of *Islam Hadhari* also has the added task of purging UMNO's image as corrupt and riddled with money politics. The prime minister's anti-corruption drive and the formulation of a code of ethics for government officials, together with *Islam Hadhari*, will serve as initiatives for state reform.

Thirdly, *Islam Hadhari* will serve as a set of values for Malay capitalists in the age of globalisation. The ten principles of *Islam Hadhari* above "have been devised to empower Muslims to face the global challenges of today" and "for Malays to be more successful global players".[50] The prime minister went on to assert that "Malays must have a global mindset, understand the global scenario and be able to face the challenges of the global environment". This "global mindset" can only be developed with the emphasis of the broader principles of Islam over religiosity and form. By loosening the tight fundamentalism-secularism binary proposed by "PAS Islam", *Islam Hadhari* emerges as a legitimate space where the *Melayu Baru* (new Malay) may retain his or her "Muslim" character while engaging in cosmopolitan practices. This space allows the *Melayu Baru* to display his or her skills and competence in manoeuvring between cosmopolitan and national identities without being accused of being "un-Islamic". *Islam Hadhari*, however, echoes the message of *Vision 2020* in the way it attempts to purge Bumiputera expectations of special privileges. According to Abdullah in the same speech, "It is necessary for UMNO members to understand the impact of the global economy on the Malay race. We must understand that at the global level, it is unlikely that a policy will be formulated with the purpose of helping Bumiputeras. The global economy does not recognise quotas; it will not allocate special projects for Bumiputeras. The global economic lexicon only acknowledges terms such as competition, competitiveness, productivity, innovation, creativity, originality, excellence and efficiency." As such, *Islam Hadhari* is tasked with the two-fold purpose of providing Malay Muslims with a code of morals and ethics to accompany their global mindset in the age of globalisation, and to reinforce *Vision 2020*'s message of Bumiputera independence from state handouts.

And lastly, on a broader global scale, *Islam Hadhari* allows Malaysia to position itself as a model Muslim society in a post-September 11 world. Malaysia has "progressed, its people benefited, and today, countries that have had more wealth and natural resources than Malaysia, and which are mired in misery and poverty, now look at Malaysia as their own model. The answer for the Islamic world is there to see, in Malaysia's success".[51] *Islam Hadhari*, a lynchpin in this deeply self-conscious construction of Malaysia as a model for the rest of the Islamic world, appears to be bearing fruit. Middle Eastern countries, traditionally the core for Islamic teachings and political thought, are expressing interest in *Islam Hadhari*[52] while Malaysian missionary envoys are venturing into south Thailand to spread "correct understandings of Islam".[53] It is clear that post-September 11 global cultural and political shifts have increased the international stakes of a "moderate" Islam discourse; and the discourse of *Islam Hadhari*, while administratively vague, has garnered immense political value for Malaysia on the international stage. In this sense, one difference between the "Vision Islam" of Mahathir and Abdullah's *Islam Hadhari* is the way in which a vastly different global political landscape has made it necessary for Malaysia's official Islam to move beyond its national audience to appeal to an international one.

Conclusion

The politics of "progressive" Islam has been playing out in the Malaysian political landscape since the 1970s. As such, the politics of *Islam Hadhari* is part of a long trajectory of interpretations and contestations within Malaysian domestic politics. This trajectory is locked within a resolutely national framework as participants struggle for legitimacy and power from various constituencies. The interpretation and contestation of Islam has not only increased the volume of political challenges and counter-challenges, but also, and on a more positive note, opened up new political and civic spaces for non-governmental groups such as Sisters in Islam (SIS).

SIS, formed in 1988, comprises highly-educated and professional Muslim women who raise women's issues from an Islamic perspective. New political and civil spaces have allowed SIS to eschew fundamentalist interpretations of the Quran for more moderate ones. For example, "[e]ven where the Qur'an places unequivocal constraints on dress and access to public for women, the Sisters' argument centres on the universality of the scriptural message; in this spirit, it should not be expected that society be frozen in a seventh-century Arabian mould, but that it should be open to suitable adaptation to the needs of changing times and circumstances".[54] SIS skilfully manoeuvres between the "fundamentalist" and "progressive" elements of Islam. The group makes it clear that "the only authentic source is the text of the Qur'an" thus winning religious legitimacy, while, at the same time, benefiting from the work of feminist studies in pointing to the fallacies of male-biased exegeses and historically-determined Hadith.[55]

The emerging discourse of *Islam Hadhari* is symptomatic of increasing and shifting pressures on the state from both the local and global communities. Local politics, influenced by the global politics of Islamisation, democracy, civil liberties, and so on, have made it necessary for the state to formulate Islamic discourses that appeal to as broad a spectrum of ideological, class, and ethnic constituencies as possible. That its legitimacy hinges on its appeal to such a spectrum is very much in keeping with the multicultural character of modern nation-states. Conversely, there will be multiple interpretations of such discourses and a variety of ways in which different individuals and groups may adapt them for their own interests. Global changes have also made it politically expedient for the state to synthesise Islam and modernity. Such a synthesis has, for better or worse, become the primary means to win international legitimacy as a "progressive" and "moderate" Muslim member of the global community.

NOTES

1. Robert W. Hefner and Patricia Horvatich, eds., *Islam in an Era of Nation-States: Politics and Religious Renewal in Muslim Southeast Asia* (Hawaii: University of Hawaii Press, 1997), pp. 5, 6.

2. K.S. Jomo and Ahmad Shabery Cheek, "Malaysia's Islamic Movements", in *Fragmented Vision: Culture and Politics in Contemporary Malaysia*, edited by Francis Loh Kok Wah and Joel Khan (Sydney: Allen & Unwin, 1992); A.B. Shamsul, "Identity Construction, Nation Formation, and Islamic Revivalism in Malaysia", in *Islam in an Era of Nation-States: Politics and Religious Renewal in Muslim Southeast Asia*, edited by Robert Hefner and Patricia Horvatich (Hawaii: University of Hawaii Press, 1997).

3. Saliha Hassan, "Islamic Revivalism and State Response to Islamic-Oriented Non-Governmental Organisations in Malaysia" (paper presented at the Islamic Revivalism and State Response: The Experiences of Malaysia, Indonesia and Brunei Workshop, Singapore, 2–3 June 1997), p. 10.

4. Shamsul 1997, p. 214.

5. Ibid.

6. Syed Ahmad Hussein, "Muslim Politics and the Discourse on Democracy", in *Democracy in Malaysia: Discourses and Practices*, edited by Francis Loh Kok Wah and Khoo Boo Teik (Surrey: RoutledgeCurzon, 2002), p. 85.

7. *The Sunday Times* (Malaysia), 26 August 1951, as quoted from Alias Mohamed, *PAS' Platform: Development and Change 1951–1986* (Selangor: Gateway Publishing House, 1994), p. 31.

8. Farish Noor, *The Other Malaysia: Writings on Malaysia's Subaltern History* (Kuala Lumpur: Silverfish Books, 2000), p. 58.

9. "Facing the Fundamentalist Challenge", *The Straits Times*, 9 January 2003.

10. R.S. Milne and Diane K. Mauzy, *Malaysia: Tradition, Modernity, and Islam* (Boulder & London: Westview Press, 1986), p. 52.

11. Cheah Boon Kheng, *Malaysia: The Making of a Nation* (Singapore: Institute of Southeast Asian Studies, 2002), p. 167.

12. Meredith L. Weiss, "The Changing Shape of Islamic Politics in Malaysia", *Journal of East Asian Studies* 4 (2004): 153.

13. Syed, *Democracy in Malaysia: Discourses and Practices*, p. 88.

14. R.S. Milne and Diane K. Mauzy, *Malaysian Politics under Mahathir* (London: Routledge, 1999), p. 85.

15. <http://www.ikdasar.tripod.com/ikd/objective.htm>. My thanks to Lee Hock Guan for pointing out IKD to me.

16. Donald L. Horowitz, "The Quran and the Common Law: Islamic Law Reform and the Theory of Legal Change", *American Journal of Comparative Law* 42 (1994): 233–93.

17. Farish Noor, "PAS Post-Fadzil Noor: Future Directions and Prospects" (working paper 8, Institute of Southeast Asian Studies, Singapore, August 2002, p. 3).

18. Alias, *PAS' Platform: Development and Change 1951–1986*, p. 179.

19. Scott (1976, p. 240) quoted in Farish (2002, p. 11).

20. Harold Crouch, "Authoritarian Trends, the UMNO Split and the Limits to State Power", in *Fragmented Vision: Culture and Politics in Contemporary Malaysia*, edited by Francis Loh Kok Wah and Joel Khan (Sydney: Allen & Unwin, 1992), p. 34.

21. Judith Nagata, "How to be Islamic without being an Islamic State: Contested Models of Development in Malaysia", in *Islam, Globalisation and Postmodernity*, edited by Akbar S. Ahmed and Hastings Donnan (London: Routledge, 1994), p. 84.

22. Jomo & Ahmad, *Fragmented Vision: Culture and Politics in Contemporary Malaysia*, p. 102.

23. R.K. Khuri, *Freedom, Modernity and Islam: Toward a Creative Synthesis* (New York: Syracuse University Press, 1998), p. 6.

24. Mahathir Mohamed, *Malaysia: The Way Forward* (Kuala Lumpur: Malaysian Business Council, 1991c), p. 17.

25. Nagata, *Islam, Globalisation and Postmodernity*, p. 75.

26. Syed Othman AlHabshi, *An Inspiration for the Future of Islam: A Brief History and Objectives of the Institute of Islamic Understanding Malaysia (IKIM)* (Kuala Lumpur: IKIM, 1994), p. 20.

27. Mahathir Mohamad (speech at the Opening of the International Institute of Islamic Thought and Civilization (ISTAC), Kuala Lumpur, 2 June 1993*a*).

28. Mahathir Mohamad (speech at the Opening of the Islam and Industrial Conference, Kuala Lumpur, 21 January 1993*b*).

29. Mahathir Mohamad (speech at the 10th Anniversary Celebration of the International Islamic University Malaysia, Selangor, 24 August 1993*c*).

30. John Hilley, *Malaysia: Mahathirism, Hegemony and the New Opposition* (New York: Zed Books, 2001).

31. Ibid.

32. Amrita Malhi, "The PAS-BN Conflict in the 1990s: Islamism and Modernity", in *Malaysia: Islam, Society and Politics*, edited by Virginia Hooker and Norani Othman (Singapore: Institute of Southeast Asian Studies, 2003).

33. Anwar Ibrahim, *The Asian Renaissance* (Kuala Lumpur: Times Books International, 1996), p. 113.

34. Farish Noor, "Malaysia's Islamic Fanaticism", *Daily Times*, 14 October 2004 <http://www.dailytimes.com.pk/default.asp?page=story_12-6-2004_pg3_2>.

35. Francis Loh Kok Wah and Johan Saravanamuttu, eds., *New Politics in Malaysia* (Singapore: Institute of Southeast Asian Studies, 2003).

36. Syed, *Democracy in Malaysia: Discourses and Practices.*

37. Anwar, *The Asian Renaissance.*

38. Phar Kim Beng "*Islam Hadhari* vs *Islam Madani*", *Malaysiakini*, 8 September 2004 <http://www.malaysiakini.com/columns/29830)>.

39. "Abdullah Offers 'Inclusive' Islam", *The Straits Times* (Singapore), 9 March 2004.

40. "A Balanced Approach that is *Islam Hadhari*", *New Straits Times (Malaysia), 1 August 2004.*

41. "PAS and UMNO Beginning to Look Alike", The Straits Times (Singapore), 13 March 2004.

42. "Triumph for Progressive Vision of Malaysia", *The Straits Times* (Singapore), 22 March 2004.

43. Phar, *Malaysiakini.*

44. Antony Black, *The History of Islamic Political Thought: From the Prophet to the Present* (Edinburgh: Edinburgh University Press, 2001), p. 172.

45. David Martin-Jones, "Badawi to the Bone?: Post-Mahathir Malaysia at the Polls", *The Review* 29, no. 4 (April 2004).

46. Radio Singapore International, "What Lies Ahead for Anwar's Political Future?", 3 September 2004 <http://rsi.mediacorpradio.com/english/newsline/view/20040903155034/1/.html>; "Return of a Rebel: Former DPM Poised to Unite Opposition", *The Straits Times* (Singapore), 16 September 2004.

47. Abdullah Badawi (speech at the 55th UMNO General Assembly, Kuala Lumpur, 23rd September 2004).

48. "A Balanced Approach that is *Islam Hadhari*", *New Straits Times*.

49. "*Islam Hadhari* Unit for State", *The Star* (Malaysia), 5 August 2004.

50. Abdullah (speech at the 55th UMNO General Assembly).

51. "Malaysia as a Model Islamic Nation", *New Straits Times* (Malaysia), 2 October 2004.

52. "Other Muslim States Show Interest in *Islam Hadhari*", *The Straits Times* (Singapore), 29 September 2004.

53. "Malaysia to Send Islamic Scholars to Thai South", *The Straits Times* (Singapore), 15 October 2004,

54. Nagata, *Islam, Globalisation and Postmodernity*, p. 80.

55. Ibid., p. 79.

3

Bangsa Malaysia: Vision or Spin?

OOI KEE BENG

Slogans as Initiators of Discourse

Mahathir Mohamad was probably unwavering throughout his political life as far as his hopes for Malaysia were concerned. However, given the pragmatics of politics, one would expect the numerous slogans he forged over 22 years to direct the political focus of his countrymen to vary in efficacy, in seriousness, and in function. For them to rally the masses to directed discourse, these chosen phrases had to be loose yet suggestive. This form of policy promulgation characterised much of his image, and can be accredited for the impact his ideas had on the political consciousness of Malaysians.

Where economic policies were concerned, Mahathir's measures may have been varied, some working better than others, but the end he sought was always nationalistic. As noted by K.S. Jomo:

> [O]n the whole, it can be said that economic policies from the early 1980s seek to transform Malaysia into a newly industrialized country (NIC) like South Korea, less dependent on the developed industrial nations, and under genuine Bumiputera capitalist entrepreneurial leadership. Most of Mahathir's economic policies seem to aim to achieve that end.[1]

His policies were interestingly of a kind that needed to capture the imagination of the populace and pave the discursive path of the nation. For example, the Look East Policy announced in 1981 was an economic initiative insofar as it courted the governments and the businessmen of Japan and Korea to invest in Malaysia and in the process allow technical know-how to flow to Malaysia's advantage. At the same time, it was also very much a socio-cultural programme "wherein the Malaysian government itself seeks to inculcate a supposed Japanese work ethic through various propaganda devices and through concrete promotion and implementation of the policy in the private and public sectors".[2]

The propaganda of "Malaysia Inc." was another conscious attempt to associate Malaysia with the example of Japan Inc., not only as an ideal where cooperation between the government and the private sector would make "greater contributions to national development", but also, again, as a socio-cultural programme to foster strong links between the public and private sectors, and to connect government services to national profit: "More efficient and prompt government services would increase the companies' prospects for profits. Larger profits in turn ensure more taxes for the government."[3] Incidentally, "Japan Incorporated" was initially a derogatory term connoting an overly materialistic culture concerned only with work and money, and not with the finer things in life. However, sustained growth has turned that culture into a developmental model considered worthy of emulation.

The Mahathir regime was thus prone to sloganeer with a dual purpose. Slogans tended to provide a comprehensible idea about a wide-ranging policy, while reminding the populace that some major change was needed of them: "We are doing our bit, you must do yours."

The socio-political atmosphere in 1991 was generally optimistic: The New Economic Policy (NEP) (1971–1990) had ended, though not the general policy of preferential treatment for Malays, and had created an apprehensive atmosphere for what was to follow; Mahathir and Anwar had both recently secured their political position, while the economy boomed; the NEP had been successful to no mean extent, and there was growing confidence among Malays in their ability to develop and modernise; Malaysian international pride and influence was rising; and inter-ethnic tension was on the decline.

What Did Mahathir Say?

Alongside the Look East Policy, one may parade a few others that expressed Mahathir's disapproval of the Eurocentrism he perceived in Malaysian cultural consciousness. The "Asian Values" debate later championed by Mahathir, among others, was, for example, an attack on the hegemony of Western presumptions of cultural superiority, just as the East Asian Economic Caucus (EAEC) initiative was an attempt to break Western control over Asia's right to internal conference.

On the global stage then, Malaysia under Mahathir developed a regionalistic profile that turned both eastwards towards the Confucian world, and westwards towards the Islamic world, even as he postured himself as a fearless spokesman for the non-Western world at large. On the domestic stage, his goals had been the raising of the status of the Malays in all areas within an expansive economy. It is not difficult to imagine strategic connections between the pragmatics of the two. While securing Malay supremacy may have been a necessary measure against inter-racial clashes, a pervasive institution for affirmative action does not enhance Malaysia's aim of becoming a shining example of non-European pluralistic, even Islamic, progress.

Whether *Bangsa Malaysia* — variously translated as "Malaysian nationality",[4] "Malaysian nation",[5] "Malaysian people",[6] or "United Malaysian People"[7] — will go down in history as a visionary carrot that worked or as a political spin that wasted sorely-needed intellectual capacity will depend on Malaysia's future economic health and her future level of inter-ethnic harmony.

The term *Bangsa Malaysia* was first dropped in a speech made by Mahathir in Kuala Lumpur on 28 February 1991 to 61 businessmen, senior bureaucrats, and politicians who were members of the Malaysian Business Council. In effect, a direction was being fixed for life after the NEP. This was *Wawasan 2020*, or *Vision 2020*. To be credible, *Vision 2020* required at least a mention of strong ethnic unity as a necessary condition for continued growth. In fact, the establishment of a *Bangsa Malaysia* was the first of the "nine central strategic challenges" that Mahathir was convinced that the nation must face.[8] Although the nine were admittedly not listed in any order of priority, "it would be surprising if the first strategic challenge which I have mentioned — the establishment of a united Malaysian nation — is not likely to be the most fundamental, but the most basic".[9] Significantly, *Bangsa Malaysia* was mentioned but only *once*, and at the beginning of the speech. This mention nevertheless was tantamount in the eyes of hopeful observers to an admission that NEP logic and race-based politics must be abandoned. The paragraph containing the term runs as follows:

> The first of these [nine central strategic challenges] is the challenge of establishing a united Malaysian nation with a sense of common and shared destiny. This must be a nation at peace with itself, territorially and ethnically integrated, living in harmony and full and fair partnership, made up of one "Bangsa Malaysia" with political loyalty and dedication to the nation.[10]

The speech led to serious discussions about what was in store for the country, especially where inter-ethnic relations were concerned. While one analyst focused on how "Late Mahathirism" had in fact embarked on a process of "restructuring Malay society — and thus Malaysian society — in class terms",[11] another perceived how socio-economic changes during the 1980s now required "a more *hegemonic* form of authority" that relied on "the cultivation of *consent* within the arena of civil society, as opposed to *coercion* via the strong arm of the state". This meant that Malaysia's new self-image had to be more inclusive, unlike "the old forms of ethnic balancing towards post-ethnic nationalism".[12]

A further significance of this event lay in the fact that sustained economic development was the underlying agenda. The speech was indeed aimed at businessmen, and the larger part of *The Way Forward*, as the speech was titled, was about the "economic infrastructure", including government commitment to aid the private sector. The factor vital to the success of this program, as Mahathir understood it, was "the development of human resources".[13] This last point involved creating a citizenry united by middle-class values, tinged on the part of the Malays by moderate Islam, and not divided by ethnic tensions:

> [It] is blindingly clear that the most important resource of any nation must be the talents, skills, creativity and will of its people .... Without a doubt, in the 1990s and beyond, Malaysia must give the fullest emphasis possible to the development of this ultimate resource.

He went on later to say:

> We cannot afford to neglect half the population i.e. the Bumiputeras. If they are not brought into the mainstream, if their potentials are not fully developed, if they are allowed to be a millstone around the national neck, then our progress is going to be retarded by that much.[14]

Apparently, the *Bangsa Malaysia* of 2020 will consist of entrepreneurial patriots living in an "economically just society" where "backwardness is [not] identified with race".[15] While the rationale of the NEP did continue to inform the reasoning of *Vision 2020*, the goals had certainly changed since 1970. Now, the sky was the limit, and for that limit to be reached, statistical means and legalistic measures would no longer suffice. The difference between the NEP and the National Development Plan (NDP) (1991–2000), it is generally conceded, is in the more accommodative style of *Vision 2020*, where *Bangsa Malaysia* replaces Bumiputera as the ethnic orientation, and where statistics are about national growth and not inter-ethnic disparities.

Does this amount to a subtle discarding of the principle of indigeneity as the legitimate basis of political and cultural dominance? On an analytical level, it would appear so, although how perceptions emanating from the ground will rise to engage political conceptualisations is another question altogether. In an insightful discussion on the Malay word *bangsa* and the Chinese term *minzu* — both of which may liberally be understood as "cultural community" — Tan Liok Ee concludes that, while indigeneity as the basis for dominance in the Malay discourse did not hold in the face of groups with a better claim to being the original peoples of the region, the Chinese alternative, enhanced by a diasporic reality, gave too much legitimacy to disparate cultural units for it to provide "the reference point for ... a shared sense of national consciousness". In her analysis, "*bangsa* demanded unity of political and cultural identity" while "*minzu* for the Chinese-educated allowed for a distinction between political and cultural identity".[16] The "nation-of-intent" that Mahathir amounted to proposing through *Vision 2020* relied on the assimilatory, or at least integrative, power of sustained economic development, and suggested a national unity that would not rely on ethnic elements. The Chinese, surviving well economically despite, and some say thanks to, decades of constraints, may not feel as strong a need to accommodate culturally in the coming years.

The "nine strategic challenges" to be overcome before a "fully developed Malaysia" can exist, as formulated in the speech, overlap considerably and should not be taken too seriously in their detailed formulation. In essence, what Mahathir envisioned was that Malaysians — this *Bangsa Malaysia* — will be a "territorially and ethnically integrated people" with strong ethical and religious moral values living in a prosperous, just, liberal, and caring model democracy based on the family system, and who are technologically innovative.[17] This generous and rhetorical rendition of Malaysia's future character would not have been such a pivotal event had it not been for two things. First, the best-before date of the NEP had passed and apprehension about what was to take its place was widespread, and second, the use of the alluring term of *Bangsa Malaysia* in a country that suffers chills at every public mention of inter-ethnic ties offered badly-needed discursive space for renewed debates outside the Malay community on "nations-of-intent", which furthermore may include issues beyond Malay hegemony and political Islam. Two days after the speech, the *New Straits Times*, a daily newspaper controlled by the United Malays' National Organisation (UMNO), quoted Mahathir saying that he was merely putting forth a concept that "discourages any manifestation of exclusivity, be it economic nationalism, racial chauvinism, or religious fundamentalism".[18] Was the NEP really over?

Strictly speaking, *Bangsa Malaysia* was not launched as a slogan in any sense, and its common use expressed a need for such a term more than it did a substantial policy. Non-Malay leaders within the ruling coalition came to lay ample stress on *Bangsa Malaysia* during the April 1995 general election and National Day celebrations that same year. The Malaysian Chinese Association (MCA) allowed a lengthy supplement in *The Star*, a party-controlled paper, on the subject.[19] Mahathir admitted in a talk with Malaysian students in the UK later that year that a shift in ethnic focus was needed for practical reasons:

> Previously, we tried to have a single entity but it caused a lot of tension and suspicions among the people because they thought the Government was trying to create a hybrid. There was fear among the people that they may have to

give up their own cultures, values and religions. This could not work, and we believe that the *Bangsa Malaysia* is the answer.[20]

Mahathir said further that in realising *Bangsa Malaysia*, one "does not have to give up one's culture, religion or language".[21] This amounted to a rejection of cultural assimilation as "the way forward" for Malaysia. While *Bumiputera* is in practice an excluding term, *Bangsa Malaysia* is inclusive, and given the high ambitions that Mahathir now had for the country, and the centrality of global status and success in this vision, this epistemic innovation appeared necessary. Mahathir further made a statement that Lim Kit Siang, the national chairman of the major non-Muslim opposition party, the Democratic Action Party (DAP), at that time publicly proclaimed to be "the most enlightened comment [Mahathir] has made on nation-building for some time". Mahathir had said that *Bangsa Malaysia* was about being Malaysian and not about being Malay, Chinese, Indian, Iban, or Kadazan. It was about "people being able to identify themselves with the country, [speaking] Bahasa Malaysia and [accepting] the Constitution".[22]

Integration or Assimilation, Plural Society or Pluralist Society?

The ethnographic framework within which Mahathir introduced *Bangsa Malaysia* necessitates a theoretical analysis of what such a *bangsa* can be. In an earlier quote, it is noted that, in realising *Bangsa Malaysia*, one "does not have to give up one's culture, religion or language", it is apparent that *bangsa* here does not refer to ethnicity. This makes the use of the term rather quaint. If nothing ethnic was being referred to, then why use a term that so strongly signifies ethnicity? This lends support to the perception that Mahathir had not meant anything controversial by the term *Bangsa Malaysia*, and that what he had wanted to stress in the *Vision 2020* speech was merely the uncontroversial unity of a Malaysian nation. He was essentially saying that unity was basic to Malaysia's continued development. The phrase "made up of one *Bangsa Malaysia* with political loyalty and dedication to the nation" was a careless rhetorical flourish that became popular because of the contradiction it injected into the delimiting Bumiputera discourse. This perspective shall be called the *Inadvertence Interpretation*.

Be that as it may, Mahathir had nevertheless allowed Malaysians, especially non-Malays, to envision a development that no longer threatened their cultural or religious uniqueness. This explains the common usage of the term, especially among non-Malay politicians who made full political use of Mahathir's careless choice of words, despite the obvious lack of substance. This may be called the *Opportunity Interpretation*.

However, for those who suspected that Mahathir did not mean anything radical by his statement and who were not in a position to capitalise on the discursive window *Bangsa Malaysia* opened, a natural response has been to ignore the whole issue as a storm in a *kopi-o* cup. The understanding that *Bangsa Malaysia* is nonsensical and that Bumiputera hegemony would remain unchanged despite the end of the NEP, may be called the *Hot Air Interpretation*.

However, if Mahathir did truly hope for a united Malaysia as a result of *Vision 2020*, then he was denouncing forced assimilation. This leaves unity among Malaysians to be achieved through spontaneous assimilation, or acculturation, on the one hand, and a development away from a plural society towards a pluralistic society on the other. The integration of different ethnic groups would presumably occur through the expansion of economic life to such an extent that it actually de-politicises ethnicity. One may be assuming that the "plural society" common in Southeast Asia's colonial societies, as described by J.S. Furnivall in 1948,[23] had in Malaysia's case been transformed by the NEP's creation of the *Melayu Baru* (new Malay).[24] This new Malay, having new middle-class values, will find it not impossible to integrate socially and economically with the new Chinese or the new Indian, with their similar though not-so-new middle-class values. This is the *Pluralism Interpretation*.

A further viewpoint may be termed the *Hegemony Interpretation*. This considers Mahathir's initiative as a necessary adaptation to the rise of civil society in Malaysia and other profound socio-economic changes, where the efficacy of power was now forced to rely more on consent than outright coercion. Instead of merely accepting Bumiputera advancement as a prerequisite for inter-ethnic peace, non-Malays would now actively agree to the creation of a pluralistic society in the hope that that may somehow dissolve the institutional preference given to Bumiputeras.

A vital question, considering how little has been openly done to leave blatant preferential treatment behind, is how long the government can continue to administer a general policy based on bias against non-Malays. Regardless of the integrative qualities of a globalising and healthy economy, the longer the government retains the legal and institutional structure of preferential treatment, the stronger the likelihood, given the diminishing non-Malay population, that *Bangsa Malaysia* will lose all content and become merely another term for the Malays, new or not. As long as constructive measures are lacking, *Bangsa Malaysia* may thus be seen as a gimmick for buying Malay nationalism more time. This may be called the *Buying Time Interpretation.*

An interesting dualism discussed by Wang Gungwu concerns the "local" and the "national", ahead of "ethnic" identity and "national" identity. The former allows for an anthropological more than an ethnological understanding of ethnic divisions within a single nation-state. The statement "traditions are ultimately local" and how this connects to the nation-building process at large is of vital importance. In the case of the Malaysian Chinese, the postponement of equal national status had enticed them "to be modern through adapting their local community traditions to the demands and opportunities of the world outside their country".[25] For the heightened ambitions of the post-NEP state to be realisable, grassroots contribution has had to be secured from all groups concerned, whether these identify themselves communally, ethnically, or religiously. Such considerations made it necessary for the national discourse to transcend the inflexible categories of Bumiputeras and non-Bumiputeras. Many factors are involved when resituated traditions adapt to new environments, such as absolute size or size in relation to other groups, extent of the history of the migration, the profundity of socio-political changes, etc. Since such diversity cannot be denied and time is of the essence, one way to proceed is to subsume this diversity under the flexible rhetorical umbrella of *Bangsa Malaysia.* This is the *National Maturity Interpretation.*

A final possible perception of the discourse of *Bangsa Malaysia* emanates from the insight that terms shift in meaning with the passage of time, i.e. not only does the signified, given time, reject the embrace of the signifier, the signifier itself attains new associations and rationale, and in effect abandons the signified. It is not at all improbable that Mahathir, when he said *Bangsa Malaysia*, had intended more logically to say *Kebangsaan Malaysia*, Malaysian nationality. The word *bangsa* might have been short for *Kebangsaan* in the moment of expression. We may call this the *Kebangsaan Malaysia Interpretation*.[26]

A Present Term with a Future Reference

It is interesting that the term *Bangsa Malaysia* usually receives an obligatory reference in most books about Malaysia after 1991. A thorough debate seems impossible, given the tentative nature of the term and the care that must be exercised in handling a discussion that is forbidden by the Malaysian Constitution. Certainly, the notion of *Bangsa Malaysia* is subsumed under the wider frame of *Wawasan 2020*, in keeping with the fervent hope throughout Malaysia's history that economic growth will defuse the ethnic dynamite. Critical studies of ethnography have never been popular in Malaysian research, fragmented as the country is by ethnic defensiveness.[27] Nevertheless, let us try to gain some idea of how *Bangsa Malaysia* has been put to use by sampling how it is mentioned (more than discussed) in various contexts.

Tellingly, despite the term having been in popular circulation for over a decade, it does not lend itself easily to analysis. This has a lot to do with the fact that positive institutional measures have been lacking. Through this, we are able to glimpse an important significance of *Bangsa Malaysia*. The Malay nationalism that was needed alongside economic growth if racial violence was not to become a signature of Malaysian politics has been successful to a large extent. However, such a development is always fragile, and in accordance with capitalist rationale, the only way to go is forward, economically. Going forward, however, now requires a socio-cultural structure unhampered by restrictions that were previously necessary. The significance of *Bangsa Malaysia* lies in its coy challenge to the terminology of Malay nationalism, to the institutional structure of race-based parties, and to the sustaining of preferential treatment.

The rhetoric has generally been well received by non-Malays, as many analysts have noted. The emphasis on the market, and not the public sector, is taken as "a sign of good faith" in the regime's commitment to reduce intervention.[28] The Chinese "were particularly struck by the multi-culturalist *Bangsa Malaysia* concept, for Malay leaders had previously employed the word *bangsa* within an exclusivist Malay nationalist context to denote Malay race or Malay nation (*Bangsa Melayu*)". Mahathir was thus "breaking from the chauvinistic conventions of Malay political and economic nationalism".[29] Indeed, he did say that the future nationality of Malaysia would be "ethnically integrated".[30] It is hard not to see a shift being initiated here where *bangsa* understood as "race", as implied in the nation-state, was being abandoned for the more republican understanding of *bangsa* as "nation", as in state-nation. This foreboded an end to Malay nationalism, and it is not surprising that non-Malays should grab this offer by Mahathir to substantiate *Vision 2020* as the enlightened aim of a Malaysian patriarch, and not as the narrow goal of a Malay nationalist.

The "explicit commitment" to transcend "ethnic identities and loyalties … greatly encouraged the non-Malays [to respond] enthusiastically".[31] Apparently, this enthusiasm also held among some Malays. As Abdul Rahman Embong's research tells us, "many informants … welcome the interethnic peace and harmony prevailing in Malaysia today, but also express the feeling that Malaysia still has a long way to go in transforming itself into *Bangsa Malaysia*".[32] Loh Kok Wah, however, notes that some Malay intellectuals had not been as euphoric about *Bangsa Malaysia* as non-Malays, warning that a "pluralism" that was not properly embedded, i.e. a formal and false pluralism, might evolve.[33] Malay leaders, such as Tengku Razaleigh Hamzah, did indeed express concern that the concept threatened to put Malay culture "in the backseat".[34]

Khoo Boo Teik rightly notes that *Bangsa Malaysia*, in correlation with *Wawasan 2020* (*Vision 2020*) and *Melayu Baru* (new Malays), was the "mature ideological representation" of Mahathir's renderings of his political thought over the years, tempered by his considerable political experience.[35] This maturity was thus highly informed by a vision of a developed Malaysian citizenry whose majority nevertheless were Malays but of a newly engineered variety suffused with middle-class values. Put another way, one may perhaps conclude that *Bangsa Malaysia* is but another term for the citizenry of an economically affluent and politically influential Malaysia integrated through vested interests in the country's political economy, consisting of "new Chinese", "new Indians", "new Kadazans", and "new Ibans".[36] This is a popular-enough aspiration in most modern states, where "common values" are part and parcel of the common absorption into the capitalist economy of production, savings, investment, and consumption, and where divergent religious and cultural values are emptied of political significance. Since Mahathir was the champion of *Melayu Baru*, one can understand his campaigns against the sultans, his proclamation of Malaysia as a legitimate Islamic nation (practising a moderate form of Islam now entitled *Islam Hadhari* — civilisational Islam — by his successor Abdullah Badawi), and his promotion of English, in the wake of the socio-economic successes of the NEP, as the very redefining of Malayness itself.

Central to the concept of *Melayu Baru*, unavoidably the major component in *Bangsa Malaysia*, as understood by A.B. Shamsul, is "entrepreneurship". This enterprise of transforming traditional Malay cultural life to cohere with the synchronically-changing entrepreneurship of other ethnicities to achieve a profound and stable socio-economic integration requires broad changes: village life must play a lesser defining role than urban life, even as class mobility undermines aristocratic traditions in favour of meritocratic trends; economic modernity must also occur in, if not on, Muslim terms, or at least must not challenge Islam too openly (this helps explain the importance given to *Islam Hadhari* by the new regime); finally, these socio-economic changes must lead to a weakening of traditional UMNO politics. "Money politics" is one of the more dramatic aspects of this change, and has led to measures taken by UMNO, such as the exclusion of the posts of presidency and deputy presidencies from open competition, to protect "the core of Malay power".[37]

In general, academics have not been enthusiastic about the term *Bangsa Malaysia*. More concrete objects of study, such as the Multimedia Super Corridor (MSC), the Second Outline Perspective Plan (OPP2) for 1991–2000, and the Sixth Malaysia Plan (6MP) for 1991–1995, have provided much more meat to devour.[38]

What Goes up ...

While academics had a hard time taking the term seriously, non-Malay politicians recognised its rhetorical appeal *and* the possibilities that were on offer to push the boundaries of ethnic discussion. In an atmosphere where the overhanging fear had been forced assimilation, *Bangsa Malaysia* suggested a non-essentialistic and pragmatic notion of nationhood that would result from global and domestic economic expedience. There were indeed signs of a thawing in the relationship between the state and non-Malays. Between 1991 and 1995, the state doubled its funding of Chinese primary schools even as the Tunku Abdul Rahman (TAR) College, sponsored by the MCA, received a tenfold increase in financial support from the state.[39] It should be added, however, that the number of Chinese primary schools between 1987 and 1998 actually diminished from 1,295 to 1,283 although the number of national primary schools, by definition instructing in Malay, increased by 10 per cent.[40]

By the time the financial crisis hit in 1997, "a common, cosmopolitan *nouveau riche* consumer style culture" had started to emerge through the workings of economic forces.

> While the common English-educated Westernized backgrounds of the UMNO and MCA elites served as the basis for multiracial political cooperation during the Alliance years, the second generation of Malay and Chinese elites is held together as much by linkages of business as by common educational and cultural experiences.[41]

How far *Bangsa Malaysia* could be translated into a licence to discuss Malay special rights was rudely decided by the *Suqiu* episode of 2000. The Malaysian Chinese Organizations Election Appeals Committee (*Suqiu*) was a collection of Chinese lobbyists that raised a 17-point appeal preceding the 1999 general election. The political atmosphere of the time was admittedly jittery, strongly influenced as it was by the 1997 crisis, the implementation of currency controls in 1998, the prolonged Anwar Ibrahim trial, and the general election itself. *Suqiu* called for the following: (1) promote national unity; (2) advance democracy; (3) uphold human rights and justice; (4) curb corruption; (5) a fair and equitable economic policy; (6) review the privatisation policy;

(7) develop an enlightened, liberal, and progressive education policy;
(8) allow multi-ethnicity to flourish; (9) protect the Malaysian environment; (10) develop and modernise New Villages; (11) housing for all;
(12) protect women's rights; (13) a fair media; (14) restore confidence
in the police force; (15) upgrade social services; (16) respect the rights
of workers; and (17) provide for indigenous peoples.

The appeal, merely stating apparently uncontroversial points, was
initially endorsed by the ruling Barisan Nasional (BN), and even by
the Cabinet, but was later countered by a 100-point demand from the
Federation of Peninsular Malay Students Associations (GPMS), the latter
claiming that *Suqiu* was questioning Malay rights, something forbidden
in the Malaysian Constitution. In the face of aggressive protests from
UMNO Youth, which included threats to burn down the Selangor
Chinese Assembly Hall in Kuala Lumpur, Mahathir chose to condemn
Suqiu for acting as "extremists and like communists".[42] In the end, *Suqiu*
had to back down and retract seven of its appeal points. This was despite
the fact that "there is no expression in the text claiming the abolition of
the special rights. The demands that may be interpreted to indicate the
wish of abolition refer to, for example, economic equality".[43]

The significance of this inter-ethnic quarrel lies in the reminder
that issues of ethnicity are always current and explosive, and that
non-Malays are always the weaker party when things come to a head.
Any ambition to foster a *Bangsa Malaysia* must take these points into
serious consideration. The plural-societal nature of Malaysian life and
politics can only shift towards pluralism if the infrastructure of Malay
nationalism is constructively engaged. Elements that can contribute to
making the latter more accommodating include continued economic
growth, competitive pressure from international markets, the reform of
Islam into a less defensive way of thought, inter-ethnic integration of
business structures, and perhaps continued effective sidestepping of the
institutions of Malay nationalism by non-Malays.

Politicians and activists, with the exception of the religious
opposition, have tended to accept *Bangsa Malaysia* as a concrete goal
that Malaysia must aim for, whether they are speaking for or against
the regime. Disagreement about *Bangsa Malaysia* appears otherwise to
be more about the government's political will than about the goal as

such. Politicians within the ruling front commonly call for support for policies through references to how these can foster a *Bangsa Malaysia*, while those who oppose policies will use it as a benchmark for illustrating inconsistencies and hypocrisy on the part of the establishment. For example, in opposing a government decision to include religious belief as a category in the national identity cards in 1999, Loh Kok Wah, the secretary of the reform movement, *Aliran Kesedaran Malaysia*, argued "the BN government must get serious about creating a Bangsa Malaysia".

> Its efforts to create a *Bangsa* Malaysia must move beyond the superficial efforts of holding "open houses" and multicultural spectacles at opening ceremonies, national day and other *pesta* parades. There must be a rethink of government policies [that] continue to divide us into bumiputra and non-bumiputra .... Too often [ethnic-based political parties] have resorted to fanning ethnic sentiments to gain votes and to maintain power.[44]

In the midst of the *Suqiu* crisis in 2000, DAP head Lim Kit Siang despondently suggested in a press statement that *Bangsa Malaysia* and *Vision 2020* were becoming "obsolete Barisan Nasional concepts".[45]

BN constituent parties tend to call for the fostering of a *Bangsa Malaysia* without feeling the need to substantiate the term. Ling Liong Sik, the former long-term president of the MCA, held the optimistic view that BN may smoothly shift from being a body for inter-ethnic compromise to being a representative of "the community of *Bangsa Malaysia*".[46]

Conclusion: Not a Unique Problem

This chapter will end with a few points that I consider of major importance. One is the strong suspicion I now have that the term was highly rhetorical and, in its immediate textual context, was used to stress an uncontroversial point, namely that of national unity. It was a minor spin that soon spun out of control, but in a fashion that Mahathir did not mind, or that he later chose to utilise. It was an inadvertent opening from the regime of Malay nationalism that non-Bumiputeras living in the subdued and cramped atmosphere of Malaysian ethnic discourse did not fail to utilise — a crowbar for non-Malays to pry the closed doors of Bumiputeraism. While its academic function has been tellingly minor, its political and populistic effect has been considerable. This argument is further substantiated by the fact that while *Bangsa Malaysia* is used once in the official English version of the speech, the term does turn up twice in the Malay version,[47] where the second mention is actually written as "united Malaysian nation" in the English version. This united Malaysian nation was apparently what Mahathir meant by *Bangsa Malaysia* on that first occasion. No grand design of integration or assimilation was intended. What was intended was most probably the attainment of a people united through full involvement in the routines and rituals — "the cultural infrastructure" — of the envisioned advanced economy of Malaysia. This connects to the further suspicion that Mahathir might have meant *kebangsaan* (nationality) and not *bangsa* (race). Words do shift endlessly in meaning and are transformed through easy and lazy associations.

When one considers the first challenge facing the nation to be merely the attainment of a "united Malaysian nation" (*sebuah negara bangsa yang bersatu*), the mystery of this new race, nation, people, or nationality dissipates. Apparently, the type of unity conceived by Mahathir was one that came as a natural result of rapid economic advancement in a globalising world. For example, in his retort to a question at the seminar *Towards a Developed and Industrialized Society: Understanding the Concept, Implications and Challenges of Vision 2020* in December 1991, he reportedly said:

> If this country achieves its target of becoming a developed nation by the year 2020, then people will say they are Malaysians. There is no need to append the word *bangsa* or race, just Malaysians. To me, I think that is good enough. Then … national unity … will also come about without having to [be forced].[48]

The basic assumption made in the early 1970s at the conception of the NEP, which continued to be salient during Mahathir's privatisation and industrialisation drive in the 1980s, i.e. that inter-ethnic tension caused by the preferential treatment of the Malays would dissipate or diminish significantly in the face of continual economic success, remained unchanged. Analyst Lee Hwok Aun, though critical of NEP policies, agrees that economic growth had brought "general satisfaction" and narrowed ethnic divisions. Consumerism itself, along with cultural liberalisation during the 1990s and the privatisation of higher education in 1996 are other changes that have "dampened ethnic-based claims on policy formulation".[49]

The second point concerns the sensitiveness of Malaysian politicians to any mention of ethnicity. This is understandable since most of them cannot deny the communalist nature of their profession, and of their base of support. The "opportunity" offered by Mahathir's use of *Bangsa Malaysia* may thus contribute inadvertently to the perpetuation of ethnic politicking and of nation-state rationality itself, where "national unity" continues to be incomprehensible without a consensus among ethnicity-based parties on what this projected nation, race, *bangsa*, or people is. One may rightly ask how ethnicity-based parties shall transcend their structure and legitimising terminology and if the BN leopard can change its spots. If *Bangsa Malaysia* comes of itself, given economic success, then mentioning it in advance will not necessarily help matters.

The third point is that regardless of how much Mahathir had meant to challenge normal Malay usage of *bangsa*, subsequent discussions show that the term was no longer the emotive issue of contention and "the sole and ultimate focus of loyalty" that it had once been, for example as expressed in the broad rejection 40 years earlier of Datuk Onn Jaafar's suggestion that UMNO be made to stand for United *Malaya* (and not *Malays*) National Organization and that non-Malays be allowed to join as full members.[50] In the event, Onn Jaafar gained the dubious reputation of being the first Malay leader to be branded a "race traitor" — *durhaka*.[51] By qualifying *bangsa* with *Malaysia*, Mahathir in effect transferred the word from a primordial setting to a situationalistic one. Had he said *orang Malaysia*, merely denoting *people of Malaysia*, the discursive consequences would probably have been minimal.

The fourth point is the fact that Malaysian discourses, socio-cultural development and political institutions today are largely the resultants of decades of powerful and undeterred Malay nationalism. No doubt, the limited but politically sufficient success of the NEP allowed for the NDP and *Vision 2020* to shift policy focus to hard-core and relative poverty, to the rapid development of a Bumiputera Commercial and Industrial Community (BCIC), to restructuring through private sector-led growth, and to human resource development.[52] Long-term political stability, strong economic performance coupled with boosted Bumiputera confidence, increased national pride in controversial mega-projects, and a general uplift in economic welfare are some of the motivations identified by analysts for the new confidence evident in the NDP.[53] The socio-economic changes have thus been encouraging. However, if Mahathir's claim that "a united Malaysian nation" should be the first priority in the race towards 2020, then whatever is stopping Malaysians from feeling united with each other must be seriously addressed. His regime was of course aware of this, and perhaps here we see that the spirit may have been willing but the flesh was not. The political challenge for the ruling coalition is how Malay nationalism can be abandoned as the national ideology without grassroots support being lost. The promulgation of *Islam Hadhari* should be understood within this context where Malayness, insofar as Islam defines it, is being redefined as less parochial and less defensive, and as a progressive trait. For the Chinese and other ethnicities, the matter hangs on how preferential treatment is diminished in practice, and how much the government is perceived in the future to be a Malaysian, and not a Malay-favouring government. This will involve changes in legal structures and in the level of political participation. Coining new terms is just a beginning. Fostering a *Bangsa Malaysia* requires a *Kerajaan Malaysia* (Malaysian government) infused with the ambition to do just that. What is envisioned is apparently not a melting pot for ethnicities but a pluralistic citizenry in which assimilation and inter-ethnic cooperation occur spontaneously, and tolerance of cultural and religious differences is encouraged by successful economic restructuring.

The fifth point has to do with the international significance of the Malaysian problem. Malay nationalism "came from behind" so to speak, to restructure the multi-ethnic nation to the advantage of the majority group. However, rapid migration and refugee streams have recently put many once homogenous nation-states, or states where the national culture had been unchallenged, in a position similar to that of Malaysia's. In these cases, ethnic tensions and inter-ethnic disparities are taking over the political agenda. The idea of the nation-state is being eroded by accelerated multi-ethnicity, and we can expect to witness many policies being implemented throughout the world to settle inter-ethnic strife, some of which will be reminiscent of Malaysia's solutions.

As mentioned earlier, the *Melayu Baru* is central to the constitution of *Bangsa Malaysia*. Khoo Boo Teik summarised his analysis of Mahathirism thus:

> [The] "prehistory" of the Malays has ended. Their history, and, by extension, the history of *Bangsa Malaysia* may perhaps begin. In the beginning, so to speak, a race set out to remake itself in class terms: that was the promise of Mahathirism. It has largely succeeded. In the end, so it appears, a new class offers itself as the social basis of a new nation.[54]

This may perhaps have been Mahathir's private vision. The road from the *Malay Dilemma* to *Vision 2020* may have been long, but the goal had remained the same, i.e. the creation of a progressive nation whose socio-cultural core is Malay. Be that as it may, Mahathir is not Malaysia, and as this chapter has perhaps shown, there are many who have their own perceptions on what is needed for inter-ethnic peace in the future.

The sixth point has to do with the diminishing significance of *Bangsa Malaysia* today when Mahathir is no longer the baton conducting the nation's voices. In the wake of recent events, inter-ethnic relations are being redefined by the issue of Islam. Abdullah Badawi's concept of *Islam Hadhari* — civilisational Islam — promises sufficient flexibility to subsume issues that once relied on *Bangsa Malaysia* for discursive space. While *Bangsa Malaysia* is without international significance, *Islam Hadhari* proposes a model for modernising Islamic nations. This shift has obviously been brought on by profound changes in Malaysian politics since 1997, and in Malaysia's international standing; racial tensions are no longer as explosive as intra-Muslim and intra-Malay contentions have become. With the new focus on terrorism in the region and the world, an articulation of Islam's role in multicultural nation-building and an innovative definition of the religion in the modern context appear much more important than discussions about and substantiations of *Bangsa Malaysia*. Several relevant points should be mentioned here concerning the importance of Malay Muslim redefinition:

1. *Melayu Baru* requires an *Islam Baru*. *Islam Hadhari* redefines Malayness, insofar as Islam defines Malayness, as tolerant and progressive.
2. It acknowledges local historical and social conditions, and the *embeddedness* of Islam in the region, in contrast to ideas of a pristine religion.
3. It is Islam as non-Malays, non-Bumiputeras, and non-Muslims in general would like it to be, suggesting the accommodative purpose behind its formulation.
4. It provides Malaysia's secular government with a religious label. Economic modernity must occur, if not on *Muslim terms*, at least in *Muslim terms*.
5. Its definition of Islam as moderate discourages extremist interpretations.
6. While *Bumiputera* involved ethnic exclusion, and *Bangsa Malaysia* suggested ethnic inclusion, *Islam Hadhari* focuses on the *relationship* of Islam and the Malays to other ethnicities, and to economic growth, urbanism, and scientific thought.

A year after the first mention of *Islam Hadhari*, details of what it is supposed to be were unveiled at UMNO's 55th general assembly in September 2004 by Abdullah Badawi in his maiden speech as party president. This new attempt at the Islamisation of the Malays apparently involves drastic changes in the "mindset among Malays".

> The Malay society must be a society that embraces knowledge, skills and expertise in order to build capacity. Islam makes it compulsory for Muslims to embrace knowledge in all fields. The misconception that there exists a difference between so-called secular knowledge and religious knowledge must be corrected. Islam demands the mastery of science and technology and the enhancement of skills and expertise. Many verses in the Quran that touch on the need to master science and technology should be studied.[55]

Islam Hadhari's ten main principles are as follows: (1) faith and piety in Allah; (2) a just and trustworthy government; (3) a free and independent people; (4) mastery of knowledge; (5) balanced and comprehensive economic development; (6) a good quality of life; (7) protection of the rights of minority groups and women; (8) cultural and moral integrity; (9) safeguarding the environment; and (10) strong defenses.

Indeed, only the first point is undeniably religious while all the others could just as easily have been said by any secular government. There is an apparent attempt to end the division between "secular knowledge and religiousness knowledge". The change in mindset that is sought here seems to be a "mental revolution" where the religion seeks the same things as the nation-building project does.

Bangsa Malaysia was not mentioned at all, neither in the English nor the Malay version of Abdullah's speech. It could have been out of place at the UMNO congress, and it could most probably have been received as an effrontery. However, the stress on merit, knowledge, and competitiveness indicate that the proposed *Islam-informed* development of the Malays must comply with the demands of globalisation, which in all probability must include inter-ethnic tolerance and open markets.

I shall end with a presentation of some illuminative comments about *Bangsa Malaysia* made by some of my respondents in Kuala Lumpur on a recent related research project. One of them considered it a very important concept but bemoaned the lack of groundwork to achieve it, while another thought it a totally unnecessary initiative since it declared all Malaysians living today to be somehow anachronistic. Other views include observations about a widening of national goals in response to global markets, about pluralism being a fact that pressed for full acknowledgement, and about cultural criteria of development status making themselves felt. Finally, a thought-provoking opinion was put forth: What do we really lose when we are not assimilated, and what do we actually gain from being assimilated? Is cultural assimilation what people want, or merely peaceful coexistence?

NOTES

1. K.S. Jomo, *Mahathir's Economic Policies* (Kuala Lumpur: Institute of Social Analysis, 1988), p. vi.

2. Johan Saravanamuttu, "The Look East Policy and Japanese Economic Penetration in Malaysia", in *Mahathir's Economic Policies*, edited by K.S. Jomo (Kuala Lumpur: Institute of Social Analysis, 1988), p. 4.

3. Mahathir Mohamad, "New Government Policies", in *Mahathir's Economic Policies*, edited by K.S. Jomo (Kuala Lumpur: Institute of Social Analysis, 1988), pp. 1–3.

4. Khoo Boo Teik, *Beyond Mahathir. Malaysian Politics and its Discontents* (London & New York: Zed Books, 2003), p. 5.

5. Goh Beng-Lan, *Modern Dreams. An Inquiry into Power, Cultural Production, and the Cityscape in Contemporary Urban Penang, Malaysia* (New York: Cornell Southeast Asia Program, 2002), p. 42.

6. Abdul Rahman Embong, "The Culture and Practice of Pluralism in Postcolonial Malaysia", in *The Politics of Multiculturalism. Pluralism and Citizenship in Malaysia, Singapore, and Indonesia*, edited by Robert W. Hefner (Honolulu: University of Hawaii, 2001), p. 77.

7. A.B. Shamsul, "'Malay' and 'Malayness' in Malaysia Reconsidered: A Critical Review", *Communal/Plural* 9, no. 1 (April 2001*a*): 79.

8. An Abstract From Mahathir's 1991 speech, *The Way Forward: Vision 2020*:

   • There can be no fully developed Malaysia until we have finally overcome the nine central strategic challenges that have confronted us from the moment of our birth as an independent nation.

   • The first of these is the challenge of establishing a united Malaysian nation with a sense of common and shared destiny. This must be a nation at peace with itself, territorially and ethnically integrated, living in harmony and full and fair partnership, made up of one "Bangsa Malaysia" with political loyalty and dedication to the nation.

   • The second is the challenge of creating a psychologically liberated, secure, and developed Malaysian Society with faith and confidence in itself, justifiably proud of what it is, of what it has accomplished, robust enough to face all manner of adversity. This Malaysian Society must be distinguished by the pursuit of excellence, fully aware of all its potentials, psychologically subservient to none, and respected by the peoples of other nations.

   • The third challenge we have always faced is that of fostering and developing a mature democratic society, practising a form of mature consensual, community-oriented Malaysian democracy that can be a model for many developing countries.

   • The fourth is the challenge of establishing a fully moral and ethical society, whose citizens are strong in religious and spiritual values and imbued with the highest of ethical standards.

   • The fifth challenge that we have always faced is the challenge of establishing a matured, liberal and tolerant society in which Malaysians of all colours and creeds are free to practise and profess their customs, cultures and religious beliefs and yet feeling that they belong to one nation.

- The sixth is the challenge of establishing a scientific and progressive society, a society that is innovative and forward-looking, one that is not only a consumer of technology but also a contributor to the scientific and technological civilisation of the future.
- The seventh challenge is the challenge of establishing a fully caring society and a caring culture, a social system in which society will come before self, in which the welfare of the people will revolve not around the state or the individual but around a strong and resilient family system.
- The eighth is the challenge of ensuring an economically just society. This is a society in which there is a fair and equitable distribution of the wealth of the nation, in which there is full partnership in economic progress. Such a society cannot be in place so long as there is the identification of race with economic function, and the identification of economic backwardness with race.
- The ninth challenge is the challenge of establishing a prosperous society, with an economy that is fully competitive, dynamic, robust and resilient.

We have already come a long way towards the fulfilment of these objectives. The nine central objectives listed need not be our order of priorities over the next three decades. Most obviously, the priorities of any moment in time must meet the specific circumstances of that moment in time.

But it would be surprising if the first strategic challenge which I have mentioned — the establishment of a united Malaysian nation — is not likely to be the most fundamental, the most basic.

Since much of what I will say this morning will concentrate on economic development, let me stress yet again that the comprehensive development towards the developed society that we want — however each of us may wish to define it — cannot mean material and economic advancement only. Far from it. Economic development must not become the be-all and the end-all of our national endeavours.

9. Mahathir Mohamad, *The Way Forward (Vision 2020)* (Kuala Lumpur: Institute of Strategic and International Studies, 1991*a*), pp. 2–4.

10. Ibid., pp. 2, 3.

11. Khoo, *Beyond Mahathir. Malaysian Politics and its Discontents*, p. 36.

12. John Hilley, *Malaysia: Mahathirism, Hegemony and the New Opposition* (London & New York: Zed Books, 2001), pp. 7, 254.

13. Mahathir, *The Way Forward (Vision 2020)*, p. 16.

14. Ibid., p. 17.

15. Ibid., p. 15.

16. Tan Liok Ee, "The Rhetoric of Bangsa and Minzu: Community and Nation in Tension. The Malay Peninsula, 1900–1955" (working paper 52, Centre of Southeast Asian Studies, Monash University, Victoria, Australia, 1988).

17. Mahathir, *The Way Forward (Vision 2020)*, pp. 2–4.

18. *New Straits Times* (Malaysia), 2 March 1991.

19. Francis Loh Kok Wah, "Withdraw Decision to Include Religion in Our ICs", Aliran press statement, 13 October 1999 <http://www.malaysia.net/aliran/ms991013.htm>.

20. *The Star* (Malaysia), 11 September 1995.

21. Ibid.

22. "One Nation, One People. Mahathir Lays the Groundwork for Stronger Unity", *Asiaweek*, 6 October 1995 <http://www.asiaweek.com/asiaweek/95/1006/nat4.html>.

23. J.S. Furnivall, *Colonial Policy and Practice: A Comparative Study of Burma and Netherlands India* (London: Cambridge University Press, 1948).

24. J.S. Furnivall developed his concept of "the plural society" through his studies of colonialism in Burma and the Dutch Indies to capture the silent divisions existent in most societies perpetuated by "the emphasis on production rather than social life" (Furnivall 1980, p. 88).

25. Wang Gungwu, "Local and National: A Dialogue between Tradition and Modernity", in *Ethnic Chinese in Singapore and Malaysia. A Dialogue between Tradition and Modernity*, edited by Leo Suryadinata (Singapore: Times Academic Press, 2002), pp. 1–8.

26. The author is indebted to Professor Wang Gungwu for this subtle point.

27. Ooi Kee Beng, "Three-Tiered Social Darwinism in Malaysian Ethnographic History", *Tonan Ajia Kenkyu* [Southeast Asian Studies] 41, no. 2 (September 2003): 162–79; Syed Husin Ali, "The Role of Malaysian Social Scientists in a Fast Changing Society", in *Reinventing Malaysia. Reflections on Its Past and Future*, edited by K.S. Jomo (Bangi: Penerbit Universiti Kebangsaan Malaysia, 2001), p. 112.

28. Edmund Terence Gomez, *Chinese Business in Malaysia. Accumulation, Accommodation and Ascendance* (Surrey: RoutledgeCurzon Press, 1999a), p. 136.

29. Lee Kam Hing and Heng Pek Koon, "The Chinese in the Malaysian Political System", in *The Chinese in Malaysia*, edited by Lee Kam Hing and Tan Chee-Beng (Selangor: Oxford University Press, 2000a), p. 220.

30. *New Straits Times* (Malaysia), 2 March 1991.

31. Goh Beng-Lan, *Modern Dreams. An Inquiry into Power, Cultural Production, and the*

Cityscape in Contemporary Urban Penang, Malaysia (New York: Cornell Southeast Asia Program, 2002), p. 42.

32. Abdul, *The Politics of Multiculturalism. Pluralism and Citizenship in Malaysia, Singapore, and Indonesia,* p. 77.

33. Francis Loh Kok Wah, "Developmentalism and the Limits of Democratic Discourse", in *Democracy in Malaysia. Discourses and Practices,* edited by Francis Loh Kok Wah and Khoo Boo Teik (Richmond, Surrey: Curzon, 2002).

34. *The Star* (Malaysia), 24 October 1991 quoted in Loh (2002, p. 34).

35. Khoo, *Beyond Mahathir. Malaysian Politics and its Discontents,* p. 4.

36. A.B. Shamsul, "The Economic Dimension of Malay Nationalism. The Socio-Historical Roots of the New Economic Policy and its Contemporary Implications", *Developing Economies* XXXV (September 1997): 259.

37. A.B. Shamsul, "The Redefinition of Politics and the Transformation of Malaysian Pluralism", in *The Politics of Multiculturalism. Pluralism and Citizenship in Malaysia, Singapore and Indonesia,* edited by Robert W. Hefner (Honolulu: University of Hawaii Press, 2001*b*), pp. 220, 221.

38. Edmund Terence Gomez and K.S. Jomo, *Malaysia's Political Economy. Politics, Patronage and Profits* (Cambridge & Melbourne: Cambridge University Press, 1997), pp. 166–84.

39. Lee & Heng, *The Chinese in Malaysia,* p. 220.

40. Tan Liok Ee, "Baggage from the Past, Eyes on the Future: Chinese Education in Malaysia Today", in *Ethnic Chinese in Singapore and Malaysia: A Dialogue between Tradition and Modernity,* edited by Leo Suryadinata (Singapore: Times Academic Press, 2002), p. 159.

41. Heng Pek Koon and Sieh Lee Mei Ling, "The Chinese Business Community in Peninsular Malaysia, 1957–1999", in *The Chinese in Malaysia,* edited by Lee Kam Hing and Tan Chee-Beng (Selangor: Oxford University Press, 2000), p. 155

42. "Malaysian Chinese Party Leader Criticizes State TV Station for 'Distortion'", *Malaysiakini,* 18 November 2002 <http://www.asu.edu/educ/epsl/LPRU/newsarchive/Art1398.txt>.

43. Claudia Derichs, "Looking for Clues: Malaysian Suggestions for Political Change" (project discussion paper no. 10/2001, Discourses on Political Reforms and Democratization in East and Southeast Asia in the Light of New Processes in Regional Community Building, Institut für Ostasienwissenshaften [Institute for East Asian Studies/East Asian Politics] Duisburg, Germany, February 2001) <http://www.uni-duisburg.de/Institute/ OAWISS/neu/downloads/pdf/orange/discuss10.pdf>.

44. Loh, Aliran press statement.

45. Lim Kit Siang, "UMNO Exploitation of Suqiu is Going to be Greatest Test as to Whether Vision 2020 and Bangsa Malaysia are Obsolete Barisan Nasional Concepts to be Consigned to the Dustbin of History", DAP press statement <http://www.malaysia.net/dap/lks0597.htm>.

46. Ling Liong Sik, "Address at the 48th Annual General Meeting of the MCA, 4 August 2001" <http://www.mca.org.my/story.asp?file=/articles/speeches/2001/576.html&sec=Speeches>.

47. Mahathir Mohamad, *Wawasan 2020* (Kuala Lumpur: Institute of Strategic and International Studies, 1991*b*), p. 5.

48. Ahmad Sarji, ed., *Malaysia's Vision 2020. Understanding the Concept, Implications & Challenges* (Petaling Jaya: Pelanduk Publications, 1993/1997), p. 14.

49. Lee Hwok Aun, "The NEP, Vision 2020, and Dr. Mahathir: Continuing Dilemmas", in *Reflections. The Mahathir Years*, edited by Bridget Welsh (Washington DC: Southeast Asia Studies Program, Johns Hopkins University SIAS, 2004), p. 277.

50. Khong Kim Hoong, *Merdeka! British Rule and the Struggle for Independence in Malaya 1945–1957* (Petaling Jaya: Strategic Information Research Development, 2003), p. 239.

51. Tan Liok Ee, "The Rhetoric of Bangsa and Minzu: Community and Nation in Tension. The Malay Peninsula, 1900–1955", p. 16.

52. Gomez & Jomo, *Malaysia's Political Economy. Politics, Patronage and Profits*, p. 173.

53. K.S. Nathan, "Vision 2020: Implications for Malaysian Foreign Policy. Part 1", *Asian Defence Journal* (January 1992): 10, 11.

54. Khoo Boo Teik, *Paradoxes of Mahathirism. An Intellectual Biography of Mahathir Mohamad* (Shah Alam: Oxford University Press, 1995), p. 338.

55. Abdullah Badawi, "Forward Towards Excellence" (presidential speech given at the 55th General Assembly of the United Malays National Organization (UMNO), Putra Jaya, 23 September 2004) <http://thestar.com.my/umno/story.asp?file=/2004/9/24/umno/8966474&sec=umno>.

4

The 2004 Malaysian General Elections: Economic Development, Electoral Trends, and the Decline of the Opposition

EDMUND TERENCE GOMEZ

Introduction

This chapter argues that the rise of the influence of the Opposition during the 1990s was primarily due to the outcome of key policies implemented by former prime minister, Mahathir Mohamad, on the economy and Malaysian society. One key reason why Prime Minister Abdullah Ahmad Badawi managed to lead the ruling Barisan Nasional (BN, or National Front) coalition to a phenomenal victory in the 11th general election in 2004 was his pledge to introduce economic reforms to respond to the needs of the poor, especially rural Malays, and to rectify social ills, particularly rampant corruption, that had emerged during the Mahathir era.

This chapter first provides an overview of Mahathir's economic agenda for Malaysia, focusing on the outcome of his developmental plan.

The second segment outlines Abdullah's promises of change following his ascendancy to the premiership and during the 2004 elections campaign. An analysis is then provided of electoral trends during the period 1990 to 2004, to support the contention that the Opposition's rise during the 1990s was primarily the result of Mahathir's economic policies.

The chapter concludes by arguing that if the BN is not able to deliver on its economic reform pledges, the decline of the Opposition may only be a temporary phase. However, as the electoral trends over this nearly 15-year period also indicate important demographic changes in Malaysia, the possibility of the emergence of a strong Opposition will depend on the implementation of institutional reforms that adequately respond to changes in society.

Malaysia under Mahathir

In October 2003, Mahathir relinquished power to his chosen successor, Abdullah, after having served more than 22 years as prime minister of Malaysia. During his tenure, the political system under Mahathir had come to be one characterised by a concentration of power in the hands of the executive. The structure of the state had become so extremely personalised that the term "Mahathir hegemony" was liberally applied in most analyses of Malaysian politics.[1] In July 1981, when Mahathir assumed the premiership, the Malaysian political system was then characterised as one of "UMNO hegemony", that is where the multi-party BN coalition, supposedly practising a form of consociational democracy, was under the control of the prime minister's party, the United Malays' National Organisation (UMNO).[2]

Mahathir's administration was also noted for its close nexus with business, typified by selective patronage of businessmen, ostensibly as a means to achieve three primary goals: first, the creation of a dynamic, entrepreneurial community with the capacity to compete internationally; second, to achieve fully-developed industrialised nation status for Malaysia by 2020; and finally, to create a new class of internationally recognised Malay capitalists.[3]

The consequences of the government's developmental agenda, also involving the implementation of the affirmative action-based, 20-year New Economic Policy (NEP), introduced in 1970, was the rise of a "new middle-class" which included the emergence of an independent, dynamic, mainly professional Malay community.[4] This new Malay middle-class was also reputedly a disgruntled community because they could not break into the elite cohort that was capturing most state concessions, or "rents",[5] created to attain Mahathir's development agenda for Malaysia. This Malay middle-class would eventually become the primary supporters of the new opposition party, Parti Keadilan Nasional (Keadilan, or Malaysian National Justice Party), led by Anwar Ibrahim, former deputy prime minister and UMNO deputy president, after he was ousted from office by Mahathir in 1998.

Despite the implementation of the NEP, which aspired to eradicate poverty by 1990, when Mahathir retired from public office in 2003, the persistence of this problem remained a serious issue among rural Malays, a community that had long provided staunch support to UMNO. By the mid-1990s, these Malaysians, situated in the so-called "Malay heartland" of Kelantan, Terengganu, Kedah, Perlis, Pahang, and northern Perak, had begun to question why affirmative action had not helped them. These Malays increasingly saw UMNO not as their "protector"[6] but as having committed to nothing more than a series of broken promises.[7] They viewed the government's focus on heavy industries, privatisation, and the promotion of big business as policies contributing little to alleviate the plight of the poor, especially those still involved in agriculture, fishing, and cottage industries.

Apart from their poverty and feeling of economic marginalisation, rural Bumiputeras were also growing anxious over the influence of Western-style modernism on Malaysian, especially Muslim, society. By the mid-1990s, an outcome of rapid urbanisation and modernisation was new social problems, including a rise in divorce rates among Malays, *bohsia* (promiscuous behaviour), and *lepak* (loitering in malls), primarily among Malay youths, escalating gangsterism among poor ethnic Indians who had migrated to urban shanty areas, and a burgeoning drug problem among youths, including the abuse of the drug ecstasy by young ethnic Chinese. These factors contributed to growing support for the Islamic party, Parti Islam SeMalaysia (PAS, or Pan Islamic Party), from the early 1990s, as the party offered Islam as the answer to the social malaise enveloping the country.[8] By the late 1990s, feelings of marginality and exclusion were being expressed more by Malays than by non-Bumiputeras, an indication of the emergence of new intra-ethnic class divisions as a consequence of policies implemented to promote rapid industrialisation.

Within the corporate sector, as a result of the rapid rise of a number of big businesses — the supposed new "captains of industry" — where much wealth was concentrated, allegations of unbridled corruption in politics and business were hurled on the Mahathir administration. Following the 1997 currency crisis, when a number of these large enterprises nurtured by the government required government support to fend off bankruptcy, this led to further allegations of favouritism, nepotism, and abuse of power by the government.[9] By the time Mahathir had decided to step down as prime minister in late 2002, even he had to acknowledge that his attempts to develop a new breed of privately-owned Malay conglomerates had failed miserably.[10]

There was evidence to support Mahathir's astonishing admission that his efforts to promote Malay capital and effectively privatise and industrialise Malaysia was unsuccessful. In 2000, of the top ten firms quoted on the Malaysian stock exchange, the government had majority ownership of seven of these firms.[11] The remaining three firms were Chinese-owned.[12] None of these top ten companies was owned by Malays. No company in the top ten was involved in the industrial sector, indicating that the government had failed to develop huge enterprises with an active participation in manufacturing. Among the top 20 firms, only two were involved in manufacturing, the once-privatised but subsequently re-nationalised Proton, manufacturer of the Malaysian car, and foreign-owned Rothmans, producer of cigarettes.[13]

Other evidence to substantiate Mahathir's argument that the enterprises his government had scrupulously nurtured were not sustainable was the impact of the 1997 currency crisis on these firms. Among the companies that were reportedly "bailed out" included Renong, controlled by Halim Saad, a firm reputed to represent the rise of Malay capital. Before Halim's takeover of the Renong Group, its associated companies had been owned by UMNO, and were privy to a number of lucrative privatised projects, including the multi-billion Ringgit North-South Highway. Proton had to be bought from the debt-ridden DRB-HICOM by the government-owned and cash-rich petroleum firm, Petronas. The loss- and debt-ridden Malaysian Airlines (MAS), the nation's privatised airline, had to be re-nationalised to rescue it from imminent bankruptcy. MAS was then controlled by the well-connected Tajuddin Ramli who also owned the privatised mobile phone operator, Celcom, which was taken over by government-controlled Telekom. The government's acquisition of debt-ridden businesses owned by Mirzan Mahathir, the former prime minister's eldest son, was mired in much controversy. Mahathir's deputy, Anwar, had objected to Mirzan's "bailout", an issue that reputedly contributed to the split between the two leaders.

Mahathir's controversial dismissal of Anwar as deputy prime minister and UMNO deputy president in September 1998 and the latter's subsequent arrest under widely-believed trumped-up charges of sexual impropriety and corruption led to the emergence of the *reformasi* (reform) movement. The *reformasi* quickly evolved into an unlikely coalition that united socialists, Islamists, and social activists. The newly-established, multi-party coalition, the Barisan Alternatif (BA, or Alternative Front), comprised the leading opposition parties, PAS, and the socialist-oriented, multi-ethnic Democratic Action Party (DAP) which had hitherto been unable to forge a common pact. Anwar's dismissal helped bring non-governmental organisation (NGO) activists into mainstream politics through the formation of the Keadilan, whose members included an UMNO faction.[14] The socialist-based Parti Rakyat Malaysia (PRM, or Malaysian People's Party) was the other component party in the BA. Anwar was declared the *de facto* leader of this new Opposition coalition.

The BA further undermined UMNO's waning influence in the Malay heartland. During the 1999 general election, PAS not only retained control of Kelantan, but wrested power of the Terengganu state government from the BN and made considerable inroads into the rest of the Malay heartland. The 1999 election results in the Malay heartland deeply embarrassed UMNO and eroded Mahathir's diminishing legitimacy as a Malay leader.[15]

Between 1999 and 2004, seven parliamentary and state by-elections were held in the Peninsula of which the BA won only two. Although this suggested a decline of the Opposition, one study indicated that the BN had still not managed to retrieve overwhelming Malay support.[16] The two by-elections won by the BA were both in Kedah, Mahathir's home state, indicating that his controversial leadership remained a problematic issue for UMNO.

Malaysia under Abdullah

Abdullah's Economic and Reform Agenda

Immediately after his appointment as prime minister, Abdullah adopted a populist agenda, voicing his desire to implement policies to help, in particular, the rural poor who had been abandoning UMNO in large numbers since the mid-1990s. One key pledge by Abdullah was that his government would endeavour to eradicate poverty by promoting agriculture, a sector in which many rural Malays were involved. Unlike Mahathir, who was deeply committed to the development of big business, Abdullah actively promoted the development of small- and medium-scale enterprises (SMEs). Abdullah went so far as to suggest that his government would provide big capitalists little support. One issue given much media prominence was the new administration's desire to eradicate corruption, suggesting that this malaise had thrived because of Mahathir's form of selective patronage. Not long after Abdullah's ascendancy to the premiership, one of Mahathir's closest business allies, Eric Chia, who had been appointed to develop Perwaja Steel, an enterprise introduced under the heavy industries initiative, was arrested on charges of criminal breach of trust. By stressing his desire to clean up the state, Abdullah was undermining a key issue emphasised by the Opposition to garner electoral support in 1999.

While it appeared that Abdullah was distancing himself from the excesses of the Mahathir administration and some of the latter's controversial and unpopular developmental plans, the new prime minister had, historically, shown little support for his predecessor's entrepreneurial and industrial agenda. Abdullah had been a member of the so-called "UMNO Team B" that had controversially challenged Mahathir's presidency of the party in 1987. Team B, led by then trade and industry minister, Tengku Razaleigh Hamzah, and comprising a number of Mahathir's cabinet members, justified this extremely divisive and unprecedented challenge on the grounds that the prime minister's heavy industrial policies and ill-conceived patronage of select businessmen, specifically Daim Zainuddin, had undermined the economy. Mahathir was accused of concentrating decision-making power in a kitchen cabinet comprising his closest associates and businessmen, including Daim, who had been appointed to the posts of finance minister and UMNO treasurer in 1984.[17] Razaleigh and many members of Team B, but not Abdullah, formed a new opposition party, Semangat '46 (Spirit of '46 Party) which, in separate coalitions with the DAP and PAS, posed a serious threat to UMNO during the 1990 general election.[18]

Abdullah had shown little interest in the corporate sector, even though his brother and son had emerged as prominent business figures by 2003.[19] While Abdullah may have been genuinely interested in the development of the SME sector, especially as an alternative means to promote the development of Malay enterprise, this new endeavour potentially served as an opportunity for him to dispense patronage at a lower, more discrete level as he attempted to consolidate political power in UMNO. Moreover, this initiative enhanced the reputation he was trying to cultivate as a Malay populist.

Prior to the 2004 election, the themes of equitable economic development and good governance were publicised as the priorities of Abdullah's government, probably the key issues preoccupying the minds of the urban middle-class and rural Malays, two groups that had supported Keadilan and PAS respectively in the previous election. Following his appointment as prime minister, Abdullah established a royal commission to review the activities of the police as part of his campaign to stamp out corruption in the public service, called off a RM14 billion railway double-tracking project apparently linked to a businessman well-connected with Mahathir, and directed the Anti-Corruption Agency (ACA) to act without fear or favour to haul up any corrupt individual, both in government and the private sector. In his ten-point election manifesto, the battle against corruption and infrastructure and economic development in the Malay heartland were the dominant campaign issues. In Terengganu, to help promote farming and fisheries, the government stressed that the poor involved in these sectors would be privy to education to help them develop the potential of these sectors. The Eastern Industrial Corridor (EIC) initiatives, stretching from coastal Kelantan to Johore and encompassing Sabah and Sarawak, initiated in the mid-1990s, was to be given a new boost through the promotion of government-aided projects.[20]

Electoral Trends: 1990 to 2004

During the 2004 Malaysian general election, the BN secured a massive endorsement, securing victory in 198 out of the 219 parliamentary seats and 453 out of the 504 state assembly seats under contest.[21] In 2004, the ruling coalition recorded its best ever performance by capturing about 90 per cent of the parliamentary seats, up from 75 per cent in 1999. In terms of popular support, the BN secured 64.4 per cent of the vote, still moderately less than the 65 per cent it secured during the 1995 general election.

The Opposition obtained a respectable 35.36 per cent of the popular vote: PAS secured 15.14 per cent, Keadilan 8.27 per cent, DAP 9.78 per cent, and independent candidates 2.17 per cent. The results indicated that UMNO had rather successfully and remarkably recaptured much of the ground in the Malay heartland that it had lost to the Opposition, bucking the trend of declining rural Bumiputera support since 1995. The BN recaptured control of the state government of Terengganu from PAS, very narrowly failed to regain control of Kelantan, and improved its electoral performance in Kedah, Pahang, and Perlis. A review of the electoral trends between 1995 and 2004 would suggest, however, that the BN's electoral victory may only be a false dawn for the coalition in terms of renewed electoral support.

Table 4.1 indicates the share of votes secured by the BN during the 1990, 1995, 1999, and 2004 general elections in Bumiputera-majority areas in the Malay heartland states of Kelantan, Terengganu, and Kedah. In the 31 parliamentary seats listed in Table 4.1, Malays constitute 80 per cent or more of the electorate. During the 1995 general election, when the BN secured its best ever electoral victory, Table 4.1 indicates that between 1990 and 1995, Malay support in Kedah and Terengganu for UMNO had begun to slump. This loss of Malay support in Kedah and Terengganu had occurred even though, between 1990 and 1995, the Malaysian economy had experienced a massive boom, during which the Opposition coalition comprising PAS and Semangat '46 had

Table 4.1

Difference in Support for Barisan Nasional in Bumiputera-majority Parliamentary Constituencies in the 1990, 1995, 1999, and 2004 General Elections (in Percentages)

State	1990	1995	1990–95 Difference	1999	1995–99 Difference	2004	1999–2004 Difference
Kedah							
Baling	61.4	55.7	–5.7	48.0	–7.7	53.5	5.5
Sik	59.4	53.6	–5.8	49.0	–4.6	50.5	1.5
Jerlun	59.5	53.9	–5.6	49.0	–4.9	52.9	3.9
Padang Terap	58.4	54.4	–4.0	48.0	–6.4	53.9	5.9
Pendang	52.9	51.0	–1.9	46.0	–5.0	49.9	3.9
Yan	57.2	55.7	–1.5	50.0	–5.7	—	—
Kubang Pasu	75.4	74.2	–1.2	65.0	–9.2	67.3	2.3
Kuala Kedah	52.8	52.3	–0.5	49.0	–3.3	58.1	9.1
Pokok Sena	53.8	54.0	0.2	46.0	–8.0	56.9	10.9
Terengganu							
Kemaman	62.9	57.6	–5.0	48.0	–9.6	63.9	15.9
Kuala Nerus	53.6	51.5	–2.1	40.0	–11.5	54.5	14.5
Dungun	54.0	50.5	–3.5	39.0	–11.5	55.1	16.1
Marang	48.2	47.6	–0.6	37.0	–10.6	50.1	13.1
Hulu Terengganu	53.1	52.5	–0.6	43.0	–10.1	59.7	16.7

Table 4.1   cont'd

Setiu	55.7	55.5	-0.2	46.0	-9.5	58.5	12.5
Besut	50.4	54.6	4.2	45.0	-9.6	59.7	14.7
Kuala Terengganu	45.3	53.5	8.2	35.0	-18.5	51.6	16.6
Kelantan							
Tumpat	33.1	46.1	13.0	35.0	-11.1	48.3	13.3
Pengkalan Chepa	26.1	29.6	3.5	25.0	-4.6	41.1	16.1
Rantau Panjang	38.1	40.4	2.3	36.0	-4.4	48.8	12.8
Bachok	32.8	42.0	9.2	38.0	-4.0	53.5	15.5
Kuala Krai	30.8	42.5	11.7	43.0	0.5	53.4	10.4
Kota Baru	29.3	41.6	12.3	38.0	-3.6	51.9	13.9
Pasir Mas	33.9	44.3	10.4	39.0	-5.3	40.7	1.7
Tanah Merah	33.7	46.9	13.2	43.0	-3.9	54.3	11.3
Pasir Puteh	35.0	44.1	9.1	40.0	-4.1	46.2	6.2
Machang	32.6	43.4	10.8	40.0	-3.4	50.2	10.2
Peringat	35.3	50.5	15.2	43.0	-7.5	—	—
Gua Musang	22.7	21.9	-0.8	56.0	34.1	66.1	10.1
Jeli*	—	51.1	—	49.0	-2.1	63.8	14.8
Kubang Kerian*	—	33.5	—	27.0	-6.5	42.4	15.4

* New seats in the 1995 general election.

begun to encounter serious problems.[22] In 1999, compared to the 1995 election, the BN gained more electoral support in only two of these 31 seats, indicating a further and serious erosion of Malay support. Where the BN registered an improved performance was in Kelantan, where Razaleigh, who had returned to the UMNO fold, retained one of the two parliamentary seats the BN had won. Razaleigh's seat was the only parliamentary constituency in Kelantan won by the BN.[23]

Of the 104 parliamentary seats that UMNO contested in the 1999 election, the party secured victory in only about 69 per cent of these constituencies, that is, 72 seats. In the 1995 election, UMNO had won 89, or 87 per cent, of the 102 parliamentary seats it contested. This was the first time in UMNO's history that the party commanded less than half the total number of seats in parliament.

In Kedah, the fall in electoral support for the BN between 1995 and 1999 was by more than 4 percentage points in all but one of the nine Bumiputera-majority parliamentary seats. Although the BN retained control of Kedah in the state-level elections,[24] PAS won eight of Kedah's parliamentary seats compared to UMNO's victory in only five of the 13 constituencies it contested.[25] The largest decline in support for the BN was in Mahathir's Kubang Pasu constituency, with a fall of nearly 11 percentage points between 1990 and 1999. UMNO lost to PAS in seven of these nine Bumiputera-majority seats, but the margin of support that the BN secured was between 46 and 49 percentage points, suggesting that a small swing was sufficient for UMNO to retain control of these seats.

During the 2004 general election, following the departure of Mahathir as prime minister, the BN recorded an increase in support in all nine constituencies, and secured control of all but one of the Malay-majority parliamentary seats in Kedah. The swing in support to UMNO increased appreciably ranging from 10.9 percentage points (in Pokok Sena) to 1.5 percentage points (in Sik). However, in all but one seat, UMNO secured less than 58 per cent of the popular vote, and in five of these constituencies, the BN support was less than 54 per cent. This suggested that a small swing in favour of the Opposition in the next election would be sufficient for it to again undermine UMNO's territorial gains in the 2004 election. In all these Malay-majority parliamentary seats in Kedah, the BN's main opposition is PAS, indicating that the Islamic party remains an influential force there.

In Terengganu, diminished Malay electoral support for the BN between 1990 and 1999 was even more striking, with an almost double-digit percentage point fall in support in all constituencies, contributing to the BN's loss of control of the state to PAS in the 2004 general election. In 1999, UMNO did not win any of the eight parliamentary seats it contested in Terengganu.[26] In Dungun, for example, the fall in support for the BN between 1990 and 1999 was a massive 15 percentage points, while in Kemaman it was 14.6 percentage points, Kuala Nerus 13.6 percentage points, Marang 11.2 percentage points, Hulu Terengganu 10.7 percentage points, and Setiu 9.7 percentage points. During the 1999 general election, in the constituency of Kuala Terengganu, the fall in support for the BN that year was a colossal 18.5 percentage points! In six of these eight constituencies, the BN's level of support was less than 45 per cent of the popular vote, suggesting that the ruling coalition faced an uphill struggle to regain control of the state government in Terengganu in the next election.

For this reason, the BN's capture of the Terengganu state government during the 2004 election was an extraordinary achievement. The swing in support from the Opposition to the BN in all parliamentary seats was in double-digit figures, ranging from 16.7 percentage points (in Hulu Terengganu) to 12.5 percentage points (in Setiu). However, in four of these eight seats, the BN's margin of victory was less than 5 percentage points, again suggesting that while the BN had recovered much ground, UMNO could still lose support in the future if the government it led did not deliver on its pledges.

The BN's performance was almost as impressive in PAS's stronghold of Kelantan as it was in Terengganu in 2004. A comparison, however, of the voting trends in Kelantan during the elections in 1999 and 1990 (when UMNO failed to win a single parliamentary and state seat) indicates that, in a majority of the state's parliamentary seats, the proportion of Malay support for the BN was higher in 1999.[27] During the 2004 election, the BN further improved its performance, registering an increase in support in all parliamentary constituencies in Kelantan. In 11 of the 13 parliamentary seats under review, the increase in support was in double-digit figures. The percentage point increase ranged from 16.1 (in Pengkalan Chepa) to 10.1 (in Gua Musang) to 6.2 (Pasir Puteh). In only one constituency, Pasir Mas, was the margin of increase of support below 5 percentage points.

Table 4.1 also indicates that during the period 1990 and 1995, UMNO had managed to regain lost ground (following the emergence of Semangat '46 which had helped PAS secure control of Kelantan in 1990). In 1999, however, in spite of the return of Razaleigh to UMNO, but following the Anwar debacle that undermined Mahathir's legitimacy, the BN again registered a loss of support in all but two constituencies, Bachok (0.5 percentage point increase) and Gua Musang (a massive 34.1 percentage point increase); Gua Musang is Razaleigh's constituency. In 1999, the BN's level of popular support in 12 of the 14 parliamentary constituencies was between a mere 25 per cent and 43 per cent. Under these circumstances, the BN's victory in seven of the 13 constituencies in 2004 suggested a major return of support for UMNO. However, in all but two of these seven constituencies won by the BN, the margin of victory was by less than 5 percentage points, again suggesting that UMNO's position in Kelantan was still quite tenuous.

PAS's performance in 2004, in terms of seats in the new parliament, was dismal, dropping from 27 to a mere seven, a severe regression for a party seemingly on the rise. Six of these victories were recorded in Kelantan, the remaining one in Kedah. PAS failed to win a single parliamentary seat in Terengganu, a major reversal of its fortunes compared to 1999 when the party denied the BN representation in any of the eight constituencies in that state. The Islamic party was not able to win a single seat in Perlis, Selangor, and Pahang, states in which PAS was reputed to be growing in influence.

The results for PAS were similarly dire in the state-level elections. While the Islamic party had a total of 98 state seats going into the 2004 election, its total was reduced to a mere 36 when the results were declared. Although PAS had the largest number of seats among the Opposition, 24 of these victories were in Kelantan. Of the remaining 12 seats under PAS, five were in Kedah, four in Terengganu, and one each in Perlis, Penang, and Johore. The victory in Johore was by default when the BN's nomination papers were rejected on technical grounds. Following the 1999 election, PAS had 41 state seats in Kelantan, 28 in Terengganu, 12 in Kedah, and three in Perlis. The party was not able to secure any representation in Pahang, where it had control of six seats going into the election, in Selangor, where it had four assemblymen after the 1999 state elections, or in Perak, where it previously had three representatives in the state assembly. In Kelantan, of the 24 seats won by PAS, in five of these constituencies, the BN was narrowly defeated by razor-thin majorities of less than 100 votes. In seven other constituencies, PAS's margin of victory was by less than 1,000 votes. According to one estimate, PAS's support in the Malay heartland fell by about 11 percentage points between 1999 and 2004, from 56 per cent to 45 per cent.[28]

Table 4.2 shows the difference in voter-support for the BN in Chinese-majority parliamentary constituencies between 1990 and 2004. In these constituencies, the Chinese constitute at least 45 per cent of the electorate.[29] The percentage point difference in votes secured by the BN between the 1990 and 1995 general elections indicates a substantial Chinese swing to the coalition during this period. This was due primarily to the consistent growth rates recorded by the Malaysian economy during the early 1990s. Apart from this, the government's economic and cultural liberalisation policies in existence since the early 1990s helped the BN secure enormous Chinese support.

Although it is widely assumed that the BN obtained considerable Chinese support in the 1999 election, a comparison of the results between 1995 and 1999 reveals a considerable fall in support for the BN in 64 per cent, or nearly two-thirds, of these Chinese-majority constituencies. However, Table 4.2 also indicates that in 1999, although the BA had won the Chinese-stronghold seats of Bukit Bintang, Seputeh, Cheras, and Kepong in the Federal Territory of Kuala Lumpur, all contested by the DAP, the BN managed to secure increased support in these areas.[30] In the 2004 election, however, the BN registered an increase in support in 24 constituencies and a decline in only 10. In one constituency, Bukit Bintang in Kuala Lumpur, there was no change in support for either the BN or the Opposition, with the DAP retaining this constituency.

Table 4.2

Difference in Support by the Chinese Electorate for Barisan Nasional in Chinese-majority Parliamentary Constituencies in the 1990, 1995, 1999, 2004 General Elections (in Percentages)

State	Percentage of Chinese Electorate 1995	1990	1995	1990–95 Difference	1999	1995–99 Difference	2004	1999–2004 Difference
Penang								
Tanjong (D)	87.0	29.1	40.7	11.1	45.0	4.3	44.8	–0.2
Bukit Bendera (D)	73.8	36.6	51.8	15.1	50.0	–1.8	61.7	11.7
Bukit Mertajam (D)	67.3	46.7	60.9	14.1	47.0	–13.9	40.2	–6.8
Jelutong (D)	65.3	39.2	48.2	9.0	51.0	2.8	58.8	7.8
Bagan (D)	64.4	45.9	48.7	2.8	47.4	–1.3	45.7	–1.7
Bayan Baru (K)	64.3	46.6	54.5	7.8	58.0	3.5	73.6	15.6
Nibong Tebal (K)	48.0	50.7	59.4	8.8	46.6	–12.9	59.5	12.9
Perak								
Ipoh Timur (D)	86.0	40.6	49.4	8.8	52.0	2.6	39.8	–12.2
Ipoh Barat* (D)	66.3	—	54.2	—	54.0	–0.2	49.3	–4.7
Batu Gajah (D)	75.7	37.1	50.5	13.4	47.0	–3.5	41.9	–5.1
Kampar (D)	61.2	48.1	65.6	17.5	59.7	–5.9	62.9	3.2
Beruas (D)	52.7	50.1	65.9	15.8	52.0	–13.9	58.4	6.4
Gopeng (K)	50.8	60.6	71.0	10.4	57.5	–13.5	65.8	8.3
Lumut (K)	45.4	50.9	77.9	27.0	50.7	–27.2	63.4	12.7
Teluk Intan (K/D)	45.1	51.5	65.5	13.9	54.0	–11.5	55.5	1.5
Johor								
Senai	57.9	54.7	69.3	14.6	68.7	–0.6	—	6.1
Bakri (D)	55.1	52.5	60.5	8.0	68.0	7.5	74.1	–1.2
Kluang (D)	49.2	52.4	70.6	18.2	71.0	0.4	69.8	7.5
Gelang Patah* (K)	49.2	—	72.1	—	74.0	1.9	81.5	

Table 4.2 cont'd

Segamat (D)	47.9	51.7	68.4	16.7	62.0	-6.4	63.9	1.9
Pontian (K)	46.9	58.4	83.4	25.0	82.0	-1.4	82.9	0.9
Labis (D)	45.4	56.6	69.8	13.2	71.0	1.2	74.2	3.2
Kuala Lumpur								
Kepong (D)	93.5	29.2	44.2	15.0	47.2	3.0	47.9	0.7
Seputeh (D)	90.6	28.7	43.7	14.9	44.5	0.8	37.6	-6.9
Cheras (D)	84.1	40.0	33.5	-6.5	40.0	6.5	37.2	-2.8
Bukit Bintang (D)	79.5	20.8	41.5	20.7	48.0	6.5	48.0	0.0
Segambut* (D)	52.6	—	65.9	—	60.0	-5.9	71.6	11.6
Selangor								
Serdang (D)	56.6	45.8	54.3	8.6	53.0	-1.3	59.8	6.8
Klang (D)	55.4	42.0	52.1	10.1	54.6	2.5	63.0	8.4
PJ Selatan* (K)	50.5	—	61.3	—	54.0	-7.3	66.6	12.6
Negeri Sembilan								
Rasah (D)	60.0	51.4	58.1	6.8	51.0	-7.1	55.0	4.0
Seremban (D)	45.0	48.3	62.1	13.8	58.0	-4.1	64.3	6.3
Telok Kemang (D)	45.0	66.6	72.1	5.5	61.0	-11.1	72.7	11.7
Malacca								
Kota Melaka (D)	66.7	35.6	44.0	8.4	42.0	-2.0	50.2	8.2
Pahang								
Bentong (D)	45.0	65.7	73.6	7.9	65.0	-8.6	72.5	7.5
Kedah								
Alor Setar (D)	46.0	54.3	68.6	14.3	68.0	-0.6	67.2	-0.8

* New seats in the 1995 general election.
D = DAP, K = Keadilan, these being opposition parties contesting in the constituencies.

In all but one of the ten constituencies that the BN registered a decline in support, the opposition it faced was the DAP. This suggested a marked improvement in the DAP's electoral performance compared to 1999.

Keadilan, on the other hand, reduced the BN's support only in Alor Setar in Kedah; even here the percentage point decline was a mere 0.8. This suggested that in Chinese-majority constituencies, Keadilan — in the BA with PAS — was facing much difficulty garnering support. The DAP appeared to have fared much better among the Chinese electorate after its departure from the BA, but this statement needs to be qualified. In the seven Chinese-majority constituencies that the DAP contested in Penang, the BN recorded a major margin of increase in four constituencies, ranging from 7.8 to 15.6 percentage points. In Malacca, the DAP lost its stronghold seat of Kota Melaka, whose member of parliament was its secretary-general, Kerk Kim Hock, albeit by a slim margin of 219 votes.[31]

In the 15 constituencies in Perak and Penang, the Opposition recorded an improved performance in only seven contests in 2004. However, during the 1999 election, the Opposition had recorded an improved performance in 11 of these 15 constituencies, suggesting increased Chinese support for the BN.[32] These results were replicated in the BN's stronghold state of Johore. In 1999, in Johore, even though the proportion of popular support for the BN was 70.55 per cent, the highest in the country, the ruling coalition registered an erosion of support in four of seven Chinese-majority constituencies. In 2004, the BN improved its performance in all but one constituency. In the five constituencies in the Federal Territory of Kuala Lumpur — where all seats were contested by the DAP — the results were mixed, with the Opposition registering an improved performance in two seats and a decline in another two; there was no change in one constituency. In the three constituencies in Selangor, the Opposition registered a very poor performance, losing an appreciable volume of support to the BN. In Negeri Sembilan, the BN not only continued to retain control of all three Chinese-majority constituencies, it registered a marked increase in electoral support. During the 1999 election, there had been a marked drop in electoral support for the BN in all these three constituencies.

Among the Opposition, the DAP was the only party that recorded a rise in the number of seats won, compared to its performance in the 1999 election. The DAP had nominees running in 44 parliamentary constituencies and 106 state seats. The DAP's representation in parliament rose from ten to 12, while in the state-level elections, the number of the party's assemblymen nationwide increased from 11 to 15. The electorate returned to parliament DAP stalwarts Lim Kit Siang and Karpal Singh, the former winning the Ipoh Timur seat in Perak and the latter narrowly victorious in Bukit Gelugor in Penang; both had been rejected in 1999 in Penang. The DAP's best performance was in Perak where the party won seven state seats, where previously it had four seats. But otherwise, the DAP's performance in the other state assemblies was dismal — two each in Malacca, Negeri Sembilan, and Selangor, and one each in Penang and Pahang. In Negeri Sembilan, however, the Opposition had no representation in the state assembly before the 2004 election and in Selangor the DAP increased its representation by one. In Malacca though, the DAP had four seats after the 1999 election, indicating a loss of support. The DAP had no representation in any of the Malay heartland states of Kelantan, Kedah, Terengganu, and Perlis, indicating its limited capacity to mobilise Bumiputera support. The electoral results for the DAP were mixed at best, with marginal gains in some states, but overall, its departure from the BA had not contributed to a return of support of the type it commanded during, say, the 1990 general election, when it recorded its best ever electoral victory, capturing 20 parliamentary seats and 45 state seats.[33]

The DAP's performance in some prominent urban, predominantly middle-class, seats once considered their stronghold indicated its position with the electorate. In Petaling Jaya Utara, a Kuala Lumpur suburb, the incumbent Malayan Chinese Association (MCA) candidate increased her margin of victory against the DAP nominee by more than 15,000 votes. The number of seats won by the Gerakan and MCA combined increased from 35 in 1999 to 41 in 2004. The DAP also lost further ground to the BN is traditional strongholds such as Bukit Bendera and Bayan Baru (in Penang), Kampar and Teluk Intan (in Perak), and Klang and Serdang (in Selangor).

Keadilan probably fared the worst among the Opposition, winning narrowly just one of the 58 parliamentary seats it contested, that is Permatang Pauh, formerly held by Anwar and represented by his wife and Keadilan president, Wan Azizah. The party did not win any of the 121 state seats it contested. Following the 1999 election, Keadilan had five representatives in parliament and control of four state seats. As Table 4.2 indicates, of the nine Chinese-majority parliamentary constituencies that Keadilan contested, the party registered an increase in support in only one, in Alor Setar in Kedah, and that too by a mere 0.8 percentage points. Keadilan recorded an appreciable decline in support in urban middle-class areas like PJ Selatan, where the party was expected to be received more favourably. In this constituency, although the Keadilan's candidate was a senior party leader and a prominent human rights lawyer, the party's decline in support was by nearly 13 percentage points compared to 1999. In the last election, the Opposition had managed to reduce the BN's majority by nearly 8 percentage points in this constituency.

The situation was similarly dire for Keadilan in other urban constituencies like Bayan Baru and Nibong Tebal in Penang, where the decline in support was by 15.6 and 12.9 percentage points respectively; in Gopeng and Lumut in Perak, by 8.3 and 12.7 percentage points respectively; and in Gelang Patah in Johore, by 7.5 percentage points. Keadilan had, however, contested primarily in constituencies that could be considered "mixed" areas, seats normally retained by the BN with ease.[34] Among Kuala Lumpur's large middle-class population, where the BA, particularly Keadilan, was reputed to have some support, the party was unable to secure substantial support, losing all the seats in the city area that it contested. The 2004 election results suggested that Keadilan had lost much of the urban middle-class electorate, and the non-Bumiputera community, support that it had secured in 1999.

Following the 2004 general election, Keadilan leaders blamed PAS and the latter's stand on promoting an Islamic state in Malaysia for its disastrous showing in the polls. According to Abdul Razak Ahmad, Keadilan's Johor leader, "They [PAS] failed to see that Malaysia is a multi-racial country and they would frighten people, including the

Muslims in Johor who are a moderate group of believers."[35] Razak also attributed Keadilan's poor performance to the dissipation of the "*reformasi* spirit" and the disunity among the Opposition, drawing specific attention to the departure of the DAP from the BA.[36]

Opposition Decline or Support for Reform?

The 2004 electoral trends reflect a number of pertinent issues. First, the results suggest that the BA does not appear to be a viable alternative to many Malaysians, an issue that became apparent following the 1999 election.[37] While analysts of the 1999 election had argued that the "split" among the Malays had contributed to UMNO's loss of Bumiputera support to PAS in the economically less-developed Malay heartland, the BN maintained the community's support in the southern states of the Peninsula. Although this indicated intra-ethnic Malay class dichotomies, the 2004 results also suggest that the BA, and the ostensibly multi-racial Keadilan in particular, could not muster support in more economically-developed mixed constituencies.

A similar ambivalence is apparent among the Chinese electorate. While the Chinese support for the BN in 1999 had declined compared to the 1995 election, the 2004 results show a small swing back to the ruling coalition even though the DAP garnered two more parliamentary seats. Gerakan lost only two of the 12 parliamentary seats it contested — in the DAP strongholds of Tanjung in Penang, and Kepong in KL Federal Territory — and just one of the 31 state seats — in Traing in Pahang — where it fielded candidates. As in the case of the DAP, Gerakan's electorate performance improved in 2004, with the party increasing its parliamentary seats from seven to 10, while the number of its state assemblymen rose from 21 to 30. In Chinese-majority Penang, Gerakan won all the 13 state seats it contested, yet it lost a parliamentary seat in this state. The MCA contested 40 parliamentary seats and won 31, and secured victory in 76 of the 90 state seats where it put up candidates. Going into the 2004 elections, the MCA had 28 parliamentary seats. In Penang, the MCA won nine of the 10 state seats it contested, yet three of its four parliamentary candidates lost to the Opposition. Since the BN and BA have not managed to secure mass Bumiputera support and the Chinese were reluctant to support the Opposition in 1999 while not standing firmly behind the ruling coalition in 2004, this indicates a need for political parties to consider institutional and organisational reforms.[38]

Second, the 2004 results support the contention that Mahathir's development plans appear to have steadily alienated poor rural Malays from the early 1990s, while UMNO's failure to redress this problem contributed to the rise of PAS. Abdullah's economic reform pledge probably was sufficient for UMNO to revive the support of much of this community. In 1999, UMNO's decline in Bumiputera support generally, including that of the urban middle-class electorate, was attributed to rampant corruption and abuse of power for vested political and economic interests. Abdullah's well-publicised image as a "clean politician" and his promise to deal stringently with corruption in government and business and rid UMNO of money politics was probably sufficient to effectively undermine a key issue adopted by Keadilan to muster support.

Third, the BN's phenomenal victory in the 2004 election was primarily due to the problems within the Opposition, specifically their inability to articulate a common stand that could unify Malaysians. The DAP's acrimonious departure from the BA and PAS's continued propagation of a purportedly conservative form of Islam, which alienated non-Muslims, did not help the cause of the Opposition. Keadilan's alliance with PAS had hindered the party's capacity to secure electoral victories in non-Bumiputera areas, reinforcing the issue of the sustainability of the BA that was apparent in 1999. In 2004, even some prominent Keadilan leaders, in their post-mortem of the election, acknowledged the repercussions of PAS's brand of theocratic politics on their campaign.[39]

Fourth, while Keadilan's almost total rejection, PAS's abysmal performance, and the DAP's negligible increase in support despite its withdrawal from the BA suggest that the Opposition is a spent force, the results in the Malay heartland indicate that the Islamic party retains some influence. The electoral trends since 1990 reveal that PAS has persistently had about 40 per cent of the support in the Malay heartland. A small swing in support is sufficient to allow the BA to regain a dominant presence in Terengganu, re-establish its control in Kelantan, and increase its number of seats in the rest of the

Malay heartland. In fact, the 2004 results indicate that PAS's share of popular support had increased by 0.8 percentage points, to 15.8 per cent, compared to 1999,[40] suggesting that the Islamic party remained a serious threat to UMNO. Even though the BN secured control of about 90 per cent of the seats in parliament, UMNO's support in the Malay heartland amounted to only 55 per cent,[41] further indicating that a modest swing would be sufficient for the Opposition to undermine the ruling coalition's electoral gains in 2004.

However, while PAS remains the main opposition to UMNO, the electoral trends over the past 15 years suggest that the Islamic party did not gain ground on the BN because of its ideological stance. PAS's national influence is limited, and it is unable to record electoral gains outside of the Malay world — the party secured a state seat in Johore for the first time in its history by default. Apart from promoting in multi-racial Malaysia a system of governance that is hardly inclusive, PAS has reputedly alienated, through its rather conservative policies, two important groups: women and the youth. According to one estimate of the voting pattern of 800,000 new predominantly young voters, a majority of them supported the BN. One prominent PAS leader, Harun Din, was quoted as saying, "I would say that from the early reading of the results, we did not get as many new voters as BN."[42] UMNO, probably recognising the alienation of women by PAS, had moved effectively to cultivate the support of this group, by, among other things, establishing a new government ministry of women and family development to promote, for example, gender equality, and by fielding more women candidates in the 2004 election.

Of the 55 women candidates that the BN fielded in parliamentary and state seats, 49 of them secured victory. Thirty-five of these 55 women candidates were UMNO members, and only four of them failed to secure victory; one lost by default. In the Opposition, however, of the 38 women candidates fielded, only seven won in these contests. Of the 15 women candidates fielded by Keadilan, only one won, while just two of the ten PAS female candidates fielded secured victories, both in Kelantan. This was the first time since 1969 that PAS has fielded women candidates. The DAP fared much better with four of the nine women candidates it fielded winning seats.[43] In urban areas contested by BN women candidates, usually taking on Keadilan, the BA fared very poorly. In Gelang Patah (in Johore), Ampang (Selangor), and Lembah Pantai (KL Federal Territory), the BN's margin of victory was huge, approximately 31,600, 15,000, and 14,000 votes respectively. All the ten women candidates fielded by the BN in the Selangor state election won their seats with comfortable majorities.[44] Meanwhile, prominent BA women candidates fared poorly. The PAS women's wing deputy president, Lo' Lo' Mohamed Ghazali, lost her bid to win the Bukit Gantang parliamentary seat in Perak, while the Keadilan president, Wan Azizah, was nearly unseated in her Permatang Pauh constituency in Penang.

The voting trends in 2004 — and in 1999 — suggest important developments in Malaysian society that have not been adequately addressed by the BN and the Opposition though there is increasing recognition by politicians of demographic changes and the need to respond to these new trends. Most political parties in Malaysia have, for example, acknowledged the importance of securing and maintaining the support of the young. After the 1999 election, among the BN component parties, UMNO and Malaysian Indian Congress (MIC) responded to the issue of limited youth support by establishing *Puteri* (young women) wings. The leaders of the BN Chinese-based parties, the MCA and Gerakan, have acknowledged that they have faced much difficulty getting young Malaysians to join their parties. These two parties are presently involved in talks about a merger, even to the extent of the possibility of evolving into a multi-racial party.

Among the Opposition, DAP leaders have admitted that the party had not been able to garner the support of the younger generation. The DAP has also been incapable of getting young Malaysians to join the party in large numbers. Probably in recognition of this problem, after the 2004 election, Lim Kit Siang proposed a merger between the DAP and Keadilan, claiming that this would help the Opposition transcend the politics of race and religion which had been rejected by the electorate. The proposed merged enterprise, seen by Lim as a secular democratic platform, served as a means to regain urban, especially Malay, support to complement the Chinese support that the DAP could still muster. Lim is quoted as saying: "The DAP is prepared to work closely and fully with Keadilan to preserve and promote the 46-year Merdeka social contract of Malaysia as a secular democracy with Islam as the official religion, but not an Islamic state, if it is prepared to leave the Barisan Alternative which is compromised by PAS's Islamic state document."[45] Keadilan made a non-committal response; it welcomed mergers with multi-racial parties, but without any conditions attached.[46]

This acknowledgement by BN and BA leaders of the need for institutional reforms to accommodate important transitions in society is probably attributable to the need for them to remain relevant to the Malaysian electorate. A number of studies have begun to highlight the profound changes that have transpired in Malaysian society, especially in terms of "identity formation" among the younger electorate.[47] These changes in Malaysian society have been conceptualised as "new politics",[48] though it could also be seen as the emergence of "new identities",[49] involving differences along generational lines in the way Malaysians view and understand national and ethnic identities.

The challenge for the Opposition — and the BN — is to recognise the changing configurations in society and to create an institutional structure that is acceptable to a majority of Malaysians. If these institutional reforms are not instituted in the future, the Opposition may only manage to secure a meaningful presence in parliament and the state assemblies if the electorate refuses to vote for the BN for failing to deliver on its campaign pledges. To the Opposition's further detriment, some BN component parties have commenced discussions on institutional reforms and Prime Minister Abdullah has been actively promoting the idea of creating a "Malaysian identity" as opposed to discourses along religious and racial lines. In these circumstances, if the Opposition hopes to stem further loss of support, it needs to immediately commence meaningful and inclusive-based institutional reforms.

NOTES

1. See, for example, Hilley (2001), Hwang (2003), Khoo (2003), and Gomez (2004).

2. See Means (1991) and Crouch (1996). The other major parties in the BN, comprising about 14 organisations, include the ethnically-based Malaysian Chinese Association (MCA) and Malaysian Indian Congress (MIC), the socialist-based

Gerakan Rakyat Malaysia (Gerakan, or Malaysian People's Movement), the People's Progressive Party (PPP), the Sarawak-based Parti Persaka Bumiputera Bersatu (PBB), and the Sabah-based Parti Bersatu Sabah (PBS, or Sabah United Party).

3. See Gomez & Jomo (1999), Sloane (1999), Gomez (1999*b*), and Gomez (2002).

4. For an insightful analysis of the emergence of this new Malay middle class, see Abdul Rahman (2002). See also Khan (1996).

5. See Gomez & Jomo (1999) and Jomo & Gomez (2000).

6. See Chandra (1979).

7. See Gomez (1996).

8. See Gomez (1996).

9. See Jomo (2001).

10. See Mahathir's speech entitled *The New Malay Dilemma*, which was delivered at the Harvard Club of Malaysia dinner on 27 July 2002.

11. These seven firms were Telekom Malaysia, Malayan Banking, Tenaga Nasional, Petronas Gas, Malaysian International Shipping Corporation (MISC), Sime Darby, and Commerce Asset-Holding.

12. These three firms were Resorts World and Genting (both of the same group owned by Lim Goh Tong) and YTL Corporation (owned by the Yeoh family).

13. However, none of the top ten was owned by a foreign enterprise. This was an indication of the government's success in protecting the domestic economy, specifically the banking sector, from coming under the control of foreign enterprises.

14. In Anwar's absence, his wife, Wan Azizah Wan Ismail, led Keadilan.

15. See Weiss (2000), Funston (2000a; 2000b), and Loh & Saravanamuttu (2003).

16. See Welsh (2004). Traditionally, since the BN is able to focus attention and resources during by-elections, the Opposition faces overwhelming odds to perform well in such contests.

17. See Shamsul (1988) for an in-depth account of this struggle for power in UMNO that nearly led to the unseating of Mahathir as party president and prime minister.

18. For an analysis of the 1990 general election, see Khong (1991).

19. In the late 1980s until the early 1990s, when Abdullah was in the political wilderness following his ouster from mainstream UMNO politics by Mahathir for his involvement in Team B, he had delved into business as a travel agent. The business venture was hardly a thriving success.

20. See *New Straits Times* (Malaysia), 24 March 2004.

21. In the 1999 general election, the BN had lost 42 parliamentary seats and 113 state seats to the Opposition.

22. In spite of this decline in support in the Malay heartland, after the 1995 election, Mahathir did little to address the economic and social concerns of rural Bumiputeras. For this reason, it is probable that the BN would have faced further erosion of Malay support in many of these Bumiputera-majority constituencies even if Anwar had not been sacked as deputy prime minister. Undoubtedly, however, the manner in which Anwar, who had presented himself as having a more populist orientation, was dismissed, contributed to the scale of Malay swing against UMNO, specifically in Terengganu and Kedah. It is also probable that discontent among the UMNO grassroots over Anwar's dismissal and the choice of party candidates for this general election contributed to the party's poor performance in Kedah and Terengganu. Prior to the 1999 election, PAS had no parliamentary seats in Kedah and only one in Terengganu (down from two in 1990).

23. Of the 58 parliamentary constituencies where UMNO faced a direct fight with a candidate from PAS, the BN won only four more seats than the Opposition. UMNO barely secured 51 per cent of the popular vote in these 58 parliamentary seats. A majority of the contests between members from PAS and UMNO were in parliamentary constituencies in the Malay heartland.

24. The BN component parties won 24 seats, while PAS won in all the other 12 state constituencies. UMNO won 16 of the 28 state seats it contested in Kedah.

25. The BN's MCA won the two other parliamentary seats in Kedah.

26. Of the 31 state seats in Terengganu that UMNO contested, the party won in only four constituencies.

27. The BN secured two seats in the state-level election in Kelantan in 1999.

28. See *New Straits Times* (Malaysia), 28 March 2004.

29. These figures do not include the Indian or other non-Bumiputera communities.

30. In Penang, where ethnic Chinese are the majority population, the BN obtained 51.4 per cent of the total votes cast. In Perak, another state with a large Chinese population, the BN secured about 55 per cent of the popular support. In Selangor, Negeri Sembilan, and Johor, all states with a large Chinese electorate, the BN secured victories in all the parliamentary seats under contest.

31. This was the first time in 35 years that the DAP had lost control of the Kota Melaka constituency. Kerk resigned from his position in the DAP following this defeat.

32. In Penang in 1999, the Opposition had improved its performance compared to the 1995 election. While, in 1999, the BN secured victories in six of the 11 parliamentary constituencies, in the 1995 election, the ruling coalition won eight

of these 11 constituencies. In the state level election in Penang, the Opposition won three seats, two more than the number it held after the 1995 election.

33. See Khong (1991).

34. See Loh (2003). In "mixed" constituencies, the division of the electorate along Bumiputera and non-Bumiputera lines is almost equal.

35. See *The Star* (Malaysia), 25 March 2004.

36. See *The Star* (Malaysia), 25 March 2004.

37. See Gomez (2004).

38. See Gomez (2004) for an in-depth discussion on this ambivalence in the voting trends in 1999. The ambivalence in voting patterns in 1999 was attributed to the kind of race- and religion-based politics propagated by the BA and BN.

39. See *The Star* (Malaysia), 25 March 2004.

40. See *New Straits Times* (Malaysia), 24 March 2004.

41. See *New Straits Times* (Malaysia), 28 March 2004.

42. See *New Straits Times* (Malaysia), 24 March 2004

43. See *The Star* (Malaysia), 25 March 2004.

44. The BN Selangor set a new record in state elections by nominating ten women. See *The Malay Mail* (Malaysia), 27 March 2004.

45. See *The Sun* (Malaysia), 25 March 2004.

46. See *The Star* (Malaysia), 25 March 2004.

47. See, for example, Nair (1999), Shamsul (1999), Gomez (1999c), Abdul Rahman (2002), Loh & Saravanamuttu (2003), and Mandal (2004).

48. See Loh & Saravanamuttu (2003).

49. For a discussion on the concept of "new identities" — and "new ethnicities" — adopted in an analysis of identity transformation in Britain, see Hall (1992).

5

The UMNO-PAS Struggle: Analysis of PAS's Defeat in 2004

AHMAD FAUZI ABDUL HAMID

Overview of the Results of the 2004 General Election

The outcome of the 11th Malaysian general election of 21 March 2004 was staggering not because of the ruling Barisan Nasional (BN) coalition's triumph, but rather because of the magnitude of its victory. Garnering 63.8 per cent of the popular vote, the result meant that BN now controlled 199 out of 219, or 90.9 per cent, of parliamentary seats, rendering an unprecedented BN domination of parliament. Out of 445 state legislative assembly seats contested in Peninsular Malaysia, BN won 394, or 88.5 per cent.

In contrast, the erstwhile main opposition party, Parti Islam SeMalaysia (PAS), had its representation drop from 27 to 6 in parliament and from 98 to 36 state legislative seats. After one term in PAS's hands, Terengganu was regained by BN, who almost achieved a similar feat in Kelantan, whose 45 state legislative assembly seats are now almost evenly divided between PAS's 24 to BN's 21. The mainly Chinese-based opposition party, the Democratic Action Party (DAP) maintained its ground by winning 11 parliamentary seats and 15 state seats, as compared to ten parliamentary seats and 11 state seats in the previous elections in 1999. The other major opposition party, the National Justice Party (Keadilan), declined from representing five parliamentary and four state constituencies in 1999 to holding only a single parliamentary seat in 2004. This sole seat was won by Dr Wan Azizah Wan Ismail, wife of Anwar Ibrahim, the former deputy prime minister sacked from all government and ruling party posts in September 1998 over allegations of corruption and sexual impropriety.[1] Dr Wan Azizah held on to Penang's Permatang Pauh parliamentary seat which had been represented by her husband from 1982 until 1999, and even then, with a slim majority of 590. This pales in comparison with her 9,077 majority in 1999, and apparently reflects a nationwide decline in the people's enthusiasm for the *reformasi*, the Anwar Ibrahim-led reform movement which strives to eradicate corruption, cronyism, and nepotism and thereby seeks to restore justice throughout society.[2]

While the opposition as a whole suffered its worst defeat, PAS was particularly humiliated. Even in states where it was strongest — the Malay heartland of northern and northeastern states of Peninsular Malaysia — PAS struggled to maintain ground. Losing Terengganu and barely holding on to Kelantan, PAS's self-professed target of capturing Kedah and Perlis was reduced to shambles. There was undeniably a swing of sentiment favouring BN among both Malay and non-Malay voters.[3] Taking into account the straight battle between PAS and the United Malays' National Organisation (UMNO) — the dominant Malay partner in BN — in the Malay heartland, thus narrowing our focus to the rural large Malay-majority parliamentary seats, we find that BN registered a rise in support from 48.5 per cent of votes in 1999 to 59.1 per cent of votes in 2004. This translates into a gain from 22 such seats (out of a total of 52) in 1999 to 53 seats (out of a total of 60) in 2004.[4]

Mandate for the BN and the Decline of *Reformasi*

That BN would win the 11th general election was never in question.[5] BN's victory was quickly hailed by the mainstream press as indicating a resounding mandate to govern Malaysia. The success was BN's as much as it was a personal triumph for Abdullah Ahmad Badawi, who had taken over the premiership from Dr Mahathir Mohamad for almost four months. While a feel-good sentiment surrounding a new prime minister had always worked in favour of BN in past elections, Abdullah's personal touch and his successful projection of *Islam Hadhari* (civilisational Islam) as a fundamental tenet of his administration were the oft-cited reasons for BN's landslide win.[6] Both factors had influenced the Malays to return to BN, whom they had deserted in huge numbers in 1999 in the wake of the *reformasi* euphoria.[7]

Reformasi had given hope that change was possible in what seemed to have been a confused nation in 1998–99, but having failed to wrest power from the BN, *reformasi* had failed to fulfil the people's expectations. The party most commonly associated with *reformasi* aspirations, Keadilan, had been constantly beset by intra-party squabbles, such as the vain attempt by former activists of the Angkatan Belia Islam Malaysia (ABIM, or Muslim Youth Movement of Malaysia) to take over Keadilan's leadership during the party's convention in November 2001. The episode was followed consequently by ABIM's effective withdrawal from Keadilan despite ABIM's unflinching support of *reformasi* from its beginnings and its members' emotional attachment to *reformasi* as a movement headed by Anwar Ibrahim, ABIM's former and most prominent leader.[8] The friction among camps within Keadilan exposed the leadership's failure to unite rank and file members who had joined the party from different backgrounds. They had included former members of UMNO, members of Islamic movements such as ABIM and Jemaah Islah Malaysia (JIM, or Society for Islamic Reform), former members of other non-governmental organisations (NGOs), and previously apolitical professionals who were disillusioned with the status of Malaysia's politico-economic establishment.[9] Between 1999 and 2004, leadership crises erupted as prominent leaders either quit out of dissatisfaction or were detained without trial under the infamous Internal Security Act (ISA) 1960,[10] giving way to a haphazard electoral organisation. This culminated in the re-entry of 12 of its leaders into UMNO in February 2004.[11]

Keadilan performed dismally in presenting itself as a credible alternative response to demands for politics run along non-ethnic lines which focuses more on issues of "good governance". Keadilan's failure reflects not only weaknesses in party organisation and leadership, but also the ineffectiveness of *reformasi* as a coherent ideological tool in binding the masses together.

Reformasi developed in its initial stages as a movement with cherished ideals popularly associated with Anwar Ibrahim's struggle since his *entrée* into UMNO and the government in 1982: the struggle for justice, a strong identification with the plight of those at the bottom of the socio-economic ladder, and the eradication of graft and abuses of power. Undoubtedly influenced by its Indonesian counterpart, which in May 1998 had managed to capitalise on street demonstrations to topple long-serving President Soeharto, *reformasi* vehemently attacked the allegedly widespread practices of corruption, cronyism, and nepotism within the upper echelons of Malaysian society. Such practices were said to have been institutionalised by Prime Minister Mahathir's policies in his ruthless drive towards the creation of a fully-developed country by 2020. While the meaning of "development" in Mahathir's blueprint, *Vision 2020*, claimed to be multi-dimensional, it was clear that the economic dimension was pivotal towards its success.[12] Policies reflecting this emphasis included economic deregulation and "Malaysia Incorporated" under the National Development Policy, which replaced the New Economic Policy (1971–90). This created a political culture termed by Loh Kok Wah as "developmentalism", which valorised "economic growth, rising living standards, ... consumerist lifestyles [and] political stability ...".[13] *Reformasi* was, therefore, a socio-political reaction to such a materially competitive culture, which so characterised the buoyant years of 1990–97.

But its "anti-developmentalist" agenda, as evident from Anwar Ibrahim's "Permatang Pauh declaration" of 12 September 1998,[14] was not sufficient to maintain the momentum that the masses had gathered through the street protests and demonstrations of 1998–99. *Reformasi* remained a vague and ambiguous concept, lacking exhaustive content. It demonstrated diverse influences, ranging from modern democratic reform to Islamic righteousness, that conveyed different meanings to different people.[15] Hence, the simultaneous appearance, accompanying the unjust treatment meted out to Anwar, of the opposition-NGO alliances: Gerakan Keadilan Rakyat Malaysia (GERAK) headed by PAS and Gagasan Demokrasi Rakyat (GAGASAN) led by the human rights organisation, Suara Rakyat Malaysia (SUARAM). Both championed *reformasi*, which was understood and represented differently by both groups, but was seen by both as providing the common solution to Malaysia's problems. Ironically, it was precisely the general character of *reformasi*, without being translated into a specific politico-ideological project, that made it feasible as a short-term mobilising tool in periods of crises.[16] Crowds demanding *reformasi* came from a myriad backgrounds and influences, with different interests, but they were all united in their stance that the process of nation-building had been awfully mismanaged by the country's ruling elites.[17] But as a long-term political solution, *reformasi* was doomed to fail as it struggled to maintain the cohesiveness of its disparate elements whose political loyalties were diverse.[18] *Reformasi*'s main contribution to Malaysia's political economy was general in nature: Widespread political mobilisation among huge numbers of hitherto apathetic citizens whether in a formal or informal setting.[19] Politics had become common property, spread with the helped of the democratisation of ideas via modern information and communications technology.

In terms of formal party politics, the winner of the *reformasi* euphoria was PAS. Ever since the eruption of the Anwar saga, PAS has persistently been the centrestage of anti-state political mobilisation.[20] PAS leaders were quick to capitalise on their long-term friendship with Anwar in portraying PAS as the torchbearer of *reformasi*. PAS projected itself as an indispensable component of *reformasi*, and by means of being the largest opposition party, emerged as its leader and pacesetter, at least as far as the masses were concerned. As the biggest election contender among *reformasi* elements, PAS was catapulted into leading the assorted *reformasi* groups by default.[21] *Reformasi* groups, out of practicality and convenience, had to accept PAS's leadership despite sharing with it only one long-term aim: the restoration of justice, as embodied in the treatment of Anwar Ibrahim. Their short-term goal was simply the exoneration of Anwar. In 1999, to the newly politically-awakened Malays, voting the Barisan Alternatif (BA) — the opposition coalition consisting of PAS, Keadilan, DAP, and Parti Rakyat Malaysia (PRM, or People's Party of Malaysia), was equivalent to supporting social and political reform. Furthermore, in constituencies where PAS candidates were left as solitary Opposition candidates in one-on-one contests against BN, there was little avenue left to express one's reformist sentiments, apart from voting PAS. The leap in the number of votes and seats of PAS in the 1999 elections was due to the euphoric support for political and social reform rather than serving as an endorsement of PAS's policies which were based on a juridical interpretation of Islam. In short, PAS was the greatest beneficiary of, rather than the main contributor to, *reformasi*.

Reasons for PAS's Defeat: The PAS-driven Factors

As the 11th general election neared, PAS's spokesmen became ever more convinced that Malaysia was on her way to becoming an Islamic state by means of states within the Malaysian federation falling one by one in a domino-like fashion to PAS in consecutive elections. In fact, PAS proclaimed their confidence in conquering the Malay heartland in the northern belt of Peninsular Malaysia, comprising the states of Terengganu, Kelantan, Kedah, and Perlis.[22] For them, PAS's methods had been verified. PAS did not acknowledge that its commendable performance in 1999 might have been due to the understanding effected with its secular and non-Muslim counterparts in BA. In other words, the improvement in votes for PAS was indicative of the people's hunger for social and political reform, which UMNO and BN had failed to deliver.[23] Participation in the BA alliance had positively improved PAS's image from a rural-based "fundamentalist" party to a broad-based reformist party commanding the confidence of the young, the middle-class and the professionals.[24] PAS's misinterpretation of its rise in support as an endorsement for its juridical brand of Islam was misplaced and was to cost it heavily in 2004.

The need for PAS to moderate its Islamic agenda, based on a rigid interpretation of an Islamic state as the preferred form of governance for Malaysia, was spelt out by its non-Muslim allies even before BA's creditable performance in the 1999 elections.[25] Central to such an Islamic state is the implementation of Islamic criminal laws known as *hudud*.[26] The implementation of *hudud* laws as the cornerstone of PAS's Islamic state sparked off a major debate even in the anti-establishment media, revolving especially around the question of their legality in view of the Federal Constitution's guarantee of freedom of religion and equality of every citizen before the law.[27] The inefficacy of such *hudud* legislation in the Malaysian context is shown by the incapacity of Kelantan's PAS's state government to enforce the Syariah Criminal Code (II) Enactment 1993,[28] despite having been passed by the Kelantan state legislature on 25 November 1993. Since then, arguments and counter-arguments have been issued on the alleged "Islamicity" or "unIslamicity" of PAS's *hudud*, as opposed to UMNO's piecemeal adoption of Islamic laws.[29] After PAS's agreement to drop the "Islamic state" agenda from the BA manifesto in 1999,[30] there is reason to believe that, both non- and liberal Muslims felt betrayed by PAS's insistence on forcing through its proposed *hudud* Bill in Terengganu, which it wrested from BN and was supposed to be a model of how PAS would rule if it were given national political power. On 8 July 2002, despite widespread reservations, the PAS-controlled Terengganu state legislature passed the Syariah Criminal Offences (Hudud and Qisas) Enactment. However, this law, being in contravention to the Federal Constitution, has remained inoperative.[31]

PAS's most glaring weakness with respect to its governing style appeared to be its "holier than thou" attitude, which triggered an innate inability and even unwillingness to consult the public, especially the non-Muslims. This tendency could be seen in its effective dismissal of non-Muslim worries of the implications of being under an Islamic state.[32] Having been elected, PAS regarded it as its right to fulfil what it had long been calling for, without acknowledging that many had voted for them despite, and not because of, their "Islamic state" agenda. Despite efforts to reach out to non-Muslims, such as the offer of associate membership of the party,[33] PAS had failed to convince non-Muslims that its version of an Islamic state would confer on them a proper policy-making role as equal citizens under the law.[34] PAS did not see itself obliged to propagate effectively its message of an Islamic state to non-Muslims, rather it placed the onus on the non-Muslims to learn and convince themselves of the relevance of an Islamic state. For example, PAS created an unfair burden on its non-Muslim coalition partners, insisting that they explain the applicability of an Islamic state to their party rank and file.[35] PAS's intransigence and inability to communicate effectively with potential non-Muslim allies eventually resulted in the DAP withdrawing from the BA in September 2001.[36] Despite later being offered time by PAS to reflect upon PAS's supposedly accommodative Islamic state model,[37] DAP asserted that any doors for negotiation was closed so long as PAS was insistent on the creation of an Islamic state.[38]

Within a few days of PAS losing its most significant non-Muslim partner, Prime Minister Mahathir further outwitted PAS by pre-emptively declaring that Malaysia was already an Islamic state.[39] In support of the prime minister, it was argued by government members and Islamic think-tanks that the facts that significant elements of the country's legal and administrative systems had Islamic foundations[40] and that Islam was increasingly prominent in the economic, educational, and constitutional spheres, qualified Malaysia as an Islamic state.[41] In fact, the unequivocal agreement on Malaysia's Islamic state status was reached after an Islamic State Discussion (*Muzakarah Daulah Islamiah*) on 3 August 2001. Chaired by Dr Abdul Hamid Othman, religious advisor to the prime minister, this gathering of 70 religious scholars, notables, and academics decided, on the basis of scholarly opinions since the Umayyad and Abbasid caliphates, that Malaysia qualified as an Islamic state.[42] UMNO had picked up the gauntlet thrown by PAS and backed it up with religio-intellectual arguments. It was a direct challenge to PAS to come up with an operational blueprint of an Islamic state of its own.[43] This was a challenge it could not deliver instantly, and indeed this failure on the part of PAS to detail what an Islamic state entailed was the source of criticism of PAS from impartial observers for some time.[44] Two years later, similar criticism was delivered by PAS's Youth wing, obviously disappointed by the leadership's sluggishness.[45]

By the time PAS launched its Islamic State Document (ISD)[46] on 12 November 2003, the damage had been done. In launching the ISD, PAS president Abdul Hadi Awang reaffirmed PAS's commitment to accomplish justice and equality cutting across race, religion, culture, language, and political persuasion; to parliamentary democracy; to the ending of draconian legislation such as the ISA; and to women's involvement in mainstream national and social development.[47] While these reassurances appeared to have allayed fears of a PAS-sponsored theocracy in the event of a BA victory in the forthcoming elections,[48] the

ISD was primarily aimed at the Malay heartland, the focus of the battle between PAS and UMNO.[49] Released just before the 2004 election, it was dismissed by the ruling establishment as another election ploy of PAS.[50] Moreover, the public could obtain PAS's serialised explanation of the ISD only through its official organ, *Harakah*, whose circulation since March 2000 had been severely curtailed to twice a month and restricted to PAS members only.[51] In order to show that PAS was not truly sincere in its endeavour, the mainstream media exposed inconsistencies of views among the PAS leadership regarding the establishment of an Islamic state.[52] Apart from that, the government released its own booklet rebutting the ISD. The booklet claimed that the ISD added nothing new to the Islamic state discourse. The ISD had the ulterior motive of legitimising PAS's state governments in Kelantan and Terengganu, but ended up reaffirming the position of Malaysia as already an Islamic state. A further nine points were enumerated to argue for Malaysia's Islamic state status, viz. (1) Malaysia's head of state was Muslim, (2) Islam was Malaysia's official religion, (3) Malaysia's administration was based on parliamentary *syura* (council for deliberation), (4) Malaysia's legal system was Islamic in substance albeit modified to suit contemporary circumstances, (5) Malaysia's laws were practised in other Muslim states, (6) Malaysia was a leader in Islamic commerce and business, (7) Malaysia was recognised as an Islamic state by the Grand Sheikh of Al Azhar — the highest legal authority among Sunni Muslims worldwide, (8) the existence of freedom of worship for Muslims, and (9) the Islamic emphasis of educational infrastructure and political planning.[53]

Lacking time and media strength, the public issuance of the ISD merely served to compound the effects of PAS's alienation of the DAP and non-Muslims. Previously, the participation of the DAP in the BA alliance, although seemingly led by PAS, provided assurance for undecided non-Muslims who might have hesitated in voting for PAS. This "assuring factor" had lost relevance by 2004, and PAS's appeal was reduced to its traditional Malay heartland and, by virtue of its alliance with Keadilan, middle-class Malays still dissatisfied with the establishment. Such middle-class Malays, who have been responsible for the democratic ferment in Malaysia since 1998, are concentrated in the urban areas of industrialised states such as Selangor, Penang, and

Negeri Sembilan, states where UMNO registered its most substantial losses in 1999.[54] PAS's hopes of expanding its wings beyond the Malay heartland depend very much on its ability to maintain support among these urbanised Malays, who may not be all too comfortable with PAS's Islamic state ambitions, and whose loyalties are capricious particularly during economic upswings. Beyond the Malay heartland, the number of ethnically-mixed seats increased in quantity, further circumscribing PAS's hopes of expansion. Hence, as Maznah Mohamad has argued, it is only in Kelantan, Terengganu, Kedah, and Perlis that "optimal conditions for PAS's highest electoral success" could be met, and "Barisan Nasional is guaranteed of victory as long as UMNO continues to contest and win in mixed seats".[55]

In spite of attempts to enhance its non-communal reputation, it has not struck PAS leaders that PAS really cannot bank its hopes of electoral success on the Malay community alone. The non-Malays interpreted the ISD declaration as an "indirect acceptance that it [could not] win significant non-Malay/non-Muslim electoral support".[56] Khoo Boo Teik called PAS's Islamic state advances just before the elections a "strategic mistake" which "alienate[d] potential allies who remember[ed] PAS for defending a 'democratic state' in 1999".[57] Non-Muslims continually see PAS's leaders as harbouring an image and style that are too idealistic and distant from daily concerns of life. PAS's political programme is feared for its presumed restrictions on various aspects of non-Malay social life. From their observations of world politics, non-Malays have the impression of "Islamic states" as non-democratic, ruthless, backward, and foreign-influenced. As such, they treat PAS's attempts to impose an Islamic state as an unwelcome intrusion of universal Islamic ideas into Malaysian politics and society, when Malaysians should really be searching for solutions which take into account its unique ethno-cultural composition probably not founded elsewhere in the Muslim world.[58]

The reputation of PAS's leadership, having been briefly enhanced by its active involvement in democratic opposition alliances, suffered a downturn following the untimely death of its president-cum-leader of the Opposition, Fadzil Noor, on 23 June 2002.[59] Rightly credited with successfully bringing PAS into the mainstream of Malaysian politics with his brand of accommodative opposition politics, Fadzil Noor oversaw the formation of the Islamic-based coalition, the Angkatan Perpaduan Ummah (APU) in 1990 and the broader-based coalition BA in 1999. Fadzil Noor's perceived moderateness strongly contributed to PAS's capture of Kelantan in 1990 and Terengganu in 1999, and its successful inroads into Kedah, Pahang, and Selangor. Even the mainstream media acknowledged Fadzil's political achievements.[60] In response to speculation that Malay unity between PAS and UMNO could only be achieved under Fadzil Noor's less than radical leadership, Fadzil Noor admitted in an interview that "the political scenario keeps changing".[61] Apparently compromising statements, and his willingness to appear on stage and shake hands with Dr Mahathir Mohamad in public, such as during a function to commemorate the struggle of the Palestinians at the Dewan Bahasa dan Pustaka (DBP, or National Institute of Language and Literature) on 8 May 2002, made Fadzil Noor the target of criticisms by PAS's radical wing worried about a possibility to re-incorporate PAS into the ruling BN. Aware of such criticisms, which were uttered even in PAS's official mouthpiece, *Harakah*, Fadzil used his closing speech to the 48th PAS general assembly on 2 June 2002 to explain his disputed actions.[62] It was his passing away that ultimately stopped criticism of his moderateness.

Following Fadzil Noor's death, Abdul Hadi Awang, the deputy president-cum-chief minister of Terengganu, took over the duties as party president. But Abdul Hadi's image as a fiery and radical firebrand worsened PAS's reputation among non-Muslims and moderate Malay-Muslims.[63] That Abdul Hadi would steer PAS away from an accommodating approach in multi-ethnic cooperative politics towards a decidedly uncompromising stance in pursuit of its Islamic state dream, seemed to have been confirmed by the 49th PAS general assembly in 2003, which officially installed Abdul Hadi as president, and elected Senator Hassan Shukri in favour of lawyer Mustafa Ali as PAS's deputy president. Hassan was practically the representative of the conservative *ulama*, while Mustafa was believed to have commanded the support of the fast emerging professionals. One would have thought that Mustafa's sophisticated image and political experience at state level would nicely balance Abdul Hadi's clerical style, but despite the upcoming role of professionals in the party, it was clear that its rank and file was not ready to dispense with the concept of "*ulama* leadership".[64] In terms of furthering its electoral prospects, the consequences were disastrous.

The 50th PAS general assembly, held in August 2004 in Kota Bharu, Kelantan, amidst the gloom and despair of the election results, was historic for PAS Youth's launch of an unprecedented attack on the *ulama* leadership's obsolete ways. Unlike the leadership, which continually blamed external factors for delivering PAS's shattering electoral defeat,[65] PAS Youth admitted that PAS lost due to its own over-confidence and lack of preparation for the elections.[66] PAS Youth's criticisms centred around the *ulama*'s failure to adapt their thinking to changing circumstances and the leadership's inconsistency in recognising election results it insisted to be fraudulent.[67] PAS Youth also called for the formation of a women's youth section which paralleled the highly successful Puteri UMNO.[68] The leadership and conservatives appeared to have stood up against the internal opposition, with Abdul Hadi adamantly defending PAS's record and valiantly rebutting PAS Youth.[69] While such intransigency, spelt out in idealistic rather than realistic terms, seems to dent PAS's future electoral prospects, concerns raised by PAS Youth did not ring hollow. For instance, regarded as an enemy of modern entertainment culture, PAS surprised the odds by recently hosting a pop concert at PAS's headquarters in Taman Melewar, Kuala Lumpur.[70]

Reasons for PAS' Defeat: The UMNO-driven Factors

UMNO-BN's control of the media, the government machinery, and money was exploited to the fullest to deliver its large victory in 2004.[71] Control of the three components meant that UMNO was able to turn politically harmless circumstances into situations advantageous to the ruling party. Two examples strongly illustrate this scenario. Firstly, UMNO exploited the global political climate after terrorist attacks by militant Islamist on the World Trade Centre in New York and the Pentagon near Washington DC on 11 September 2001 (hereafter September 11). By no fault of its own, PAS found itself being implicated with sympathy for and perhaps even direct involvement in terrorism. For example, it never escaped the attention of the mainstream media that activists arrested for involvement with the Mujahidin Group of Malaysia (KMM, or Kumpulan Mujahidin Malaysia, later sensationalised

as Kumpulan Militan Malaysia) and the Jemaah Islamiah (JI), both
of which were allegedly linked to the Al-Qaeda international terrorist
network, were former or active PAS members. This included a son of
Nik Aziz Nik Mat, PAS's chief minister of Kelantan, Nik Adli Nik Aziz,
who was detained under the ISA together with nine others in the first
wave of KMM arrests in early August 2001.[72] While this happened
before September 11, KMM was alleged to have launched attacks on a
police station and on non-Muslim religious sites, and assassinated Dr Joe
Fernandez, a Kedah BN state legislative assembly member notorious for
his evangelising activities among Malay-Muslim youths.[73]

After September 11 and the US attack on Afghanistan, emotional
outbursts of sympathy for the Taliban and Osama bin Laden's Al-Qaeda
network shown by PAS's leadership easily fell prey to the mainstream
media. Added to this were PAS-orchestrated anti-USA demonstrations,
briefly recreating the tumultuous scenes surrounding the *reformasi*
agitations of 1998–99.[74] In January to February 2002, the country's
premier television channel, Radio Televisyen Malaysia (RTM), repeatedly
played video clips of the Memali tragedy, in which police stormed upon
a community of wretchedly-armed PAS villagers in Memali, Kedah,
resisting the arrest of their leader, Ibrahim Libya, who was among
the 14 PAS followers who perished in the countdown alongside four
policemen.[75] PAS rightly regarded the airing of the clips as UMNO
propaganda, but insofar as it prompted PAS into stoutly defending its
claim that Ibrahim Libya and his comrades were martyrs,[76] UMNO
had achieved its aim of linking PAS with violence and terrorism. One
year later, acting PAS president Abdul Hadi Awang's presence at an
Islamic congress in Makassar, South Sulawesi, Indonesia, in October
2000, was made into a big issue as participants at the congress included
prominent Indonesian militants such as JI leader Abu Bakar Basyir and
Laskar Jundullah leader Agus Dwikarna.[77] PAS retorted that Abdul
Hadi had attended the congress upon invitations from Hasanuddin
University and Indonesian NGOs in his capacity as leader of the
Terengganu state government, and had spoken of the implementation
of Islamic administration and laws in Terengganu and Kelantan.[78] On
the whole, the impact of September 11 and in particular UMNO's and
the government's manipulation of the event, by inciting renewed fear

of Islamic extremism, was to confirm the frightening impression non-Muslims and liberal Muslims had of PAS.[79] No doubt, their skepticism about PAS persisted until the 2004 election.

The second example relates to the succession of Abdullah Ahmad Badawi to the premiership on 31 October 2003. While he may have been the chosen successor of Dr Mahathir, Abdullah Badawi had to quickly show the nation that he was neither Dr Mahathir's clone nor his puppet. He had to balance carefully the need to avoid the displeasure of Mahathirites in UMNO and the government with the need to distance himself from Dr Mahathir, whose unpopular administration had been tainted with corruption, injustice, one-man domination, and lack of identity with people at the bottom of the economic ladder. There is no hiding the fact that for many who had been inspired by *reformasi*, Dr Mahathir was the nemesis. The ills of the nation had been blamed on his ruthless disposition and despotic character, hence earning him the unsavoury nicknames of *mahazalim* (most cruel), *mahafiraun* (most pharaonic), and so on. The excesses of the Mahathir regime had been so highlighted by the *reformasi* imbroglio, such that even slight signs of departure from Dr Mahathir's ways would have been significant for the average Malaysian. In this, Abdullah Badawi was indebted to *reformasi*.[80] Herein lay the political opportunity for him to prove that he was his own man. His "de-Mahathirisation" moves, while not overhauling the country's politics and society, was to be adequate to convince the populace that he was intent upon reforming Malaysia. Dr Mahathir had overstretched the nation, and now it was Abdullah Badawi's task to restore its normalcy and sobriety. Abdullah Badawi's first step towards legitimacy was to demonstrate that his administration would be a different one in style if not in substance.[81] But he had to have a loyal media machine in order to accomplish a turnabout from the Mahathir era. One of the first steps he took in this direction was dismissing Abdullah Ahmad, editor-in-chief of the *New Straits Times* and a well-known Mahathir loyalist. While the dismissal was ostensibly a punishment over an article implicating the Saudi Arabian government with complicity in September 11, many quarters saw Abdullah Ahmad's replacement by Kalimullah Hassan as sparking off the subtle "de-Mahathirisation" process, for Abdullah Ahmad had prematurely attempted to impose Dr Mahathir's choice as deputy prime minister, Najib Razak, upon Abdullah Badawi.[82]

For a start, Abdullah Badawi projected the image of a leader in close touch with the grassroots and the youth. His celebrated exhortation to the people to work with him and not for him[83] was an early sign of a personal charm that would persist into the 2004 election. His retention of the avuncular sobriquet, Pak Lah, despite solitary calls by his ministers that he be properly addressed as "Datuk Seri Abdullah",[84] displayed a determination to distance himself from feudal Malay political culture which, by unduly over-honouring leaders, created an immeasurable gap between leaders and the people.[85] The public was fed with images depicting his closeness with his family, such as that of him hugging his wife Endon Mahmood, whom he described as his foremost supporter amidst her struggle against breast cancer.[86] Even more spectacular was the visuals of Abdullah venerating his mother during her life and paying his last respects upon her death in February 2004; such portrayals were repeatedly aired on television during the election campaign.[87] He refused to cede moral ground to the opposition Islamists. Coming from a respected lineage of *ulama* and himself a graduate in Islamic studies,[88] Abdullah did not shy away from staking his claim to religious leadership, for example, by leading prayer sessions held among ministers and UMNO members.[89] To the Malay community, such images were not superficial. In the era of Islamic resurgence, Malay leaders needed the religious edge over their rivals, and the Islamic tilt needed to be demonstrated intellectually as well as ritually. Thus, politicians well-versed in religion held a distinct advantage. Some suggest that it is for this reason that Abdullah was selected as Dr Mahathir's deputy in 1999 in replacement of Anwar Ibrahim, whose reputation was that of a self-made Islamist.[90]

Of greater significance, especially to the well-educated population, was the change of emphasis in Abdullah Badawi's policies. He reversed Dr Mahathir's penchant for big-spending mega-projects and instead stressed Malaysia's agricultural roots. Symbolic of this was the indefinite suspension of the country's would-be largest infrastructure project: a billion ringgit construction of a double-track railway system across the country. The award had been controversially awarded to the Malaysian

Mining Corporation (MMC)-Gamuda consortium in the final days of Dr Mahathir's administration, but now Abdullah Badawi was insisting that government contracts be awarded on the basis of open tenders.[91] High-profile personalities such as Eric Chia, former executive director of Perwaja Rolling Mill and Development and a Dr Mahathir favourite, and Kasitah Gaddam, minister for land and cooperative development, were charged in court for corruption allegedly committed during Dr Mahathir's administration.[92] Such was the nation's excitement that speculation sharply rose as to which of the "big sharks" would be next to be indicted.[93] In July 2004, Abdullah Badawi revealed that most corruption cases involving high-profile figures such as former state executive council members, former members of parliament, and former heads of government departments and agencies, had been brought to court.[94] Such moves reflected his overall war against corruption and bureaucratic inefficiency. Even members of parliament of the ruling BN would not escape; they would need to submit report cards detailing their performance, twice to thrice a year.[95] All these were inter-related, and translated into popular parlance as "good governance".[96] The anti-corruption drive, although still poor by international standards and as yet inconclusive,[97] did wonders in beguiling the nation into believing that it was really on the threshold of a new age under "Mr. Clean".[98] For immediate purposes, it delivered Abdullah Badawi a convincing election victory and a mandate to govern Malaysia as prime minister in his own right.

As an alternative to PAS's Islamic state, UMNO hammered through the idea of *Islam Hadhari* as a fundamental theme of Abdullah Badawi's administration. Officially translated as "civilisational Islam", *Islam Hadhari* can be understood as a progressive form of Islam which espouses a joining of forces between the *ulama* and professional technocrats, a rational acquisition of knowledge, a balance between spiritual and material development, and religious tolerance.[99] In a nutshell, it is an effort to rediscover an understanding of Islam from its original sources, the Quran and the *Sunnah*, by looking at the contemporary reality and historical development of Muslims.[100] In a direct reference to PAS's "Islamic state" agenda, *Islam Hadhari* is contrasted with *Islam Siasi* (political Islam), which asserts that acquisition of political power was a prerequisite to a comprehensive practice of Islam.[101] *Islam Hadhari*, on the contrary, merely calls for values and principles of a state to be compatible with Islam, without necessarily forging a state which incorporates the Islamic legal framework, for this is understood as being constantly prone to change. This is consistent with Abdullah Badawi's recent exhortation for a reappraisal of past *ijtihad* (legal opinions) for they may not be in tandem with contemporary developments.[102] In the Malaysian context, *Islam Hadhari* had been around since 2001, when it was proposed at a gathering of UMNO *ulama*, intellectuals, religious bureaucrats, and Islamic think-tanks.[103] It remained in the political and intellectual backyard despite a formal introduction of the concept in September 2002 by Abdullah Badawi, then deputy prime minister. It really gained ground just one week before the elections, when Abdullah Badawi suddenly presented it in front of a massive audience of 25,000.[104] PAS's reply to *Islam Hadhari* was a meek accusation that UMNO was propagating a new religion, a claim that rang hollow among ordinary Malay-Muslims, many of whom were convinced that PAS's Islamic state was neither existent in the scriptures nor feasible.[105]

After the elections, the strongest direct articulation of *Islam Hadhari* to date has been Abdullah Badawi's keynote address at the 55th UMNO general assembly in Kuala Lumpur on 23rd September 2004. In this speech, Abdullah proclaimed *Islam Hadhari* to be a comprehensive form of Islam which emphasised all-encompassing economic and civilisational developments. In a globalised world, *Islam Hadhari* would potentially empower Malays by raising their competitiveness. For the first time, Abdullah outlined ten fundamental principles of *Islam Hadhari*: (1) faith and piety in God, (2) a just and trustworthy government, (3) a free and independent people, (4) a vigorous mastery of knowledge, (5) a balanced and comprehensive economic development, (6) a good quality of life, (7) protection of the rights of minority groups and women, (8) cultural and moral integrity, (9) conservation of the environment and (10) strong defence capabilities.[106] Under *Islam Hadhari*, according to Abdullah, Malaysia proudly projects itself as a successful, modern Muslim country — a model nation-state in the Muslim world.[107] With such an emphasis, religious debates and personalities acquired wider prominence in the 55th UMNO general assembly which officially installed Abdullah as UMNO's sixth president.[108] Judging by its success, it is fair to say that such a religious trend, which was manifested by UMNO's fielding of well-known religious candidates during the 11th general election,[109] is set to increase in the politics of Malaysia's ruling establishment.

PAS's Response and Concluding Remarks

PAS's response to its defeat in the 11th general election was to heap blame on a biased media and poor monitoring standards of the Election Commission (SPR, or Suruhanjaya Pilihanraya) and National Registration Department.[110] From available evidence gathered via the alternative media, the Opposition claims of fraud may well be true. As soon as the election was over, reports of irregularities emerged from all over the country. These included unexplained tremendous increases in voter turnouts, discrepancies between votes polled in parliamentary constituencies and corresponding state constituencies, large discrepancies between ballot papers issued and ballot papers returned, different versions of electoral rolls denying many the right to vote, wanton breaking of rules by SPR officials, and discoveries of abandoned identity cards at polling stations and of SPR-sealed ballot papers in dustbins outside polling stations.[111] So rampant and intense were fraudulent practices this time round that even the state-sponsored Human Rights Commission of Malaysia (SUHAKAM, or Suruhanjaya Hak Asasi Manusia Malaysia) was reportedly outraged.[112] Fraud was said to be especially rife in Selangor and the frontline states of Terengganu, Kedah, and Pahang, all of which were states where BA had made successful inroads in 1999.[113] Terengganu was especially targeted because BN needed to avert a pending court action by PAS's state government against the national oil company, Petroleum Nasional (Petronas) for illegally converting oil royalties to the state government into *wang ihsan* (compassionate money) dispensed by federal government.[114]

Added to these was "legalised" fraud in terms of electoral gerrymandering and amendments to electoral rules which made it more difficult for opposition parties with meagre resources to seek redress in the event of a miscarriage of justice. The constituency redelineation exercise of 2003 created 26 new parliamentary seats and 63 new state seats. Not only were these seats concentrated in states where BN had a convincing edge over BA in 1999, but most of them were also semi-urban, ethnically-mixed seats, which had a good record of returning BN candidates. BN not surprisingly won in 25 of the 26 new parliamentary constituencies. Moreover, electoral boundaries were substantially redrawn, even in BA-targeted states which received no additional seats.[115] A year before, in 2002, amendments to the Election Act 1958 dismissed any possibility of challenging the validity of electoral rolls once gazetted, raised compensation payable to anyone unjustifiably accused of being a "phantom voter" in an electoral roll from RM200 to RM1,000, and raised the deposit demanded from candidates from RM5,000 to RM20,000, plus an additional RM10,000 to ensure swift removal of posters and other campaign material after the election.[116] The Election Offences Act 1954 was amended to raise spending limits of a state seat candidate from RM30,000 to RM100,000 and a parliamentary seat candidate from RM50,000 to RM200,000, in effect legalising what had already been practised by BN candidates. Another amendment made it an offence

> to act or to make any statement with a view or with a tendency to promote feelings of ill-will, discontent or hostility between persons of the same race or different races or of the same class or different classes of the population of Malaysia in order to induce any elector or voter to vote or refrain from voting at an election or to procure or endeavour to procure the election of any person.[117]

The overall impact of the 2002 amendments was to relieve SPR from any shame at having committed intentional or inadvertent technical mistakes, to make the whole election process into a very expensive affair, and to muzzle freedom of expression during campaigning.

Combining the effects of fraud, gerrymandering, changes to electoral legislation, and the failure of SPR to oversee the election process fairly, all of which worked to the advantage of the ruling party, PAS had a valid case in point. But focusing on these issues diverts attention away from PAS's own weaknesses and the efficiency of UMNO's election machine, both of which would have delivered the 11th general election to BN anyway, without the existence of electoral irregularities.[118] Because irregularities are not alien to Malaysian politics, complaints surface in all elections. The transformation of SPR from an independent commission to a body which ensured that constituency redelineation exercises worked in favour of the ruling coalition, had been in place since the 1960s, and this favouritism was strongly demonstrable in past redelineation exercises in 1974, 1984, and 1994.[119] In 2004, SPR bore the brunt of criticism for widespread inefficiencies and malpractices found to have occurred during the election, and these criticisms came from both ruling and opposition parties.[120] Also, the bias against opposition parties shown by the mainstream media was nothing new. Wong Kok Keong's study of the mainstream media's coverage of the 11th general election merely confirms what has already been observed during past elections.[121]

PAS might as well blame its defeat, as outlined in the section on "Reasons for PAS's Defeat" above, on PAS-driven factors, in particular its over-confidence and over-estimation of the size of the pro-Islamic state constituency.[122] It can then ponder and rework a strategy which captures the realities of Malaysian society. PAS did not lose ground among its traditional supporters, but its hardcore base alone could not conceivably deliver victory for PAS at the national level. In order to expand its wings beyond the Malay heartland, whose population is slowly becoming more urbanised and ethnically-diverse, PAS needs to project a more amenable image to both moderate Malay-Muslims and non-Muslims. Short-term support may come in the form of paroxysmal rebellion against the status quo ala *reformasi*, but in the long term, the onus is left on PAS to broaden its appeal beyond its hardcore supporters. Prior to the general elections, PAS had been warned that UMNO was regaining Malay support,[123] while both PAS and Keadilan were not heeding lessons of several by-election defeats.[124] In conclusion, BN's victory in the 11th general election was a *fait accompli*, and PAS needed only to blame itself for the setbacks it had suffered in 2004.

NOTES

1. Having spent almost six years behind prison bars, Anwar Ibrahim was released on 2 September 2004, having had his High Court conviction for sodomy overturned by the Federal Court. However, on 15 September 2004, the Federal Court upheld his conviction for corruption, the jail term for which he had served. Anwar is thereby barred from political activity until 2008. At the time of writing, Anwar is in Munich, Germany, recuperating from an operation to remedy his spinal back

injury which had worsened during incarceration due to a beating he received at the hands of the then inspector general of police, Abdul Rahim Noor.

2. Statistics of the 11th general election may be obtained from national newspapers following the election. See, for example, "Keputusan Penuh Pilihan Raya 2004", *Utusan Malaysia* (Malaysia), 23 March 2004. The statistics quoted above already takes into account minor revisions that have occurred since polling day on 21 March 2004. These are the victory of BN for the Pahang state legislative assembly seat of Sungai Lembing after delayed polling on 28 March 2004, due to a printing error of ballot papers; and the High Court declaration on 22 June 2004 that the parliamentary seat of Pasir Puteh in Kelantan had actually been won by BN candidate Che Min Che Ahmad, who had filed a petition claiming that the result had been wrongly announced by the Election Commission's officer during election night.

3. Jeyakumar Devaraj, "The 2004 BN Victory: By Fair Means or Foul?", *Aliran Monthly* 24, no. 5 (2004): 13.

4. Francis Loh, "Understanding the 2004 Election Results: Looking Beyond the Pak Lah factor", *Aliran Monthly* 24, no. 3 (2004): 8–9.

5. Khoo Boo Teik, "Malaysian Politics in 2004: Transitions and Elections", in *Political and Security Outlook 2004: Political Change in Southeast Asia*, Trends in Southeast Asia Series monograph 7 (Singapore: Institute of Southeast Asian Studies, 2004), p. 11.

6. Cf. "Landslide for BN", *New Straits Times* (Malaysia), 22 March 2004; "Resounding 'yes' for Abdullah", *New Straits Times* (Malaysia), 22 March 2004.

7. "Perubahan sikap Melayu bantu kemenangan BN", *Utusan Malaysia* (Malaysia), 23 March 2004.

8. "Jangan kaitkan lagi ABIM dengan Keadilan", *Berita Minggu* (Malaysia), 25 November 2001; "Keadilan lupa jasa pemimpin ABIM", *Utusan Malaysia* (Malaysia), 26 November 2001. See also the media interview with ABIM President, Ahmad Azam Abdul Rahman, "Orientasi politik ABIM berbeza", *Utusan Malaysia* (Malaysia), 19 November 2001.

9. Baharom Mahusin, "Keadilan di Ambang Kehancuran", *Mingguan Malaysia* (Malaysia), 21 October 2001; "Seorang Lagi Pemimpin Keadilan Letak Jawatan", *Berita Harian* (Malaysia), 27 October 2001.

10. Among leaders who left Keadilan were UMNO renegade Marina Yusoff and prominent social activist-cum-academic Dr. Chandra Muzaffar. See Khoo Boo Teik, "Die Hard: The New, the Old and the Ugly in Parti KeADILan Nasional's Turmoil", *Aliran Monthly* 20, no. 5 (2000): 2–6; "Apa Dosa Dr. Chandra Kepada Keadilan', *Utusan Malaysia* (Malaysia), 11 March 2002. The top Keadilan leaders arrested under the ISA were Ezam Mohamed Nor, Tian Chua, Saari Sungib, Dr. Badrulamin Baharon, Hishamuddin Rais, Lokman Noor Adam, Raja Petra

Kamarudin and N. Gobalakrishnan. See Johan Saravanamuttu, "'Reformasi Activists Under Detention': ISA is the refuge of the incompetent", *Aliran Monthly* 21, no. 3, (2001): 2–6; "Protest against the 2001 ISA Arrests: Memorandum Submitted by ALIRAN, HAKAM & SUARAM", ibid., pp. 7–8.

11. "12 pemimpin kanan Keadilan sertai UMNO", *Utusan Malaysia* (Malaysia), 12 February 2004. See also the media interview with former Keadilan information chief, Ruslan Kassim, "Keadilan sudah tidak relevan lagi", *Mingguan Malaysia* (Malaysia), 22 February 2004.

12. Mahathir Mohamad, *Malaysia: The Way Forward* (speech presented at the First Conference of the Malaysian Trade Council, 28 February 1991) (Kuala Lumpur: Biro Tatanegara Jabatan Perdana Menteri Malaysia, 1991), pp. 21– 27.

13. Francis Loh Kok Wah, "Towards a New Politics of Fragmentation and Contestation" in *New Politics in Malaysia*, edited by Francis Loh Kok Wah and Johan Saravanamuttu (Singapore: Institute of Southeast Asian Studies, 2003), p. 261.

14. Farish A. Noor, "Looking for *Reformasi*: The Discursive Dynamics of the *Reformasi* Movement and its Prospects as a Political Project", *Indonesia and the Malay World* 27, no. 77 (1999): appendix (a).

15. Ibid., pp. 6–10.

16. Ibid., pp. 12–13.

17. Khoo Boo Teik, "Can There be Reformasi Beyond BA? Reaffirm the Continuing Relevance of Reform", *Aliran Monthly* 22, no. 1 (2002): 5.

18. For example, in mid-2003, a disillusioned Dr. Farish Noor, hitherto identified as a prolific *reformasi* thinker, abandoned writing in the anti-establishment news website malaysiakini.com, citing *reformasi*'s allowing itself to be taken over by religious zealots and traditionalist defenders who were reluctant to steer the movement towards its logical conclusion. Ideological imperatives had been compromised to suit electoral priorities of some PAS leaders. Needless to say, since BN's electoral victory in 1999, it was only a matter of time before liberal social activist segments of *reformasi* felt alienated by PAS's domination of Barisan Alternatif (BA) – the opposition coalition. See Lee Ban Chen, "Paradoks pemikiran dan emosi Farish Noor", *Suara PRM*, 15 June 2003.

19. Meredith L. Weiss, "The 1999 Malaysian General Elections: Issues, Insults, and Irregularities", *Asian Survey* XL, no. 3 (2000): 421.

20. Muhammad Syukri Salleh, "Reformasi, Reradikalisasi dan Kebangkitan Islam di Malaysia", *Pemikir*, bil. 20 (2000): 39–41.

21. Ibid., p. 44.

22. From primary sources gathered by the present author, for instance, firstly, the speech by Abdul Hadi Awang, acting PAS president, in a fundraising dinner

organised by Kedah's PAS Youth, at the Cinta Sayang Club, Sungai Petani, Kedah, 24 August 2002. Secondly, an interview with Mohd Hamdan Abdul Rahman, PAS assemblyman for the Permatang Pasir state legislative seat, at his state constituency office in Permatang Pasir, Penang, 26 June 2003. Thirdly, "Islamic State Document Released", *Harakah English section*, 1–15 December 2003. See also, Khoo Boo Teik (2002), *Aliran Monthly* 22, no. 1 (2002): 6–7.

23. Dr. Maznah Mohamad, "The Challenge of Islam Within and Beyond Democracy. It is Time to Take Stock of this Issue Squarely", *Aliran Monthly* 21, no. 9 (2001): 8–9.

24. Sangwon Suh and Santha Oorjitham, "Battle for Islam: UMNO and Pas are Locked in a Struggle for the Malay Soul. The Outcome may Irrevocably Change Malaysian Society", *Asiaweek*, 16 June 2000.

25. Cf. "DAP Keluar Pakatan Jika PAS Mahukan Negara Islam", *Utusan Malaysia*, 26 October 1999; "DAP Tetap Menentang – Walaupun Karpal Minta Maaf Isu Pembentukan Negara Islam", *Mingguan Malaysia* (Malaysia), 7 February 1999.

26. From the singular *hadd*, meaning "limit", *hudud* refers to criminal punishments as instituted by the Quran and *Sunnah* (words, deeds and life of the Prophet Muhammad), such as amputation of the hand for thieves, flogging of eighty lashes for consuming intoxicating liquor, flogging for libel, stoning to death for adultery and flogging of one hundred lashes for fornication.

27. Cf. "Q and A on the Hudud and Qisas Enactment", *Aliran Monthly* 22, no. 6, pp. 25–29.

28. *Pelaksanaan Hukum Hudud di Kelantan* (Kota Bharu: Telda Corporation, 1994).

29. For pro-PAS' arguments, see Anual Bakhri Haron, *UMNO Tolak Hudud* (Kota Bharu: Pustaka Qamar, 2002). For arguments on UMNO and the government's side, see Hasnul Rahman, *Hudud: Siapa Khianati Hukum Allah, UMNO atau PAS?* (DLSB, 2001).

30. "Jenayah Idealisme PAS", *Utusan Malaysia* (Malaysia), 27 October 1999.

31. "Hudud: Pusat Bertindak Jika Bercanggah Perundangan", *Utusan Malaysia* (Malaysia), 28 October 2003; "Hudud mungkin tidak dapat dikuatkuasa", ibid.

32. Cf. "Bukan Islam Jangan Campur Tangan Usaha Laksana Hudud — Halim", *Utusan Malaysia* (Malaysia), 25 December 1992.

33. Cf. Syed Hussein Alatas, "PAS Perlu Banyak Berfikir: Nasib Ahli Bersekutu Dan Kedudukan Wanita Perlukan Kajian", *Mingguan Malaysia* (Malaysia), 6 June 1999; Prof. Ramlah Adam, "PAS Gadai Perjuangan", *Utusan Malaysia* (Malaysia), 11 June 1999; Zulkiflee Bakar, "Moral Politik PAS Jika Terima Ahli Bukan Islam", *Utusan Malaysia* (Malaysia), 14 June 2004.

34. Village Idiot, "Is Any Opposition Better Than No Opposition?", *Aliran Monthly* 22, no. 9, (2002): 4–6; Mustafa K Anuar, "The Mousedeer, The "Taliban" and a Sorry State: The Result may be to Produce Two 'Extremist' Elephants that may Well Trample All Mousedeer Caught between Them", *Aliran Monthly* 22, no. 7 (2002): 5.

35. "Tindakan DAP Keluar Pakatan Untungkan PAS – Nik Aziz", *Utusan Malaysia* (Malaysia), 24 September 2001.

36. "DAP Keluar Pakatan: Kegagalan Rundingan Isu Negara Islam Dengan PAS Punca Tindakan", *Mingguan Malaysia* (Malaysia), 23 September 2001.

37. "DAP Diberi Masa Fikir Mengenai Negara Islam", *Utusan Malaysia* (Malaysia), 3 June 2002.

38. "DAP Enggan Bincang Jika PAS Mahu Tubuh Negara Islam", *Berita Harian* (Malaysia), 4 June 2002.

39. "Malaysia Negara Islam — PM: Dr. Mahathir Sahut Cabaran Fadzil Noor", *Mingguan Malaysia* (Malaysia), 30 September 2001.

40. "Pentadbiran Negara Berasaskan Islam", *Utusan Malaysia* (Malaysia), 1 October 2001.

41. "Malaysia Boleh Diikitiraf Negara Islam Sejak Merdeka", *Utusan Malaysia* (Malaysia), 1 October 2001; "Banyak bidang Dilaksana Berasaskan al-Quran, Sunnah", *Utusan Malaysia* (Malaysia), 4 October 2001.

42. "Kita Negara Islam Contoh", *Mingguan Malaysia* (Malaysia), 5 August 2001; "UMNO Akan Terangkan Status Malaysia Sebagai Negara Islam", *Utusan Malaysia* (Malaysia), 1 October 2001.

43. Cf. "NGO Mahu PAS Jelas Ciri-ciri Negara Islam", *Utusan Malaysia* (Malaysia), 1 October 2001; Mustafa K Anuar, "Public Response to the "Islamic State" Poser", *Aliran Monthly* 21, no. 9, (2001): 10–11.

44. Muhammad Syukri Salleh, "Establishing an Islamic State: Ideals and Realities in the State of Kelantan, Malaysia", *Southeast Asian Studies* 37, no. 2 (1999): 235–56; Ahmad Fauzi Abdul Hamid, "Reforming PAS?", *Aliran Monthly* 23, no. 6 (2003): 11–13.

45. "Mana Memorandum Negara Islam PAS?", *Berita Minggu* (Malaysia), 14 September 2003.

46. The contents of the ISD may be accessed at <http://www.parti-pas.org/IslamicStateDocument.php>.

47. Dato Seri Tuan Guru Abdul Hadi Awang, "The Islamic State Document: Allay fears of a Theocracy", *Harakah English section*, 1–15 December 2003.

48. "Dokumen lerai kebimbangan: 'Negara Islam' Hujah Mantap — Anwar", *Harakah*, 1–15 December 2003.

49. M.G.G. Pillai, "PAS Throws Down its Gauntlet with its Islamic State Document. Would UMNO Pick it Up?", *Harakah English section*, 1–15 December 2003.

50. Cf. Leslie Lopez, "The Islamic Challenge: An Opposition Party Ups the Ante in the Battle for the Hearts and Minds of Ethnic Malays with a Plan for a Fully Fledged Religious State", *Far Eastern Economic Review*, 27 November 2003.

51. Cf. Mustafa K. Anuar, "The Forbidden Fruit Called Harakah: Malaysians Hungry for Alternative Views will Continue to be Drawn to the Popular Tabloid Despite the Latest Curbs", *Aliran Monthly* 20, no. 2 (2000): 13–14; P. Ramakrishnan, "Clampdown on Harakah: Prompted by Fear of Eroding Support", ibid. p. 15.

52. Cf. "Hadi, Mustafa Tidak Sekata Hasrat Tubuh Negara Islam", *Berita Harian* (Malaysia), 1 October 2003; "PAS Tidak Pernah Bercita-Cita Tubuh Negara Islam — Hassan", *Utusan Malaysia* (Malaysia), 15 October 2003.

53. Abd. Manaf Bin Haji Ahmad, *Negara Islam: Satu Analisa Perbandingan* (Kuala Lumpur: Yayasan Dakwah Islamiah Malaysia, 2000), pp. 87–91, 98, 99.

54. Francis Loh Kok Wah, *New Politics in Malaysia*, pp. 256–258; Maznah Mohamad, "The Contest for Malay Votes in 1999: UMNO's Most Historic Challenge?" in *New Politics in Malaysia*, edited by Francis Loh Kok Wah and Johan Saravanamuttu (Singapore: Institute of Southeast Asian Studies, 2003), p. 75.

55. Ibid., p. 77.

56. Khoo Boo Teik, *Political and Security Outlook 2004: Political Change in Southeast Asia*, p. 13.

57. Khoo Boo Teik, "A Transition and Two Elections: Between the General Election and the UMNO Election, Abdullah has Two Choices", *Aliran Monthly* 24, no. 2 (2004): 4.

58. Khoo Boo Teik, "Masyarakat Cina, Politik Malaysia dan Dunia Islam" (paper presented at Seminar Politik Kelantan, Pusat Kajian Strategik, Kota Bharu, 23 March 2004).

59. A native of Alor Star, Kedah, with an ancestry running to honourable families of *ulama* (traditional Islamic scholars) hailing from Patani, southern Thailand, Fadzil Noor was 65 years old upon his death. It was reported in the *New Straits Times*, 24 June 2002, that about 50,000 people attended his funeral, but PAS sources put the figure higher at around 250,000. Fadzil's humble demeanour and open-mindedness had endeared him to people of all affiliations, as testified by the paying of last respects to him by senior UMNO figures, including then Deputy Prime Minister Abdullah Ahmad Badawi, Defence Minister Najib Tun Razak and UMNO Secretary General Khalil Yaakob. Holder of a B.A. (Hons.) in Islamic Law from Al Azhar University, Cairo, he taught at his *alma mater*, the *Maktab Mahmud* in Alor Star, and lectured at the Universiti Teknologi Malaysia (UTM), Kuala Lumpur, before contesting the Kuala Kedah parliamentary seat and

the Alor Merah state seat in the 1978 general election, losing both. However, he held the Bukit Raya state seat for four terms (1982–99), before moving to Anak Bukit in 1999. The 1999 general election, which saw PAS capturing a record 27 parliamentary and 98 state seats throughout Malaysia, gave him his first taste of electoral victory at parliamentary level. This enabled him to be chosen the new leader of the Opposition. He had held the posts of secretary general of the Persatuan Ulama Malaysia (PUM, or *Ulama* Association of Malaysia) (1974–76) and deputy president of ABIM (1974–78). In PAS, he was vice president (1981–83), deputy president (1983–89) and president (1989–2002). For details on Fadzil Noor's background, see the PAS-published official eight-page tribute, *Almarhum Dato' Haji Fadzil Noor Dalam Kenangan 1937–2002* (2002).

60. Cf. Zin Mahmud, "Fadzil Keluarkan PAS Daripada Pinggiran Politik", *Utusan Malaysia* (Malaysia), 24 June 2002; Zulkiflee Bakar, "Hala Kepimpinan PAS Pasca-Fadzil", ibid.

61. Interview with Fadzil Noor: "Pengalaman 1974 Menjadi Peringatan Yang Cukup Mendalam - PAS Tidak Minat Kongsi Kuasa", *Mingguan Malaysia* (Malaysia), 2 June 2002; "Senario Politik Berubah-ubah", *Utusan Malaysia* (Malaysia), 24 June 2002.

62. Mohd. Kamil Yusuff, "Muktamar Pilihanraya", *Utusan Malaysia* (Malaysia), 4 June 2002. See excerpts of his speech in PAS, *Almarhum Dato' Haji Fadzil Noor Dalam Kenangan 1937–2002* (2002).

63. Cf. Abdullah Hassan, "Amanat Haji Hadi Bawa Padah: Pejabat Utusan Pernah Diancam Dibom Kerana Isu Kafir-mengkafir", *Mingguan Malaysia* (Malaysia), 13 June 2004; The interview: "PAS is not a Racist Party: Hadi Awang on Minorities and Islam", *Asiaweek*, 16 June 2000.

64. Joceline Tan, "Hassan's Win Shows Ulama Still has Grip on PAS", *The Star* (Malaysia), 15 September 2004.

65. "Hadi Enggan Akui Kelemahan Diri", *Utusan Malaysia* (Malaysia), 28 August 2004.

66. "Pemuda Akui Terlalu Yakin Punca Kalah Teruk", *Utusan Malaysia* (Malaysia), 27 August 2004.

67. "Ulama hits out at PAS Youth: Improve Yourself First, Wing Told", *The Star* (Malaysia), 27 August 2004; "Pimpinan Parti Tidak Konsisten — Pemuda PAS", *Utusan Malaysia* (Malaysia), 27 August 2004.

68. "PAS didesak tubuh Dewan Srikandi", *Utusan Malaysia* (Malaysia), 27 August 2004.

69. Joceline Tan, "Hadi's Leadership Put to Test", <http://www.malaysia-today.net/english/MT010904.htm>; "Hadi Bidas Pemuda PAS — Reaksi Terhadap Kritikan Kelemahan Pucuk Pimpinan", *Utusan Malaysia* (Malaysia), 28 August 2004.

70. "PAS Tries to Woo Youths with All-male Concert", *New Straits Times* (Malaysia), 1 October 2004; "PAS Softening its Stand on Accepted Popular Culture", *New Straits Times* (Malaysia), 9 October 2004.

71. Cf. Francis Loh, "Understanding the 2004 Election Results: Looking Beyond the Pak Lah Factor", *Aliran Monthly* 24, no. 3 (2004): 10.

72. N. Ganesan, "Malaysia in 2002: Political Consolidation and Change?", *Asian Survey* XLIII, no. 1, (2003): 151.

73. "Anak Nik Aziz Ditangkap: Disyaki Antara Tokoh Terpenting Kumpulan Mujahidin Malaysia", *Mingguan Malaysia* (Malaysia), 5 August 2001; "Ramai Lagi Akan Ditangkap: Abdullah — Polis Mendapati Kegiatan Mujahidin Di Negara Ini Sudah Serius", *Utusan Malaysia* (Malaysia), 6 August 2001.

74. K.S. Nathan, "Malaysia: 11 September and the Politics of Incumbency", *Southeast Asian Affairs 2002*, pp. 164–165.

75. "Memali: PAS pertikai arahan Majlis Fatwa Kebangsaan", *Utusan Malaysia* (Malaysia), 13 March 2002.

76. PAS (2002), *Isu Memali: Hakikat dan Realiti* (Kuala Lumpur: Jabatan Penerangan PAS Pusat).

77. "Kehadiran Hadi di Makassar bukti Pas Cenderung Keganasan", *Utusan Malaysia* (Malaysia), 10 February 2003; "Hadi Boleh Dikenakan Tindakan Undang-undang", *Utusan Malaysia* (Malaysia), 11 February 2003.

78. PAS, *Ulasan Terkini ... Tuan Guru Ab. Hadi Restui Pengganas?* (Tanjong Karang: Dewan Pemuda PAS, 2003).

79. Claudia Derichs, "A Step Forward: Malaysian Ideas for Political Change", *Journal of Asian and African Studies* 37, no. 1, (2002): 50–51; Lee Hock Guan (2002), "Malay Dominance and Opposition Politics in Malaysia", *Southeast Asian Affairs 2002*, pp. 191–192.

80. Khoo Boo Teik, "De-Mahathirising Malaysia: Abdullah Badawi's Debt to Reformasi", *Aliran Monthly* 23, no. 8 (2003): 2–6.

81. Khoo Boo Teik (2004), *Political and Security Outlook 2004: Political Change in Southeast Asia*, p. 8.

82. Leslie Lopez, "He's No Mahathir, and that's OK", *Far Eastern Economic Review*, 25 December 2003; James Wong Wing On, "Abdullah Ahmad's Vicissitude of Fortune", <http://www.malaysiakini.com/opinionsfeatures/20031123004145 2.php>, <http://www.malaysiakini.com/opinionsfeatures/200311280041454. php>.

83. The interview: "Kerjasama Dan Maklumat Tepat Penekanan Pak Lah", *Berita Harian* (Malaysia), 12 November 2003.

84. "Henti Panggil Perdana Menteri Pak Lah — Rafidah", *Utusan Malaysia* (Malaysia), 19 November 2003.

85. Abdul Razak Ahmad, "A Great Obsession with Niceties of Protocol", *New Straits Times* (Malaysia), 7 September 2004; cf. Nidzam Sulaiman (2002), "Anjakan Paradigma Budaya Politik Melayu Dari Feudal Kepada Neo-Feudal" in *Prosiding Persidangan Antarabangsa Melayu Beijing ke-2 Jilid 1: Agama, Budaya, Pendidikan, Ekonomi, Sejarah dan Seni,* edited by Abdullah Hassan (Kuala Lumpur: Dewan Bahasa dan Pustaka, 2002), pp. 612–17.

86. "Endon — Wife and Loyal Supporter", *The Sun* (Malaysia), 1 November 2003; Andrew Aeria, "An Open Letter to Abdullah Ahmad Badawi", *Aliran Monthly* 24, no. 3 (2004): 19–20.

87. "A Caring and Dependable Son", *The Sun* (Malaysia), 1 November 2003; "Abdullah Mencium Tangan Ibu Mohon Restu", *Mingguan Malaysia* (Malaysia), 2 November 2003; "Jenazah ibu PM Dikebumikan", *Utusan Malaysia* (Malaysia), 4 February 2004; Wong Kok Keong, "The Pak Lah Factor: The BN's PR Boys Promoted a Carefully Constructed 'Brand' Image of Abdullah Badawi", *Aliran Monthly* 24, no. 3 (2004): 40.

88. Abdullah was a grandson of Haji Abdullah Fahim, a scholar credited for having chosen the date of independence for Malaysia, 31 August 1957, based on its equivalent date in the Islamic calendar. Abdullah's father, Haji Ahmad Badawi, was a scholar and active UMNO politician who had been a member of Penang's state legislative assembly continuously from 1959 until his death in 1978. Loyal to the family tradition, Abdullah opted to read Islamic studies at the University of Malaya, even though he had obtained a scholarship to read economics. Upon graduating in 1964, Abdullah joined the civil service until 1978, when he contested in the general elections and became UMNO/BN member of Parliament for Kepala Batas, Penang. Since then, he has held posts at federal level continuously, except for a brief lull in 1987–91, when he was thrown into the political wilderness for having sided with Dr Mahathir's opponents during the UMNO factional crisis of 1987. See, "Turbulent Journey to Putrajaya", *The Sun* (Malaysia), 1 November 2003; "The Pak Lah His Friends Know", ibid.; Zulkifli Jalil, "Abdullah Fahim Tetapkan Tarikh Kemerdekaan", *Utusan Malaysia* (Malaysia), 24 August 2004; Abdullah Ahmad Badawi, "My Grandpa, Merdeka and I", *New Straits Times* (Malaysia), 1 September 2004; Yahaya Ismail, *Pak Lah dari Kepala Batas ke Putrajaya* (Petaling Jaya: Usaha Teguh Sdn. Bhd., 2004), pp. 36–41.

89. Cf. "Abdullah Berbuka Puasa Bersama Pemimpin UMNO Negeri", *Utusan Malaysia* (Malaysia), 19 November 2003; front page cover of Abd. Manaf Bin Haji Ahmad, *Negara Islam: Satu Analisa Perbandingan* (2004).

90. Yahaya, *Pak Lah dari Kepala Batas ke Putrajaya,* pp. 30–31.

91. MMC-Gamuda is controlled by Syed Mokhtar al-Bukhary, a business darling of Dr Mahathir. See Eddie Toh, "Scrapped — Syed Mokhtar's Concession for RM2.5b Project", *Business Times* (Singapore), 4 December 2003; Simon Elegant, "A New Vision for Malaysia: Malaysians Expected Prime Minister Abdullah Ahmad Badawi to be Cautious, but He has Quickly Emerged as a Bold Reformer", *Time*, 22 March 2004.

92. "Eric Chia Diikat Jamin RM2j: Tidak Mengaku Salah Pecah Amanah RM76.4 Juta Dana Anak Syarikat Perwaja", *Utusan Malaysia* (Malaysia), 11 February 2004; "Kasitah Gaddam Didakwa: Hadapi tuduhan Menipu, Rasuah Babitkan Saham Bernilai RM24 Juta", *Utusan Malaysia* (Malaysia), 13 February 2004.

93. "Tiada Menteri Ditahan: Rais Ulas Spekulasi Lagi Anggota Kabinet Ditangkap Kerana Rasuah", *Utusan Malaysia* (Malaysia), 19 February 2004.

94. "11 Kes Rasuah VIP Ke Mahkamah", *Berita Harian* (Malaysia), 15 July 2004.

95. Leslie Lau, "Abdullah to MPs: Hand in Report Cards", *Straits Times* (Singapore), 13 July 2004.

96. Lopez, *Far Eastern Economic Review*; Khoo Boo Teik (2004), *Aliran Monthly* 24, no. 2 (2004): 2, 4.

97. Cf. "Not Yet Out of Mahathir's Shadow: Abdullah Badawi has Done Some Good Things, but the New Prime Minister has Fought Shy of the Most Important Ones", *The Economist*, 29 January 2004; "Who will Watch the Watchdogs? Despite a Few Encouraging Signs, South-East Asia's Record on Fighting Corruption at the Top is Still Mostly Lamentable", *The Economist*, 19 February 2004.

98. Cf. Brendan Pereira, "Abdullah Changing Way of Doing Business: While He Champions Malaysia Inc, the New PM is Putting his Foot Down on Giving Special Treatment to a Select Few", *Straits Times* (Singapore), 2 December 2003; Leslie Lau, "Exit Dr M… it's Gripes Aplenty Now", *Straits Times* (Singapore), 20 June 2004.

99. "Islam Hadhari Perjelas Nilai Rasional Agama", *Berita Harian* (Malaysia), 14 June 2004; interview with Nakahie Ahmad: "Hala Tuju Ulama Dalam Islam Hadhari", *Berita Harian* (Malaysia), 26 June 2004; Datuk Seri Abdullah Ahmad Badawi, "Peranan, Cabaran Ulama Jana Pemikiran Positif Masyarakat", *Berita Harian*, 30 June 2004; Mohd Shauki Abdul Majid, "Toleransi Agama Dalam Islam Hadhari", *Utusan Malaysia* (Malaysia), 9 July 2004; "Islam Hadhari Gabung Ulama, Profesional", *Berita Harian* (Malaysia), 28 July 2004; "Islam Hadhari Bukan Ajaran Sesat: Abdullah", *Utusan Borneo* (Malaysia), 31 July 2004.

100. Nakhaie Ahmad, "Misi Islam Hadhari bentuk acuan Wawasan 2020", *Berita Harian* (Malaysia), 2 July 2004.

101. Ibid.

102. "Teliti Semula Ijtihad — PM — Langkah Memastikan Umat Islam Sekarang Lebih dinamik", *Utusan Malaysia* (Malaysia), 5 August 2004.

103. Astora Jabat, "Malaysia Model Islam Hadhari", *Mingguan Malaysia* (Malaysia), 25 April 2004.

104. Rose Ismail, "Bringing Islam Hadhari into the Mainstream", *New Straits Times* (Malaysia), 27 July 2004.

105. In a forum entitled "The Concept of the State in Islam" held in Georgetown, Penang on 24 April 2004, the prevalent opinion among the presenters was that no specific reference to the concept of an Islamic state could be found in the Quran and *Sunnah*. The nearest term matching such a concept was "a territory fair and happy, and a Lord Oft-Forgiving" (Quran: chapter 34, verse 15). The panelists were the author of this chapter, Astora Jabat — religious columnist for *Mingguan Malaysia* and editor of the *Al Islam* magazine, and Kassim Ahmad — a modernist scholar notorious for his controversial views on the *hadith* (oral traditions) of the Prophet Muhammad. See also, "Malaysia Laksana Islam Hadhari", *Utusan Malaysia* (Malaysia), 29 March 2004; and Radzuan Halim, "The Islamic State Document", *The Edge Malaysia*, 22 December 2003.

106. Datuk Seri Abdullah Ahmad Badawi, "Menuju Kecemerlangan" (keynote address at the 55th UMNO General Assembly, *Utusan Malaysia* (Malaysia), 24 September 2004); "Islam Hadhari Perkasakan Bangsa Melayu — Abdullah", *Utusan Malaysia* (Malaysia), 24 September 2004.

107. Abdullah Ahmad Badawi, "Muslim World Needs a Meeting of Minds" (speech delivered at the Oxford Centre for Islamic Studies on 1 October 2004), *New Straits Times* (Malaysia), 5 October 2004; Kalimullah Hassan, "Malaysia as a Model Islamic Nation", *New Sunday Times* (Malaysia), 3 October 2004.

108. Cf. "Pirdaus 'ustaz' Kedua Muncul Dalam Pemuda", *Utussn Malaysia* (Malaysia), 24 September 2004; "Bersih Imej Negatif", *Berita Minggu* (Malaysia), 26 September 2004; "Lima PM Usaha Terapkan Rukun Islam", *Berita Minggu* (Malaysia), 26 September 2004; "Kaji Semula Program TV — Rancangan Tidak Bermoral Halang Pelaksanaan Islam Hadhari", *Utusan Malaysia* (Malaysia), 27 September 2004.

109. Among well-known religious personalities fielded by UMNO in the elections were Dr Mashitah Ibrahim — lecturer at the International Islamic University of Malaysia (IIUM); Dr Abdullah Mohd. Zain, ex-deputy rector of the Islamic University College of Malaysia (KUIM); Dr Amran Kasimin, lecturer at the National University of Malaysia (UKM); Che Min Che Ahmad, ex-deputy director of the Islamic Development Department (JAKIM); and Pirdaus Ismail, former imam of the National Mosque in Kuala Lumpur. All were triumphant except for Pirdaus Ismail, who lost narrowly to Wan Azizah Wan Ismail in Permatang Pauh, Penang. See "Pencalonan Tokoh Agama Disokong", *Utusan Malaysia* (Malaysia),

11 March 2004; "Tokoh Agama Kini Bukan Lagi Milik Pembangkang", *Berita Minggu* (Malaysia), 21 March 2004.

110. "Hadi Tuduh Media, SPR Punca PAS Kalah", *Berita Harian* (Malaysia), 14 June 2004.

111. Philip Khoo, "A Brave New World? Worrying Implications for Democracy", *Aliran Monthly* 24, no. 3 (2004): 4; Ramdas Tikandas, "An Election Day under Guardian Angels", *Aliran Monthly* 24, no. 3 (2004): 13, 14.

112. Raja Petra Kamarudin, "X-Files: Unexplained Mysteries in Malaysia's Worst Ever Election", email posting to the discussion group <http://groups.yahoo.com/group/kini-malaysia/> (accessed 3 April 2004).

113. Devaraj, *Aliran Monthly* 24, no. 5 (2004): 10–11.

114. Raja Petra Kamarudin, "Analysis of the 11th General Elections 2004 — Kuala Terengganu", email posting to the discussion group <http://groups.yahoo.com/group/kini-malaysia/> (accessed 25 March 2004); Raja Petra Kamarudin, "More Unexplained Mysteries in 11th GE", email posting to the discussion group <http://groups.yahoo.com/group/kini-malaysia/> (accessed 27 March 2004); Raja Petra Kamarudin, "Malaysia's 11th General Election Fraud: Press Conference Today", email posting to the discussion group <http://groups.yahoo.com/group/kini-malaysia/> (accessed 14 April 2004).

115. Raja Petra Kamarudin, "Why Barisan Nasional will Win the Election: A Prediction by Seruan Keadilan", email posting to the discussion group <http://groups.yahoo.com/group/kini-malaysia/> 24 March 2004; Janadas Devan, "Shaping the Votes of Victory", *The Straits Times* (Singapore), 26 March 2004.

116. Francis Loh, "New Threats to the Electoral System: The Last Remaining Democratic Institution is under Siege", *Aliran Monthly* 22, no. 3 (2002): 5–6; Lim Hong Hai, "New Rules And Constituencies for New Challenges? Appearances of Unfairness Can Erode the Credibility of the Election Commission", *Aliran Monthly* 23, no. 6 (2003): 7.

117. Loh, *Aliran Monthly* 22, no. 3 (2002): 6, 7; Lim, *Aliran Monthly* 23, no. 6 (2003): 7.

118. Cf. "Vote For Democracy", *Aliran Monthly* 24, no. 2, pp. 40, 34–37; Philip Khoo (2004), "A Brave New World? Worrying Implications for Democracy", p. 7; Dr Jeyakumar Devaraj, (2004), "The 2004 BN Victory: By Fair Means or Foul?", p. 13.

119. Lim Hong Hai, "The Delineation of Peninsular Electoral Constituencies: Amplifying Malay and UMNO Power" in *New Politics in Malaysia*, edited by Francis Loh Kok Wah and Johan Saravanamuttu (Singapore: Institute of Southeast Asian Studies, 2003), pp. 25–52; Lim Hong Hai, "The Transformation of the

Election Commission: A Shell of its Original Self", *Aliran Monthly* 22, no. 3 (2002): 9, 10.

120. Cf. "Pilihan Raya: SPR Dikritik — BN Pulau Pinang Akan Hantar Memorandum Bantah Kelemahan", *Utusan Malaysia* (Malaysia), 24 March 2004; "SPR Buat Laporan Polis Kertas Undi Salah Cetak", ibid.; Raja Petra Kamarudin, "LOST BALLOTS: 67,174 Postal Votes not Returned, Says Commission", email posting to the discussion group <http://groups.yahoo.com/group/kini-malaysia/> (accessed 15 April 2004).

121. Wong Kok Keong, "Propagandists for the BN (Part 1): RTM and TV3 were the Main Culprit", *Aliran Monthly* 24, no. 5 (2004): 14–17; Wong Kok Keong, "Propagandists for the BN (Part 2): The Star and the NST Could Learn a Thing or Two from the Sun — Though, Overall, Journalistic Integrity was in Short Supply", *Aliran Monthly* 24, no. 6 (2004): 13–17.

122. Cf. Rajen Devaraj, "Keadilan: The Need for Introspection", *Aliran Monthly* 24, no. 4 (2004): 21, 22.

123. Maznah, *New Politics in Malaysia*, p. 79.

124. Cf. Raja Petra Kamarudin, "The Wakeup Call That Did not Wake Us Up", email posting to the discussion group <http://groups.yahoo.com/group/kini-malaysia/> (accessed 3 April 2004); Raja Petra Kamarudin, "All That Glitters is Not Gold: Keadilan Should Have Learnt Some Lessons from the Indera Kayangan by Election", *Aliran Monthly* 24, no. 3 (2004): 15–17.

⑥

The Malay Electorate in 2004: Reversing the 1999 Result?*

JOHN FUNSTON

On 21 March the ruling National Front (Barisan Nasional, or BN) swept to its greatest electoral victory ever, winning 199 of 219 seats. The Opposition won only 20 seats, down from 45 in the smaller outgoing parliament. The Democratic Action Party (DAP) increased its representation by two to 12, but Parti Islam SeMalaysia (PAS) declined from 27 to six, and Parti keADILan Malaysia (Keadilan) retained only one of its five seats. Unexpectedly, the BN even routed PAS and coalition ally Keadilan in the Malay heartland states. In 1999, it won 11 of 40 parliamentary seats in the four northernmost states; this time it took 33, representing a swing in the popular vote ranging from 4 per cent in Kedah to 16 per cent in Terengganu (refer to Tables 6.1 and 6.2). It reversed the 1999 result for the Terengganu state assembly (28 to four), strengthened its hold on the Kedah and Perlis assemblies, and just fell short of PAS in Kelantan (24 to 21).

---

* The author is grateful to Bridget Welsh for her comments on an earlier draft of this chapter.

Table 6.1
Results of 1999 and 2004 General Elections

	2004	1999
Number of registered voters	10,276,173	9,566,188
(Terengganu)	455,924	387,339
Number of registered voters excluding		
those in uncontested wards	9,762,720	9,546,303
Number of parliamentary seats	219	193
Number of valid votes	6,895,729	6,658,999
Percentage of votes	70.63	69.75
(Terengganu)	85.5	79.9
(State)	86.9	79.9
	Number of seats won	
BN	199	148
(UMNO)	110	72
PAS	6	27
DAP	12	10
PKM (Keadilan)	1	5
Other	1	3
	Number of contested seats	
BN	219	193
PAS	84	63
PKM	58	59
DAP	44	46
	Number of votes won	
BN	4,414,513	3,762,556
PAS	1,056,110	996,437
PKM	586,980	767,969
DAP	694,356	848,040
	Percentage of parliamentary vote	
BN	64.02	56.5
PAS	15.32	15.0
PKM	8.51	11.5
DAP	10.07	12.7
	Percentage of parliamentary seats	
BN	90.90	76.69
PAS	2.70	13.99
PKM	0.46	2.60
DAP	5.48	6.20

Table 6.1   cont'd

	2004	1999
For Peninsula Malaysia only		
Number of valid votes	6,158,988	5,698,489
	Number of votes won	
BN	3,931,678	3,157,426
PAS	1,051,889	990,437
PKM	546,089	699,851
DAP	618,288	771,145
	Percentage of parliamentry vote	
BN	63.84	55.4
PAS	17.08	17.4
PKM	8.87	12.3
DAP	10.04	13.5

Source: Malaysian Election Commission. Adjusted to include the Pasir Puteh (Kelantan) seat initially declared for PAS but awarded to BN on appeal, but not the revised count for this electorate as it has not yet been issued by the EC.

The conduct of the elections and the result were warmly welcomed by world leaders and the international media. A US official congratulated Malaysia "on the conduct of the election and how the process was handled … the decision was made by the people of Malaysia and we're happy the election went well".[1] *The Australian* declared that Malaysian elections "are free and fair … and they are very good news for everybody who understands that democracy is the best antidote to the Islamic fundamentalism [meaning PAS] that fosters political terrorism".[2] The *Christian Science Monitor* went even further: "The sweeping victory of Malaysia's secular rulers … emphasises the narrow appeal of Muslim hard-liners in Southeast Asia, where strict religion-based politics run up against multiethnic realities. Muslim voters dealt a potentially knock-out blow to the conservative PAS."[3]

The results were, however, more complicated than these analyses suggested, since the percentage of those supporting PAS actually slightly increased (from 15 per cent to 15.3 per cent). Why then did the National

Table 6.2
Number of Contested Seats, Total Number of Votes, and Percentage of Votes in the 1999 and 2004 General Elections by State

State	Party	2004 General Election			1999 General Election		
		No. of Contested Seats	Total No. of Votes	Percentage of Votes	No. of Contested Seats	Total No. of Votes	Percentage of Votes
Perlis	BN	3	58,188	63.7	3	46,326	56.2
	PAS	3	33,132	36.3	2	26,162	31.8
	PKM	—	—	—	1	9,872	12.0
Kedah	BN	15	388,943	59.8	15	315,622	55.8
	PAS	10	184,850	28.4	10	171,825	30.4
	PKM	5	77,101	11.9	4	65,371	11.6
	DAP	—	—	—	1	13,258	2.34
Kelantan	BN	14	262,377	50.1	14	187,102	38.9
	PAS	11	202,103	38.6	11	228,111	47.5
	PKM	3	52,824	10.1	3	64,763	13.5
Terengganu	BN	8	219,861	56.4	8	127,700	41.2
	PAS	7	149,299	38.3	7	161,052	52.0
	PKM	1	20,635	5.3	1	20,715	6.7
Penang	BN	13	284,110	59.4	11	247,870	51.4
	PAS	2	19,109	4.0	1	8,810	1.8
	PKM	5	39,673	8.3	3	54,987	11.4
	DAP	7	135,125	28.3	6	169,973	35.2

Table 6.2 cont'd

State	Party	2004 General Election			1999 General Election		
		No. of Contested Seats	Total No. of Votes	Percentage of Votes	No. of Contested Seats	Total No. of Votes	Percentage of Votes
Perak	BN	24	456,031	59.6	23	415,112	55.5
	PAS	11	106,022	13.8	7	93,454	12.5
	PKM	8	68,703	9.0	7	80,067	10.7
	DAP	8	135,056	17.6	9	156,110	20.9
Pahang	BN	14	270,384	67.6	11	215,003	57.4
	PAS	8	73,636	18.4	6	81,984	21.9
	PKM	3	31,081	7.8	3	50,711	13.5
	DAP	3	24,991	6.3	2	26,786	7.2
Selangor	BN	22	651,139	65.8	17	470,248	54.8
	PAS	10	143,946	14.6	5	95,643	11.1
	PKM	9	125,758	12.7	7	161,575	18.8
	DAP	4	68,636	6.9	4	106,905	12.5
Federal Territory (Kuala Lumpur)	BN	11	263,915	58.6	10	220,492	50.2
	PAS	2	19,183	4.3	1	17,111	3.9
	PKM	4	57,033	12.7	3	62,600	14.3
	DAP	5	109,343	24.3	5	116,776	26.6
Federal Territory (Putrajaya)	BN	1	4,086	88.33	—	—	—
	PKM	1	540	11.67	—	—	—

Table 6.2 cont'd

Negri Sembilan						
BN	8	69.9	211,760	7	168,185	59.2
PAS	4	10.2	31,010	2	25,239	8.9
PKM	2	6.4	19,480	2	23,585	8.3
DAP	2	13.5	40,752	3	68,526	24.1
Malacca						
BN	6	71.6	189,053	5	132,803	56.6
PAS	2	5.9	15,653	2	25,239	10.8
PKM	2	7.9	20,834	2	43,051	18.3
DAP	1	14.5	38,370	1	33,611	14.3
Johore						
BN	26	79.6	671,831	20	611,053	72.9
PAS	12	8.8	73,946	5	57,273	6.8
PKM	5	3.8	32,426	7	62,554	7.5
DAP	7	7.8	66,015	6	79,200	9.5
Federal Territory (Labuan)						
BN	1	77.7	11,087	1	8,687	71.3
PAS	1	22.3	3,186	1	1,318	10.8
Sabah						
BN	25	64.3	196,683	20	258,656	59.4
PAS	—	—	—	2	2,244	0.5
PKM	9	11.6	35,471	3	18,344	4.2
DAP	2	2.7	8,512	2	973	0.2
PBS			Joined BN	16	141,166	32.4
Sarawak						
BN	28	66.0	275,065	28	337,787	65.9
PAS	1	0.3	1,035	1	2,438	0.5
PKM	1	1.3	5,420	12	49,774	9.7
DAP	5	16.2	67,556	7	75,922	14.8

Source: Malaysian Election Commission. Adjusted to include the Pasir Puteh (Kelantan) seat initially declared for PAS but awarded to BN on appeal, but not the revised count for this electorate as it has not yet been issued by the EC.

Front win such an overwhelming majority? Has it won back the Malay electorate? What are the longer term implications for Malay politics — in particular, does it represent the triumph of secularism?

The 1999 Elections and Aftermath

In 1999 the BN was returned with a comfortable majority, winning 77 per cent of the parliamentary seats. But in an election dominated by Prime Minister Dr Mahathir's sacking of deputy Anwar Ibrahim, Anwar's black eye at the hands of the head of the police, his controversial trials, and the rise of *reformasi*, UMNO had its worst result ever. Its parliamentary seats declined from 94 (89 elected in 1995) to 72. Four of its ministers and five deputy ministers were defeated.[4] Many others experienced a massive reduction in their majorities, including Education Minister Dato' Najib (from 10,793 to 241), and Trade Minister Datuk Rafidah (10,649 to 2,774). Dr Mahathir's own majority fell from 17,226 to 10,138 and his deputy, Datuk Abdullah, from 17,834 to 11,175. PAS retained power in Kelantan and took control of Terengganu for the first time since 1959, with massive majorities in each assembly (41 of 43 in Kelantan and 28 of 32 in Terengganu). Its 27 seats in the national parliament gave it leadership of the Opposition. The newly-established Keadilan, headed by Anwar's wife Wan Azizah, also gained broad national support, winning 11.5 per cent of the vote though securing only five federal and four state seats. Around half the Malay vote — much more by some UMNO calculations — went to the Opposition.

Subsequent by-elections showed little evidence of Malay support returning to UMNO. In November 2000, Keadilan unexpectedly won a by-election for the Kedah state seat of Lunas, depriving the National Front of a psychologically important two-thirds majority in the assembly. Federal and state Kedah by-elections in July 2002, after the death of former PAS leader Fadzil Nor, were a critical test, and UMNO invested a massive effort in the campaign. In what had been an UMNO stronghold until the 1999 election, the party wrestled back the federal constituency by a narrow margin, but PAS retained the state seat. UMNO gained more support from non-Malays, but made no inroads into the Malay electorate.

Developments Favouring UMNO

Nonetheless, by the time elections approached in 2004, UMNO (and the BN) was considerably better placed to perform strongly than it had been in 1999. Several factors contributed to this.

September 11, 2001

The political atmosphere in Malaysia was profoundly changed by September 11. In 1999 non-Malays had kept the government in control, though some had voted for the Opposition, and more did so in pre-September 11 by-elections. The dramatic attacks on the World Trade Centre and Pentagon reinforced many non-Malay fears about Islam, turning them back to the government and away from the PAS-led Opposition. This benefited particularly the non-Malay BN parties, but UMNO also stood to gain in predominantly-Malay electorates with a significant non-Malay component.

Opposition Disarray

The post-September 11 environment also worked against the Opposition. The DAP's break with the Opposition coalition (Barisan Alternatif, or BA) was in train before September 11 — over the predominantly-Chinese party's opposition to PAS's advocacy of an Islamic state — but this event sealed the issue, and greatly inhibited the capacity of the DAP to cooperate with other opposition parties. It also provided some legitimacy for government arrests under the draconian Internal Security Act (ISA). This weakened Keadilan when several key leaders were arrested in April 2001, and five of them held for over two years.

Opposition parties, particularly PAS and Keadilan, also suffered from other tough government actions directed at restricting their political activities. Shortly after the 1999 election, the PAS newspaper *Harakah* was allowed to publish only twice a month instead of twice a week and other pro-opposition newspapers were closed down. Several Opposition leaders were detained for alleged offences against the Sedition or Official Secret's Acts, before resorting to the ISA. A ban was placed on almost all public gatherings, with police even intervening to break up a PAS meeting held on its own premises in January 2002.

The government also moved to undermine PAS finances, withdrawing petroleum royalty payments from Terengganu in September 2000, even though these were guaranteed under legal agreements in 1975 and 1987. Worth more than RM810 million in 2000, royalties comprised over 70 per cent of state revenue and were widely viewed as a resource that could be used to entrench and expand PAS influence.

The death of popular leader Fadzil Nor in June 2002 was also a great setback for PAS. His replacement by Terengganu Mentri Besar Dato' Seri Tuan Guru Abdul Hadi Awang moved the party in a more conservative direction. At party elections in September the following year, a damaging contest took place for the deputy leader's post, and although Hadi supported the liberal Datuk Mustafa Ali, the veteran *ulama* Senator Hassan Shukri prevailed. Indeed, throughout 2003, the party often sought to address concerns that it was too conservative — by, for example, promising to reverse a 40-year position and stand women candidates in elections — but such efforts were undone by the publication of a conservative Islamic state blueprint in November.

Keadilan, for its part, descended into a series of debilitating factional conflicts after the arrest of its top leadership. It eventually agreed to merge with Parti Rakyat Malaysia, creating the new Parti Keadilan Rakyat in August 2003 (though the Registrar of Societies only accorded legal recognition after elections on 29 March 2004[5]). But, partly because of this merger, several high profile leaders quit the party, the Islamic youth group Angkatan Belia Islam Malaysia (ABIM) distanced itself, and on the eve of the 2004 election, three more leaders defected to UMNO.

Economic Pickup

The Malaysian economy had begun to emerge from the depths of the 1997/98 Asian economic crisis by the time of the 1999 election, but its impact was still keenly felt. While the economy had not returned to pre-crisis levels and the local corporate sector remained mired in debt, high budget deficits had sustained growth at reasonable levels. As the 2004 election approached, GNP had improved to around 6 per cent and the stock market was moving upwards, ensuring what the media described as a "feel good" factor.

Electoral Changes

A further package of factors working in UMNO's favour included an electoral redistribution, changes to electoral laws, and a "cleansing" of the electoral roll.

An electoral redistribution carried out by the Election Commission (EC) added 26 seats to parliament, most in areas favourable to UMNO in the south (Johore from 20 to 26, Selangor 17 to 22), and Sabah (20 to 25). The northern states of Kelantan, Terengganu, and Kedah had no additions. Furthermore, several seats in Kedah won by PAS in 1999 were reorganised with a higher proportion of non-Malay voters, making a repeat PAS victory unlikely. A columnist in the pro-government *The Star*, noted that constituencies for the PAS secretary-general and the party's former youth chief, had been redrawn to include a sizeable number of non-Muslim voters who were previously in other constituencies. "The Barisan", he noted, "is putting in extra efforts to win back the lost seats because gerrymandering, common in all democracies, has always benefited the ruling parties."[6]

In the lead up to the 2004 election, the government also amended electoral law; the Elections Offences (Amendment) Act 2002 (Act A1177) came into effect on 16 January 2003. This introduced a number of changes to tighten government control over the election process. Amongst other matters, it provided the EC with increased powers, together with the police, to stop a candidate doing anything that might be construed as instigating tensions. This was strengthened by a complicated Code of Ethics released (though never formally gazetted) just before the election.[7] The EC was also empowered to raise the deposit for candidates. For 2004, it was doubled to RM5,000 for state seats and RM10,000 for federal seats, with an additional deposit of RM3,000 and RM5,000 in case candidates did not clean up election advertising afterwards — a substantial new impost for poorly-funded opposition parties. A further change was that once the electoral rolls had been gazetted they could not be legally challenged. In the past, results had been overturned when voters had been fraudulently included in particular electorates.

After 1999, the EC also began a process of cleaning up the electoral rolls, announcing in January that some 50,000 had been deleted as a result.[8] In fact, an even more substantial reorganisation must have taken place. As can be seen from Table 6.1, the total eligible voters increased to 10,276,173 from 9,566,188, an addition of 709,985 (7.4 per cent). It should have been much larger. At the end of 1999, at least 680,000 were on the rolls but not gazetted at the time of the election. Increased EC efforts to enroll voters after this should in the next four years have added at least 1,200,000,[9] resulting in a cumulative total of 1,880,000, which even allowing for 50,000 deletions and other routine changes, was not reflected in the 2004 electorate. The NGO Aliran was among those that discovered several anomalies in the rolls, including, for example, the fact that in Sungai Siput, Perak, an operations centre for Malaysian Indian Congress leader Samy Vellu, "which is an office, had 12 registered voters. Large numbers of voters were falsely registered at fictitious addresses where there were no houses … in Pandamaran in Klang a one-room flat had 150 registered voters."[10]

Many such anomalies may have been unintended errors, but several commentators were left suspicious. An Aliran spokesman commented that in Sungai Siput, for example, "we are told that some 5,000 voters from outside this constituency have been registered to vote here".[11] The increase in voter numbers in the critical state of Terengganu by 17.7 per cent, against the average of 7.4 per cent, (see Table 6.1), raises further questions about the roll reorganisation.

Prime Minister Abdullah's Honeymoon

Like most new political leaders, Prime Minister Datuk Seri Abdullah Ahmad Badawi enjoyed a honeymoon period after taking over from Dr Mahathir on 31 October 2003. While Mahathir went out on an apparent high, with extravagant praise for his career in the pro-government media, his passing was more regretted by non-Malays than Malays. The controversy surrounding his sacking of Anwar, his autocratic and confrontational style, and his opaque management of the economy, remained issues for most Malays. Abdullah, dubbed by the media as "Mr Nice Guy", "Mr Clean", and "Pak Lah" (short for Uncle Abdullah) contrasted with Mahathir in such areas, and in his initial weeks, he acted effectively to highlight this contrast.

Abdullah began by lowering the tone of confrontation in dealing with PAS and the Opposition. He did not brand PAS leaders "liars" and "hypocrites" as Mahathir had. And his release of 19 ISA detainees with alleged ties to extremist groups (15 al-Ma'unah and four associated with Kumpulan Militan Malaysia/Jemaah Islamiah) at the end of the fasting month in November was perhaps a cautious step to demonstrate a less punitive approach to Islamic groups.

Abdullah also highlighted his Islamic background. He has strong credentials: his father and grandfather were prominent Islamic preachers, and he graduated in Islamic Studies (though this was not a theology degree as often claimed). He received saturation publicity when leading Muslims in prayer during the fasting month. And the media repeatedly projected him as pious and learned, well-placed to counter the Islamic claims of PAS.

Abdullah also addressed a number of the issues raised by *reformasi*. His first speech as prime minister was to parliament, a gesture intended to emphasise the importance of this key democratic institution. He also, amongst other things, called on the party and public to provide him with correct information, eschew flattery, and "work with me, not for me".

Similarly, Abdullah said the right things about the need for greater transparency, accountability, cutting bureaucratic red tape, and above all, less corruption. He had positioned himself on such issues even before taking over, giving several speeches proclaiming zero tolerance for corruption. He announced a national integrity plan and, in his first address to parliament, promised to lead a "clean, incorruptible, modest and beyond suspicion" administration. He then urged the Anti-Corruption Agency to speed up several outstanding corruption cases, including a prominent case involving national steel corporation Perwaja. One month later, he announced the allocation of RM17 million to establish a regional Anti-Corruption Academy, and promised Malaysia would sign the United Nations Anti-Corruption Convention. Finally, during a major speech on the economy on 13 January 2004, he promised improved transparency in applications for government contracts, with open tendering the norm.

In early December, Abdullah took more concrete action. He suspended a controversial RM14.5 billion rail construction project, which was taken away from Chinese and Indian firms and given to a close associate of Mahathir's, Syed Mokhtar Al-Bukhary, ten days before the close of his administration. He declared that the controversial Bakun hydroelectric dam in Sarawak would not be privatised, again disadvantaging Syed Mokhtar. And at the end of the month he announced a Royal Commission into the police, to address the issue of corruption amongst others.

In early 2004, the gloss began to wear off this buildup slightly when, on 7 January, Abdullah appointed a Cabinet almost identical to the one he inherited from Dr Mahathir. He made Dato' Najib Tun Razak his deputy, a move Mahathir had urged, though he was widely seen as a rival to Abdullah. The anti-corruption campaign appeared to lose momentum, particularly when the details of the Police Royal Commission announced on 4 February contained no mention of corruption, focusing only on general issues such as "the role and responsibility of police in implementing law".

An additional complication were serious US allegations, appearing in the media on 4 February, that Abdullah's son Kamaluddin part-owned a company producing centrifuge components suitable for developing nuclear weapons on the black market. The Malaysian police were quick to deny that nothing illegal was involved, but Kamaluddin's Sri Lankan business partner was later detained under the ISA.

At this time of uncertainty, the anti-corruption campaign took a new and to many unexpected turn. On 9 February, the former head of Perwaja, Tan Sri Eric Chia, was arrested and charged with dishonestly approving a payment of RM76.4 million in 1994. On 12 February, an UMNO politician, land and cooperative development minister, Tan Sri Kasitah Gadam, was charged with cheating on share transactions in his capacity as chairman of the Sabah Land Development Board in 1996 (the prosecution said one transaction was worth RM24 million). Shortly after, the de facto law minister, Rais Yatim, warned that at least another 18 high-profile corruption cases were with authorities awaiting further action.

Election Campaign

These prosecutions, and a sustained media buildup, regained the initiative for Abdullah. On 3 March, he announced that parliament would be dissolved to permit general elections. This occurred the following day, and on 5 March, the EC set 13 March for the nomination of candidates and 21 March for the election. In addition to 219 national seats, elections for state assemblies were held simultaneously, except in Sarawak. A total of 505 state seats were at stake, 63 more than 1999.

The Candidates

Around 30 per cent of the ruling BN parliamentary candidates are normally new faces. This was so again, with sweeping changes in Kelantan and Terengganu (where only one UMNO candidate was elected in 1999) but relatively minor adjustments in most other states. Several new faces were, however, political veterans who had not previously stood for election, such as deputy minister of information, Datuk Zainuddin Maidin, and deputy minister of education, Datuk Abdul Aziz Samsudin.

Before the nominations were announced, much media speculation focused on major changes to rid the party of those identified as corrupt or pro-Mahathir. This was to include easing out four or five state leaders (*mentri besar* or chief minister) by "promoting" them to the federal level. Eventually, only one was moved. One or two who were pro-Mahathir failed to gain nomination, the most conspicuous being controversial former Selangor Mentri Besar Muhammad Muhammad Taib. (Mahathir himself opted not to stand, but ran the BN campaign in the important northern Kedah state.) Few of those commonly suspected of being corrupt were excluded, with the obvious exception of Tan Sri Kasitah Gadam.

One clear difference from earlier elections was an increase in the number of Islamic figures, a move designed to outflank PAS. Most were not traditional UMNO Islamic leaders, but high-profile public figures. Five or six parliamentary candidates came from this background, most notably the *imam* of the national mosque, Datuk Pirdaus Ismail, and the young personable university lecturer and television personality, Datuk Dr Mashitah Ibrahim.

Traditionally, the head of the BN has a final say on all candidates. Mahathir used this power in the past and Abdullah was quick to claim a similar right. In practice, however, Abdullah deferred to state-level heads. In a departure from tradition, candidates were announced on a state-by-state basis, not by a national official.

Opposition parties mixed veterans with the young. PAS fielded a large number of professionals, including doctors, engineers, and lecturers, seeking to distance itself from accusations that it was a narrowly-religious party. It fielded an ex-general against Deputy Prime Minister (concurrently Defence Minister) Dato' Najib — one of several generals and senior civil servants who came out to endorse PAS in the lead up to the election. And it fielded ten women candidates, the same number as BN.

The Issues

The Malaysian media defined this election as giving a personal mandate to Abdullah, to overcome the now acknowledged shortcomings of Mahathir, particularly excessive corruption. It urged strong popular support since "the margin of victory will make a lot of difference to how far Abdullah will be able to take the nation on the path of stable growth with high standards of performance and accountability".[12] Abdullah was the centrepiece of a sustained media campaign. Government television repeatedly featured a four-minute special during the news entitled "Together with the Prime Minister" ("*Bersama* PM"), emphasising the conciliatory, almost saintly qualities of the man. A commercial had images of Abdullah and a voice-over by one Hj Mohamad Lajim Kurim lamenting the problems in Malaysia and imploring the electorate to "[p]lease look after this man who is looking after us. I ask this not for myself, I am already in my 70s. I ask this for the country."[13] Many of Malaysia's elite were reportedly moved to tears.

Continuing an emphasis apparent since the transfer of power, BN's campaign stressed two issues: Islam and anti-corruption. The government-controlled media highlighted Abdullah's personal Islamic credentials, and the selection of several prominent Muslim leaders as candidates reinforced his commitment to advancement of Islam. The official BN manifesto promised to introduce the teaching of the Quran for all Muslim students in state schools, while promoting "a progressive and modern Islam *hadhari*", a new concept that government leaders promised would be explained in the near future.

PAS sought to force Abdullah on the defensive by asking why he failed to lead prayers at his mother's recent funeral, questioning the behaviour of his wife (for not covering her head with a *tudong*) and riches acquired by his son, and asking him to state his position on the implementation of Islamic law (*Syariah*). Opposition parties also challenged Abdullah to resume payments to independent Islamic schools withdrawn by Mahathir, and linked the continued detention of alleged Muslim extremists (including a son of PAS spiritual leader and chief minister of Kelantan, Nik Aziz) under the ISA, with a lack of Islamic compassion.

Government leaders highlighted anti-corruption actions taken hitherto, and promised more to come. The message was the same to all communities, but reached its height in a full-page advertisement in Chinese newspapers saying that Malaysia had become "corrupt and rotten to the very core with no single aspect of life untouched by corruption". Abdullah, the advertisement continued, needed a strong mandate to address this.[14]

Opposition parties were quick to dismiss Abdullah's anti-corruption campaign as tokenism. They regretted the lack of any mention of corruption in the terms of reference for the Police Royal Commission. They argued that prominent personalities brought to court were no longer significant corporate or political players — Chia was a reclusive and ailing 71-year-old and Kasitah UMNO's least significant minister. The sums involved were relatively small and the RM76 million in Chia's case was an insignificant part of Perwaja's losses of over RM11 billion. They noted also that the charges involved alleged corruption in the 1990s, for cases that had been finalised by the Anti-Corruption Agency years ago, and could have been pursued at any time, but Abdullah chose to do this just before an election.

The issue of injustice against Anwar Ibrahim was again part of the Opposition's campaign, with pictures of his infamous black eye featured prominently. But it was a much less influential issue this time, partly because time had dulled sensitivities, and partly because, unlike Mahathir, Abdullah refused to go on the offensive against Anwar.

Both sides campaigned on their records — BN for bringing development and maintaining communal harmony; PAS on its promotion of Islam in Kelantan and Terengganu. BN warned that the Opposition threatened violence. Non-Malays were warned that a vote for the Opposition could result in a Taliban-style Islamic system, while Malays were told it represented support for the pro-Chinese DAP. Opposition parties also criticised the absence of democracy, transparency, and independence for government institutions and the judiciary.

Electoral Politics

Traditionally, the "three Ms" — media, money and machinery — are the key determinants of Malaysian elections, not issues. (It used to be the "four Ms", before Mahathir retired.) The BN controls all television and radio stations and all major newspapers, either through its control of government or party ownership. It uses this control to sell the virtues of the BN and to denigrate the Opposition. An independent voice does exist in the form of the on-line newspaper *Malaysiakini*. Some opposition parties and NGOs also have their own publications on the internet and/or in hard copy. But such publications cannot reach a wide audience.

Money is a key component for any electoral campaign. According to well-honed practice, just before elections, the BN arranges for the government to spend millions on fixing immediate village problems, such as repairs to schools, roads, water and electricity utilities, and the like. Thousands of people need to be employed to assist with campaigning — camping out in the villages to win over the opposition electorate, erecting information booths, bringing voters to the polling station, and putting up flags and posters. Large amounts of election material must be purchased, including flags and posters, T-shirts, and the like. (Three months after the election, at least RM100 million worth of National Front election paraphernalia had not been paid for.[15]) In some cases, "donations" are made directly to voters.

Machinery is perhaps the most important ingredient of all. In part this refers to party organisation. UMNO and its partners in the BN have more experience in mobilising voters than other parties. And UMNO went into these elections desperate to regain ground and strengthened by a new Women's Youth wing (Puteri UMNO), perhaps the most successful of UMNO reforms after the 1999 debacle.

But the BN was also able to achieve much more than it could acting alone by utilising a wide range of government organisations. Traditionally, the EC has acted in a range of ways so as to assist the government, and it did so very conspicuously this time (see the next section). The Information Ministry acts in a manner designed to spread the BN message — a partisan role that was underlined when it held a dinner to celebrate the BN election win.[16] Security agencies, particularly the police, often make life difficult for the Opposition, while facilitating campaigning by the BN. In 2004, the district officer in Abdullah's constituency even assisted by compiling and distributing a book detailing the life and contributions of the prime minister.

Amongst the Opposition, PAS has the most sophisticated electoral machinery. However, to many observers and some party officials, PAS approached this election over-confidently, expecting that the 1999 gains would without effort be replicated this time round.

EC Oversight

The most controversial aspect of the 2004 election campaign was its management by the EC. The election was the most disorganised and contested ever. In some cases, this may simply have reflected incompetence, but EC activities frequently provided direct benefits to the BN, as they had in the revisions of electoral boundaries and membership of the electoral roll. Some of the highlights were:

- On 4 March, the EC chair Tan Sri Abdul Rashid Abdul Rahman announced that three of Keadilan's top leaders would not be able to stand because they had court convictions. But all three were appealing their sentence, and as recently as 23 October 2003, Abdul Rashid had declared that "an election candidate sentenced to more than a year in jail and RM2,000 fine can still contest if the candidate is allowed a stay of execution pending appeal".[17]
- The EC then announced the shortest campaign period ever of eight days. Critics were convinced that this reflected the government's bidding. Aliran commented: "When the EC rushed to hold the

election in the shortest possible time, it is clearly meant to favour the BN and put the Opposition and the independents in a quandary ... There is hardly any time to print posters and prepare banners and other election paraphernalia. The BN's arsenal of armoury is already in full swing because they are the ones who knew the timing of the election."[18]

- Polling stations were not announced until the day before elections. Many voters went to their usual station and found they had been registered elsewhere.
- Contrary to the electoral law, the EC announced two days before voting (19 March) that party-run information booths would be permitted just outside polling stations. The BN had already constructed theirs, while the Opposition had no time to do so.
- Numerous opposition reports cite instances of the EC (and police) turning a blind eye to BN illegalities, while closely policing the Opposition (for example, by insisting that only the party flag of any opposition candidate be flown, while never requiring this of UMNO, which technically had to be represented by the BN flag).[19]
- The EC provided the BN with names and addresses of 600,000 voters registered in constituencies outside their place of residence, enabling the prime minister to write a moving personal letter urging them to vote and have a safe journey.
- The EC claimed to have gazetted all voters on 3 April, but the lists provided to political parties cited gazetting on various dates, including 15 March, 16 March, and in one case 23 March. Moreover, these lists were not identical, nor were they provided to political parties. Some voters went to polling stations and found that their names were not on the list held by the EC but on the list held by the BN.[20]
- In Selangor, the EC extended the voting for a further two hours, though this was against the electoral law. According to the BA, "this was not done in writing or supported by a proper and authorised document but was merely conveyed by phone or SMS to the returning officers on duty, or in some cases through the police personnel at the centres via walkie-talkie. In most cases, the extension was conveyed close to [the closing time of] 5.00 pm and in some a few minutes after 5.00 pm."[21]

- On election day, thousands went to vote and found that their names were not on the list, or that they had been registered elsewhere. Keadilan claimed that, at a conservative estimate, 500,000 were denied the right to vote, 250,000 in Selangor alone.[22] In one electorate the wrong party symbol was used, causing the EC to order a re-election. Even the pro-government *New Straits Times* lamented that: "The Election Commission's handling of some constituencies in Sunday's election caused embarrassment to anyone with any faith in Malaysian democracy."[23]

- When election results began to appear on the EC website from the eve of 21 March, many of the results were greeted with incredulity. In the Kuala Terengganu parliament seat, 98.7 per cent were recorded as having voted. This constituency also recorded 10,254 "unreturned" ballots, while unreturned ballots for the constituency's state seats — which should have been similar — amounted to only 124. A total of 17,960 ballots, or 57.5 per cent, were recorded as unreturned in the Kuala Selangor parliamentary seat. And for the state seat of Pangkor in Perak, a total of 5,108 ballots were recorded as unreturned out of the 6,712 issued. When these discrepancies were pointed out in *Malaysiakini*,[24] the figures suddenly disappeared to be replaced by new ones. Even so, the EC chair said in mid-April that more than 67,000 postal votes, 35,190 for parliamentary seats, and 31,984 for states, had gone missing. This represented 17.53 per cent and 15.4 per cent, respectively, of a total of 200,712 postal ballots issued.

- Besides such anomalies, voting figures in areas that have generally favoured the Opposition were abnormally high. The increase in voter turnout in Terengganu, for example, by nearly 6 per cent at the federal level and 7 per cent for the state, to 85.5 per cent and 86.9 per cent respectively, is particularly difficult to understand in an election where overall voter turnout only just exceeded that of 1999. Such levels had never been achieved in the past.

In the face of very broad concern over EC activities, its chairman proposed an independent inquiry into EC conduct. Prime Minister Abdullah quickly rejected this, telling the EC to conduct its own internal inquiry.

Results

As noted at the beginning of this chapter, the election results in terms of parliamentary seats was the best BN had ever achieved. It also gained 64 per cent of the voter support, just below the previous best of 65 per cent in 1995, and indeed this may understate support since 13 seats were won on the day of nomination without a contest. Particularly unexpected was the substantial inroads made into opposition strongholds, most notably in Terengganu. In addition, the growing middle-class around areas such as Kuala Lumpur and Penang demonstrated its volatility by swinging sharply back to the government for economic benefit this time, though of course many of its members were non-Malays who had been led back to the BN by the events of September 11.

Nonetheless, as far as the Malay electorate is concerned, it was not the overwhelming UMNO victory many claimed. Even EC figures put PAS support at slightly above its record 1999 result (see Table 6.1). Its total vote went from 1,056,110 to 996,437. In absolute terms, it maintained its support in most of the northern states, though UMNO increased its number of votes. The inclusion of Sabah and Sarawak in these figures causes a slight statistical aberration, but on the Peninsula, it virtually maintained its percentage of votes (from 17.4 per cent to 17.1 per cent). A study of 22 constituencies in which Malays represented over 90 per cent of the voters found both UMNO and PAS very much on level terms: 50.7 per cent UMNO and 49.3 per cent for PAS. In terms of seats, however, this translated into 16 for UMNO and six for PAS.[25]

These figures do need to be qualified. PAS contested 21 extra seats and may have had greater leverage within the BA to select more favourable constituencies. However, the significance of the former should not be exaggerated in an election that had 26 extra seats. Moreover, 13 of the new PAS seats were in Johore, Perak, and Pahang and resulted in only 20,893 additional votes. In its heartland, PAS's parliamentary vote was almost as high as 1999.

Keadilan suffered a more significant decline, down from 12.3 per cent to 8.9 per cent on the Peninsula. But this decline was probably largely attributable to a smaller non-Malay vote. The party's votes decreased particularly in states with a large population of non-Malays, but remained strong in predominantly-Malay Kedah.

On the Peninsula, BN's vote increased by about 8.4 per cent, but only 3.7 per cent of this was at the expense of the Malay Opposition. The predominantly Chinese DAP also declined 3.5 per cent, despite increasing its seats by two.

Implications

The result was nonetheless a strong endorsement of UMNO and a personal triumph for Abdullah. How much of this was due to Abdullah's own attributes, or simply the departure of Mahathir, is open to conjecture. But Abdullah was the centrepiece of the BN campaign and in charge of Terengganu state where coalition gains were the most remarkable. He increased the majority of his personal vote from 11,175 to 18,122, brushing aside an image as an accidental prime minister.

The victory strengthened Abdullah's hand before UMNO elections in late September, ensuring he was nominated unopposed to the party presidency. Nonetheless, UMNO's success at these elections strengthened different factions in the party. Among those who gained was his deputy, Dato' Najib, who many see as a future rival; his winning margin soared stratospherically from 241 to 22,922. And electoral success has never guaranteed UMNO leaders a dominant position over the party. The September party elections were described as "shocking" by the establishment media, when Abdullah failed to get key supporters elected to top party posts, and a majority fell to allies of former Prime Minister Mahathir and Najib.

The controversial and contested nature of the election did, howover, cast a shadow over Abdullah's victory. No one doubts that the BN had majority support, but the actions of the EC caused uncertainty over the real extent of the victory. The subsequent "deal" between UMNO and PAS, whereby both sides dropped election appeals against the other in Kelantan, Terengganu, and Kedah, and agreed to accept the status quo (except for one extra parliamentary seat going to UMNO), is perhaps an illustration of how UMNO was weakened by electoral controversy. On balance, the deal seemed to favour PAS, confirming its three-seat win in the Kelantan assembly, which many believed would have been overturned in UMNO's favour were it left to the courts.

Abdullah would also have been disappointed that, despite a decline in seats, PAS and Keadilan virtually maintained their share of the Malay vote. This leaves work to do if he is to overcome the polarisation of the Malay society started by Mahathir's sacking of Anwar in 1998, and revealed starkly in the 1999 election.

Nonetheless, the Opposition did receive a major setback. PAS has experienced such fortunes before — in 1986 it won only one parliamentary seat — and accepted the result calmly. Since the death of Fadzil Nor, it has had difficulty reconciling professionals, who joined or became active during the *reformasi* period, with traditional Islamic leaders (*ulama*). Resolution of this issue, which also pits some *ulama* on the side of the professionals against the traditionalists, is crucial if PAS is to re-emerge as a credible challenge to UMNO. To its credit, PAS is debating the issue openly, and not simply blaming defeat on an unequal electoral playing field.

With only one parliamentary seat, Keadilan seemed unlikely to survive beyond the current parliament, representing the failure of yet another attempt to promote a non-communal alternative to the communally-based BN. The unexpected release from prison of Anwar Ibrahim on 2 September 2004 has, however, given it a chance to revive its fortunes.

The DAP will return to a familiar role as leader of the Opposition. Despite a decline in its popular vote, it made some gains from two additional seats and the re-election of veteran leaders, in particular, party elder statesman, Lim Kit Siang. At the same time, however, this puts further obstacles in the path of rejuvenating the party and broadening its basis of support.

From a broader perspective, the election results may well prove an obstacle to the reforms that Abdullah has promised. Democracy was not enhanced by the election process. It will likely suffer from the polarisation of a Malay-led government with a Chinese-led opposition. The decimation of the Opposition will reduce the importance of parliament. And indeed the size of Abdullah's victory after years of deterioration in areas such as democracy, human rights, justice, and transparency may reinforce the notion that toughing it out rather than reform is the best policy. Similarly, a tiny opposition will reduce Abdullah's leverage to act against corruption. And in the post-September 11 era, no foreign pressures will be mounted on such issues — Malaysia's cooperation in the war on terror is too important for that.

Finally, the implications for Islamic issues may be more problematic than the expectations of the international media. Abdullah's own moderation on such matters are not in question. Nonetheless, what UMNO did in the election campaign was to try and outbid PAS, not promote secularism. Recent Malaysian history has shown that attempts by either UMNO or PAS to outbid the other have pushed Malaysia steadily towards a more conservative Islam.

NOTES

1. *The Star* (Malaysia), 24 March 2004.

2. *The Australian*, 23 March 2004.

3. *Christian Science Monitor*, 24 March 2004.

4. The ministers were Datuk Dr Abdul Hamid Othman, minister responsible for Islamic affairs in the Office of the Prime Minister; Datuk Seri Megat Junid Megat Ayub, internal trade and consumer affairs; Datuk Mustapa Mohamad, second finance minister and minister for entrepreneur development; Datuk Annuar Musa, rural development. The deputy ministers were Datuk Ibrahim Ali, Office of the Prime Minister; Datuk Dr Ibrahim Saad, transportation; Abu Bakar Daud, science, technology and environment; Dr Tengku Mahmud, agriculture; and Idrus Jusoh, entrepreneur development.

5. *Suara PKM* (Malaysia), September 2004, p. 2.

6. *The Star* (Malaysia), 27 February 2004.

7. This was so complicated that BN candidates were issued with a 74-page "Election Manual for BN Candidates". *New Straits Times* (Malaysia), 13 March 2004.

8. *New Straits Times* (Malaysia), 30 January 2004.

9. The EC never published cumulative figures on enrolment, but its secretary announced in January 2004 that nearly 400,000 had been enrolled in 2003 (*New Straits Times* (Malaysia), 3 January 2004). Enrolment is not compulsory, but around 80 per cent of those eligible do, so with the secretary estimating 350,000 Malaysian reaching voting age each year, an estimate of 1,200,000 new registrations should be conservative.

10. Speech delivered at a forum — *General Election 2004: Democracy and You*, jointly organised by the Penang Office for Human Development and Aliran on 18 March 2004. The speech was featured in "Malaysian General Election 2004 Special", *Aliran Monthly*.

11. Ibid.

12. *New Straits Times* (Malaysia), 14 March 2004.

13. *New Straits Times* (Malaysia), 19 March 2004.

14. Lim Kit Siang, "Call on Abdullah to ensure that the Special Code of Ethics for ministers includes their public declaration of assets and those of their next-of-kin or he will spark a second round of nation-wide disappointment over his pledge for a clean and incorruptible government after the 2004 general election", media statement, 2 April 2004

15. "BN Owes Us RM100m for Poll Merchandise, Claim Firms", *Malaysiakini*, 7 July 2004.

16. "Ministry Celebrates BN Win", *Bernama* (Malaysia), 29 April 2004.

17. *Utusan Express* (Malaysia), 5 March 2004.

18. "The Election Commission is Not Free and Fair", Aliran press statement, 10 March 2004.

19. See, for example, Raja Petra Kamarudin, "An Uneven Playing Field, the Putrajaya Experience", *Harakah* (Malaysia), 17 March, and several other reports on campaigning in the Putrajaya electorate by the author on the "Free Anwar Campaign" website.

20. See, for example, "Malaysia's Recently Concluded 11th General Election Can Be Deemed Illegal", Barisan Alternatif media release, 14 April 2004.

21. Ibid.

22. "Application for Judicial Review Filed Against Election Commission", *Malaysiakini*, 29 April 2004.

23. *New Straits Times* (Malaysia), 23 March 2004.

24. "Massive Gaps in EC's Ballot Figures", *Malaysiakini*, 25 March 2004.

25. Marzuki Mohamad, "2004 General Election: ABIM and the New Politics of Fragmentation" (unpublished).

7

UMNO and BN in the 2004 Election: The Political Culture of Complex Identities

ZAINAL KLING

Introduction

This chapter focuses on the pattern of the relationship between United Malays' National Organisation (UMNO) and its partners in the Barisan Nasional (National Front, or BN) and the factors regulating their relationship especially in the context of the 2004 general election. The pattern of the relationship and the fundamental factors affecting them provide insights into the dynamics of power relations between the political parties. These patterns and factors affect the general perception of actors within the complex grouping, and the manner by which each component group and its internal constitution would perceive its own role and identity, and, in turn, how they would react towards each other and towards the outside world. With each component upholding its fundamental objective of existence, which is perpetuating the group identity, their interactions will inevitably generate tension, rivalry, and a certain degree of conflict. In the long run, a political culture sustaining the group cohesion will emerge. To maintain and perpetuate the complex grouping, each component would always have to make adjustments between the idealism of its subjective demands and the reality of group cohesion. The interplay of such adjustments is reflected in the complex web of inter-group and interpersonal identity maintenance and cohesive relationships among members. In the long run, the relationships would allow the sedimentation of the pattern within which the identities are maintained and interactions carried out. The case of the Malaysian elections, specifically the recent 2004 general election, provides us with an insight into the perpetuation of the culture of complex identities.

The March 2004 Malaysian general election is a historic event viewed in the light of the leadership of the new Malaysian prime minister, Abdullah Ahmad Badawi. Not only is the prime minister new to his post, but to call an early election and emerge victorious can be considered a personal triumph. With more than four-fifths of BN candidates returned (198 out of 219) and an increase in the popular vote of 64 per cent as opposed to 55 per cent in 1999, it completely debunked the euphoria of anti-UMNO/BN largely displayed by many analysts of the 1999 general election.[1] With some writers already quick in calling the 1999 election as "new politics in Malaysia", even governments outside of Malaysia were already in dialogue with the Pan Malaysian Islamic Party (PAS) leadership on possible future relationships in the face of BN possible demise as a government.[2] The 2004 election has therefore surprised many observers and analysts when the rate of swing was almost unthinkable.

Inevitably, the 2004 results also aroused the suppressed jubilation of the ruling coalition which at that time, seemed to verge on mocking the Opposition with grandiose headlines and comments in the press calling it the "Abdullah tsunami", "resounding 'yes'", and "blue waves demolishing opposition". The results indeed completely reversed the faltering position of the BN in 1999 and has attracted a great deal of analyses on the underlying reasons for the unexpected failure of PAS and the Barisan Alternatif (BA, or Alternative Front) as well as the achievement of Abdullah, UMNO, and BN. Several analyses have focused on the fatal conditions of PAS, Keadilan, and the Democratic Action Party (DAP) before and after the election while simultaneously accusing the BN government of electoral misconducts, much of which were seemingly based on rumours and unproven accusations. Unfortunately, this time round, the Election Commission had done a very messy job of running the election that resulted in several electoral inadequacies even though the entire electoral operation was generally accepted as fair and clean. This eventually cast some doubts on the results.

While the Opposition weaknesses contributed to their dismal performance, several factors related to the operation and functioning of the ruling parties in the run up to the election must be closely and objectively examined in order to fully understand BN's electoral success. The analysis here is mostly ethnographic, and describes observable situations and relates the larger issues with the general outcome of the recent election. Factors such as the personal appeal of the leadership, historical and current situations of the political parties, and other underlying dynamics are argued to have played crucial roles in the overall outcome of the election. The author would like to focus on the seemingly cohesive nature of the BN components prior to the election as the major contributing factor in the rout of the Opposition. This must take into consideration a deeply historical view of inter-party interactions among BN members, for history provides a better guide to understanding much of political behaviour.

Outwardly, the personal appeal of Abdullah Badawi seemed to have a kind of counter-balancing and harmonising effect on the mind of the general electorate.[3] The more amicable and gentle personality displayed by him is a contrast to the more combative Dr Mahathir. A genial and more compromising Abdullah seemed to sooth many feelings and lightened the general mood. At the same time, the BN generally and most of the component parties in particular displayed a great deal of internal cohesiveness to face the election. This is not to claim that there was no friction within the BN coalition which was evident within Parti Bangsa Dayak Sarawak (PBDS), Sarawak National Party (SNAP), Malaysian Chinese Association (MCA), and even UMNO prior to nomination and during the election itself. Nonetheless, more than the Opposition parties such as Keadilan and PAS could have achieved, the BN components displayed greater stability and general cohesion. Above all, the intense utilisation of all the known strategies of mobilising and forming public opinion by the BN, and UMNO especially, by building upon the personality icon and traits of Abdullah seemed to assure the voters of the commitment of their chosen leaders and the need to provide an overwhelming mandate for them. A resounding victory to Abdullah, UMNO, and the BN was called for to ensure the continued prosperity for Malaysia as "never been seen before".

An analysis of the strategies of UMNO and the BN components in the conduct of the election would clarify several contentious issues related to both their victory and the failure of the Opposition. Given the general perception that UMNO has always played the dominant role in the complex relationship of the BN coalition, the focus must be on understanding the determining factor underlying the dynamics of power interplay between component members during the election as well as throughout its history from the early 1970s. After more than three decades of cooperation and working together, sharing power among their leaders, a situation frequently described as "consociationalism" inspite of its departure from the ideal proposed by Arend Lijphart,[4] there seems to be a commonly-accepted formula of cooperation between them. For example, the method of seat allocation seemed to have found consensus among members so much so that they have generally managed to avoid open inter-party challenges, clashes, and disagreements for the sake of the common victory. This is especially true during the last election when all the component party leaders were each, as usual, consulted with regards to the number of candidates to be fielded. Everyone expressed general satisfaction with the formula of allocation even if some leaders did qualify their statement, a situation one commentator described as a "paragon of political stability".[5]

Officially formed in June 1974 by the second prime minister, Tun Abdul Razak, in an attempt to avoid too much politicking within the Malaysian political contestation and to achieve consensus on national development and progress, the BN has been in existence for the last three decades since the formation of the UMNO-MCA alliance which contested the first municipal election in 1952 and later the UMNO-MCA-MIC alliance of 1954 to contest the first Malayan general election in 1955. Looking through the entire history of the alliance and coalition since then, the dynamics of power relationships can be understood as a kind of long-term inter-group adjustment among political groups working closely together in power contestations.

Historical Consciousness

It is this dynamics of power contestations that characterised the ebb and flow of leadership and elite circulation among the racial groups in contact. Grounded in somewhat dissimilar perspectives of history and group positioning within the entire political spectrum, the early attempt at cooperation in the form of the Alliance was arguably driven principally by a superficial but common motive of achieving *merdeka*, an objective already clearly enunciated by at least the Malay and Chinese groups long before Malaysia's independence. Whether in the form of communist insurgency or Malay nationalism, each of them spelled out a deep-seated struggle to liberate the country and the "nation" from the colonial yoke. Nevertheless, the pre-war British colonial situation was one of global dominance in many of the colonised territories. The British did not entertain demands for independence until its defeat in the eastern war theater during World War II at the hands of the Japanese.

It was this possibility of defeat that fired the nationalistic imagination in many colonised territories to demand or fight for national independence. Similar conditions seemed to have driven the Malays to talk of *merdeka* during pre-war days but especially more so after the Malayan Union. It was a project and a deliberate attempt by the British to betray and deprive them of their legal right and historical standing as the recognised ruling nation of the Malayan states within the provision of a series of formal treaties entered between them and Malay rulers since the Pangkor Treaty in 1874. With much coercion and threat to the Malay rulers to relinquish their sovereignty, the Malayan Union was proclaimed immediately after the war. The Malays reacted with emotional uproar and immediately and unanimously rejected the Union. This eventually led to the birth of UMNO. A sleepy nation was aroused into action to make a stand against the dictate of a global power and to reclaim their rightful status and sovereignty over their own country. Since then the Malay mind and psyche has been galvanised into an almost monolithic drive to safeguard sovereignty, defend unity, and lately, promote development as the basis of survival within a multi-ethnic nation-state and an open globalised world.

The Malay perception of sovereignty completely differentiated them from the ideology behind the Communist, anti-colonial stand during the pre-war period. Since the early 20th century, the Malays have already discussed and reviewed their impoverished and weak standard of living *vis-à-vis* other races, especially the Chinese, in the context of colonialism.[6] They were already aware of the threat to their sovereignty and the related consequences of poverty. There was also a reliance on the integrity of the British as the "protector" of Malay sovereignty within the perception of being a "protectorate" in the treaties signed with the various Malay Sultans of the Malayan states. In that context, it is wrong to regard British attitude and policies as being "pro-Malay" since the British were administrating on behalf of the Malay rulers. While British intervention was already beyond mere protection and on the verge of colonisation, the Malays still regarded the British as protectors.[7]

The Communists were largely alien as they were focused on their own nationalistic ambition, reflected in their opposition to the invasion of China by the Japanese, beginning with Manchuria and the rest of China in 1937. Anti-British movements and insurgencies and the eventual Chinese support of the anti-Japanese movement during and after the war was an extension of this alien nationalism. They cannot be equated with Malay national consciousness since the former was related to territorial sovereignty based on legal and historical claim, while the latter is as good as colonisation by an alien ideological force over the Malayan states. This situation became the single most important factor that shaped and galvanised the mind and psyche of the Malays in general and the UMNO ideology particularly when they unexpectedly rose against the British who had long regarded them as nothing more than ignorant, lazy, and treacherous natives.

The immediate post-war experience of the bleak and bloody weeks prior to the establishment of the British Military Administration (BMA) in September 1945 when the Communist assumed power in most Malayan townships and effected revenge against the Malays for what they perceived as the Malay wartime collaboration with the Japanese, gelled into deep suspicion and hatred of the Chinese, as reflected in clashes that followed. This and other events in later years, which led to many inter-racial clashes even in recent times, were part of the manifestation of the Malay fear and deep suspicion of the "alien" intention in their country and over their sovereignty. The fact that they eventually rose and fought against the Malayan Union, which was meant to reward the Chinese for their wartime efforts, became the cornerstone of their historical struggle to ensure continuity and perpetuity of that sovereignty. It was almost akin to a political "amok" for them to realise that they have been deprived of their rightful territorial claim merely because they have been accused of not being anti-Japanese and betraying the British to the detriment of British colonial power, sentiment, and pride.

To the Malays, both the British and the Japanese were colonials. Inspite of the suffering experienced by other races during the Japanese occupation, the Malays were promised freedom after the war and saw this possibility with the defeat of the British. The Japanese occupation and the imposition of an alien agenda on their sovereignty shaped the Malay mind and their perception of politics and political power in relation to "others". The fact that UMNO was the most important political party to fight for and assume the protection of Malay rights since the Malayan Union debacle, has implanted in the Malay mind the singular role of UMNO as the only reliable Malay party. To its advantage, UMNO has replayed and manipulated this tune. While the 1999 election has somewhat challenged this perception, PAS nevertheless remained very cautious and sceptical of their ability to encroached into the "Malay sovereignty" mind. PAS challenge to this "sovereignty", through its concept of the universal Islamic state, has been regarded as a deviation from the Malay cause and were accused of "betrayal" especially when they embraced the DAP in the BA alliance, which has clearly and openly rejected the Malay claim of sovereignty and primacy in their concept of "Malaysian Malaysia". To a certain extent, UMNO has also manipulated and countered an earlier accusation by PAS of UMNO being *kaffir* (infidels) for having shared their power with the MCA and Malaysian Indian Congress (MIC) now that they are involved in an identical coalition.

This deep-seated historical pattern constituting the Malay psyche generally and UMNO in particular became a dynamic force in shaping the interaction of UMNO with the various political parties within the

BN. Dato' Onn bin Ja'afar relied heavily on the Malay sense of historical justice when he rallied Malays to unite and persuaded them to reject and oppose the Malayan Union in his campaign across the country, and finally formed UMNO in the palace of the Johore Sultan[8] on 1 March 1946. Tunku Abdul Rahman has been regarded as more liberal, yet his reliance on history was unmistakable during the period of challenges from the People's Action Party (PAP) in the Malaysian parliament early in Malaysian history and even in later years.[9] This dynamic was followed even more consciously by Tun Abdul Razak and subsequent Malay leaders and UMNO.[10]

In this respect, much of the political analyses have also been slow to explain and clarify several issues relating to fluctuations in the relationship between UMNO, BN and the components of the BA. While current factors have an immediate effect in swaying public opinion especially during election campaigns, yet collective memories of past events and ideological and historical causes have a significant impact on the electoral outcome — history frequently plays a very significant role in the strategies and manipulation of campaign issues. The 1969 Kuala Lumpur riot has become the bedrock of reminders and emotional orchestration during election campaigns ever since its occurrence to this day. History is the spectre of influence in the oscillation of perception determining many political choices. In the Malaysian political dynamics, this point must always be taken into consideration to understand the mind of inter-party and inter-racial players.

Another significant element to be considered for a more meaningful assessment of Malaysia's future, specifically that of the relationship of UMNO and BN under the new leadership of Abdullah Ahmad Badawi, is the legacy of Dr Mahathir whose image and rule[11] cast a huge shadow on the possible method of administration by Abdullah. Perhaps it is still too early to observe and understand the impact of the Mahathir legacy and the probable achievement of Abdullah's administration as it has only been a year since his ascendancy. While policies and intentions have already been stated and generally spelled out as one of continuity from preceding policy statements, yet subtle changes or modifications have already been put in place. A number of so-called mega-projects have been discontinued, corruption has become the biggest target, and administrative integrity and personal responsibility have been stressed. However, at this juncture, they are at best rhetoric and perhaps empty promises. Observers are still in doubt and waiting for concrete evidence of, for instance, tackling corruption and inefficiency within the government. A minister in the Prime Minister's Office has commented on high profile cases that have yet to be indicted in court.[12] Several cases of shoddy public works by contractors have been ear-marked for blacklisting and legal indemnity for uncompleted construction projects.

The short time frame since Abdullah assumed the role of prime minister, therefore, does not do justice to the analysis of the political culture animating Abdullah's leadership especially in relation to the influence he might have on inter-party interaction within the BN and the entire Malaysian political culture. Nevertheless, his involvement in politics for more than two decades would already provide ample indication of the probable steps he may take in the future.[13]

Inevitably also, in order to counter-balance the lack of depth as a result of the short time frame of Abdullah's administration, a broader and more longitudinal analysis that examines a period spanning several leaders than the current leadership alone is needed. Although the 2004 election results will demonstrate certain conditions and trends of voting behaviour and inter-group political dynamics, they do not make up the total consequence or a functional inter-play of the current political climate. The author believes that other significant factors have been influenced by historical variables which have been sharply mobilised to achieve political victory and justification for the exercise of options and choices within the complex interactions of constituting groups in the BN. The length of history studied may not be necessarily lengthy. Even the conventional practices of the last four decades since the emergence of the Alliance and the BN coalition would suffice to justify the basis of current decisions. It may be presumed that such a practice must have been cited in order to achieve the kind of smooth acceptance of political consensus on the allocation of seats to candidates during the recent election.

The Mahathir Legacy

The Mahathir administration in Malaysia was phenomenal. After more than two decades, Dr Mahathir has, in the words of C. Kessler, "created a world in his own image, according to ideas and visions made possible yet also constrained, perhaps even foreshortened or distorted, by his own mental and intellectual horizons".[14] This "rule" has been called "personalised", "paradoxical", "semi-democratic", and "authoritarian" by critics. Yet it can be agreed that he left a tremendous legacy particularly in raising the Malay confidence through material and occupational achievements. To the Malays, he has been considered a guiding light, providing a strong vision for achieving possibilities unheard of in life. The job of running and developing the country into a recognisable global player necessitated the presence of a strong and visionary leader and like many of such leaders in developing countries, Mahathir was never absolutely regarded as an "authoritarian" by supporters, especially among his Malay supporters. Although there were opposing voices and accusations of Mahathir being *mahazalim* (very cruel) and "pharaohnic" (oppressive) mainly by the Opposition, his policies found favour with a forgiving general public. The perception was that he has been very *tegas* (steadfast and unfaltering), *berdisplin* (disciplinary), and *berani* (brave) in his mission of raising the *mertabat* (status) and *harkat* (dignity) of the nation. Businesses particularly favoured Dr Mahathir's policies as they were seen to support the general economic development and prosperity of the country. This was presumably one of the major contributing factors which provided electoral support for the BN in the 1999 election.[15] Undoubtedly, he has left a perpetual and indelible mark on the Malaysian political landscape and the psyche of Malaysians.

Of particular significance is his well-known visionary framework for future development initially known as "The Way Forward", later came to be popularly cited as *The Vision 2020*, which defined, in very general terms, the vision of a developed Malaysia for the next couple of decades. Prior to this, Dr Mahathir had implemented various policies and changes in all areas of administration such as the bureaucracy, judiciary, economy, politics and had even amended certain sections of the Constitution to achieve what he has personally visualised as the means towards achieving the goals of democracy and development. Until the final days of his prime ministership, he was still trying to put in place a new national school system to achieve his vision of a united Malaysia of the future. At the same time, he was still travelling to other countries within the

Organisation of Islamic Conferences (OIC) and Non-Aligned Movement (NAM) blocks to persuade others to put up a united front in facing the current realities of unipolar global politics of the US.

Mahathirism,[16] as some analysts would call it, has worked in ways that many Malaysians regarded as generally beneficial. It has laid down fundamental structures in the political, economic, socio-cultural, and religious domains. They have become the foundation of many areas of administration that any successor would find difficult to replace. For this reason, it is most significant that his successor, Abdullah Ahmad Badawi, when asked what his vision would be after the smooth handover of the country's leadership, replied unequivocally, "My vision for Malaysia is Vision 2020."[17] Perhaps Abdullah has other option to offer immediately after the transfer but to remain locked within the general framework of various Mahathirian policies and structures. It was very obvious that such a stance would only push him to an unprecedented situation of a weak leader, tied down and enmeshed within a network of existing policies and merely playing the role of an implementer.

Abdullah, however, did not wait long before spelling out his own brand of leadership by consulting and requesting from the people for a very strong mandate to continue with the development and growth of the country. He created a personal vision, seemingly tempered with deep-rooted ideas within the Islamic political traditions which was also considered to be a democratic and civil vision of the *siyyasah syariah* system, when he loudly proclaimed on his first arrival as prime minister at the Bayan Lepas airport, Penang, his home state: "This is my hope. I do not ask of you to work for me but work with me for the sake of the nation and country."[18] This utterance immediately became the slogan of the new government and the prime minister. Subsequently, when he decided to call for a general election on 15 March 2004, the call to "work with me" became the party's catch word which was eventually transformed into a political manifesto with "excellence, glory, and determination" (*cemerlang, gemilang, terbilang*) as the formula for moving beyond the Mahathirian glorious years.

The mood was, therefore, set for an open and more inclusive government by a very subtle but clear shift from the pervasiveness of the Mahathirian legacy. At once, a feeling of relief and unuttered easiness among all classes of people seemed to emerge now that "Pak Lah" (as he is dearly addressed) would be more answerable to the people. This was a deliberate change in style of leadership or "de-Mahathirisation" as some would call it, and certainly was a test of confidence of the people and willingness to provide a mandate in the general election.

Speculation was rife that an election would be called during 2003, just before the year end *Hajj* (pilgrimage) when many Muslims, presumably supporters of PAS, would be away. Previously, the Islamic party had challenged the venerable position of UMNO and the BN in the Malay heartland, and this caused some anxiety within the BN government for the upcoming election. The 1999 election results had quickly sent the massage that UMNO was already very vulnerable which was, to an extent, weakened by PAS's "green wave". The Malays and especially the younger generation were rejecting and abandoning their "protector" and their racial politics for more democratic and just political parties. Keadilan has emerged as a symbol of political participation of the youth following the exhortation of Anwar Ibrahim, the ex-deputy premier, who was taken to court for misuse of power and sexual misconduct by Mahathir and dismissed from the party and the government in late 1998. This presumably was a big mistake which finally found its fateful impact in the Malay heartland with the lost of Trengganu and the strengthening of PAS position in Kelantan and in all Malay majority states in the 1999 election. Keadilan therefore became an alternative party for Malays against the UMNO and BN racial politics.

UMNO's reaction was predictable. While PAS was seen as riding the crest of the Anwar wave of general dissatisfaction as well as manipulating religious issues in the name of Islamic religiosity and piety, there was a feeling of UMNO's loss of relevance to the Malay cause. Inspite of Mahathir's success in raising Malay dignity and economic well-being, he also seemed to have abandoned the rural Malays through an overemphasis on industrial development and sidelining cultural issues dear to Malays especially the replacement of Malay with English as the language of instruction of the sciences in schools. There was a feeling of general neglect by the Malays in favour of Chinese causes with the extension of private higher education, a reminder of the tightly-fought case of Merdeka University in 1987, and industrialisation which benefited mostly Chinese businesses and small-scale industries.

Keadilan, on the other hand, has been the focus of UMNO's public campaign within the context of traditional cultural and Islamic values. Keadilan has been accused of inculcating ungratefulness among the younger Malay professionals whose university education within and outside the country has been almost totally sponsored by the government. To forget the government's commitment towards their well-being is considered, to use the proverbial saying, *kachang lupakan kulit* — the ungrateful pods of peanuts. This ungrateful attitude was confounded by another accusation of gross disregard for the Islamic teaching of *syukur* (ever grateful to God). Such a teaching reflects the false claim of Anwar as an Islamic reformer who misled the youth. Destructive actions of Keadilan members during their demonstrations were portrayed as the work of deviants that justify much of the physical and legal actions taken against them during most of their protests.

UMNO regarded them as a threat of divisiveness towards Malay society which would open incisive opportunities for other "races" to split and weaken Malay unity. This was the view eventually taken by UMNO when the *Suqui* 83 demands were made during the 1999 election. While the Suqui demands, which questioned issues such as the granting of economic assistance solely to ethnic Malays, were not publicly well-known during the election, it was known in the newspapers after the election as something of a "hell break loose", and the uproar created was heated enough for Dr Mahathir, then prime minister, to retract whatever had been said much earlier and to decide that the demands were against the "social contract" of the Constitution. Since then, the idea of a social contract has come to the foreground as a reminder of the very basis for inter-party relationship in the BN. The perceived threat to Malay sovereignty made the demands unacceptable. This threat remains a sensitive issue and a challenge to Malay politics. This was the underlying fear that drove UMNO to undertake strategic action and mobilisation of opinion after the 1999 election debacle.

Given that the Malay votes were already fragmented and Malay unity was threatened, several strategic positions were undertaken by the BN to deny PAS of its Islamic content:

1. PAS was just another political party and not an Islamic party. UMNO highlighted several occasions where PAS leadership had uttered vulgar and distasteful remarks against UMNO defying Islamic teachings. Such remarks include calling fellow Muslims *kaffir* (infidels), *taghut* (idolaters), and "Yahudi" (jews), and allowing vulgar remarks by either Nik Aziz or Hadi Awang to be carried in mainstream newspapers, publicising their irreligious and uncalled for behaviour as *ulama* and pious political leaders. At the height of PAS's confidence, Nik Aziz even alluded to "working with Satan" if it could win them votes. Of course, he and Hadi Awang embraced DAP's party leader, Lim Keat Siang, during that period, but the latter eventually rejected PAS's "Islamic state" ideology. Even more serious were some of the blasphemous remarks by Nik Aziz in equating God with "gangsters" and attributing God with using vulgar words. This was a war of attrition with Dr Mahathir to win the spiritual heart of the Malays.

2. UMNO's tactic of equating a vote for PAS based on Islamic salvation as blasphemous. Throughout the years, PAS has been giving *ceramah* (speeches) either in open rallies, on their own premises, or in *surau* (prayer houses). Many of the *ceramah* were not rational analyses of the BN and UMNO government but jocular remarks on government personalities and programmes. Yet this appealed to the audience who were mainly PAS members from other districts who came to listen to the "latest jokes". Typical of these *ceramah* were those held at the party headquarters in Gombak, Kuala Lumpur. A common theme that normally runs through such speeches is that human beings would have to face God's judgment after death. The implication is that only PAS can help a Muslim attain salvation and therefore a vote for PAS is a ticket to salvation in the world of the dead (*alam barzah*). Presumably this campaign hit its mark among rural Muslims who gave them overwhelming votes in the Malay heartland. This promise of salvation was eventually used by the BN to demonised PAS of its blaspheme.

3. Denied PAS the use of *surau* (prayer houses) and mosques for

anti-government campaigns and restrict the circulation of its newspaper — *Harakah*. The *surau* and mosques are under the administration of religious departments and councils which by law are within the jurisdiction of the Sultan as head of state, who have often issued religious instructions to disallow anti-government speeches and *khutbah* (sermons). Members of the Committee of Administration of each prayer house were also threatened with dismissal for their discretion to allow such campaigns. When newspapers published the misdeeds of PAS, *surau* committees allowed anti-government campaigning and not religious sermons or teachings. When *Harakah* published news regarded as *fitnah* (slander, libel, and defamation), it was almost suspended. It was allowed to continue for the readership of its members and for weekly publication.

4. An attempt at reconciliation with PAS to preserve unity at the behest of Malay intellectuals. A call was made by several intellectuals for unity of Malays and for the leaderships to come together to air their common concern for Islam and the Malays instead of causing divisiveness among Malays. The attempt was met with unenthusiasm among PAS members who felt that they should not compromise with UMNO. UMNO on the other hand treated the idea with caution and apparently rehearsed the meeting which was videotaped. Eventually, nothing came out of the move except for an uneventful participation by Dr Mahathir and Fadzil Noor in a forum on Palestine. Nonetheless, the call reflected the common concern of various sectors in the Malay society concerning unity and its probable divisiveness. Similar efforts were undertaken earlier in the 1980s when disunity appeared on issues related to the amendment to the Constitution, deregistration of UMNO and the resignation of leaders from the government. Unity and its probable impact on sovereignty remained a major concern of the Malay community and UMNO.

The strategy adopted in relation to Keadilan was to portray it as a party lacking in real substance, and that their sole objective was to obtain a release for Anwar from impending court appearances and probable conviction. At the same time, internal squabbles among the leaders within Keadilan were fully highlighted to sow the seeds of dissatisfaction and incredulity among its supporters. The incessant attacks probably created, to a certain extent, internal dissent among senior leaders that eventually led to breakaways and resignations that weakened Keadilan considerably.

Simultaneously, a special government information agency was reorganised and given the specific task of clarifying government policies and action to the public especially the Malays. Year-long *ceramah* and courses were conducted in all states to convince the Malays of the efficacy of UMNO as their only hope for progress and development. A decade of non-development in Kelantan and probably Trengganu by the PAS government was cited as having only led them to poverty, underdevelopment, and stagnation. Developmentalism remained the major basis of the campaign for the Malay heart and mind in spite of rebuttals by PAS as a non-convincing issue. In Trengganu, the "blue wave" programme of *Islam Hadhari*, in contrast to PAS's "Islamic state" ideology, was introduced to spearhead the challenge and provide a modern conceptual alternative to PAS orthodoxy. Finally, Dr Mahathir made the daring declaration that Malaysia is already an Islamic state, thus, PAS's drive for an Islamic state was redundant. In this respect, PAS and Keadilan has had to constantly face the ruling government's actions both in tactical and legal terms throughout the inter-electoral years.

The non-Malays, on the other hand, were enticed to support UMNO through more liberal economic, political, cultural, and education policies and promises. Industrialisation and economic development have benefited Chinese businesses tremendously and contributed to their regained superiority in the share of the national economy. The degree of Chinese participation in Cabinet decision-making and power-sharing was increased and a channel to the prime minister was opened with the appointment of a Chinese political secretary in order to keep him informed of Chinese issues. Chinese cultural activities were encouraged and Chinese New Year celebrations were raised to that of a national celebration with the presence of the Yang di-Pertuan Agong. Private education was opened up, allowing for the Chinese to acquire educational qualifications. This was further relaxed with the granting of university status to their professional college, the Universiti Tunku Abdul Rahman. Finally, their demand for meritocracy in educational placement was implemented in all public universities and 10 per cent of the total seats were allocated to the Chinese in the Mara Junior Science College which was, up till then, exclusively for the Malays. Perhaps, in answer to many demands for equality, a subtle criticism of special rights and privileges accorded to the Malays was publicly made as a persistent reminder to the Malays not to depend so much on government assistance and to do away with a subsidy mentality. Therefore, several policy adjustments were tactical in winning non-Malay votes which, to some extent, determined the balance of power for the BN and UMNO in the election.

In reality, the BN and UMNO leadership were never demoralised after the 1999 election debacle, even with the lost of Trengganu. Dr Mahathir immediately launched several political steps to recover lost ground. These steps included blocking the distribution of royalty[19] of Petronas, the national oil company, to Trengganu, withdrawal of financial support for private religious schools which purportedly supported PAS, and proclaimed Malaysia as an Islamic state to outbid the PAS manifesto. A series of meetings with state *muftis* (highest religious authority) were organised to cajole them into making statements rebutting PAS pronouncements on religious matters. Seminars at national and international levels were also organised to defend the Islamic constitution of the government.

In addition, BN's achievements in Islamic development were highlighted frequently. Within the concept of social Islamic development or *fardhu kifayah*, the Islamic banking system, insurance (*takaful*), credit system, and pawn institutions were frequently highlighted as the crowning examples of Malaysia's Islamic governance. The Institute for Islamic Understanding Malaysia (IKIM) was tasked to deliberate on various issues from an Islamic perspective. A series of national seminars on "The Closing of Malay Mind" were organised to combat and win over the minds of staunch PAS supporters.

News *blitzkrieg* was undertaken to nullify PAS achievements. The government media machine constantly aired and reported on any shortcomings of the two states under PAS. There were reports of an increase in crime, cases of Muslims becoming apostates in Kelantan, increasing prostitution in Kelantan, poverty and declining employment, and Kelantan's dependence on remittances from their migrants who work in other states. Even television programmes were geared towards increasing viewership in the east coat states through *Salam Pantai Timur* ("Hello East Coast"). However, inspite of all these initiatives, there was still a great deal of uncertainty with regards the support of the Malays by the time Dr Mahathir announced his retirement in 2003. This did not help UMNO to prepare for the 2004 election. A series of by-elections in Negeri Sembilan, Pahang, and Kedah also did not fully reveal their political leanings.

September 11 contributed an unexpected gift to UMNO. It provided a moral legitimacy for the detention of several opposition members and pro-Islamic militants, some of whom were related to PAS leaders. It captured the imagination of the non-Malays who later rejected PAS and its support of the DAP. The DAP understood the implications and reminded PAS of the changing climate of opinion of the idea of an "Islamic state". However, PAS refused to budge on this issue and the DAP had no choice but to leave the BA which considerably weakened the fragile coalition of the BA. As the election drew near, Keadilan suffered defections from its senior leadership and eventually its survival was called into question. This whole situation contributed towards the failure of the Opposition as a whole to mount a concerted challenge to the BN.

Abdullah was very mindful of the public mood and understood the Malay issues well. In the 2003 UMNO annual general assembly, he addressed the delegates as well as the "the ordinary members who are not in our midst". He purposely mentioned the latter to emphasise that their interests were very much in his heart. He recognised that he needed a spectacular formula to win back the Malay vote which has been eroded to the extent that all the grassroots support was threatened with the possibility of having for the first time an Islamic government in power. The PAS euphoria was echoed everywhere even in neighbouring countries, and the PAS leadership began to allude to such a possibility with confidence.

By the time of the transfer of stewardship in October 2003, Abdullah knew he needed to gather the support of all the people behind him as a demonstration of his mandate to govern. At that time, his position was merely a shadow of an untested popularity without electoral legitimacy. More importantly, he needed to obtain the real support of the Malays which at its core is the foundation of UMNO.

During the inter-election years, especially after the move to modify the language policy and putting English as the medium of instruction for science subjects in primary schools in 2002, UMNO had been openly accused of abandoning the Malay cause. The refusal of Dr Mahathir to listen to the plea of Malay cultural organisations on this issue led many to accuse UMNO of abandoning Malay constitutional and cultural rights. Many formally left UMNO to join Keadilan and PAS. PAS tried to exploit the issue to the full which was considered contrary to universal Islamic ideology to identify totally with ethnic and sectarian cultural issues. Nevertheless, they organised a cultural show in Kota Bharu and dubbed it as the real Malay/Islamic cultural presentation.

While Abdullah understood and tried hard to diffuse the discontent, he made no move to undercut Dr Mahathir on the language issue. In his report to the prime minister after several meetings with various cultural groups including some of the more prominent associations such as Gapena, Peninsular Malay Students Federation (GPMS), Muslim Youth Movement of Malaysia (ABIM) and Malay teachers associations, he alluded to the general dissatisfaction of the Malays. In his typical mode of combative politics, Dr Mahathir accused the opposing groups as linguistic chauvinists and threatened them with the ISA. He dismissed the complaints as being unduly emotional and improper for the Malay race in the face of globalisation.

In summary, several outstanding major issues were already weighing heavily as legacy for the new prime minister. There seemed to be no honeymoon for him in the face of a threatening on-coming general election. The electorate was still vague and uncertain in its support. The threat of the Opposition winning the election was therefore real and it was probably already a situation of political quicksand, ready to suck the unmindful players.

Change and Continuity

The few months prior to and after the 2004 general election were certainly a period of stress and one of confidence-building for Abdullah after two decades of Mahathirian economic achievements. As part of the election promises, senior government officers and ex-CEOs of government-linked corporations (GLC) were allowed to be tried in court for breach of trust and corruption. Abdullah has been known as "Mr Clean". He needed to demonstrate a certain quality of steadfastness and resolve to muster support to face the major challenges in the coming election. He needed to make some radical changes while remaining outwardly supportive of existing policies. At least certain new emphases must be made to demonstrate the emergence of a new leadership with a clear mandate.

Two major points of contention were on his mind even before the power transfer: corruption and Islamic challenges. He has championed the move for a strong anti-corruption stance and closely related to that was the build up of an ethical base upon which the country must move forward and be able to handle the two international organisations which Malaysia is heading: the OIC and the NAM. Both moves are in fact part and parcel of a new political strategy that he was beginning to reveal. After his first Cabinet meeting, he announced the need to form what he called the National Integrity Plan "which is a comprehensive framework in which best practices, new mechanisms, committees and structures would be formalized and implemented to promote good governance, particularly within the public sector,"[20] and to build a Malaysian Institute for Integrity with the major function of collecting data on national integrity, continuous monitoring of the processes of corruption, and make policy recommendations to the government on how to increase national integrity. The Cabinet secretary began planning for both objectives and both programmes were launched on 23 April 2004.[21]

Then, on 3 December 2003, he proposed the setting up of the Anti-Corruption Academy for which the government allocated a sum of RM17 million. There were also sweeping actions initiated to clean local authorities of corrupt officials and place the tender system under a transparent and open system for interested bidders. He also began to take note of some of the salient comments made on the so-called mega-projects, most of which were approved earlier by Dr Mahathir. As a result he postponed the RM16 billion project of laying a double tract for the railways and restructuring the Bakun hydroelectric construction equity. This was part of the need to close the widening budget deficit of which he personally was not in favour as a mechanism of development.

Another major initiative was the formation of the Royal Commission for the Improvement of the Police Force in late December 2003. He gave the widest possible power to the commission to reassess the role of the force, its operating procedures, recruitment, and training practices. Its primary aim is to end brutality and graft within the ranks, while increasing professionalism and instilling a greater respect for human rights. For that purpose, two ex-lord presidents were selected, with one as chairman, together with several independent members including the more vociferous chairman of the Bar Council. It was certainly a very surprising move on his part. Being the minister of internal affairs, it would reflect his failure to whip the police force into a clean and efficient organisation and yet he was now proposing the set up of the commissions to overhaul the force thoroughly. This move was largely received favourably by the public.

Abdullah has therefore made several radical moves to achieve a clean and fair government early in his leadership which was also the objective of Mahathir when he took office in the middle of 1981 through the well-known slogan "*bersih, cekap, amanah*" (clean, efficient, trustworthy). There seemed to be a degree of continuity between the two leaders at least in their stated intentions. It was certainly received positively by concerned Malaysians and has been the benchmark of the new government. Inspite of the good intention, Mahathir's rule over the previous two decades have been marked by a number of financial and economic blunders, political turmoil, and more importantly, socio-cultural degeneration into the dark alleys of corruption.

Islamic Challenges

One of the major problems left behind by the Mahathir administration was the Islamic issue. Throughout its history, UMNO has always been troubled by the presence of PAS as an alternative Malay party. Although

UMNO has totally rejected the possibility of creating Malaysia as an Islamic state, the persistence of PAS to advocate it and question the legitimacy of UMNO as the party of Malays (being Muslims) occasionally touched a sensitive nerve within the party. As a result Tun Abdul Razak, the second prime minister and president of UMNO, incorporated PAS as part of a "Government of National Unity" which later became the BN in 1974. This lasted for a while until 1977 when PAS withdrew from the coalition largely due to the rivalry they had with UMNO in the state of Kelantan where PAS ruled. The federal government took over the administration of Kelantan when violent demonstrations and looting erupted in the state capital, Kota Bharu. This direct intervention enabled UMNO to capture Kelantan from PAS but created disunity among Malay supporters of both parties.

The 1970s were marked by the rise in Islamic revivalism around the world. Radical Muslim *dakwah* (missionary) groups appeared along with the more orthodox *Perkim* (*Persatuan Kebajikan Islam Malaysia*). They included urban middle-class groups and university students headed by UMNO leaders such as Sunusi Junid and a young student leader Anwar Ibrahim, the *Tabligh* movement as an off-shoot of the Indian sub-continental group, and the *Darul Arqam*, a mass movement of various memberships from professionals to small-time traders and university students. At the same time, a number of smaller groups emerged to demand a purer Islamic life and destroy "infidel symbols" by attacking Hindu temples as well as capturing police stations to demonstrate millenarian (*al-Mahdi*) revivalism. By the end of the 1970s, Iran broke in an influential fundamentalist Islamic revolution, overthrowing the Shah dynasty and becoming a source of inspiration for Muslims at large as a symbol of Islamic government. This inspired orthodox PAS *ulama* (religious leaders) to adopt a more radical stance for an Islamic state for Malaysia which only gelled into a more coherent formula two decades later, during Abdullah's premiership.

By the early 1980s, a new brand of radical Islam took over the PAS leadership under Dato' Asri Muda whose stance was more nationalistic, in line with UMNO. This new brand of Islam gave rise to young advocates such as Fadzil Noor and Haji Hadi Awang. They played the role of ideologists within PAS and began more open and scathing attacks on the lack of religiosity of UMNO, and thus increasing the rivalry and conflict within the Malay community. This culminated in the prescription by Hadi Awang in the late 1980s when he decried UMNO as *kaffir* (infidels) and that the blood of UMNO members were *halal* (permissible) to be shed. Since then, UMNO has viewed PAS as an enemy to be discredited if not destroyed. Attempts were presumably made to create a rift within the PAS leadership particularly between the more genial Nik Aziz, the *Tuan Guru* (religious teacher) and chairman of the Ulama Council, and Hadi Awang, the fire-brand president who replaced Fadzil Noor after his untimely death in 2003. Hadi Awang constantly came under attack for much of what he had to say. A column in the *Utusan Malaysia* newspaper devoted and constantly highlighted his shortcomings in Islamic affairs. In the end, he came to be seen as an arrogant leader who needed to be replaced.

Meanwhile, Dr Mahathir made his impact on the global stage by highlighting the modernity and moderateness of Islam in Malaysia inspite of his questionable labelling of the country as a "fundamentalist Islamic state", signalling a return to the true interpretation of Islam as a peaceful (*salam*) religion. A series of national and international seminars participated by well-known scholars were organised to support the contention. It was of course strongly criticised by PAS who rejected the contention. Nevertheless, UMNO continued with this strategy, after which the DAP came into the forefront as a strong Opposition which they tried to propagate in Ipoh.

On taking over the leadership, Abdullah's strategy in the face of the PAS threat and apparent popular appeal among the Malay peasants and new professionals, was to disassociate from the combative stance adopted by Mahathir. He was more approachable and avoided playing to the galley of the PAS leadership. Biting comments by Hadi on his role as *imam* in prayers was regarded as trivial. He was more concerned with the larger issue of providing a clear and imaginative alternative to PAS's "Islamic state" programme. Finally, he made his stand on Islam by redefining the civilisational role of Islam or *Islam Hadhari* as suggested by modern Islamic thinkers. He went even further to depict not only the historical role of Islam as a civilised ideology but, more importantly, on the modern role of creating harmony and peace with others in the face of very real challenges at the global level. As such he made it a key point to assert the civilising function of religion in his formulation of a strategy to face the challenge of the "Islamic state" by PAS. The publication of PAS's concept of the "Islamic state" in December 2003 provided the much needed bullet for his subtle attack on the Opposition's strategy and programmes which he dismissed as "anachronistic and outdated". Much of the formulation had already been achieved by UMNO and the BN government for many years since *merdeka*.[22] There was a streak of confidence in his remarks that PAS had nothing new to offer in their programme, except "to fish for votes in the coming election".

Therefore, *Islam Hadhari* was propagated to define the UMNO version of Islam in the face of global challenges. It was not merely a specific strategy for outbidding PAS but a general framework for the development of the Muslim *ummah* in the modern world, away from the violent trend of *jihad* and militaristic options undertaken by many Islamic groups the world over, the most famous of which is al-Qaeda of west Asia and Jumaah Islamiah of Southeast Asia. Even within Malaysia, the experience of militant movements since the communist revolt in 1948 and the al-Maunah and KMM attempts at *jihad* in 2002 and 2003 have provided valuable information on the objectives and organisation of the groups. Most of them were bent on adopting the violent interpretation of *jihad* as a Qur'anic injunction. But Abdullah as well as Dr Mahathir openly criticised and disavowed the violent streak in the Islamic *jihadist* movement. As such the formulation and propagation of Islam *Hadhari* provided the needed framework for the Muslim community to move forward in Islamic terms and for non-Muslim citizens to understand the peaceful mission of Islam and probably accept it as the rallying call for the new government.

Islam Hadhari was first proposed in 2001 by several Islamic thinkers within UMNO who grappled with the loss of 22 seats, the defeat of senior UMNO figures, and PAS's win of a state government seat in the 1999 general election. A special information unit was formed within the Ministry of Information to combat the growing violent message of Islam by various factions in society and members of PAS. Islamic programmes were launched to search for the most appropriate strategy and to reduce the effect of the message of violence. By 2002, Abdullah, as the then deputy prime minister, began to speak of *Islam Hadhari* as a general concept for Islamic development, in line with the thoughts of several renown world Islamic thinkers such as Yusuf Qardawi, Muhammad Amarah, and Sy. Mohamad al-Ghazali. These thinkers were regarded as the modern manifestation of earlier Islamic reformists such as Jamaluddin al-Afghani, Muhammad Abduh, and Rashid Redha whose influence had made an impact on Islamic reformist movements in many Muslim states during the colonial period.

Nevertheless, PAS did not sit quietly with the propagation of *Islam Hadhari*. They began to attack the concept as *bi'dah*, revisionism of Islamic tenets and injunctions — and highlighted the failure of the concept to relate the foundation of Islam to the *syariah* law and its necessity in an Islamic state. A roadshow was undertaken among its members to spread the message that *Islam Hadhari* was *haram* (unlawful) under Islamic *syariah* law. It is a new Islam, departing from the truth. Abdullah, on the other hand, mobilised the special Islamic Information Unit to explain the concept to various interest groups. Finally, it became the slogan for the general election in the heartland of Malay voters. Abdullah Badawi's *Islam Hadhari* made its point as the rallying call for the development of the Muslim and the non-Muslim party components began to take notice of the *Islam Hadhari* agenda and examined the implications of the project. In his usual style, Abdullah assured non-Muslims that "[a]s a Prime Minister of Malaysia, I am not a leader of Muslims, but a Muslim leader of all Malaysians."[23] He was aware that the deep skepticism of non-Muslims would have an impact on Islamic ideas within the country and as such he assured the people that he had no other agenda. Nevertheless, the MCA and Gerakan were still sceptical of the implications of the idea.

The idea had been the centerpiece of sloganeering during the first by-election on 28 August 2004 in Kuala Berang, Trengganu, where the BN won the seat with an increase in majority. Simultaneously in Kota Bharu, PAS had its annual assembly in which, for the first time, party members, especially from the Youth Movement, openly criticised the leadership of Haji Hadi Awang as failing in his duty to clarify the party's weaknesses and setbacks during the recent general election. PAS was presumably demoralised and Hadi's comment further placed the younger generation in a state of disbelief when he likened them to Coca-Cola, the temporary wheezing of carbonate out of a bottle which has been reduced to quietness. Perhaps, Abdullah now has the upper hand in the political arena of Malaysia after 12 months at the helm of the nation.

Managing a Coalition

The coalition of 14 major ethnic political parties of the BN is not a simple coming together of various groups.[24] More than any other combination, it is a dynamic coalition of racial groups whereby each group understands and upholds their ethnic mission. While the major groups are avowedly racial in their membership, catering for specific major racial groups in the country, there are members who are avowedly less racial. They maintain a certain degree of mixture in memberships although the majority and core members are from one racial group. UMNO, MCA, MIC, and Parti Bansa Dayak Sarawak (PBDS) are by definition racial parties. Several others such as Parti Bersatu Sabah (PBS) and Sabah Progressive Party (SAPP) consists of Kadazandusuns, and the People Progressive Party (PPP) largely consist of Indians. Although the Sarawak Progressive Democratic Party (SPDP) consists mainly of Orang Ulus, they are only non-racial in name as their members are from one of the major races in the country. Only Gerakan, United Pasokmomogun Kadazandusun Murut Organization (UPKO), and Pertubuhan Bangsa Bersatu (PBB) maintain a semblance of openness, yet their core members are constituted from either one of the core groups: the Chinese for Gerakan or a combination of two major racial groups: Murut and Kadazandusun for UPKO; and Malay, and Melanau and Iban for PBB. Therefore, racial and political groupings constitute the political order within which power is distributed.

A wealth of experience has accumulated during the more than four decades of coalition among the BN components. The prime minister, being the president of UMNO and the chairman of the BN, had practised what he perceived as the right formula in managing a large multi-ethnic coalition. Some commentators have likened the method practised by Dr Mahathir as putting the Chinese "in a box" while others are happy with Dr Mahathir's policy of liberal and free enterprise in business and the policy of multi-ethnicity and religious freedom.[25] The first prime minister, Tunku Abdul Rahman, had been described as being a "pluralist" and "inclusivist" in his attitude towards nation-building. By the time Tun Razak took over, the experience of racial tension and conflict had influenced him to pursue Malay dominance and equitable distribution of economic resources. This was followed by a strong conservatism and resistance to change during the administration of Tun Hussain Onn.[26]

In the case of Abdullah, there is a considerable deliberateness to be more inclusivist and to perpetuate the liberal attitude of Tunku Abdul Rahman and Dr Mahathir. In a speech as chairman of the BN given at the 58th MIC general assembly in Shah Alam, Selangor, on 21 August 2004, he reminded the assembly that he is a Muslim prime minister of all Malaysians who is intent on preserving the multi-ethnic, multi-religious harmony of the country. He also reiterated his promise to "walk the talk" of being moderate and to put national interests above communal interests. His reference to Malay issues frequently followed the Mahathir practice of berating the Malays and the Bumiputera community for their failures in development and harbouring a subsidy mentality, even equating them, like other Malaysians, with a "third world mentality within a first world infrastructure".

On closer examination, a great deal of his proposals so far are a continuation of earlier policies which have not been fully realised or practised by the government within the entire political process. This is notwithstanding certain practices that have become almost a sacred convention and customary rule among members. These include the formula for seat distribution and the right of the prime minister to finalise the candidates for each election.

The formula of seat distribution among BN components inevitably reflects the conventional wisdom of the primacy of UMNO within the BN which, in turn, is a reflection of the physical delineation of electoral constituencies. Criticism of gerrymandering in favour of BN and perhaps against the Opposition does not necessarily mean it is an undemocratic practice since ruling and opposition parties alike would resort to it when they are in power. Objectively viewed, it is already a political strategy of many ruling groups in democratic states to perpetuate hegemony and power. Under such circumstances, UMNO has found it convenient to redistribute power bases within the electorates to its constituencies and component members. Abdullah himself has apparently left it to the Election Commission to administer the delineation of constituencies and ensure its transparency within the democratic system.

The last election illustrates the BN wisdom of power-sharing which retains its primacy in political terms. With the enlarged parliament and state constituencies to 219 and 505 respectively, the advantage traditionally practised by UMNO over others does not show a marked difference. From 1950 till 2004, the delineation of constituencies remained on a rural-weighted basis and has almost fixed its delineation advantage of around 12 per cent for Malay-majority constituencies since 1974. While it is true that malapportionment and gerrymandering, apart from natural population increase, could have caused the eventual electoral advantage however, as already fully demonstrated by the 1999 election, it never guarantees electoral success. The fact that there has always been a Malay opposition party for the last 50 years inspite of its failure to get mass recognition, the constituency advantage merely provides an illusion of superiority which could swing to the Opposition given the right strategy and conditions on their part.

The other point which must be considered here is the racial basis of the Malaysian ruling groups, Malay being the dominant group. This concept of racial retention and maintenance of the political order has proved to be of great significance to all Malaysians in view of the worldwide process of "retribalisation" by post-colonial states. Be it in Africa, South Asia, Oceania, the Balkan states, and Central Asia, decolonisation has broken many states into racial chaos, civil war, endless inter-state rivalries, and even wars. Centuries of subjugation did not obliterate racial identities and pride. The "great narratives" of the cold war years in the form of democratic states, socialism, or communism have only given impetus to their emergence after their liberation in recent decades, especially after the fall of the Soviet Union. The idea of the unity of citizens through class integration or solidarity never provided the real answer to colonially-engineered territorial union. A nation-state is also never the final answer to such colonial legacy. In most cases, unity and integration are always engendered through some form of racial dominance and political supremacy of a group. Therefore, to demand institutional changes to racialised political groups, changes to the entire foundation of the state and mind that maintained it and its legal basis have to be made.

It is true that in recent years there has been a greater awareness of the possibility of the non-race-based alternative as demonstrated by the failed attempt of the MCA-Gerakan merger or the call for a single Dusunkadazan political group. However, the possibility of a race-based framework to rework itself into a more flexible structure has also been tried and accepted by its members. This possibility has been the experiment of UMNO *vis-à-vis* its non-Malay, non-Muslim members among the Siam- and Portuguese-descended groups in the north of the Peninsula and among all the Bumiputeras of Sabah. The fact that PAS was willing to accept to non-Muslim members can be interpreted as equating Islam with ethnic-Malays and others as non-Malays. Needless to say, if history is of any guide to the Malay mind thus far, the denial of the party's ethnic label and consciousness by any UMNO or, for that matter, Malay leader, be it Dato' Onn, Tengku Razaleigh (for working with the DAP), Tunku Abdul Rahman (in terms of language), and several others, has met with disapproval and total rejection through the various electoral contests. PAS has attempted to displace this ethnic loyalty with an Islamic call and yet its success in 1999 was more or less on the wave of other dissatisfactions rather than its Islamic appeal.

The BN political consensus has served the nation well and therefore Abdullah, as the current chairman, has always reminded BN members to stick to the rules of the game by being sensitive to the interests of others. Table 7.1 shows the number of seats contested and won by each component party through its participation as a group in parliament after the 2004 election.

The distribution figures indicate that UMNO controls just over half (53.4 per cent) of the total number of seats contested and won 93.1 per cent of its allocation and the rest controls 46.6 per cent of the seats and won 87.3 per cent (MCA won 77.5 per cent; MIC 100 per cent, Gerakan 83.3 per cent, and others 100 per cent; SUPP and LDP small lost). Obviously, UMNO alone cannot have a dominating position with an almost equal number of allocation of seats as the rest. Even more glaring is its shaky position of forcing its will on others when its

Table 7.1
Barisan Nasional's Performance in the 2004 Election

Party	No. of Seats Contested	Seats Won	
		No.	%
UMNO	117	109	53.4
MCA	40	31	18.3
MIC	9	9	4.1
Gerakan	12	10	5.5
Others			18.7
PPP	1	1	
PBB	11	11	
SUPP	7	6	
PBDS	6	6	
SPDP	4	4	
PBS	4	4	
UPKO	4	4	
SAPP	2	2	
LDP	1	0	
PBRS	1	1	
Total	219	198	100.0

Note: PAS won five out of 84 seats; DAP won ten out of 44 seats.

dominance is in fact illusory when viewed within a democratic process of decision-making. In a council of coalition members, UMNO can never carry any decision without a consensus from its members. Under such a circumstance, UMNO has to play its game very cautiously, principally using a consultative and circumspect bargaining method to reach a common decision. This formula has always been the approach within the BN. It is not clear how such a compromise might have been achieved among component parties but what has transpired from numerous meetings is that the prime minister would make the final decision on certain issues related to any particular ethnic groups after an open debate and information-sharing.

Abdullah has revealed that, "All have the right to speak, even if the issue involves matters related to specific races or specific religions. In the BN style, we are always confident that we can discuss all issues, even if they involved sensitive topics, in a wise manner and come to a consensus. The key to this is that we must engage in discussion in an attitude of moderation."[27]

Presumably, the traditional BN-UMNO coalition has continued with the understanding that each and every political party in this coalition will represent the interest of their racial group within the government. Abdullah does not seem to have made any radical changes to the nature of the relationship or the process of decision-making. UMNO seems to continue to play the dominant role as the major shareholder of power representing Malay interests, while other interests have been similarly considered within the limits of the broader perspective. The recent enlargement in the number of parliamentary seats and state legislative assemblies have been allocated to all parties within the confines of the general principle and the outcome generally has been accepted by all concerned.

Internal Dynamics of Political Parties

The basic convention governing relationships and power-sharing does not allow the leaders of component parties to intrude into the affairs of others. The internal affairs of a party are the prerogative of the party's leadership and perhaps their supreme councils. The style and pattern of administration is always left to the decision of the particular party. Friendly advice may be given at times to resolve internal disputes and dissatisfaction among members of another party. The prime minister, as chairman of the BN council, occasionally suggests solutions to certain on-going disputes which may otherwise lead to problems that would weaken a component party and eventually affect the overall BN standing. This has frequently occurred within the MCA, PBDS, and several other parties. At least for now, Abdullah has left the internal affairs of each component party to their respective governing leadership with little direct intervention. He had occasionally urged parties with internal problems, such as the PBDS, MCA, and MIC, to manage their internal affairs without jeopardising BN interests. Recent attempts by the MCA and the Gerakan to merge into a single Chinese party has not drawn any public remarks from the prime minister, nor has he commented on the attempt by another Indian political party to join the BN only after consultation with the BN's existing partner, the MIC. A recent case of a party split by the PBDS in Sarawak drew some remarks from the prime minister urging the party members to settle their internal affairs without jeopardising BN interests. The case seems to illustrate his preference for the law to take its own course when the failure to compromise between competing factions lead to their deregistration. Similarly, the practice of rotating the post of chief minister in Sabah has been discontinued after receiving the general consent of the component parties in Sabah. Abdullah is presumably happy with the traditional arrangement of pursuing common interests through positive engagement and consensus building. The general aim of his government is, to quote him, " ... to bring government back to the people. Government serves the people and its policies must empower the people with opportunities, rights and responsibilities."[28]

The more significant internal dynamics would be the role and function of specific units and factions in a political party. For most of the BN component members, there is a women's wing, a youth wing, and a supreme council which also have to play the power game. In recent months, there have been talks of forming a young women's wing in line with the Puteri UMNO wing which has demonstrated the efficacy of such an addition to attract younger professionals and sustain the party's attractiveness to the masses.

However, it seems that not everyone among the more established leadership welcomes the formation of such a wing. Wanita (Women) UMNO expressed initial dissatisfaction with the introduction of Puteri UMNO. Apparently it attracted unintended challenges to the positions of the incumbent women leaders and thus presents a threat as well as a probable manipulation on the part of the top leadership towards the more vocal and established women's wing.

Apart from such a consideration, the youth wing always demonstrated a more vocal demand for the leadership to implement policies and achieve stated short-term or long-term goals. There have been fiery demands made on certain issues such as that of meritocracy in educational placement, eradication of poverty irrespective of race, and equal opportunity in education which in some cases would draw similar demands from component youth wings. It is a working relationship among member parties that normally invites the prime minister as chairman of the BN to officiate annual assemblies and thus allow him to rebut criticisms or uphold certain policy issues while reminding them of the government's position on the issues at hand. In any case, these annual assemblies play a significant role in addressing public party interests and concerns which normally result in some form of resolution adopted for further action. Resolutions would normally be based on overall national interests and unity. Potential and latent conflicts may also be resolved internally among leaders of component parties and through meetings of the national councils of the lower-level personnel of the women's and youth wings of all component members. Therefore, in terms of maintaining cohesion and preserving unity, the BN has evolved a system of inter-group consultation whenever an issue of national interest crops up which urgently needs the establishment of a common understanding. It is perhaps within this kind of inter-group and interpersonal consultations that a great deal of fallouts have occurred within each component member whenever a challenge or deep dissatisfaction surfaces among the top leadership of the coalition. Many UMNO, MCA, MIC, Gerakan, PBDS, PBB, and other promising party leaders have been dropped or withdrawn from active participation when component members take action against them and publicly declare their differences.

The interest is, therefore, in maintaining the general racial balance and equilibrium within a functionally-harmonious political order. The balance is presumably achieved by way of empowering each racial group to express their ethnic identities openly and equitably without perceptible sense of deprivation *vis-à-vis* each other. This can only be achieved by fully understanding the needs and concerns of each racial group in relation to their common stake in the country. For this purpose, it is perhaps reasonable to assume that what the government is aiming for is to create multi-level identities within the Malaysian population whereby, at the lowest intimate level, they would be able to identify themselves as the family of a certain racial group with political representation to ensure that their voice is heard. At the higher level of inter-racial interactions, individual identities are reflected in the mass admixture of national celebrations of racial particularities such the Chinese New Year, Hari Raya, Christmas, Deepavali, harvest festivals, and the creation of opportunities for inter-racial interaction such as the custom of "open house".

At the highest level of international representation, the identity would be national which is generally based on so-called national cultural principles, i.e. based on the indigenous representation. This is observable on many occasions when national sports teams, diplomatic officers, or attendees at royal ceremonies would be dressed in the national costume. Needless to say, this can be considered as minimal demands made on various racial groups whose culture is practised daily and who are not forced to adorn a national identity. The preservation of a complex myriad of identities presents a culture of choice among Malaysians which will remain so in the future. The racial social order with minimum demands for identity change seems to be the Malaysian choice for harmonious living over and above the class consciousness mode. Class does cut across racial lines without injuring their unique consciousness as particular group identities.

The Culture of Complex Identities

Finally, I would add that the political arrangement within the BN and the inter-racial composition of the coalition has always been determined by the recognition of the principle of indigène and historical location of indigenous groups. This, of course, has been met with tacit approval and sensitively preserved. It is a fundamental principle, the questioning of which will always create waves and severe reaction among UMNO members and the Malays in general. The experience during the last four decades of government, first by the Alliance and later by the BN, indicated that this fundamental issue is not negotiable and is regarded as a sacrosanct foundation stone of the constitutional social contract among the various races of the country. The points of contention eventually were embodied in the Sedition Act which makes anyone liable to be charged in court for tendentious statements made in public. The latest controversy that emerged during and after the 1999 election illustrate the kind of uproar that can happen when a group of Chinese associations made the election appeal to political parties, known as Suqui, which among other things demanded changes in the constitutional order by eliminating the racial categorisation of citizens, away from Bumiputera and non-Bumiputera or Malay and non-Malay. The stern reaction caught the sponsor by surprise and, for a while, led to strained relations among the Chinese associations and gave rise to acrimonious allegations of disrespect for the "racial bargain" as embodied in the Constitution.

From the Malay point of view, the contract has always been the *raison d'etre*, the reason for existence, of the social order. Therefore, it carries a certain degree of obligation on the part of every racial group of citizens to respect the provisions and common agreement of the country's founding fathers. Since it has some degree of legal and constitutional standing, it would, therefore, have certain implications on the political, economic, cultural, and social dimensions of life. Translated into policies and actions, it would mean that UMNO and the Malays and other indigènes would have a slight primacy over others.

In reality, the translation of such provisions has always depended on the perception, personality, and style of leadership of the top political leaders, particularly the prime minister. He sets the tone and stamps his style on the nature of the relationship among component members and the population at large. Generally, his leadership style has seeped down to the masses of party members, among leaders at every level, and in inter-group relationships. This aura or feeling that such a style is working among the populace puts the top leader in a position of power and authority.

The first prime minister, Tunku Abdul Rahman, has always been cited as the founder of an open and "inclusivist" culture within the coalition and the masses through tolerance or a *tolak ansur* attitude. To many UMNO leaders, he was too "altruistic" with a very high threshold for tolerance of the demands of others. Cynics regarded this behaviour as being *tolak* (push), and as a result, the Malays have to *ansur* (shift) to give way to others. Nonetheless, during the last 40 years, the practice of bargaining or consultation has become a kind of fundamental and sacred principle among the BN coalition members. Perhaps the ideal racial objectives each party has attempted to achieve is tempered by the "real-politik" of other demands interacting with each other. In the end, there must be a sort of common decision and practical consensus, which may occasionally be a bitter pill to swallow for some leaders, acceptable to all racial groups. A kind of shift and change of personal paradigms has to occur in order to accommodate conflicts and expectations. Tun Razak, Tun Hussain Onn, and Tun Dr Mahathir as well as the subsequent prime ministers have shifted their personal stances in the face of strong opposition and debunking by others inspite of conventional and fundamental norms. In recent years, UMNO has seen several shifts in fundamental policies such as the opening up of MARA College to non-Malays, the practice of meritocracy in the face of rural disadvantage to many Bumiputera groups, the amendment to the Industrial Coordination Act to allow foreign ownership, and the latest being the teaching of science in English in schools which is now facing of Malay opposition. In the final analysis, the demands of circumstances, be it politics, economics, or race, made its way into what has always been defined as pragmatic decisions.

Under Abdullah, the socio-political order seems to have undergone a more flexible and, again, pragmatic evolution by stressing "Malaysianness" rather than "Malayness" or "Islamicness". The way forward for him is one of greater dialogue and consensus-building and the construction of a common vision among UMNO and BN members and even with the Opposition. He has allowed open and wider consultation as well as a greater respect for other views be it legal (parliamentary select committee on criminal laws), social (public discussions on road safety), economic (the role of GLCs), or political (UMNO's disciplinary committee, parliamentary public account committee [PAC] with the inclusion of Opposition members). Perhaps the key to his style and confidence may be found within the traditional Islamic political thought of *siyyasah syariah* with its emphasis on *syura* (consultation) and *maslahah* (public good) and the belief in the civilising force of Islam under the *Islam Hadhari* concept.

There has been no declaration of intent with regards the future political culture of "multiculturalism", but from what has been seen so far and the recognition accorded to the liberalisation of cultural practices, especially in the realms of religion and the economy, there is greater hope for a more Malaysian approach and a solution to national problems than is presently understood. This is good for the preservation of complex identities and pluralistic policies in Malaysia. Perhaps Ye

Lin-Sheng's optimism for Malaysia is well founded when he recounted his encounter with Malayness:

> "When I first read *The Malay Dilemma* it was easy for me to identify with the poverty and humiliation of the Malays and the explosive feelings mentioned by Mahathir. I have always thought that if there was a race that could understand *The Malay Dilemma* it would have been us the Chinese."[29]

NOTES

1. A series of writings, analyses, and assessments on the post-1999 election appeared euphoric on the possibility of BN and UMNO "slipping into irrelevancy" especially with the fervour of *reformasi*, the new challenges from PAS, and the rise of a new Malay middle-class. See among others, Nash (2004); Loh & Saravanamuthu (2003); Verma (2004); Ho & Chin (2001).

2. See the reply by PAS leader, Fadzil Noor, to the comment made by Lee Kuan Yew about talking to the leadership of the Islamic party (*New Straits Times* (Malaysia), 8 September 2001).

3. See the report of PAS's acceptance of the impact of the "Abdullah factor" on their dismal performance in their election post mortem (*Berita Harian* (Malaysia), 2 November 2004).

4. See Milne & Mauzy (1999, pp. 17, 18).

5. See Teo (2004).

6. See the writings of Za'ba and Syed Sheikh al-Hady during the period in Adnan Nawang (1994, 1995, 1998) and Gordon (1999) on the writings of S.S. al-Hady.

7. See Braddell (1931).

8. See Ramlah & Onn (1999).

9. See Tunku Abdul Rahman's columns, "Looking Back" (1977); "Lest We Forget" (1983).

10. Perhaps the assessment of Cheah Boon Kheng is closer to the reality of Malay perception and belief on issues related to their sovereignty and primacy in Malaysia for now and the future. See Cheah (2002, p. 72).

11. A great deal of assessment on Dr Mahathir's administration has been negatively weighted as being "authoritarian" against its theoretical ideal type construct. See Hilley (2001), Milne, & Mauzy (1999), and Verma (2004) with some comparison with other similar regimes during his leadership.

12. *Berita Harian* (Malaysia), 26 June 2002.

13. Promises made during interviews marking his first year of administration indicate his commitment for results from now on. See *New Straits Times* (Malaysia), *Berita Harian* (Malaysia), 31 October 2004.

14. C. Kessler, "Mahathir's Malaysia after Dr Mahathir", in *Reflection — The Mahathir Years*, edited by B. Welsh (Washington DC: Johns Hopkins University, 2004), p. 16.

15. See Ng (2003).

16. See Khoo (1995).

17. See Rehman (2004, p. 62).

18. See Roslan (2004, p. 11).

19. Also known as *wang ikhsan* (gift fund).

20. Speech officiating the 4th Regional Anti-Corruption Conference for Asia and the Pacific, 3 December 2003, Kuala Lumpur.

21. Speech on the launch of both programmes on 23 April 2004.

22. Quoted from Roslan (2004, p. 57).

23. An address at the Plenary Commission on Faith and Order of the World Council of Churches, 3 August 2004, Kuala Lumpur.

24. As of now the 14 component members of BN are UMNO, MCA, MIC, Gerakan, PPP, PBB, SUPP, SPDP, PBDS (recently deregistered and probably to be replaced by PRS and a faction of the opposing leadership is appealing against the deregistration), PBS, LDP, SPDP, UPKO, and SAPP.

25. See K.H. Lee's and Ong Kian Ming's articles on Dr Mahathir and Chinese politics in Welsch (2004) for the various reflections on the impact of personal policies.

26. See Cheah (2004) for a general study of the historical development of nation-building under the first four prime ministers.

27. New Sunday Times (Malaysia), 22 August 2004 front page.

28. Prime Ministerial address to the Cambridge Foundation, 10 February 2004.

29. See Ye (2003, p. 197).

8

Malaysia's Civil Service Reform: Mahathir's Legacies and Abdullah's Challenges

HO KHAI LEONG

Introduction

Since Malaysia's independence in 1957, administrative reform efforts in the country have been moving ahead at a rapid pace. Under Mahathir, such reform efforts have been further reinforced with much conviction as well as rhetoric. His administration picked up the new public management (NPM) paradigm. New civil service reform programmes, together with their problems, emerged in the mid-1990s amidst major political and economic transformations in the country.

When Abdullah Badawi was sworn in as the fifth prime minister of Malaysia in 2003, he inherited the weaknesses and strengths of the reform programmes as well as the intended and unintended consequences of Mahathir's relentless efforts in transforming the country. The perennial issues of performance, efficiency, control, and accountability (or the lack of) in the Malaysian civil service remain major challenges for Abdullah. He has pledged, after the landslide victory of the 11th general election, to take Malaysia towards "excellence, glory, and distinction".

The bureaucracy, as a tool of policy implementation, will be a major player in the process.

This chapter surveys the administrative reform initiatives in Malaysia, focusing, in particular, on developments during the Mahathir administration and the challenges that confront the Abdullah administration. It argues that both internal and external changes have forced the Malaysian administrative apparatus to adjust and respond rapidly in the Mahathir administration, and these forces will remain significant in the Abdullah administration. In addition, Abdullah's pledges to improve bureaucratic efficiency and minimising corruption would prove to be difficult to fulfil if entrenched and stubborn political and bureaucratic resistance are not removed.

Administrative Reforms: Malaysian Style

The Malaysian political elite's approach is consistent with the general belief that administrative reform is a prerequisite for significant growth on the development front.[1] Civil service reforms — broadly defined "an organizational, instrumental, problem-related change of government and the public sector to meet environmental demands and require-ments"[2] — were initiated by the United Malays' National Organization (UMNO)-dominated Barisan Nasional (BN) government in the past 40 years. These reform efforts — making the institution more profes-sional and politicised — have enabled the Malay governing elite to maintain its political supremacy and its control of resources in the country. The bureaucracy has been regarded as the last bastion of Malay power, quickly transforming the once plural polity into a Bumiputera state.[3]

Once securely entrenched, however, the Malaysian bureaucracy has been increasingly unresponsive and unaccountable, and this has caused major concern for the Malay ruling elite. Mahathir Mohammad, who assumed the premiership in 1981, took major steps towards reforming the bureaucracy by first introducing a programme for a "clean, efficient, and trustworthy" government, scrutinising mismanaged and unprofitable government-owned Bumiputera enterprises, stamping out corruption from the public sector, and improving efficiency. In the 1990s, new initiatives, in the form of new public administration-style reforms, have taken on a more urgent task in the face of regional competitiveness and globalisation.

Mahathir's New Public Management: Old Wines in New Bottles?

It was during Mahathir's administration that the term "new public management" and its variations began to surface in official rhetoric.[4] Its objectives and values were somewhat reflected in many of the initiatives taken by the bureaucracy. The NPM of course has many dimensions, which include:[5]

1. devolving authority, providing flexibility;
2. ensuring performance, control, accountability;
3. developing competition and choice, market-type mechanisms;
4. providing responsive services, client orientation;
5. improving the management of human resources;
6. optimising information technology;
7. improving the quality of regulation;
8. strengthening the steering functions at the centre;
9. private sector-style management.

In essence, the NPM is used to denote a new paradigmatic shift towards better management and service delivery by the bureaucracy to the citizenry. The Malaysian civil service officials were quick to adopt many of these themes. The new concept was best expressed in the following paragraph by the director general of the public service department, Tan Sri Dr Mazlan Ahmad:

> In order to promote and enhance knowledge and creativity in the new public administration, I would like to propose measures to redefine and refine the purpose of public administration to instill a commitment to improve the quality of citizens' life: establishing networking within the public service and the public service and clients, suppliers and private sector with a primary objective of sharing knowledge; using multi-cultural and multi-disciplinary teaming to provide diversity of idea generation; creating a learning culture that makes learning a personal adventure, creating an environment that support risk-taking, tolerance for ambiguity and failures, and rewards success; and providing resources and time for creative adventure.[6]

Official rhetoric aside, administrative reforms during the Mahathir period indeed have taken on some significant developments. They consisted of two major themes: privatisation and efficiency, and development of information technology.

Privatisation and Efficiency

Under Prime Minister Mahathir's "Malaysia Incorporated" concept mooted in 1983, the civil service was again the target of change. "Malaysia Incorporated" has the objective of establishing a symbiotic relationship between the private and public sectors to achieve the goals of development. The message to the civil service has been simple and direct: Get slimmer, be more effective and helpful, buck up or be privatised. At the face-to-face level, every civil servant wears a name tag so that poor service or corruption can easily be reported. In implementing these reform measures, Mahathir's government sought to (1) downsize the civil service to make it more affordable and to bring it into line with a new, scaled-down role of the government in economic activities; (2) provide civil servants with appropriate incentives, skills, and motivation; and (3) enhance management and accountability. As a result, by 1995, the number of civil servants had shrunk by a third.[7]

The downsizing of the public sector was achieved by privatising many of the inefficient and ineffective public agencies. Indeed, privatisation of public enterprises became a key element in the administrative reform policy in the 1980s under the Mahathir government. It sought selective sale of state enterprises to private investors or shareholders, or divestiture of government interest in state-owned and operated parastatals and commercial enterprises. It reflected the government's growing disenchantment with the government bureaucracy in managing these huge enterprises and services. At the same time, there were also efforts in deregulation and decentralisation of state authorities.

When the NEP was replaced by the National Development Policy (NDP) in 1991, the role of the state has already undergone a major overhaul.[8] While the NDP did not represent any major shift in philosophy of the government's approach to development, it did replace the emphasis on equity with rapid economic growth as lessons were learned in the recessions of the mid-1980s and the development of the international economy. Mahathir also unveiled his *Vision 2020* in 1991 which aimed to transform Malaysia into an industrialised modern state by the year 2020. In view of these major initiatives, the civil service was quickly made over to be in concert. Administrative reform was implemented "to increase the efficiency and effectiveness in the management and administration to provide a meaningful contribution towards achieving the targets and goals of national development and Vision 2020."[9]

One major development in the civil service reform was the introduction of the Client Charter in 1993. To better equip the civil service for the 21st century, Mahathir felt that there was a need for the civil service to possess the mentality to serve rather than be served. A paradigm shift was, therefore, needed from the civil servants in their attitude and approach towards their duties. In the words of Dato' Seri Ahmad Sarji, chief secretary to the government, the Malaysian civil service has to move "from [their] conventional and one-dimensional roles as rule-setters and regulators to that of facilitator and pacesetter in national development". A new civil service was needed, one that is more customer-focused, results- and performance-oriented, responsive, accountable and innovative, with the capacity and capability of providing quality services. With the implementation of the Client's Charter, quality service and meeting customer satisfaction would be emphasised in all government agencies.

The Client's Charter was supposed to be the starting point that links the empowerment of the citizenry *vis-à-vis* the civil servants, but its impact is yet to be evaluated comprehensively. Though Mahathir respected and trusted individual civil servants, he distrusted the bureaucratic process. He noted: "Our country is tied up with rules and regulations so much so that matters which clearly only involve technicalities will cause us to be unable to implement certain things."[10] According to Mahathir, civil servants took far too long to make decisions and senior civil servants were invariably shielded from consequences of their own actions.

Overall, when gauged by measures such as improvement of efficiency, accountability, and transparency, Malaysia's civil service reform initiatives made insignificant difference. Despite reform efforts, it was still operating under the influence of the British colonial administration and heavily politicised by local interests. "Despite the fact that an increasing number of the administrative and professional members of the civil service receive their postgraduate education and training in the United States and the fact that several 'renovations' of the administrative system have taken place since independence ..., the bureaucracy continues to be influenced by its colonial experience and its highly politicized local environment."[11]

Information Technology and E-government

Since the mid-1990s, with the inevitable advent of information technology, the concept of electronic government has been heavily emphasised. This marked a significant shift from the previous emphasis on the traditional method of serving the public. Indeed, Malaysian public officials firmly believed that the success of the Malaysian civil service sector would largely depend on the extensive use of information technology. A lot of effort was spent in creating the electronic government as an application for the development of the Multimedia Super Corridor (MSC). Since the beginning of the 1990s, the Malaysian government invested heavily in building the technological infrastructure of the country. For example, under the Sixth Malaysia Plan (1990–1995), RM1.36 billion was approved for projects and purchases related to IT. Under the Seventh Malaysia Plan (1996–2000), RM2.3 billion of IT-related investments in its ministries and agencies was spent, an increase of nearly 70 per cent

In the late 1990s, the National Institute of Public Administration (INTAN), the training ground for government servants, launched the electronic-government (E-G) training programme to provide IT training and basic computer skills to civil servants. The aims were to simplify work procedure and, from the government perspective, to reduce the size of the civil service.[12] Between 1995 and 1998, INTAN trained more than 10,300 personnel. Of that number, 4,055 personnel were from all levels in the Prime Minister's Department, the first agency to move to Putrajaya, the new administrative capital of the federal government.[13]

In April 1996, Dr Mahathir announced in Malta at the biennial conference of the Commonwealth Association for Public Administration and Management (CAPAM) that Malaysia aimed to be the first country in the world whose 800,000-strong civil service qualify for the ISO 9000 quality standard. He said:

> Quality has become a much sought-after target. If goods produced must meet a certain standard, surely services, government services, included, must achieve a certain degree of quality. ISO 9000 should not be for the factories of the private sector alone. Government administration must also vie for the coveted award. A good government administration cannot be of lower quality than its clients — largely the private sector. It must complement the private sector fully if it is going to serve the country and contribute towards its growth and well-being of the people.

In 1997, the Malaysian Administrative, Modernization and Management Planning Unit (MAMPU) in the Prime Minister's Department implemented five pilot projects: electronic services, electronic procurement, generic office environment, human resource management information system, and project monitoring system. The major objective is to make the civil service leaner and more responsive to the demands of its constituents. Officials believed that this would lead to improved information flow, better communication, and greater coordination and collaboration between government agencies. By 2000, 70 per cent of the agencies under the Prime Minister's Department have their own websites to disseminate information to clients and the public as it was mandatory for all government agencies to develop websites to facilitate this purpose.[14]

These recent reforms, however, have their critics. Public complaints of inefficiency and corrupt practices of the bureaucracy did not diminished in the 1990s. Opposition parties have also been criticising the UMNO-led government for "talking too much and doing too little". Democratic Action Party (DAP) secretary-general, Lim Kit Siang, who was also the Opposition leader in the parliament, attacked the Mahathir administration for its lack of commitment to IT: "Malaysia is unable to begin to provide government online services not because of lack of technology, but the absence of commitment, will and leadership by both the political and bureaucratic leadership."[15]

Political Change and Administrative Responses in the 1990s

Initially, Prime Minister Mahathir Mohamad depended very much on the civil service to uphold the image of his clean, efficient, and trustworthy government, and he introduced enthusiastically various reform measures to change the ethic of the civil service. His personal involvement in the reforms were obvious as many measures, such as the wearing of name tags and clocking in at work, were his ideas. In the later part of his administration, however, he was constantly ensnared, and his attentions were diverted, by other economic and political priorities.[16]

The financial crisis of 1997 and the sacking of his deputy Datuk Anwar Abrahim in 1998 marked a watershed in Mahathir's administration and Malaysian politics. The financial crisis exposed many of the government failures, such as corruption and nepotism, in the Mahathir administration. The Anwar debacle prompted a prolonged movement of street protests by Malay youths who were sympathetic to Anwar. The formation of the Justice Party (Parti Keadilan) under the leadership of Wan Azizah Ismail (Anwar's wife) and the subsequent formation of Barisan Alternatif (Alternative Front, or BA) challenging the BN in the general elections in 1999, significantly changed the political landscape of the country. Consequently, the Malaysian civil service was caught up in these political struggles in the Malay community and between states, and issues of ethnic quote and preferential treatment emerged as important issues once again. The old issue of privatisation and problems of inefficiency and corruption remain major points of contention within the civil service discourse.

Abdullah's Administrative Reforms: New Wines in Old Bottles?

When Abdullah Badawi took over the premiership from Mahathir, he was viewed at first as someone who is not able to escape from the latter's shadow. However, he was able to acquire a different substance and style from his predecessor and very quickly established a degree of political legitimacy. As far as the study of civil service reform is concerned, we are interested ascertain out his ideas and thoughts on the subject and his proposed solutions to the problems.

What is Abdullah's perception of "good governance"? When he was still deputy prime minister, at the 5th National Civil Service Conference on Good Governance: Issues and Challenges held in Kuala Lumpur in 2000, he embraced the concept of "good governance" which he said was most accurately defined at the 1999 World Conference on Governance in Manila as "a system that is transparent, accountable, just, fair, democratic, participatory and responsive to the people's needs". He further stated that it is certainly a vision of governance that Malaysia continues to endeavour to realise.

Since taking office, Abdullah has taken the following steps:

- His public commitment to lead a "clean, incorruptible, modest and beyond suspicion" administration;
- His surprise visit to the immigration department to underline his call for an end to red tape and bureaucracy, the introduction of a people-oriented civil service, and his message "work with me, not for me".
- His proposal to set up a regional anti-corruption academy, operational by mid-2005.
- He drew up a code of ethics for his ministers that requires them to declare their financial assets. The code also requires ministers to submit a report card to the Prime Minister's Department every three months spelling out what duties they have performed on behalf of the people.

Indeed, it was clear that Abdullah knows the political values of shaping up the bureaucracy. After his ascendancy to the premiership, Abdullah has made administrative reform a theme of his administration. In his domestic speeches and trips overseas, he repeatedly emphasised the need for an efficient and clean civil service. Apparently, he was preparing the ground for launching an aggressive agenda on administrative reform. It seems quite obvious that Abdullah needed to build a legitimacy based on a more effective government compared to the last one. Hence, he wanted to impose wide-ranging reforms and instil in public servants a high-performance culture. The strong mandate he received in the 2004 general elections certainly helped him to acquire confidence to pursue what can be called high-idealism in civil service reforms.

Eradication of Corruption

Malaysia's ranking in the Transparency International's Corruption Perception Index has fallen precipitously from 23rd place in 1995 to 37th place in 2003. The eradication of corruption, which was part of the legacy of Mahathir's administration, will be Abdullah's major challenge. High on Abdullah's agenda is corruption. In his own words:

> We need to enhance the efficiency of our institutions and continually strengthen good governance, transparency, and accountability. I have singled out corruption as a serious problem in our economy. We are taking this fight to the root and I have ordered systemic reform of the police force. New talent has been introduced to helm the management of strategic government-linked corporations. Key performance indicators have been instituted in order to promote a high performance culture and extract greater value.[17]

To demonstrate his commitment to the crusade against corruption, he launched a much-publicised crackdown against corrupt, middle-ranking politicians and tycoons. But critics charged that these were little-known personalities and the "big fish" are still not caught. Lim Kit Kiang, chairman of the oppposition DAP, however, wasted no time in crying foul. To him, Abdullah's mild actions reflected that his initial commitment to combat corruption was simply "pledges, pledges, and more pledges!"[18]

Since Abdullah has declared publicly that fighting corruption is his chief concern, the success and failure of his administration will be measured against how successful he combats corruption. Here, Abdullah faces a new set of challenges. First, de-Mahathirising the polity. The fact that Mahathir remains as an "advisor" to many national blue chip firms, such as car manufacturer Proton and petroleum corporation Petronas, shows that a break from the past administration is far from complete. No meaningful reforms can be possible if the Abdullah administration is unwilling or unable to curb the influence of the former prime minister. While there has been a decline in crony capitalism and mega-projects following the departure of Mahathir, it is unclear if the trend is due to Abdullah's effort in curbing Mahathir's influence or as a result of a natural demise of cronies in the system.

Second, controlling money politics within UMNO and getting support from UMNO members. UMNO has been transformed over the years, from a party of civil servants to a party based on patronage and crony capitalism. Money politics has been a hallmark in UMNO elections. The lower levels of the party organisation have been accused of money laundering and buying official positions and high-level posts. At the highest echelons of the party, there have also been allegations of corruption. If Abdullah is committed to minimising corruption within the party he would have to confront some of the senior party leaders. It is highly unlikely that UMNO top leaders would be seriously committed to such reforms. Indeed corruption at the highest echelons of the political party and government, such as influence on the state by vested interests, has had a profound impact on Malaysian political economy which is not easy to combat.

Eradication of Police Brutality

The Royal Malaysian police force as a paramilitary institution has enjoyed a reasonably good reputation in the public eye since independence. However, in the last decade, its image was severely damaged by a spate of allegations of police brutality, shootings of criminal suspects, and custodial violence and deaths. A series of snatch theft cases — reported in the media — also tarnished the image of the police as a security provider of the community and undermined public confidence in the commitment and capability of the police to make the community safe. The abuse of power by the police has reached a point where the public fear that the police is criminal. The rate of crime in urbanised cities has increased considerably, many of which were brutal murders. Abdullah responded to the public outcry even before the general elections and set up a royal commission to look into the operations and management of the police.

Was it a case of repairing the damaged reputation of the police force or a genuine commitment to reforming the institution? The commission, chaired by Mohamed Dzaiddin Abdullah, aware of its public responsibilities, went on a road show to gather feedback. After 26 public hearings around the country and a series of consultations, it published a critical report which pointed the entire police force as inefficient and corrupt. The commission alleged that rampant corruption occurred particularly in six areas: the commercial crimes division; narcotics department; logistics department; anti-vice, gambling, and secret societies division; and traffic police. It also uncovered evidence that excessive force had been used against detainees, leading to a number of deaths in police custody.

The report, however, was rebuked by the deputy inspector-general of police, Datuk Seri Mohd Sedek Mohd Ali. He said that the royal commission had made a "sweeping statement" when it said that corruption existed at all levels of the police force. In fairness, the police have been a neglected institution during the Mahathir administration, hampered by a lack of money, personnel, and equipment. However, these should not be excuses for its abuse of power and degradation. Abdullah responded to the commission saying that, in order to solve the problem of abuse of power, the government's long-term aim was to increase police numbers ten-fold in line with levels in developed nations, pledging to eliminate corruption in the police force with the qualification that the clean-up will not happen overnight. He said that, as an immediate measure, any report lodged against police personnel will be investigated thoroughly followed by court action if necessary.

Bureaucratic Inefficiency

Besides corruption, Abdullah is most concerned about the inefficiencies that has become a common complaint among the public. He called for a more hard-working, more efficient, and more competent civil service even before the general elections in 2004. On 30 August 2004, the day before the celebration of Malaysia's National Day, the public service department (PSD) issued a warning to all civil servants: Those who do not measure up will be sacked, demoted, or have their pay frozen. The Abdullah government plans to crack the whip on sluggish and incompetent workers. According to the PSD director-general, the ministries of domestic trade and consumer affairs; housing and local government; women, family and community development; and higher education will be spearheading the drive to reduce graft and improve public delivery systems.

Such attempts at stamping out inefficiency are not new. Past efforts have not led to anything significant. Why should it be different this time? Abdullah's challenge here is to convince the public that he is serious. However, he probably requires a different group of close advisors who can tell the "truth" which he so very much needs as a prerequisite for initiating genuine reform. The chief secretary, Tan Sri Shamsuddin Othman, was quoted in the mass media as saying that "Malaysia's corruption is not serious". Lim Kit Siang retorted: "Is he suggesting that Abdullah has been wasting everybody's time focusing on corruption and raising expectations that there would be an all-out war against corruption?"[19] This is, indeed, a classic example of resistance to reform within the bureaucracy which probably has vested interests.

Conclusions

The commitment of the Malaysian government to good governance have been earnest at times, but the lack of implementation and the negligence of certain administrative institutions have led to many social and political outcomes associated with bad governance. Bad governance is related to corruption, red tape, distortion of government procedures, inequitable growth, social exclusion, and lack of security of the community. Unfortunately, the Malaysian bureaucracy for all its dedication and commitment to efficiency, effectiveness, and responsiveness, has been plagued by graft and corruption charges, at least as perceived by the public. If the formal governance institution cannot perform functions that are deemed to be rightly theirs, then the country's leadership will need to rethink if their administrative efforts have gone to waste.

All said, Mahathir's efforts in reforming the Malaysian bureaucracy have been nothing less than dramatic, although they created a whole new set of issues and problems. His emphasis on a modern procedural management system for greater efficiency and effectiveness in the delivery of services to the public, and on IT to increase productivity, growth, and demands of a global market were well placed. It was obvious that while the quality of the Malaysia civil service had always been emphasised, it took on more urgency in the 1990s. Abdullah took up the challenge to re-emphasise the good qualities of the civil service and simultaneously wipe out the bad. Inefficiencies, lack of coordination, petty corruption, separating political interests from commercial ones, etc. were problems that Abdullah believed Malaysia's bureaucratic reforms should continue to emphasise. So far, he has placed high expectations on his countrymen and it remains to be seen if all his reform efforts will take root.

If Abdullah were serious about moving forward beyond the Mahathir era, then reforms within the bureaucracy must be sustained. With all the rhetoric of a new public administration — creativity, entrepreneurship, transparency, better delivery of service, reinventing government, etc. — we have yet to see serious political commitments to address serious problems. Instead, a mounting sense of disappointment has sunk in. Indeed, the challenge for Abdullah, if he wishes a legacy that is different and greater than his predecessor's, is to pay much more attention to administrative hardballs instead of delivering political rhetoric.

NOTES

1. Milton Esman, "Public Administration, Ethnic Conflict, and Economic Development," *Public Administration Review* (November /December 1997).

2. Heinrich Seidentopf, "Introduction: Government Performance and Administrative Reform", in *Strategies for Administrative Reform*, edited by Gerald Caiden and Heinrich Siedentopf (MA: D.C. Heath and Company, 1982), p. xi.

3. Ho Khai Leong, "Indigenizing the State: The New Economic Policy and the Bumiputera State in Peninsular Malaysia" (Ph.D. dissertation, Ohio State University, 1988).

4. Much of the material on Mahathir's civil service reform efforts have been taken from the author's article "Reinventing Bureaucracy? Malaysia's New Administrative Reform Initiatives", *The Journal of Comparative Asian Development* 1, no. 1 (Spring 2002): 87–104. These sections have been slightly updated for the present publication.

5. OEDC, *Public Management and Administrative Reform in Western Europe* (Paris: OECD, 1997).

6. *New Straits Times* (Malaysia), 18 August 1997.

7. Ho Khai Leong, "The Political and Administrative Frames: Challenges and Reforms under Mahathir", in *Mahathir's Administration: Performance and Crisis*, edited by Ho Khai Leong and James Chin (Singapore: Times Academic Press, 2001).

8. Ho Khai Leong, "The Dynamics of Policy-making in Malaysia: The Formulation of the New Economic Policy and the National Development Policy", *The Asian Journal of Public Administration* 14, no. 2 (1992): 204–27.

9. Ahmad Sarji, *The Civil Service of Malaysia: Towards Vision 2020* (Malaysia: Government of Malaysia, 1995), p. 1.

10. Govin Alagasari, Mahathir: *The Awakening* (Sabah: Uni-Strength Sdn Bhd, 1994), p. 52.

11. Sharifuddin Zainuddin, "Malaysia", in *The International Encyclopedia of Public Policy and Administration*, edited by Jay M. Shafritz (CO : Westview Press, 1998), p. 1,328.

12. *New Straits Times* (Malaysia), 28 October 1997.

13. *Computertimes Malaysia*, 22 February 1999.

14. *Bernama* (Malaysia), 4 November 2000.

15. Lim Kit Siang, *IT for All* (Petaling Jaya: Democratic Action Party, 1997), pp. 65, 66.

16. Mahmood bin Taib, Tan Sri Dato, and Johari Mat, "Administrative Reforms in Malaysia Toward Enhancing Public Service Performance", *Governance: An International Journal of Policy and Administration* 5 no. 4 (October 1992); Ho, *Mahathir's Administration: Performance and Crisis*.

17. Speech by the Honourable Abdullah Ahmad Badawi, prime minister of Malaysia, at a dinner hosted by the US-ASEAN Business Council at the Willard Intercontinental Hotel, Washington DC, 19 July, 2004 <http://www.us-asean.org/Malaysia/Badawi04/Speech.doc>..

18. <http://www.dapmalaysia.org/english/lks/dec03/lks2811.htm>.

19. <http://www.malaysia.net/dap/lks2780.htm>.

9

Reinventing Governance in Corporate Malaysia: The Challenges Ahead

MICHAEL YEOH AND
FARIZAL HJ. MOHD. RAZALLI

Introduction

Finally, Malaysia has a new prime minister in 22 years. The smooth yet historic power transition from one of the longest-serving to one of the few pre-selected prime ministers in Asia draws everyone's attention to the unique democratic procedures in Malaysia. Without any unruliness taking place in the background of this momentous event, Malaysia once again proves to the rest of the world that the local political scenario takes on a somewhat sound and stable base.

With the new prime minister installed, it is traditional to expect to see some changes, if not at all, to the administration. The most popular question remains whether or not this new administration will result in new ways of doing things or at least improved methods in dealing with issues and problems. This question takes on more importance when framed within the context of the business or corporate environment.

This chapter is simply oriented toward this interesting question. It is tempting to explore the nexus between the new administration and the forthcoming challenges facing Corporate Malaysia. The authors argue that a solid policy response from the new administration is required to empower Corporate Malaysia to enter into the new liberalised market economy. And they, therefore, foresee that in doing so, there needs to be a clear definitive role between the state and the market. Without this, Corporate Malaysia risks loosing its advantages and thus possibly damaging Malaysia's competitiveness.

In keeping with this onus, this chapter is organised in the following manner. It first introduces and defines key terms used in the chapter. It then analyses the corporate governance landscape in Malaysia whereby this overview forwards two main discussions: (1) the history of corporate governance inherited by the new administration and (2) how problems or setbacks during this history were treated and their observable effects today. The authors also put forward an analysis of the new administration's response to the issue of further reforming corporate governance as a continuous effort to enhance Corporate Malaysia. The discussions embed the framework of the state-market relationship whereby we see events unfold in reflection of such a relationship. This analysis also incorporates the foreseeable challenges that the future holds for Corporate Malaysia under the new administration. The last section concludes this chapter by readdressing the main question of whether or not the new administration's policy response bears any significance on reducing unwanted risks in Corporate Malaysia.

Defining Key Terms

The chapter contains three very important terms: (1) "reinventing governance", (2) "Corporate Malaysia", and (3) "challenges". It is very crucial for all these terms to be defined within the proper context of this chapter so as to ensure readers a better understanding of the discussion to come.

"Reinventing governance" refers to the process of reforming the management, in this case, the management of Corporate Malaysia. While semantically "reinvent" and "reform" might pose some differences, this chapter, however, treats both as interchangeable. Thus the chapter treats the linguistic inventory of both terms indifferently.

"Corporate Malaysia" here refers to two elements: public-listed companies (PLCs) in Malaysia with special emphasis on government-linked companies (GLCs)[1]. Second it also refers to the environment in which these PLCs operate. In short, Corporate Malaysia is treated as both the corporate players and the corporate environment (the rules that govern them).

While many would treat the word "challenges" as merely the foreseeable difficulties that one might have to overcome sometime in the future, this chapter goes a step further to refer to the foreseeable difficulties that might face the government (the new administration) as well as Corporate Malaysia (corporate players and stakeholders) in undertaking the reforms whereby these challenges are being assessed within the context of globalisation.

Malaysia and the Issue of Corporate Governance

It would definitely be an understatement to say that Malaysia's practice of corporate governance has been below par. While undoubtedly such practice may have been unsatisfactory and lacking, corporate governance in Malaysia, just as in other countries in the post-Enron era, has remained an issue of highest concern both to shareholders and the government as it affects investors' confidence and sentiment. The difference lies in the way and degree to which this issue is being dealt with.

Yesterday Revisited: Lessons Learnt and Actions Taken

In tracing the history of corporate governance in Malaysia, one could go back as early as 1965 when the first Malaysian Companies Act was developed which served as the primary legal framework for the country's business environment. Since then regulatory developments on corporate governance in Malaysia has taken place quite steadily. The enactment of the Securities Act 1983 and the Securities Commission Act 1993[2] strengthened the legislative and regulatory frameworks for the Malaysian capital market.[3] They prescribed the requirements for the listing of PLCs on the then Kuala Lumpur Stock Exchange (KLSE) (now Bursa Malaysia). Accompanying these Acts are a few other governing provisions, namely, the Securities Commission's Policies and Guidelines on Issue/ Offer of Securities; Code on Takeovers and Mergers 1987; Guidelines on the Regulation of Acquisition of Assets, Mergers, and Takeovers of Companies and Businesses; and Part E, Chapter 15 of the KLSE Listing Requirements.

With rather solid legislative and regulatory frameworks in place, there is every reason to believe that Malaysia complies with sound corporate governance practice. But as the saying goes, laws are made to be broken. Good and sound legal facilities are not a guarantee for good and sound legal observation and implementation. Besides regulatory frameworks are never perfect and unforeseen loopholes make it even more complicated and difficult for good legal observation to manifest itself.

More interestingly, Malaysia's experience with the issue of corporate governance came in light of the financial crisis of 1997/98. In this regard, one may want to argue that if it were not because of the financial crisis that plunged the entire Asian region into chaos, Malaysia would not have to worry about the issue of corporate governance or at least she would just have to comfortably review its practices of corporate governance. Thus, it was not the laws or the breach of rules of the game that was the main issue in Malaysia.

Nevertheless such an argument lacks the logic of reality. Had it not been the fragile compliance and enforcement of good corporate governance practices, Malaysia could have responded better to the financial crisis.[4] The fact remains that the practice of corporate governance in Malaysia prior to the financial crisis was unsatisfactory. This was reflective of the Malaysian Institute of Corporate Governance (MICG) vice president's comments during an interview with the media not long ago. He said that even though Malaysia had the necessary legal framework to combat non-compliance compared with the rest of the region, it lacked enforcement.[5] The same tone was echoed by Eric Teo in his paper at the ASEAN-China ISEAS forum:

> ... The Asian Crisis had indeed provoked a crisis of governance in some form; as democracy was being installed, many of the affected countries had in fact to build or rebuild crucial political and social institutions, which unfortunately had led to some instability.[6]

Prior to the crisis, there seemed to be some loopholes in the law that actually bred opportunities for irresponsible conduct of corporate governance to occur. The Companies Act 1965 vested the Registrar of Companies (ROC) with limited power and authority. ROC being the ultimate agency to regulate the Companies Act had been empowered to investigate potential violations and perform prosecutory functions. However, the ROC has no authority to institute civil actions on behalf of the investors who have suffered loss or damage as a result of these violations. In other words, while the ROC makes sure that companies violating the Companies Act are punished, it is helpless in safeguarding the victims of such violations. As a result, stakeholders, whose investments (rights) are at stake due to irresponsible actions taken by companies they invest in, are not adequately covered, thus exposing themselves to high risks. This issue becomes more crucial when minority shareholders are concerned.

The Securities Commission (SC), on the other hand, although empowered with wide administrative powers, did not actually have the judicial power of a court. This made SC less credible in the eyes of corporate players. SC's jurisdictional boundaries were vague and at times not determined at all. The case of the Renong takeover by UEM is the most glaring example of SC's overlapping role with the other regulatory bodies. What was supposed to be the exclusive jurisdiction of SC — granting a waiver from the requirement to make a mandatory offer for a remainder of shares — was taken over by the Foreign Investment Committee (FIC). Many argued that such a decision (of granting a waiver) should have been delivered by an independent body and not by one that directly represents the government's interest.[7]

Another prominent issue that reflected the poor corporate governance in Malaysia prior to the crisis was the absence of one regulatory body to monitor the GLCs' conduct of corporate governance. It was no secret that GLCs were indifferently managed given their status as government businesses which saw the government's dominant interest in those companies as opposed to private shareholders' interest in non-GLCs. The SC's and the Bursa Malaysia's listing requirements were meant specifically to monitor listed companies. They, however, do not have the authority to monitor the workings of unlisted GLCs. As such there is a double standard in corporate governance surveillance between GLCs and non-GLCs. Consequently, this has reduced the credibility and transparency of the conduct of corporate governance in Malaysia.

When the financial crisis manifested its full-blown devastation in late 1997, Malaysia suffered what we call the compounding effects of market management problems. While we acknowledge the loosely regulated global financial market as one of the major contributors to the financial crisis in Malaysia, we, however, found that the damaging effects were actually made more intense by the poor corporate governance practised in firms. This poor corporate governance was arguably the reason why foreign investors managed to take advantage of the weaknesses of Malaysian companies.[8]

Undoubtedly, reforms on some of the laws and regulations had been on-going prior to the crisis.[9] But obviously such reforms were not quick enough, nor were they good enough, to change the long-inherited malpractices in the system. These reforms appeared to be cosmetic rather than structural. Corporate players, while being aware of the reforms, played a less enthusiastic role in participating in the reforms by means of observing the newly-reviewed rules of the game. To make matters worse, these reforms did not appear to be marshalled by a holistic monitoring mechanism.[10]

The climax of these reforms somehow took place in March 1998 when the government formed the High Level Finance Committee on Corporate Governance. This Committee features very senior government officials, industry captains, and heads of professional organisations. The main task of the Committee was to prepare and submit recommendations to improve the conduct of corporate governance to the government.

What is interesting here is the fact that the formation of the Committee was the first ever comprehensive effort by the highest political authority to address the issue of corporate governance in Malaysia. We saw this as a real positive response to the outcry for a more dynamic Corporate Malaysia. While this effort actually began during the previous administration, the actual challenge in successfully implementing the policy recommendations remains to be that of the new administration of Prime Minister Abdullah Badawi. This is so the case as immediately after Malaysia fully recovered from the financial crisis in early 2000, the previous administration was tide up with the task of sustaining economic resilience especially when the global economy began to slow down in late 2000. Furthermore, the effect of new changes in corporate governance practices was slowly felt across Corporate Malaysia as many companies were still occupied with restructuring their own internal management.

In general the Committee's recommendations touched on four main elements relating to corporate governance: (1) transparency, (2) accountability, (3) enhanced regulatory enforcement, and (4) training and education.

A few significant achievements are observable. One single most important output of these recommendations was the issuance of the Malaysian Code on Corporate Governance. This Code codifies the principles and best practices of good governance and describes the basic standard for corporate governance structures and processes internal to the company. While it represents international best practices, it is also tailored to the needs of Corporate Malaysia. On the issue of transparency, extensive amendments have been made to laws, rules, and regulations so as to improve the accuracy and timeliness of the disclosure of adequate, clear, and comparable information concerning corporate financial performance, corporate governance, and corporate ownership. The mandatory listing requirement for adequately trained directors by Bursa Malaysia helps boost the emergence of highly-qualified directors running Corporate Malaysia. The existence of the MICG contributes to the pertinent role of training and continuous education of the corporate and capital market constituents.

The launch of the Capital Market Master Plan in early 2001 by SC has, to this day, contributed to positive developments in three key areas, namely, (1) the promotion of shareholder activism through enhancing avenues for minority shareholders exercising their rights, (2) the guarantee of higher standards of financial reporting and disclosure of information, and (3) the enhancement and continuous awareness of and accountability for the duties and obligations of company directors, financial controllers and officers as well as the strengthening of the role of auditors in PLCs.

With all these achievements thus far, what is next on the agenda? Undeniably, there is a positive impact brought about by all the aforementioned changes to the overall conduct of corporate governance in Malaysia. But corporate governance is a never-ending story. Since the reform began seriously in early 1999, we, however, have yet to see its full-blown effects.

Where Do We Go from Here?

Reforms, in one way or another, point to the role of the state in ensuring the smooth running of business as well as the economy at large. And in this regard we see a clear shift in Malaysia's neo-mercantalistic[11] character to one that is somewhat neo-liberal. The government, at least the previous administration, was ready to undertake changes irrespective of whether or not these changes might reveal some defects in the government's way of doing things. But the more important issue here is to make these reforms work in the long run and, therefore, sustain the business and economic integrity in Malaysia.

Hence, realising the full-blown effects of the reforms remains to be the main challenge facing Abdullah's new administration. While enjoying the early fruits borne by the recent reforms, the new administration saw more room for improvement. It was recognised that without on-going efforts in improving corporate governance practice, Malaysia might not be able to sustain its competitiveness and attractiveness to investors in a global climate of declining foreign investments and heightened competition.

Prime Minister Abdullah is aware of the importance that Corporate Malaysia functions within a competitive and effective business environment. He also knows that the administration must play a responsible yet accountable role in facilitating such a competitive and conducive corporate environment. Perhaps Abdullah noticed upon taking over at the helm that most reforms centre on the corporate sector (private as opposed to public). This is perhaps true, as was mentioned in the previous section, since the issue of loose corporate governance focuses on the private sector with little specific mention of sound governance within the public sector. This indirectly suggests that Malaysia's reform on corporate governance is far from complete considering GLCs play a very significant role in Corporate Malaysia.

The first response then was to address the issue of corruption in the public sector. The rampant corruption practices across government agencies, including those closely dealing with the private sector, worried Abdullah. Hence, he made a bold move to wage serious war against corruption. Although Abdullah risks his own political capital in cracking down corruption, it received overwhelming response from many quarters in Malaysia including the Opposition.[12]

Such overwhelming response came immediately after two high profile arrests involving key political and corporate personalities by the Anti-Corruption Agency (ACA). The first one was the arrest of the Perwaja tycoon, Eric Chia. The arrest took many by surprise as the scandal had been downplayed for over a decade ever since it was revealed.[13] Following suit was another public arrest where a fellow Cabinet member, Kasitah Gadam, was charged with graft and breach of trust.

These arrests were surely to signal something positive. At least from the public viewpoint, the new administration is honouring its promise during the recent elections. But such positive outcomes should be read with some degree of caution. While Eric Chia's arrest might end Perwaja's long scandalous saga, his arrest will not necessarily lead to resolving burning corporate governance issues for the rest of the GLCs, as with Kasitah's arrest. The more crucial question now is: Will there be more arrests involving other high-ranking civil servants who are proven guilty of corruption? For as long as corruption exists, the new administration bears the onus of fully convincing the public that the war against corruption is not mere political rhetoric but is equally matched by decisive actions.

The seriousness of Abdullah's administration in combating cor-ruption can be seen in the introduction of the National Integrity Plan (*Pelan Integriti Nasional*).[14] This Plan has the main objective of improv-ing the observance of good and rigorous ethics among all sectors across the system including political, economic, and social institutions. Although some may view it as a thick document with utopian and idealistic dreams, the Plan does provide guidelines and principles regarding morals and ethics that have been much forgotten in the chase for material gain and wealth. The Plan serves to be the reference point for the national code of conduct on ethics. The implementation of the Plan will be key to the successful inculcation of good values and ethics. The establishment of the National Integrity Institute indeed gives greater substance to the Plan as it is translated into concrete action.

One question remains though. With the Plan nicely put in place, there only remains its implementation. By merely being a reference point, having the Plan alone is not enough to improve the climate of corruption. The comprehensive propositions put forward in the Plan must be put into action. It is in this area that the new administration ought to give more emphasis. With regard to corporate governance, the Plan is arguably replicating and echoing similar principles contained in the various regulatory frameworks on corporate governance. The challenge facing the new administration then is to make all the philosophies and ideas in the Plan work.

Perhaps this challenge is being gradually overcome by the establishment of a High Level Corporate Governance Committee to investigate corporate wrongdoings. This new committee will provide regular progress reports to the prime minister himself regarding corporate investigations especially those that are overdue for whatever reason.[15]

This committee is undoubtedly timely and provides a structured working framework for all the relevant parties involved in handling corporate wrongdoings, namely, the SC, the Commercial Crime Division of the police, and the Company's Commission. Its existence coordinates efforts much more effectively. But again such a framework might work well theoretically. The fact that it involves three independent agencies alone may actually be a source of conflict if not uncoordination. The committee members will have to demonstrate integrity and professionalism as much as possible. They might face the challenge of giving the impression that they are representing one entity working towards a single goal.[16]

Abdullah's government continues to embark on bold moves since gaining a new mandate. This time the long-held sensitive issue of Bumiputera dominates the core of the game. On 17 June 2003, at the time when Abdullah was still a "houseman" in his prime ministership duties, the law requiring foreign investors to have Bumiputera business partners was repealed. Under the new law, foreigners may now own 100 per cent of a Malaysian company in most sectors.[17] And after taking office, Abdullah announced that non-Bumiputeras will make the line up of new CEOs and other senior management executives in GLCs.[18] The clear sign here is that the selection process will no longer depend on the race but on the merit and qualification of the candidates.

In many respects, all these moves will make Malaysia more attractive to potential foreign investors than ever before while at the same time suggest Malaysia's true compliance with international trade regimes such as the WTO which encourage countries, especially those in Asia, to reduce and finally remove all kinds of discriminations and preferences as well as barriers to the free flow of capital and labour.

This bold initiative by the new administration is responsive to global changes and is, therefore, critical to Malaysia's future survival in the face of the ever-increasing regional competition.[19] Also, this indicates the gradual dismantling of the state's strong and protective role in the economy. While it is not within the scope of the chapter to argue its merit, such a development reveals a whole new dimension to Malaysia's role in the international economic front especially in the era of WTO and the free market economy.

But reforming a system that has benefited some of the loyal supporters and political allies of UMNO might prove to be troublesome, if not difficult. And for a country like Malaysia where the dominant role of the state in protecting the interests of the elites and political savvies is quite obvious, reforms might be slightly painful for the affected parties. Hence, Abdullah's efforts in revamping the governance in GLCs may be a truly painful experience. But Abdullah has little space to maneouvre in this area. As GLCs play a key role in driving the economy, not adequately redressing the problem of governance in these GLCs may result in the next paralysis of the economy. GLCs in Malaysia account for almost 34 per cent of the Bursa Malaysia's capitalisation with some 40 of these GLCs listed on both the main and second board of the stock exchange.[20] With such a large proportion of shares in the market, GLCs are a de facto indicator of the general health of the economy. Should these GLCs fail to or poorly perform, Malaysia might risk putting its economy in jeopardy.

Abdullah has personally vowed to the public that the government would take whatever measures possible to clean up the GLCs.

In an exclusive interview with the *Far Eastern Economic Review*, he announced that his first target for a clean-up are GLCs. This statement reflects Abdullah's true boldness. While many might question the sincerity and credibility behind such a statement, the authors would rather forucs on the psychological effects of such a statement.

By appealing to the general public of his government's drive toward reforms, Abdullah psychologically affects the Malaysian public in two ways: (1) the public may view the new administration as worth relying on to see to the progress of the new administration's agenda, and (2) the corporate community at large may read this sign as a signal or warning to better reposition themselves in order to fit into the new administration "style" of governing. This is a more subtle way a state can help facilitate positive changes within companies and engage the public.

Looking at the items on Abdullah's reform agenda, it does present strong evidence that lends much credence to the aforementioned psychological influence. First, he made a firm decision on cracking down corruption, next he spoke of improving efficiency in the civil service and enhancing the delivery system, and then he hoped to improve the governance in GLCs. This chain of statements indirectly leads the general public including those in the business community to see the seriousness of the new administration. The argument against the sincerity of these statements as being merely political rhetoric might, in this case, prove to be unfounded as those statements manifested into concrete action plans.

On 14 May 2004, Abdullah appointed Azman Mokhtar to head the federal government's investment arm, Khazanah Nasional. The appointment of the 43-year-old former country head of Salomon Smith Barney consolidated the efforts of bringing the best and most qualified personalities into Malaysian GLCs. Azman was not alone on the bench as Telekom Malaysia got its new CEO, Dato' Wahid Omar, the former managing director of the UEM, who is 40 years of age. Another new face brought onto the scene of reforming GLCs is Dato' Che Khalib Mohamed Noh who is tasked to head the country's biggest energy company, Tenaga Nasional Berhad (TNB).

Being the former CEO in KUB, Che Khalib assumes the post at the age of 38.

The introduction of these young fresh faces to the board of directors of some of the prominent GLCs again reflects the drastic move by the new administration to breathe new life into these GLCs. One thing is clear, Abdullah capitalises on the young, brilliant, and energetic human resources to implement his agenda. This trend has picked up in Malaysia where more companies are now looking to hire bright young minds. This somehow suggests Abdullah's strategy of maximising the energy and intellect of the youth that was not effectively tapped in the past. And the recent announcement by the government to entice Malaysian young talents currently working abroad to return home to serve the nation emphasises this point.[21]

The real challenge here then is to ensure that the change cascades down the various management levels. While this remains the main responsibility of the newly-elected CEOs, the government is still responsible to help facilitate such a process. The appointment and use of more non-executive, independent directors to provide a check and balance on the management suggest less reason for not achieving a better and trustworthy Corporate Malaysia.

Having discussed all these recent reforms of the new administration, it must now be asked "what next?" While Abdullah's administration is off to a good start, it is more important to work on a good finish. Reforms in themselves mean nothing than merely preparing for a new way of looking at and doing things. It is the process that follows the reforms that matters most. And it is the process that harbours a myriad of issues and challenges. The final section addresses this aspect apart from redressing the significance of the new administration's policy of the betterment of Corporate Malaysia.

The Quest for a Brighter Future in a Bleak World

It is an already well-known fact thus far that the new administration is embarking on a whole new journey of reinventing governance in Corporate Malaysia. It is a journey that bears two issues: (1) the area to be reinvented and (2) the execution of such reinvention. Addressing these two issues has proven to be a real challenge for the new administration.

Also, it is interesting to note that in the course of doing so, there is a shift in the way companies relate themselves to the government, i.e. the state-business relationship.

There is no doubt that the practice of corporate governance in Malaysia prior to the financial crisis of 1997/98 was quite negligible or overlooked. But in the wake of the crisis and its aftershocks, corporate governance came under public scrutiny. Awareness of the issue of corporate governance and its relation to the crisis had substantially led to efforts to better address its practice or lack thereof. Hence, some major changes took place in subsequent years following the crisis, the highlight being the revamp of the corporate governance legal framework in 2000/01.

Having successfully undertaken these changes, one has yet to see them taking effect in enhancing corporate governance. Perhaps it is far too early to expect positive results. But time remains a weak excuse. If time is ever a constraint, efforts should be stepped up to be ahead of time, and the only possible way to do this is to continue getting the right and most qualified people into the system. Following this effort then is the development of a new mentality by means of instiling extrinsic and intrinsic motivation and merit-based performance assessment within the system that is geared toward achieving the highest standard that measures up to the global practice. The bottom line is that Corporate Malaysia urgently needs to feel the impact of these changes and see some concrete reform results not necessarily in the form of restructuring but more importantly in the form of new ideas and mentality.

Thus this is the true challenge facing the new administration. While the previous administration, toward the end of its era, had put in place the necessary frameworks and structures, the new administration bears the tougher job of ensuring all these efforts work efficiently and successfully. And the first step towards this is to be able to recognise the various sections of Corporate Malaysia in which to apply all these reform efforts.

The new administration has proven that it has passed the first step. It is something to be celebrated as it takes strong political will and determination on the part of the administration to recognise the various aspects of Corporate Malaysia to be reformed. But the passing of this first step also sees the loosening up of the state's direct control of companies, in this case the GLCs. Unlike in the past, the new administration makes the companies more accountable for their actions and decisions. With a "new team" put in place in some of these GLCs, the state is actually transferring much of its once exclusive authority and power in running the companies to the private and independent hands of capable corporate men. This reform reinforces the argument that Malaysia is gradually releasing itself from the shackles of rigid and direct state control of businesses. This particular by-product of the reform has really been an extraordinary feature of the new administration. It is indeed a clear sign of an open and liberal government.

Nevertheless as mentioned earlier there remains the second issue to be considered: the execution of the reforms. Thus far the execution process seems to be running on track. But burning issues like how holistic will the process be are still lingering. The few bold initiatives such as the introduction of new faces in the higher management and board of directors of the few GLCs, the involvement of more non-Bumiputeras in the top-level management of GLCs, the focus on key performance indicators (KPIs), greater accountability and transparency, and the redress of issues of corruption in the public delivery system, are all welcomed provided that such initiatives are undertaken in the spirit of truly benefiting the entire Corporate Malaysia. It is imperative that such bold initiatives do not end up as another political gimmick in the hope of gaining greater support from the electorate. Therefore, every single move and plan needs to be adequately clarified and made public so as to add credibility and transparency to the administration's action plans. In this regard, the parliament serves as the best ground for communicating such rationale and debating the plans. The execution of all the plans must be monitored as frequently as possible.

This is where the state helps facilitate the establishment of a workable legal framework. All the plans must work within the desired and targeted guiding principles in the most transparent and impartial way. The applicability of the principles must be made with no exception and discrimination. The government then has the responsibility to empower its federal, state, and local authorities so as to ensure the efficiency of the newly-reformed system. It is in this realm that the role of the state (government) seems to be of ultimate concern.

The other important aspect of executing these reform plans in Corporate Malaysia is to implement the execution process in conjunction with global changes and developments. Corporate Malaysia is the ultimate hope of all Malaysians for gaining a better edge in the era of globalisation. The 25-million Malaysian population depend so much on Corporate Malaysia to represent their interests and stake at the global front. Therefore, the performance of Corporate Malaysia must be stronger to face any uncertainties in today's world. The country cannot lose her reputation and credence in the eyes of her international counterparts. Strategic partnerships might prove to be so necessary in this regard. Malaysia is but a small player in the global field. And being small suggests that she has to think big. If economic and business alliances are part of the answer to her long survival, then Corporate Malaysia should consider working toward that end. In a game where evils and angels compete, observing good values alone may not be enough. Being smart and tactical also play a crucial role.

Corporate reforms in Malaysia will indeed strengthen investors' confidence in Malaysia. This can be seen in the increasing market capitalisation of Bursa Malaysia and the increase in the Kuala Lumpur Composite Index (KLCI). The greater focus on accountability and transparency and the introduction of KPIs will change the Malaysian corporate culture to one that is increasingly performance-driven. The pursuit of corporate excellence and improved shareholder value will lead to better results. What is, however, important is that there will be no back-tracking in the reform measures taken thus far. What is also important is for the younger CEOs recently appointed to head various GLCs to successfully lead their respective GLCs not only in good but also in bad times, for many of them may not have been tested during periods of cyclical downturns. Nevertheless, the corporate reform agenda of Prime Minister Abdullah Badawi has brought about a more open and transparent business environment, one where there are no chosen favourites and where only the best will thrive.

In conclusion, the authors believe that the progress made by the new administration is satisfactory. With new plans up for implementation, notwithstanding the ones already undertaken, the hope for a better Corporate Malaysia remains intact. The main question is when? Therefore, consistency is key. The new administration needs to demonstrate great consistency apart from strong determination for the action plans to work. Sustaining the efforts and human resources to do this will weather the storms of the future. Corporate Malaysia is poised to contribute significantly to Malaysia's national economic development, progress, and prosperity. More importantly, Malaysia needs corporate players and managers who are visionary, ethical, strategic, global, and performance-driven.

NOTES

1. While the term "government-linked companies" (GLCs) is deemed to be rather new in Malaysia, this chapter, however, tries to apply a term that sufficiently describes the nature of the companies in Malaysia. The term "state-owned companies" (SOCs) is rather familiar by the virtual fact that the government actually runs companies like Petronas. The government owns an overwhelming majority of the shares (almost 99 per cent) in the company. However, in other companies, the government may hold fewer shares but it possesses substantial influence in them. The authors then feel that the term GLCs, with regard to this chapter, is suitable and succinctly represent the sample of companies in the analysis. (Note: Use of the different terms in this case, however, might vary from one individual to another and therefore is not to be taken as a rigid definition.)

2. It was this Act that brought the Security Commission into existence. This financially-independent statutory establishment is answerable to the minister of finance and its accounts are tabled in parliament. It possesses wide administrative powers and closely monitors the smooth operation of the Bursa Malaysia.

3. According to an article by the Global Corporate Governance Forum, along with the ever-globalising world economy, international and domestic capital markets become more crucial for firms to raise investments. Hence, only strong, transparent, and reliable capital markets would keep a country's firms in business and competitive. See "Corporate Governance: An Issue of International Concern" <http://www.gcgf.org> (accessed 29 July 2004).

4. There are indeed many approaches to explaining the Asian financial crisis. But among the most widely cited is the role of the structure and environment. The

system with careless lending practices and careless use of financial derivatives were believed to have fatally affected the Asian economies including Malaysia's. Besides, the opaque data reporting processes fuelled the ever-burning fire of the financial crisis. See Salih N. Neftci, "FX Short Positions, Balance Sheets and Financial Turbulence: An Interpretation of the Asian Financial Crisis" (paper presented at the International Capital Markets and the Future Economic Policy) (CEPA 1998).

5. Alice Chia, "Institute: Give SC Enforcement Power", *News Straits Times* (Malaysia), 20 August 2003, sec. B, p. 5.

6. Eric Teo, "ASEAN+3: The Roles of ASEAN & China" (paper presented at the ASEAN–China ISEAS Forum, 23–24 June 2004).

7. The FIC waived the requirement for UEM to make the mandatory general offer for the remaining shares in Renong after the former's takeover of Renong. The acquisition was perceived as a bailout of a cash-starved company and its shareholders with sole regard for UEM's interest. Hence, this gave the public the impression that such acquisition was officially authorised. See World Bank Group, "Malaysia: Corporate Governance Assessment and ROSC Module", *Reports on the Observance of Standards and Codes* (1999) <http://www.worldbank.org/ifa/rosc> (accessed 2 August 2004).

8. During the financial crisis, Malaysia fell prey to short-term capital (mainly foreign portfolio investment [FPI] and foreign direct investment [FDI]) withdrawal from the market. These investors, taking advantage of the relatively loose and underdeveloped capital market, pulled out of the Malaysian capital market which left it chaotic and unstable.

9. The Financial Reporting Act 1997 established the Malaysian Accounting Standards Board, four years after the establishment of the Audit Committee in 1993. Along with the aim to enhance transparency in the securities market, the merit-based system or regulation had been replaced with the disclosure-based regime in 1995. Apart from this, the Code on Takeovers and Mergers was revamped in 1996. See Nik Ramlah Nik Mahmood, "Ensuring Higher Standards of Transparency and Accountability in Corporate Life" (speech delivered during a dinner hosted by the Securities Commission, 25 January 2003) <http://www.sc.com.my> (accessed 5 August 2004).

10. Nik Ramlah in her speech admitted that it was the financial crisis that underscored the need for a holistic approach in realising the reforms. The financial crisis had urgently called for reform efforts to be fast-tracked. Ibid.

11. Neo-mercantilism is an idealism that refers to the state's control over enterprises and businesses especially those deemed integral and strategic to national interest. Unlike neo-liberalism that emphasises on the operation of a free market with minimal state involvement, neo-mercantilism, on the other hand, emphasises the state's role in

the economy. In other words, neo-mercantilism affirms that the state leads and the market follows.

12. While not openly admitted, corruption has somehow bred across the political fractions as well as the civil service. The system is such that corruption itself, due to various interpretations it presents depending on the individual's needs and interests, seems to be rather complex and thus difficult to overcome. Hence, when the effort to get rid of corruption is publicly announced, many would be reserved as to what extent such effort will be a success. For further discussion on corruption and its impact on the national integrity system, see Jeremy Pope, *Confronting Corruption: The Elements of a National Integrity System* (Kuala Lumpur: Transparency International, 2000).

13. The Perwaja scandal saw one of the biggest corporate grafts in the country. The former managing director of Perwaja Steel, Eric Chia, was alleged of mismanaging the company and authorising some irregular transactions with a company based in Hong Kong that resulted in Perwaja Steel's bankruptcy in 1996.

14. The National Integrity Plan (NIP) was launched in May 2004. The general objective of NIP is to fulfil the fourth challenge of *Vision 2020* that is to shape a nation with strong morals and ethics. For the first five-year period (2004–08), the NIP identifies five priority targets, known as TEKAD 2008, to be achieved, namely, (1) reducing symptoms of corruption and abuse of power, (2) enhancing the performance of the public service delivery system and overcoming poor bureaucratic practices, (3) improving corporate governance and business etiquette, (4) strengthening the family institution, and (5) improving the quality of life and well-being of society. *The National Integrity Plan* (unofficial translation), July 2004.

15. Balan Moses, "Probe into Corporate Wrongdoings", *News Straits Time* (Malaysia), 15 May 2004, sec. F, p. 2.

16. This committee is supposed to take on a study and then propose changes to the allocation of responsibilities between the three enforcement agencies to minimise duplication of efforts and ensure greater effectiveness. This, however, is where the real challenge is. Each individual agency might not be so keen to surrender part of their enforcement territory or acquire additional enforcement tasks. While on the surface reallocation of responsibilities sounds attractive, losing or sharing some authority to or with the others might prove to be something undesirable.

17. Michael Shari, "Malaysia after Mahathir", *Business Week Online*, 29 September 2003 <http://www.businessweek.com> (accessed 15 July 2004).

18. Lim Kit Siang, the Opposition leader, in his media conference at the Parliament House, said that the next few appointments to head GLCs will be the acid test of the new administration's assurance on the selection of the "best and brightest"

regardless of whether they are Bumiputeras or not. See <http://www.geocities.com/CapitolHill/3939> (accessed 3 August 2004).

19. Such a change should be looked at from a global perspective. In recent years, China has been the single most important destination or the major magnet for FDIs in this region. Southeast Asian economies have seen a dramatic reduction in FDI which has outflowed to China. Thus, Malaysia cannot afford to wait too long before China writes off all of her advantages. Mr Jemal-ud-in Kassum, "Recent Trends in FDI and Challenges for Malaysia" (speech delivered at the Ministry of Finance, Putrajaya, Malaysia, 15 July 2004).

20. Michael Vatikiotis and S. Jayasankaran, "Softly, Softly Go Reforms", *Far Eastern Economic Review*, 3 June 2004, pp. 20–23.

21. The government recently announced more competitive incentives for Malaysian talents working abroad to return home and serve the nation. Although similar attempts have been made in the past, the recent appeal, however, came in light of new changes taking place in the country coupled with Abdullah's promise to provide better facilities for research and development (R&D).

10

Globalisation and Ethnic Integration in Malaysian Education

LEE HOCK GUAN

Introduction

In the 1956 Razak Report, two important roles were assigned to education in Malaysia: to facilitate economic development and nation building, or ethnic integration.[1] In the aftermath of the May 1969 ethnic riots, however, education also became a key vehicle designated by the state to advance its New Economic Policy (NEP) goal to achieve economic growth with equity, especially equity in terms of gradually eliminating the economic participation identification with ethnicity.[2] Thus, since 1971 education in Malaysia was expected to perform potentially contradictory overlapping objectives: support economic growth while expanding Malay economic participation, and foster national integration while building a Malay-dominated nation.

State planners, aware of the inherited divisive and latently explosive multi-ethnic society, had always regarded facilitating ethnic integration in the newly-independent nation as an important role of education.[3] The central dilemma encountered in developing an education system to facilitate ethnic integration in Malaysia was how to juxtapose the promotion of Malay as the medium of instruction with guaranteeing the Chinese and Indian their rights to be instructed in their mother tongues. To foster national integration and cement the ethnically-diverse society, state planners also argued that it was necessary to create a set of common values. While this view was not in dispute, nevertheless, what were and who defined the "common values" was rigorously debated and contested. A prevalent view regarded education as a means to preserve, transmit, and develop each ethnic group's language and culture. This view influenced non-Malay communities to regard the policy to build a predominantly Malay-medium education system as a move that would curb mother tongue education and lead to a gradual demise of their values, languages, and cultures.

To help increase Malay participation in the economy, education was assigned the role of improving the skill levels and varieties, especially in the management, technical, and scientific fields, of the Malay labour force. This was to be achieved through a variety of ethnic preferential policies and programmes, including ethnic quota,[4] to increase Malay enrolment in higher education. The state's rationale for using ethnic quotas was that "an admission policy which is based solely on academic merit will result in the exclusion of many Malays from universities and this will have adverse effects to promote national unity".[5] Ethnic preferential treatment, in other words, was not only crucial to expanding and upgrading the Malay labour force but also towards promoting national integration.

The manner in which the ethnic preferential policies were implemented and the prevalent non-Malay sentiment that they were deprived of equal educational opportunities and their languages, religions, and cultures were discriminated against, had negatively impacted ethnic integration in the education system. Indeed, the education system had become marked with the presence of ethnic enclaves. In this chapter, the author will show that while Malaysia has made substantial steps to upgrade its human resource capability and increase Malay enrolment in tertiary education in the face of globalisation, entrenched ethnic preferential prejudices and policies have further resulted in expanding the ethnic enclaves.

Globalisation and Educational Development in Malaysia

Broadly speaking, globalisation[6] has impacted the development of education in Malaysia in two significant ways. Firstly, since globalisation has greatly intensified the economic competition among nations, it has led the Malaysian state to recognise the urgent need to transform the Malaysian economy from a production- to a knowledge-based economy.[7] This recognition has directed the state to expand the education system, especially the tertiary level, in order to upgrade the skills and knowledge levels of the country's human resource. Secondly, the country's effort to upgrade its human resource was fortuitously assisted by the fact that globalisation has also given rise to the privatisation and internationalisation of higher education.[8]

By the 1990s, as a result of accelerating economic globalisation, Malaysia's labour-intensive and lower-end manufacturing industries were subjected to increasing competition from fast-developing, lower-wage economies, especially China. This stark reality reinforced the policy makers' decision to reposition the Malaysian economy up the skill and technological ladder. In 1991, the then prime minister, Mahathir Mohammad, publicly announced his *Vision 2020*'s objective to transform the country into a fully-modern industrialised society by the year 2020.[9] The process of transforming Malaysia into a modern industrialised society by 2020 was equated with the development of an information and communication technology (ICT)-driven, or knowledge-based, economy.[10]

To develop a knowledge-based economy would necessarily entail developing the country's human and intellectual capital that would "produce adequate supply of, support and sustain a flexible, agile, and mobile workforce with the relevant knowledge and skills".[11] Aiming to develop a knowledge economy thus led the state to significantly increase its development allocation and expenditure to the education sector, especially tertiary education.[12] Beginning in the 1990s, the state has embarked on expanding the existing public tertiary institutions as well as building new ones. For example, the number of polytechnics has increased from seven in 1990 to 11 in 2004, and the number of universities from seven to 18 during the same period.

Most importantly, substantial gains made in increasing the total tertiary enrolment were due to a policy change that enabled the private sector to play a larger role in the provision of tertiary education. Private tertiary institutions offering certificate and diploma courses have existed since independence, and although there was a huge demand, the private sector has remained relatively small because of a state policy to restrict the privatisation of education. From the late 1980s, a number of factors compelled the state to expand the role of the private sector in the provision of tertiary education.[13] By 1996, to regulate and facilitate the growth of the privatisation of education, the Private Higher Education Institutions Act was implemented. At the international level, the growth of the private education sector was assisted by the increasing numbers of tertiary institutions in the developed world driven to recruit more full fee-paying foreign students in order to generate more revenues.[14]

Allowing the private sector to play a larger role in the provision of tertiary education greatly expanded the opportunities for students to acquire both local and foreign tertiary qualifications. In particular, the internationalisation of higher education enabled Malaysian students to receive their qualifications from foreign institutions through various local private educational institutions and programs, at a much reduced cost. The growth of the private tertiary education sector has been most impressive indeed; the number of private colleges increased from 280 in 1995 to 611 in 1999, local private universities and university colleges from none in 1995 to 19 in 1999, and there have also been five foreign university branch campuses in Malaysia since 1999.

Table 10.1 shows the dramatic increase in educational development expenditure from nearly RM7 billion (13.4 per cent of total public development expenditure) in the Sixth Malaysia Plan (6MP) (1991–95) to RM17.5 billion (19.9 per cent) in the Seventh Malaysia Plan (7MP) (1996–2000). The projected allocation for the Eighth Malaysia Plan (8MP) (2001–05) was RM18.7 billion (20.6 per cent).

The emphasis on increasing enrolment in higher education has led to the channeling of more resources to expand and develop the tertiary education sector. The development expenditure for tertiary education increased from RM3 billion (43.5 per cent of the total development educational expenditure) in the 6MP to RM5 billion (28.5 per cent) in

Table 10.1
Development Allocation and Expenditure for Education,
1981–2005 (in RM Millions)

	4MP	5MP	6MP	7MP	8MP*
Primary	759.5	760	1,127.1	2,631.8	2,750
Secondary	1,381.6	1,543	1,909	5,317.5	4,862
Tertiary	2,056.8	1,727	3,039.4	5,005.1	8,900
Teacher	149	144	155.6	332.5	300
Other educational	134.5	1,208	751	4,255.3	1,848
Total	4,334.5	5,382	6,982.1	17,542.2	18,660

*Development allocation.
Source: Various Malaysia Plans.

Table 10.2
Enrolment Rates in Government and Government-assisted Institutions,
1970–2000 (in Percentages)

Educational Level	Age Range (Years)	1970	1980	1990	1995	2000
Primary	6+ to 11+	88.2	93.6	99.8	96.7	96.8
Lower secondary	12+ to 14+	52.2	79.9	83	82.5	85.0
Upper secondary	15+ to 16+	20.1	38.1	49.1	55.8	72.6
Post-secondary college	17+ to 18+	3.1	9.4	18.9	23.2	16.2
University	19+ to 24+	0.6	1.6	2.9	3.7	8.1

Source: Educational Statistics (Ministry of Education).

the 7MP and is projected to be RM8.9 billion (47.7 per cent) during the 8MP.[15]

Since 1970, the growth in school enrolment was faster than that of the school-age population, reflecting an increase in enrolment ratios, particularly at the primary and lower secondary levels. At the primary level, the ratio increased from 88.2 per cent in 1970 to about 93.6 per cent in 1980, indicating a near universal enrolment by the 1980s (see Table 10.2).[16] The enrolment rate at the lower secondary level has increased from about 52 per cent in 1970 to more than 80 per cent since 1990. For upper secondary enrolment, the rate increased only from 20.1 per cent in 1970 to 49.1 per cent in 1990. To further upgrade human resource in the country, in 1995, the state instituted an automatic promotion policy from lower to upper secondary schools. This policy change helped to raise the upper secondary level enrolment rate to 72.6 per cent in 2000.

The enrolment rate for post-secondary and college education has increased from 3.1 per cent in 1970 to 18.9 per cent in 1990 and 16.2 per cent in 2000 (Table 10.2). For university education, the enrolment has increased from 0.6 per cent in 1970 to 2.9 per cent in 1990 and 8.1 per cent in 2000. In other words, for tertiary education (combined total of post-secondary, college, and university), the enrolment rate has increased from 3.7% in 1970 to 21.5% in 1990 and 24.3% in 2000.

In 1990, the enrolment of students in public and private institutions were 122,340 and 35,600 respectively. But, by 2000, the enrolment in private institutions had surpassed that of public institutions, 203,391 to 167,507 (Table 10.3).[17] In contrast, a number of factors had contributed to the declining number of students studying overseas, from 73,000 in 1990 to 50,600 in 1995 and, especially after the 1997 financial crisis, to 13,000 in 2000. Thus, the total enrolment of students at the tertiary level has more than doubled between 1985 and 2000,[18] from 169,330 to about 380,000.

The rapid growth in school enrolment and educational achievement is well illustrated by the highest educational attainment achieved by the 20- to 24-year-old cohort in Malaysia. The percentage of 20- to 24-year-olds who finished 11 years of education has almost doubled from about 20 per cent in 1980 to nearly 40 per cent in 2000 (Figure 10.1). For

Table 10.3
Enrolment in Public, Private, and Overseas Tertiary Institutions, 1985–2000

Types of Institutions	1985	1990	1995	2000
Public institutions	86,330	122,340	189,020	167,507
Private institutions	15,000	35,600	127,584	203,391
Overseas institutions	68,000	73,000	50,600	13,000
Total	169,330	230,940	367,214	383,898

Source: Various Malaysia Plans; Educational Statistics (Ministry of Education).

Lee Hock Guan

Figure 10.1
Persons 20–24 Years Old Who Have Completed Upper Secondary or Tertiary Education, 1980–2000 (in Percentages)

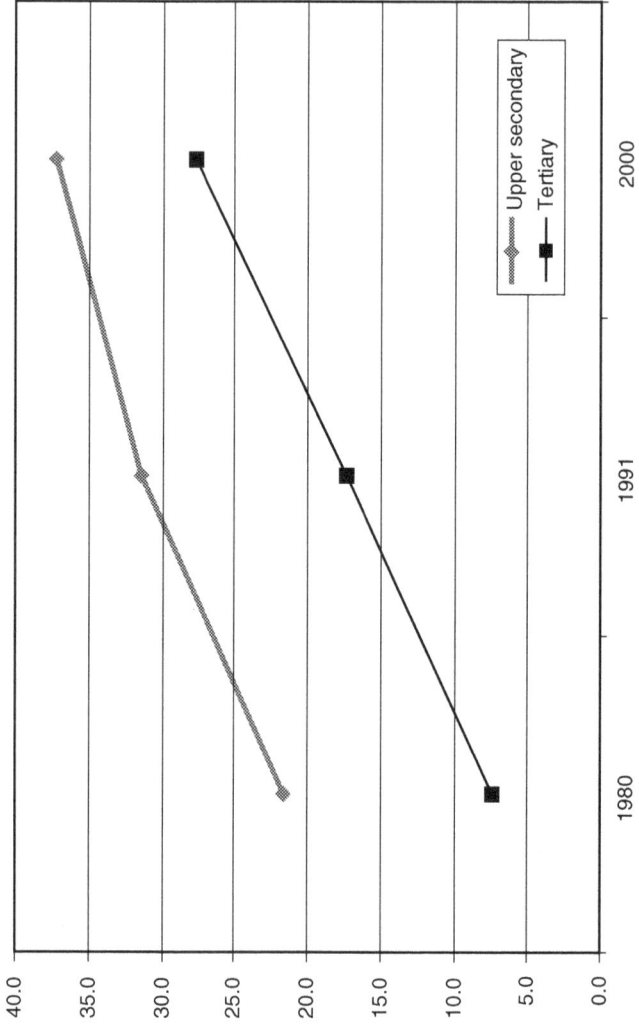

Source: Population Census, 1980, 1991, and 2000.

tertiary education, the percentage has increased from slightly less than 10 per cent in 1980 to nearly 30 per cent in 2000.

In accordance with the objective of transforming the Malaysian economy into a knowledge-based one, the state has made substantial strides in upgrading the country's human resource. More investments for the expansion of public tertiary education and a change in state policy on privatisation of education had resulted in the output of more graduates with higher educational qualifications. Globalisation's impact on higher education, through privatisation and internationalisation, has assisted the growth of private higher education in Malaysia. However, while Malaysia has made substantial gains in upgrading its human resource, its higher education enrolment rate is still lower than many of the newly-industrialised economies such as South Korea and Singapore.

Ethnic Participation in Higher Education

Since the launch of the NEP in 1971, ethnic preferential policies and programmes had been implemented to expand Malay participation in higher education. Importantly, Article 153 of the Constitution, which links safeguarding the special position of the Malays to the implementation of a system of quotas for them in employment, admission to education and training, and access to scholarships, has been invoked to argue that the preferential policies are part of Malay special rights. Indeed, Article 153 is frequently used to legalise Malay privileged access to educational scholarships, training, and enrolment in general.[19]

Prior to the implementation of the ethnic quotas policy, it was at the tertiary education level, especially in science and technical courses, that the Malays were most under-represented. The National Educational Act 1971 introduced a number of ethnic preferential policies that favoured the Malays in general, and Bumiputeras specifically, in order to raise Malay enrolment at the tertiary level. In particular, an ethnic-based admission policy made it mandatory for all higher public education institutions, especially universities, to reserve 55 per cent of their places for Malay students. In the early years of the implementation, it was argued that since Malays were under-represented in universities in the past, their proportion had to be well above 55 per cent in order to make up for the past; during the 1975–80 period, the ratio was around 66.2 per cent.

In reality, however, since 1980 the Malay admissions into local universities have continued to exceed 55 per cent. The reason was because policy makers took into account the total university ethnic enrolment figure that included enrolment in overseas universities, the majority of whom were non-Malays. With the inclusion of non-Malay students studying overseas, invariably Malay enrolment in local public universities would be higher than 55 per cent in order for the total Malay university enrolment figure to account for 55 per cent of the total university enrolment.

Tertiary enrolment has increased significantly since the implementation of the NEP in 1971, especially since 1995 with the intensification of efforts to accelerate the human resource development. In 1970, the tertiary enrolment of Malays was 54.1 per cent of the total enrolment, constituting 82.9 per cent and 39.7 per cent at certificate and diploma, and degree levels respectively (Table 10.4). These figures are only for local public institutions, and given that the majority of private and overseas students are non-Malays, the total percentage of enrolment of Malays would be lower than 54.1 per cent. For enrolment of students in public and private (including overseas) tertiary institutions, in 1980, Malays made up 46 per cent of the total, constituting 46.3 per cent and 45.7 per cent in the certificate and diploma, and degree courses respectively. By 1999, Malay enrolment made up 53.9 per cent and 58.7 per cent at the certificate and diploma, and degree levels respectively, totaling 56 per cent of the total tertiary enrolment.

An additional important feature is the change in the distribution of Malay tertiary students in the public and private education sectors. Historically, majority of Malay students were enrolled in the local public institutions. For example, in 1980, they made up 72.8 per cent of the total enrolment in local public tertiary institutions, constituting 87.7 per cent and 62.7 per cent in the certificate and diploma, and degree programs respectively (Table 10.4). In contrast, they made up only 21.1 per cent of the student population in the private tertiary sector, constituting 15.7 per cent and 26.8 per cent in the certificate and diploma, and degree programs respectively. By 1999, Malay enrolment in the private sector has made noticeable gains: 39.4 per cent of enrolments with an especially huge increase in the certificate and diploma programs where they made up 44.5 per cent.

Table 10.4
Distribution of Enrolment in Tertiary Education by Ethnic Group (in Percentages)

Type of Education	1970			1980			1999	
	Malays*	Chinese	Indians	Malays*	Chinese	Indians	Malays*	Non-Malays
Public sector								
Certificate and diploma	82.9	15.5	1	87.7	10.9	1.4	78.9	21.1
Degree	39.7	49.2	7.3	62.7	31.5	5.8	69.9	30.1
Subtotal	54.1	40.3	5.6	72.8	23.2	4	72.7	27.3
Private sector								
Certificate and diploma	—	—	—	15.7	71.2	12.8	44.5	55.5
Degree	—	—	—	26.8	59.4	13.8	16.3	83.7
Subtotal	—	—	—	21.1	65.6	13.3	39.4	60.6
Public and private sectors	—	—	—	46.3	45.7	8	53.9	46.1
Certificate and diploma	—	—	—	46.3	45.7	8	53.9	46.1
Degree	—	—	—	45.7	44.7	9.6	58.7	41.3
Total	—	—	—	46	45.2	8.8	56	44

* "Malays" includes other Bumiputeras.
Source: Various Malaysia Plans.

Undoubtedly, the effectiveness of the ethnic quota policy in enhancing Malay participation in higher education was most evident in their enrolment gains in the science and technical courses at the university level. Historically, the number of Malays enrolled in higher education, especially university level, was disproportionately found in the humanities and arts faculties such that their numbers were much lower than that of the non-Malays in the science and engineering departments. For example, between 1959 and 1970, the Malay to Chinese graduates ratio for engineering, science, and medicine were 1:100, 1:20, and 1:9 respectively. The proportion of Malay graduates in science and engineering has, however, increased significantly since the implementation of the ethnic preferential policies. In 2000, for the 25–29 and 35–39 age groups, Malays made up 48.2 per cent and 57.1 per cent and 59.9 per cent and 60.2 per cent respectively of those who had attained a certificate diploma or degree in the fields of science and engineering, construction, and skills training in electronics and mechanics (Table 10.5). In contrast, the Chinese percentages across the age groups in these two fields indicated a declining trend, with the older cohort achieving a higher proportion than the younger cohort.

The success of the ethnic preferential policies in education has led to the growth of a sizeable Malay professional class. The progress made by the Malays in becoming highly qualified professionals is evident in Table 10.6. During the 1970s and 1980s, there was limited Malay representation of architects, accountants, engineers, dentists, doctors and lawyers. Since 1990, their numbers in these professions have increased noticeably except for accountants and less so for architects and engineers. By 2000, about one in three dentists, doctors, and lawyers and one in four architects and engineers were Malays. Indeed, while the Chinese were previously over-represented in the majority of the professions, by 2000, the Malay percentage has exceeded 30 per cent except for architects, accountants, and engineers. The success in raising the participation of the Malays at the tertiary level is consequently reflected in their participation in professional employment, including their participation in the ICT sector.

Table 10.5
Distribution of Malaysian Certificate/Diploma/Degree Holders
by Main Field of Study, Age Group, and Ethnic Group, 2000 (in Percentages)

Main Field of Study	Age m Group											
	25–29 Years				35–39 Years				55–59 Years			
	Malays	Chinese	Indians	Total	Malays	Chinese	Indians	Total	Malays	Chinese	Indians	Total
Education	77.20	10.39	4.59	100.00	70.48	17.42	7.16	100.00	57.04	31.34	8.49	100.00
Humanity and arts	71.92	20.07	3.02	100.00	73.49	17.39	4.91	100.00	65.98	23.41	8.41	100.00
Social science, business, law	48.35	41.59	6.74	100.00	51.89	37.21	7.09	100.00	39.41	47.09	9.68	100.00
Science	48.24	40.42	7.70	100.00	57.10	34.36	6.04	100.00	22.92	63.32	12.39	100.00
Engineering, construction-skill training	59.87	29.56	7.88	100.00	60.21	30.93	6.65	100.00	27.54	60.10	9.93	100.00
Agriculture, forestry, fishery	72.60	10.24	3.25	100.00	80.18	9.22	2.95	100.00	43.75	43.44	8.44	100.00
Health and welfare	65.93	18.82	10.42	100.00	52.54	25.48	16.21	100.00	19.82	46.68	31.71	100.00
Service	61.47	25.09	6.81	100.00	72.56	14.22	10.26	100.00	60.58	25.00	11.54	100.00
Unknown	56.25	31.69	6.24	100.00	56.36	31.89	6.50	100.00	45.95	40.70	8.93	100.00

Table 10.6
Membership of Registered Professionals by Ethnic Group, 1970–2000 (in Percentages)

Profession	1970 (Peninsula)				1980				1990				2000			
	Malays	Chinese	Indians	Others	Bumi-puteras	Chinese	Indians	Others	Bumi-puteras	Chinese	Indians	Others	Bumi-puteras	Chinese	Indians	Others
Architects	4.3	80.9	1.4	13.4	10.7	86.5	1.3	1.5	23.6	74.4	1.2	0.8	28.9	69.3	1.5	0.3
Accountants	6.8	65.4	7.9	19.9	7.4	77.9	7.2	7.5	11.2	81.2	6.2	1.4	15.9	77.0	5.8	1.3
Engineers	7.3	71	13.5	8.3	18.5	71.3	6.3	3.9	34.8	58.2	5.3	1.7	26.5	67.1	6.4	—
Dentists	3.1	89.1	5.1	2.8	10.3	65.7	21.3	2.7	24.3	50.7	23.7	1.3	34.8	42.1	21.0	2.1
Doctors	3.7	44.8	40.2	11.3	9.7	43.7	41.7	4.9	27.8	34.7	34.4	3.1	36.7	30.9	28.4	4.0
Veterinarian surgeons	40.0	30.0	15.0	15.0	17.8	27.8	46.5	7.9	35.9	23.7	37.0	3.4	42.6	26.8	28.5	2.1
Surveyors	—	—	—	—	31.2	58.7	7.2	2.9	44.7	49.6	3.7	2.0	47.8	47.4	3.0	1.8
Lawyers	—	—	—	—	14.8	48.5	35.4	1.3	22.4	50.0	26.5	1.2	31.3	41.0	26.8	0.9

Ethnic Preferential Policies and Equality of Educational Opportunity

With the formulation of the NEP, policy makers identified the use of education as a key vehicle to be employed to address its objective of eliminating economic participation identification with ethnicity. To meet this objective, equality of opportunity in education was shelved and instead, a system of ethnic preferential programmes and policies were introduced. An outcome of the implementation of the ethnic preferential programmes and policies was the creation of ethnic enclaves in the education system. In the face of globalisation, maintaining the system of ethnic preferential programmes and policies had only further accentuated the ethnic fragmentation of the education system.

While the ethnic quota policies implemented discriminated against non-Malay admissions, it did not lead to the development of ethnic enclaves in public universities, as enrolment remained ethnically diverse. After all, the aim of the ethnic quota policy was to ensure that the enrolment in public universities would gradually reflect the ethnic composition of the general population.[20] Nevertheless, in the rush to raise the proportion of Malay enrolment in higher education, the state established several Malay-only programmes and institutions, thereby creating, consciously or not, ethnic enclaves in the education system.

The Majlis Amanah Rakyat (MARA), or Council of Trust for the Indigenous Peoples,[21] was designated as a key vehicle to realise the objectives of the NEP.[22] Initially, MARA was established to encourage, guide, train, and assist the indigenous peoples to participate actively and progressively in both commercial and industrial enterprises towards creating a strong and viable business indigenous community. As the first-among-equals indigenous group, the Malays invariably benefited the most from the various MARA programmes, particularly in the field of education where MARA arguable was most successful.

The Rural and Industrial Development Authority's (RIDA) training centre was renamed the MARA College of Business and Professional Studies and then, in October 1967, the MARA Institute of Technology (MIT).[23] Until 1999, before it was upgraded to university status, MIT was the most important component in MARA's educational programmes. Initially, it offered courses in business, accountancy, commerce, and secretarial studies and later on, applied sciences, engineering, languages, applied arts, computer sciences, and architecture. By 1986, the total number of courses reached 91, and not long thereafter, every state had a MIT branch. The institute offered a wide variety of programmes with the bulk of the courses at the certificate and diploma levels.[24] Over the years, the state has channelled relatively sizeable resources to develop and expand MIT such that its total enrolment has increased from 6,900 students in 1975 to about 9,000 in 1980 and to nearly 45,000 in 1996.

As a political compromise, the Malaysian Chinese Association (MCA), which was a member of the ruling coalition, was granted permission to establish a government-assisted college, the Tunku Abdul Rahman (TAR) College, for non-Malays to pusue certificate and diploma education. Compared to MIT, however, TAR College was a much smaller institute and over the years, funding for its development and expansion was rather limited. Not surprisingly, TAR College's enrolment has been unimpressive, from 4,036 students in 1975 to about 6,000 in 1980 and to about 9,000 in 1996.[25]

Besides MIT, MARA also established the MARA Junior Science Colleges (MJSCs) as a means to increase the number of Malay students taking up science and science-related subjects. The ultimate goal was to ensure that there would be a sufficient number of qualified Malay students to fulfil the quota allocated to them in the universities. The rationale for establishing the MJSC was that it would provide an environment in which Malay students could excel. The MJSCs were essentially residential-type schools, and because they received generous funds from the state and had the best teachers, places were highly sought-after by Malay parents. In 1984, there were ten MJSCs with 6,311 students, and in 2000, the number of schools had increased to 25, enrolling a total of 15,424 students.

Besides the MJSCs, policy planners also launched the Residential Secondary School system to help raise the number of Malay students in science and science-related courses in 1971. According to Mustapa, "the aim was to provide post-elementary education in science and science-related subjects to Malay students from the rural areas and low socioeconomic families".[26] In 1984, there were 27 residential schools in Peninsula Malaysia with an enrolment of 12,115, and by 2000, the total number of students has doubled to about 24,000.

Another important step taken by the state to increase Malay intake into the public universities was the creation of the two-year matriculation programme in 1970. In its initial implementation, during the first year, students were attached to 11 selected residential schools, and in the second year, they were fully attached to their respective university.[27] The programme had its beginnings in UPM and UTM where matriculation programmes were started to admit Malays students into diploma courses, and those who performed well in these courses were then transferred to degree courses. Later UM, USM, and UKM also introduced various matriculation science programmes to admit Malay students, who on successful completion were eligible to read undergraduate courses in science and technology.[28]

In recent years, as part of the privatisation of higher education and of efforts to increase Malay ownership of private higher education, matriculation students have also been farmed out to a number of mostly Malay-owned private colleges. MARA has also cashed in on the matriculation programs by converting a number of its MJSC into colleges to enroll matriculation students.[29] Moreover, to further expedite the entry of Malay students to take up degree courses at the university level, the matriculation programme in recent years was shortened from two to one year.

Hence, the establishment of the Residential Colleges, various MARA training and education institutions, and the matriculation programme created Malay-only education enclaves within the national education system. The non-Malay students were largely neglected and only TAR College was established to cater for the non-Malay students to receive certificate and diploma education; whatever limited resources existed were channelled to develop and expand the college. Moreover, ethnic quota admission policies made it much more difficult for Chinese and Indian students to get a place in the local public universities. Chinese and Indian students thus had to look for other avenues to pursue their higher education ambitions. In the 1970s and 1980s, the scarcity of local higher educational opportunities for Chinese and Indian students induced growing frustrations and thus tense ethnic relations.[30] Needless to say, the majority of the non-Malay parents could not afford to send their children to study overseas.

In the 1990s, with the privatisation and internationalisation of higher education, Chinese and Indian students now had more opportunities to realise their higher educational goals. Because of the pent up demand for higher education among the non-Malays, privatisation of education led to a proliferation of private colleges in Malaysia. Besides offering local certificate and diploma courses, private colleges, through a variety of twinning programs with tertiary institutions, especially universities, in developed countries, enabled non-Malays to receive foreign qualifications at less expense. Above all, their opportunities were further enhanced in the late 1990s when the government permitted the establishment of private universities in Malaysia.[31]

Predictably, the enrolment in private higher education was overwhelmingly made up of non-Malays; in 1980, for diploma and certificate courses, the Malays, Chinese, and Indians made up 15.7 per cent, 71.2 per cent, and 12.8 per cent respectively, and for university courses, the figures were 26.8 per cent, 59.4 per cent, and 13.8 per cent respectively (Table 10.4). The under-presentation of Malay students in the private higher education sector worried the state planners, in particular UMNO politicians, the dominant partner in the coalition government. By the late 1990s, steps were taken to partly address this problem.

Thus, in 1999, the ethnic breakdown evened out especially for the certificate and diploma courses where Malays and non-Malays constituted 44.5 per cent and 55.5 per cent. On close inspection, however, the increase in Malay enrolment in private higher education did not lead to the creation of a more ethnically-integrated private education sector. This was because ethnic claves continued to persist as the majority of Malays were enrolled in Malay-owned colleges,[32] while non-Malays were largely found in the non-Malay-owned colleges. The ethnic segmentation in private higher education continues to be most glaring in 1999 in the enrolment of students in the degree programs where the Malay and non-Malay student breakdown was 16.3 per cent and 83.7 per cent respectively.

In part, the implementation of the ethnic preferential policies led policy makers to establish Malay-only programs and education institutions as a means to increase their participation in higher education. In addition, to fast track the enrolment of Malays in the science and technical, including engineering, courses at the university level, special schools and programmes were created as well. Conversely, while the ethnic quota policy made it much easier for Malays to gain admission into the public tertiary universities, it deprived the Chinese and Indians of the equality of educational opportunity. While privatisation and internationalisation of higher education was a fortuitous development for tertiary education in Malaysia, however, its development only accentuated the ethnic segmentation as enrolment in the largely non-Malay-owned private colleges were overwhelmingly non-Malays.

The Education of Ethnic Minorities and Muslims

In late 2001, in response to allegations that certain national primary schools had deliberately practised segregation by race streaming, the government promptly mounted an inquiry.[33] The Ratnam Committee concluded that only "minimal" and "unintentional" segregation had taken place in the 197 national primary schools investigated, and where there were any race streaming, this was due not to deliberate or intentional segmentation, but rather to the scarcity of non-Malays enrolled in the primary schools. It revealed that out of the 2.2 million students enrolled in national primary schools in 2002, only 2.1 per cent and 4.3 per cent were Chinese and Indians respectively. In other words, there was no ethnic segregation in the national primary schools simply because there were not enough non-Malay students enrolled. Rather, the findings clearly indicted the existence of ethnic segregation in Malay-medium and Chinese- and Tamil-medium primary schools.

A paradoxical development of globalisation is that, while it is increasingly welding the world into a single global village, it has also led ethnic and religious communities in different parts of the world to revive their cultural heritage and identity. In Malaysia, the ethnic and religious resurgence has had a negative impact on ethnic integration in the development of Malaysian education. On the one hand, the revival in ethnic identity and culture has further strengthened the Chinese and Indian parents' resolve to have their children educated in their mother tongue. On the other hand, Islamic resurgence has led to giving Islamic education a new lease of life as an increasing number of Malay families sought to educate their children in their religion within a religious environment.

The Razak Report, widely regarded as drawing up the blueprint for Malaysian education, recommended making "Malay the national language of the country whilst preserving and sustaining the growth of the languages and cultures of non-Malays living in the country".[34] After emotionally-charged debates and struggles over the conception of education and its construction and implementation in the first 20 or so years after independence, a working model has evolved and has been accepted by the majority of each ethnic community.

For many years before and after independence, influenced by the vision of a nation as a culturally-homogenous population, the prevailing Malay nationalist thinking regarded homogeneity as a necessary prerequisite for the formation of a stable and united nation. As such the ethnically-diverse Malaysian society, with the prevalence of ethnic primordial attachments, was essentially viewed as detrimental to fostering national integration and thus nation building. To overcome the ethnic diversity obstacle, education was to be used as a means to breakdown "the primordial attachments towards one's own racial, language, cultural and religious groups" and to shift the attachments "towards the new nation and [give] rise to a new national identity".[35]

To assist education in developing and inculcating a set of common identities and values that would help to cement ethnically-diverse relations, many a Malay nationalist argued for the construction of a Malay-only-medium national education system sharing a common curriculum.[36] To ensure ethnic integration, educational institutions were to be made ethnically desegregated such that they could "serve as a real meeting place of the children of the different races" which would give "them the opportunity to know and understand each other right from childhood".[37]

The prevailing Malay nationalism concept of "nation" as a culturally homogenous population and insistence on a Malay-only-medium national education as the way to achieve national unity came into direct conflict with the Chinese community insisting on their citizenship rights to mother-tongue education which, the latter insisted, was crucial to the transmission and preservation of their language and culture. In terms of national integration, the Chinese argued that mother-tongue education would not hinder integration as a set of core values to foster national cohesion could be achieved, whatever the language of instruction, as long as all schools adopt a common syllabus. In short, the Chinese strongly felt that the education system should help to preserve the unique multicultural character of the Malaysian nation in general.[38]

The differing Malay and non-Malay educational demands and expectations were mediated by a consociation form of politics. This led to a compromised education system that both accommodated and displeased certain groups from both communities. While Malay was elevated to be the medium of instruction for national primary schools, and for public secondary and tertiary education, the use of Mandarin and Tamil as medium of instruction was permitted for Chinese- and Tamil-medium primary schools.[39] A contentious struggle, however, ensued over the status of Chinese secondary schools in the 1960s; the 1961 Education Ordinance gave the ultimatum that the Chinese secondary schools must switch their medium of instruction to Malay to conform to the national education practice. Failing to convert meant both losing financing and exclusion from the national education system. While the majority of the Chinese schools opted to convert and be included in the national education system, a minority decided to continue to teach in Chinese. They formed the Independent Chinese Secondary Schools (ICSS).[40]

By the 1990s, except for the occasional muted calls to do away with the Chinese- and Tamil-medium primary schools and the ICSS, one could argue that their existence is pretty much assured.[41] Even the Parti Islam SeMalaysia (PAS), the main opposition Malay party, has come around to supporting them in order to gain support from the non-Malays. For the majority of Chinese and Indians parents, they generally support the compromised model of six years' primary education in their mother-tongue language and Malay medium of instruction from secondary level onwards. This is clearly borne out by the fact that at the secondary level the overwhelming majority of non-Malay students are enrolled in the national schools and only about 45,000 students, almost all Chinese, are enrolled in the ICSS.[42]

The increasing trend of Chinese student enrolment in Chinese primary schools could be attributed to several factors: economic and educational advantages in learning Mandarin especially with the rise of China as a major economic player, declining quality of education in the national primary schools, ethnic discrimination,[43] failure of multicultural education in the national primary schools,[44] and lastly, to learn Mandarin as an identity marker and preserve their Chineseness. By 2000, more than 90 per cent of primary school-going Chinese students are now enrolled in Chinese primary schools. A more important development, and perhaps an encouraging sign, is the increasing number of non-Chinese, especially Malay, parents who are sending their children to Chinese primary schools for pragmatic reasons; in 2000, there were about 60,000 non-Chinese, usually Malay, students.

In the 1980s, Islamic resurgence in the country led to a growing dissatisfaction among an increasing number of Malay parents over what they viewed as an essentially Western-oriented secular education provided by the national education system. In addition, they wanted their children to study in a school environment that observed the Islamic precepts. Their search for alternative educational means to provide their children with an Islamic education in an Islamic environment coincided with the emergence of private Islamic schools established by Muslim social movements.[45]

Historically, Islamic religious education was provided first by the *pondok* system in the 19th century, which began to lose its popularity around the turn of the 20th century. The *pondok* schools provided free education that was open to Muslims of all ages and were scattered throughout the Peninsula. A number of reasons and factors led to the rise of the *pondok* system: As a response to British secular schools, especially Christian missionaries, "Malays saw little advantage in vernacular education unless it could be supplemented with further English education — something considered to be a privilege, since it was available only in the urban area", and the Muslim reform movement known as *Islah*, which began at the close of the 19th century, contributed greatly to the new zeal for education.[46]

At the turn of the 20th century, however, the *pondok* system came under criticism from some influential Muslim intellectuals who perceived the education provided as "narrow and its curricular content confined merely to *far 'ain*".[47] The beginning of the 20th century also marked the emergence of the *madrasah* system. Before World War II, the vast majority of the *madrasahs* provided largely primary instruction with a handful providing secondary and higher education; those who passed the higher level could continue their education in a Middle Eastern university. The Islamic College, established in 1955 in Klang, provided opportunities for further studies in Malaysia. However, a number of factors contributed to a decline in the demand for Islamic religious education from the late 1950s until the 1970s. Combined with various quality and financial problems confronted by the *madrasahs*, the number of such institutions declined. In particular, the popularity of Islamic religious schools were greatly affected by the NEP. The inclusion of religious instruction in national schools and greater educational opportunities led many Malay parents to see the advantages of sending their children to national schools than to religious schools.

However, Islamic education in Malaysia was given a new lease of life with the resurgence of Islam in the 1980s.[48] In the late 1970s, a common approach was already adopted by groups like the Malaysian Muslim Youth Organisation (ABIM) in their efforts to bring back the Malays to the "purer" form of Islam through, for example, education.[49] The general emphasis on education led ABIM to establish privately-funded *rakyat* religious schools, or *agama* schools. By the 1980s, a sizeable number of Malay parents had begun to send their children to *agama* schools. Indeed, realising the potential of influencing the Muslim public through *agama* schools led PAS to fund and establish a number of such schools throughout the Peninsula. Partly responding to the demand for religious education and partly to "contain" the rising influence of Islamic groups and later PAS, the state also started to take a number of measures, including establishing *agama* schools.

Currently, there are three kinds of *agama* schools: the national and local *agama* schools funded by the state, and the privately-funded *rakyat agama* schools. As expected, the *rakyat agama* schools emerged first to meet the demand for Islamic instruction, and later on, in an attempt to regulate Islamic instruction, the state established public Islamic schools. By 2000, the government-assisted religious secondary schools enrolled a total of nearly 24,000 students while there were a total of 33 primary and 44 secondary private religious schools with a total enrolment of about 53,000 students.

At the tertiary level, new Islamic departments were created and existing ones were expanded to increase the intake of students. The status of Nilam Puri Islamic Higher Education Foundation, a famous institution in Kelantan, was elevated to that of an institute in the University of Malaya and renamed the Islamic Academy. The faculty of Islamic Studies at UKM, the Islamic Teachers College, and the Islamic Academy provided further avenues of higher Islamic education. Above all, the state established the Islamic International University (IIU) where the majority of the local students are Malay.

The resurgence of ethnic and religious identities and cultures that accompanied globalisation has negatively impacted ethnic integration in Malaysian education. For the Chinese, this has led to a further increase in the number of Chinese students enrolling in Chinese primary schools — more than 90 per cent of the Chinese student population. For the Malays, their desire for their children to receive Islamic instruction in a religious environment has led to the emergence of, first, private and, later, public *agama* schools; needless to say, students enrolled in *agama* schools are Malay Muslims.

Conclusion

To cope with economic globalisation, the state has quickened the pace to transform the Malaysian economy from a production- to a knowledge-based one. Among other things, this economic transformation entails the availability of a highly-educated labour force. State strategies to raise the tertiary enrolment were greatly assisted by the privatisation and internationalisation of higher education, an outcome of the globalisation of education. By 2000, tertiary enrolment in Malaysia had increased dramatically. Parallel to the advances made in developing tertiary education was the success of the ethnic preferential programmes and policies to increase Malay participation in tertiary education.

The implementation of ethnic preferential programmes and policies, however, has led to the development of ethnic enclaves in the education system. On the one hand, the state established a number of Malay-only programmes and institutions[50] as a means to raise Malay student enrolments in the universities, especially in science and technical courses. On the other hand, the lack of equality of opportunity[51] for non-Malay students to study in public universities resulted in the development of an overwhelmingly non-Malay enrolment in private colleges. The privatisation and internationalisation of higher education has but only perpetuated the ethnic fragmentation at the tertiary level.

Moreover, the resurgence of ethnic and religious sensibilities that has paradoxically occurred with globalisation negatively impacted ethnic integration in the Malaysian education system. While, by 2000, more than 90 per cent of Chinese primary school students were enrolled in Chinese- and Tamil-medium schools, the growing demand for Islamic education has led to the establishment of an increasing number of private and public *agama* schools where the enrolment is wholly Malay Muslims.

NOTES

1. Abdul Razak Hussain, *Report of the Education Committee* (Kuala Lumpur: Government Printing Press, 1956), p. 1.

2. Just Faaland et al., *Growth and Ethnic Inequality: Malaysia's New Economic Policy* (Kuala Lumpur: Dewan Bahasa dan Pustaka, 1990), pp. 262–65.

3. Abd Rahim Abd Rashid, *Education and Nation Formation in Malaysia: A Structural Analysis* (Kuala Lumpur: University of Malaya Press, 2002).

4. In January 2002, the Malaysian government terminated the 31-year-old quota system, and replaced it with a "meritocratic"-based admissions policy of sorts. However, many critics pointed out the existence of questionable practices in the new admissions policy that would essentially disadvantage non-Malay applicants.

5. Abdul Majid Ismail, *Report of the Committee Appointed by the National Operations Council to Study Campus Life of Students of the University of Malaya* (Kuala Lumpur: Government Printing Press, 1971).

6. The author shall not attempt to give a definition of the globalisation concept. For a sample of the concept's definitions, see <http://www2.hawaii.edu/~fredr/glocon.htm>.

7. A factor that has enabled globalisation to fundamentally transform the flow of people and services, both globally and locally, has been the growth of modern communications technologies. Indeed, the emergence of globalisation is closely

and inescapably bound to the growth and permeation of knowledge economies of the world. Simply put, in a knowledge economy, the classic factors of production, namely, land, labour, and capital, are no longer the central factors of production — knowledge and technology have become key factors. In a comprehensive study, a World Bank Report (1998) states:

> For countries in the vanguard of the world economy, the balance between knowledge and resources has shifted so far towards the former that knowledge has become perhaps the most important factor determining the standard of living — more than land, than tools, than labour. Today's most technologically advanced economies are truly knowledge-based.

8. Philip G. Altbach, "Globalization and the University: Myths and Realities in an Unequal World", *Teritary Education and Management* 10, no. 1 (March 2004): 3–25.

9. Mahathir Mohammad, *The Way Forward* (London: Weidenfeld & Nicolson, 1998).

10. Two foundations to facilitate the development of an ICT economy were laid in 1996; the National Information Technology Agenda (NITA) was launched by the National Information Technology Council (NITC; see www.nitc.org.my/nita/index. shtml) and the Malaysian Multimedia Super Corridor (MSC) conceptualised by the Malaysian Development Corporation (MDC; see www.mdc.com.my). NITA's task was to provide the foundation and framework for the utilisation of ICT to transform Malaysia into a developed nation that is consistent with *Vision 2020*. The idea of the MSC, its physical infrastructure was completed in 1999, was to create a "multimedia environment … to enable Malaysia to be in the mainstream of activities necessary to attract knowledge workers, technopreneurs and high technology industries" (Seventh Malaysia Plan).

11. Halimah Awang, "Human Capital and Technology Development in Malaysia", *International Educational Journal* 5, no. 2 (2004): 239–46

12. Since the 1956 Razak Report, the emphasis on linking education to economic growth has led the Malaysian state to consistently allocate substantial expenditure to develop the national education system. In the early years, special focus was given to the provision of primary education, and as the economy grew together with the need to improve the skills of the labour force, the emphasis shifted from expanding the primary to the secondary educational needs from late 1980 to early 1990. And most recently, with the advance of globalisation and the need to develop a knowledge-based economy, the emphasis has shifted to expanding the tertiary level.

13. Financially, the country was losing a huge sum of money in having tens of thousands of Malaysian students studying overseas. This problem became especially painful during the 1997 financial crisis. Also, the state came to see the business potential

in education and thus proceeded with plans to make Malaysia into an educational hub in the region. An additional factor was that the brain drain of young non-Malay Malaysians — bound for Australia, the UK, Canada, New Zealand, Singapore and the US — was depriving the local economy of skilled human resource the country badly needed for its objective to be a knowledge economy.

14. Tan Ai Mei, *Malaysian Private Higher Education: Globalisation, Privatisation, Transformation and Marketplaces* (London: Asean Academic Press, 2002).

15. The sizeable increase in the amount allocated for the "other education" category is largely due to increasing the loans and scholarships for students to study at the tertiary level.

16. The drop in enrolment since 1995 is due to the emergence of private primary schools.

17. However, various quarters have raised concerns over the privatisation of higher education in the country and its consequences, such as excluding students from poor families, quality of instruction and facilities, commodification of education, and so on.

18. It should be pointed out that the percentage of students enrolled for degree programmes is still relatively low, especially in private tertiary institutions.

19. Mustapa B. Kassim, *Preferential Policy in Higher Education in Malaysia: A Case Study of Malay Graduates at the University of Science, Malaysia* (Michigan: University Microfilms International, 1991).

20. Evidence indicated that the 55:30:10 ethnic formula was never strictly followed in practice in that Malay admissions consistently superceded the allocated figure. Moreover, the distribution of students by university showed that the majority of the non-Malay students are found in University Malaya (UM) and Science University Malaysia (USM) while the percentage of Malay students in Putra University Malaysia (UPM, formerly Agricultural University of Malaysia), Technology University Malaysia (UTM), National University of Malaysia (UKM), and Northern University Malaysia (UUM) far exceeded 70 per cent.

21. In 1954, the Rural Industrial Development Authority (RIDA) established a centre to train Malays on coir- and rope-making. The training centre then developed into Latihan RIDA (Training Centre for RIDA) which provided training for Malay entrepreneurs and simple commercial education. As the largest majority and most powerful group, the Malays benefited disproportionately. In 1965, following resolutions passed by the first Economic Congress for Bumiputra, Latihan RIDA was completely reorganised into MARA.

22. Ibrahim Abu Shah, *The Use of Higher Education as an Intervention Strategy in the Economic Development of a Plural Society: A Case Study of MARA Institute of Technology in the Economic Policy of Malaysia* (Michigan: UMI, 1987).

23. It was upgraded to university status in 1999. This move in hindsight was poorly conceived as it deprived Malays who did well but not enough to get into university which was an important avenue to receive professional and skills training.

24. Besides MIT, MARA also established and operated such educational institutes like MARA Professional College and MARA Infotech Academy. Also in 1985, a College for Preparatory Studies, or MARA College, was established to provide pre-university studies for government-sponsored students, to enable them to join American, Canadian, and Australian universities at junior year. MARA operated a number of MARA Skills Institute with 13 campuses.

25. The Malaysian Chinese Association was given permission to establish University TAR in 2001.

26. Mustapa, *Preferential Policy in Higher Education in Malaysia: A Case Study of Malay Graduates at the University of Science, Malaysia*, pp. 309, 310. Malay students were selected by the Residential School Unit of the Ministry of Education and in 1978 the three criteria were:

    1. academic excellence in the Grade 5 public elementary education examination
    2. parental socio-economic status based on annual income
    3. the number of dependents

27. It has been argued that employing university faculty to teach matriculation courses was an inefficient use of scarce human resources. Also in recent years, the programme was shortened to one year because the objective was to increase the output of Malay graduates, and graduates in general, as fast as possible.

28. Mustapa, *Preferential Policy in Higher Education in Malaysia: A Case Study of Malay Graduates at the University of Science, Malaysia*, p. 340.

29. Several factors led to the decision to redirect matriculation students to private and MARA-run colleges. However, this move had generated a number of problems because of the lack of proper regulation and accreditation of private colleges conducting such programmes — poor facilities, unqualified faculty, inferior quality of education, more expensive education, etc. Lastly, there have been complaints that reducing the length of the programmes from two to one year had resulted in students who are not well prepared for university instruction.

30. An additional frustration among the Chinese was the refusal by the state to recognise the qualifications of Chinese students who graduated from independent Chinese secondary schools. This accounted for about 50,000 students though the number has been decreasing since the 1990s.

31. They are usually branches of foreign universities such as Monash University and Curtin University from Australia, and University of Nottingham from the UK. Also, the government granted MCA permission to establish TAR University in early 2000.

32. Especially from the farming out of matriculation students to private colleges. Indeed, the majority of Malay students enrolled in private colleges received financial assistance from the government. The government established a national loan fund, in the aftermath of the 1997 financial crisis, to largely assist Malay students.

33. Receiving and investigating inputs from parents and teachers, the National Union of the Teaching Profession (NUTP) contended that 209 national schools nationwide practised racial segregation. The government established the Independent Committee on Segregation in Schools (or the Ratnam Committee), which was given eight weeks to look into the allegations. The Committee's findings were disputed by several quarters.

34. Abdul Razak Hussain, *Report of the Education Committee* (Kuala Lumpur: Government Printing Press, 1956), p. 2.

35. Ibrahim Saad, *Competing Identities in a Plural Society: The Case of Peninsular Malaysia* (Singapore: Institute of Southeast Asian Studies, 1980), p. 1.

36. Aminuddin Baki, *The National School of Malaya: Its Problems, Proposed Curriculum and Activities* (Kuala Lumpur: Arkib Negara Malaysia, 1953) (reprint 1981); Asmah Omar, *Language and Society in Malaysia* (Kuala Lumpur: Dewan Bahasa dan Pustaka, 1982).

37. Aminuddin Baki, *The National School of Malaya: Its Problems, Proposed Curriculum and Activities*, p. 1.

38. In the 1960s, Chinese and Indian enrolments in national-type schools were declining while their numbers in English primary schools were increasing. This trend, however, reversed from the 1970s when English schools gradually converted to the Malay medium of instruction. The explanation was that in the 1960s the enrolment in the Chinese primary schools was decreasing because an increasing number of Chinese parents regarded an English education as helping to increase their children's educational and employment opportunities. In addition, the overall quality of education and facilities provided by English schools was generally of a higher standard than that provided by the Chinese and Tamil schools. Since the 1970s, the trend reversed precisely because of the perception that "familiarity with the Chinese language opens up additional opportunities in terms of employment and social mobility in the future. Acquiring the necessary skills — including familiarity with the Chinese language — to move into the private sector has become increasingly important because of the NEP, and in view of the fact that jobs in the public sector are perceived to be extremely limited and increasingly difficult to obtain for the non-Malays. Coupled with this was also the perceived deteriorating standard in the quality of education found in national primary schools and, on the other hand, the concurrent improvement in Chinese schools.

39. The conversion to the Malay medium of instruction was conducted gradually so as not to cause major disruptions in the education of students. It was indeed

implemented incrementally such that it took a total of about 20 years for the conversion to be complete. In the national primary schools, Mandarin and Tamil classes were offered after school hours whenever there were more than 15 Chinese or Indian students who requested it (called the Pupils Own Language). Malay and English were taught as compulsory subjects in the national-type primary schools.

40. At the secondary education level, the Razak Report suggestion was ambiguous; while it stated that more than one medium of instruction may be used, all schools will work to a "common syllabus and for common examinations" (p. 3). In late 1957, education policy dictated that for "Chinese schools to be accepted as National-type Secondary Schools they must prepare their students for the public examinations which were to be conducted in English only" (Tan 1997, p. 199). Chinese schools were faced with the choice between losing government aid or changing their medium of instruction. However, assurance was given that Chinese schools that did not accept this condition for full assistance would still receive aid on a per capita basis.

41. Their Chinese counterparts who insisted on the giving equal recognition to the Chinese medium of instruction remained a minority voice in the community.

42. Of course, one could argue that the small enrolment in the ICSS is due to the small number of schools.

43. This has been frequently cited by non-Malay parents and the most recent case was the 2001/02 report filed by the NUTP.

44. There is also the non-Malay general perception that in the national primary schools the tendency is to promote the dominant Malays' homogenising nationalism such that "integration" carries assimilationist overtones where the minority group were being "integrated into" a national culture fully defined by the Malay majority. Conversely, the minority group's own cultural integrity is not respected or taught in the national primary schools. In the advent of Islamic resurgence in the 1970s, and as part of the state's Islamisation policies, the increasing Islamisation of national primary schools further alienated the non-Malays and their reluctance to enroll their children in the national primary schools.

45. Anne S. Roald, *Tarbiya: Education and Politics in Islamic Movements in Jordan and Malaysia* (Lund: Almqvist & Wiksell International, 1994).

46. Rosnani Hashim, *Educational Dualism in Malaysia: Implications for Theory and Practice* (Kuala Lumpur: Oxford University Press, 1996), pp. 23, 24.

47. Ibid., p. 25.

48. The seed of Islamic resurgence in Malaysia in the 1970s first germinated among Malay students studying in both local and foreign universities before becoming a societal phenomenon. One of the best known groups was Angkatan Belia Islam Malaysia (ABIM, or Malaysian Muslim Youth Movement) that was established in the University Malaya in 1969, but was only officially registered in 1971. ABIM

support among the Malay tertiary students received a boost when the government imposed a series of restrictions on student activities. Its popularity made major gains beyond the universities when the charismatic Anwar Ibrahim became its president from 1974–82.

49. Roald, *Tarbiya: Education and Politics in Islamic Movements in Jordan and Malaysia.*

50. In early 2000, the government decided to open up the matriculation programme to non-Bumiputera students, about 10 per cent. The take up rate, however, was not impressive.

51. Although the ethnic quota policy has been terminated and replaced with a "meritocratic" policy, it has yet to change the ethnic distribution of students along the public and private tertiary education divide.

11

Globalisation and the Challenges Facing Malaysia's Economy

DENIS HEW

Introduction

2004 was a very good year for Malaysia. Although the Malaysian economy showed some signs of easing in the fourth quarter of 2004, strong growth in the first three quarters (averaging 7.6 per cent) delivered a robust GDP growth of 7.1 per cent for the full year. (The economy grew 5.3 per cent and 4.1 per cent in 2003 and 2002 respectively.) Although growth prospects appear fairly positive over the next year or two, is Malaysia able to sustain a strong rate of economic growth in the medium to long term?

Malaysia has undoubtedly recovered from the Asian financial crisis of 1997/98 (see Figure 11.1) but the world has changed significantly since then. Besides the US and Japan, China has in recent years become an important engine of growth for the region as well as a major recipient of foreign direct investments (FDI). The world economy has also become increasingly globalised and this poses new challenges for Malaysia. These emerging challenges may affect Malaysia's economic development and

Figure 11.1
Real GDP Growth, 1988–2004 (Based on 1987 Prices)

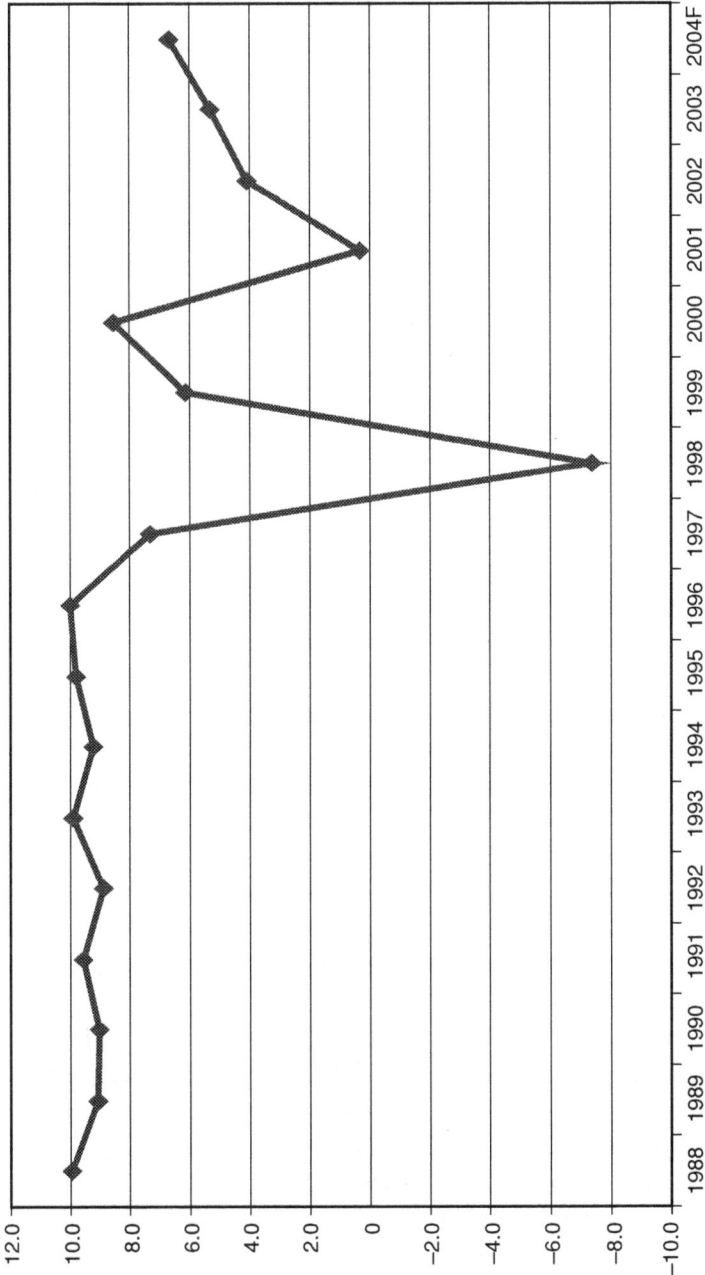

Source: CEIC Data; Malaysian Institute of Economic Research.

overall international competitiveness in the coming years. This chapter aims to identify the key economic challenges that will have an impact on Malaysia's medium- to long-term economic development.

Rising Competition for FDI

FDI inflows to Malaysia have been showing a declining trend in the 1990s. Using UNCTAD's World Investment Report 2004 database, as a percentage of developing countries total, FDI inflows to Malaysia declined from 8.7 per cent in 1992 to 1.4 per cent in 2003. According to the UNCTAD Inward FDI Performance Index, which measures the extent to which host countries receive inward FDI, there has been a sharp deterioration in Malaysia's FDI performance.

> From ranking among the top 10 till the mid-1990s, Malaysia fell in ranking every year in the latter part of the decade, reaching 75th place in 2001–2003.[1]

This is a worrying trend as Malaysia is dependent on FDI as a driver of growth.

In contrast, China has become the country of choice for foreign investment especially in manufacturing and its accession to the World Trade Organisation (WTO) could potentially pose a serious challenge to Malaysia's ability to attract new FDI. According to UNCTAD, China received US$53.5 billion worth of FDI inflows in 2003 and is now the world's largest recipient of FDI. As a percentage of developing world total, China's FDI inflows has risen from 18.8 per cent in 1992 to 31.1 per cent in 2003. Because of its potentially huge domestic market and lower unit labour costs (particularly in labour-intensive industries), China and increasingly India have become major competitors for global FDI.[2] See Table 11.1.

Greater competition notwithstanding, the quality of FDI is just as important as the quantity. Okabe[3] found that recent foreign applications for manufacturing projects appear to concentrate on higher value-added products. Since 2002, there has also been a rise in new FDI in engineering-supporting industries in the electronic sector which, albeit small projects (less than RM10 millon), are vital to maintain Malaysia's global industrial competitiveness.[4]

Table 11.1
Inflows of Foreign Direct Investment, 1992–2003 (in US$ Millions)

	1992–97*	1998	1999	2000	2001	2002	2003
Brunei	327	573	748	549	526	1,035	2,009
Cambodia	128	243	230	149	149	145	87
Indonesia	3,518	−241	−1,866	−4,550	−2,977	145	−597
Laos	67	45	52	34	24	25	19
Malaysia	5,816	2,714	3,895	3,788	554	3,203	2,474
Myanmar	359	684	304	208	192	191	128
Philippines	1,343	2,212	1,725	1,345	982	1,792	319
Singapore	8,295	7,690	16,067	17,217	15,038	5,730	11,409
Thailand	2,269	7,491	6,091	3,350	3,813	1,068	1,802
Vietnam	1,586	1,700	1,484	1,289	1,300	1,200	1,450
ASEAN	n.a.	23,111	28,730	23,379	19,601	14,534	19,100
China	32,799	45,463	40,319	40,715	46,878	52,743	53,505

* Annual average.
Source: UNCTAD World Investment Report 2003.

Industrial Challenges

The manufacturing sector has been the main driver of Malaysia's economic growth over the past three decades. This sector continues to play an important role in the country's economic development. From 1970 to 2003, the manufacturing sector's share of GDP rose from 13.3 per cent of GDP to 30.9 per cent. In 2003, the sector contributed 83 per cent of total exports and 27 per cent of total employment (see Table 11.2).

What are the Challenges in the Manufacturing Sector?

Poor industrial linkages

The different phases of industrial development reflects Malaysia's "dual" approach towards globalisation. The government allows an open policy in certain sectors (viz. electrical and electronics) while protecting other sectors for national interests (viz. heavy industries such as automobile, in this case, Proton).

This dual approach of adopting both export-oriented and import-substitution industrial policies continues to prevail today, and has resulted in uncompetitive domestic-oriented industries that remain to

Table 11.2
Share of Manufacturing in GDP, Employment, and Exports, 1970–2003

Year	Manufacturing Value added as a % of Total GDP (Based on 1978 Prices)	Manufacturing Employment as a % of Total Employment	Manufacturing Exports as a % of Total Exports
1970	13.9	8.7	11.9
1975	17.4	10.1	21.9
1980	19.6	15.8	22.4
1985	19.1	15.1	32.8
1990	27.0	19.5	62.8
1995	33.1 (33.1*)	25.7	79.6
1996	34.2 (29.1*)	26.4	80.5
1997	35.7 (29.9*)	27.1	81.0
1998	34.4 (27.9*)	27.0	82.9
1999	29.9*	26.4	85.5
2000	32.0*	26.4	86.6
2001	30.1*	27.6	85.8
2002	30.1*	26.8	85.2
2003E	30.6*	27.2	83.0

* Based on 1987 prices.
Sources: Tham (2004); Data for 2000–2004 from Economic Report 2003/2004 (Ministry of Finance, Malaysia).

be protected from external competition, e.g. the domestic car industry. However, rising competition in manufacturing (particularly from China) and regional efforts to integrate economically (via the ASEAN Free Trade Agreement (AFTA) and ASEAN Investment Area (AIA)) would suggest that this approach is no longer tenable.

This approach has resulted in a dualistic industrial structure where there is a "disconnect" between the export manufacturing activities of MNCs in Free Trade Zones (FTZs) and industrial activities of local companies for the domestic market.[5] It was evident that there were little industrial linkages between MNCs based in these FTZs and domestic industries particularly SMEs.[6]

Skilled labour deficiency

The shortage of skilled labour is a major challenge for Malaysia's industrial development. Malaysia's sustainable economic expansion from the mid-

1980s until 1997 led to severe labour and skill shortages. To fill the labour gap, there was a massive inflow of predominantly low-skilled foreign workers to Malaysia that reached about 15 to 20 per cent of the total labour force in 1997. This would surely delay the restructuring of Malaysia's industries into higher value-added manufacturing activities which tend to be skill- and capital-intensive.

Skill intensity (as measured by the ratio of skilled and semi-skilled workers to the total workforce) was relatively stagnant during this period of high economic growth, while technical and tertiary institutions were unable to cope the growing demand for skilled workers.[7] Meanwhile, the World Bank[8] found that the skill intensity of labour actually fell from 0.43 in 1985 to 0.35 in 1991.

The shortage of skilled workers is reflected by the high wage premium particularly for science and engineering employees.[9] If these problems are not addressed, it would clearly pose serious challenges to Malaysia's industrial competitiveness in the medium to long term.

In the 1990s, the Malaysian government has undertaken several initiatives to raise skill levels such as the Human Resource Development Fund (HRDF)[10] and the liberalisation of the education sector in 1995 to allow the establishment of new private universities. It may be too early to determine whether these initiatives would be effective in addressing the skill deficiency problem.

Low productivity and poor technological capabilities

Technological capabilities of the manufacturing sector were found to be poor. Total factor productivity (TFP) growth (which essentially measure technological progress) in Malaysia's manufacturing sector was found to be low or negative in the 1980s and 1990s.[11] Why? The easy availability of unskilled foreign workers created little incentive for local manufacturers to invest in training, R&D, and automation. Hence, it is not surprising that the manufacturing sector suffers from low productivity.

Despite various government initiatives to support industrial technology development, R&D expenditure remains low. R&D expenditure increased from RM549.1 million in 1996 to RM1.1 bilion in 1998. In terms of percentage of GDP, it rose from from 0.2 per cent to 0.4 per cent. There was also a heavy reliance on foreign R&D capacity due to a lack of skilled personnel and limited financial resources and infrastructure for R&D.[12]

Over-dependence on the electronics industry

Over the past two to three decades, the electrical and electronics (E&E) industry has become the most dominant subsector in Malaysia's manufacturing sector. The industry is the largest contributor to manufacturing output, employment, exports, and imports.

In 2003, E&E products contributed 28.3 per cent of total value-added and 66.2 per cent of total exports. Between January and August 2003, the industry employed 390,249 persons or 39 per cent of total employment in the manufacturing sector.

This dominance reflects uneven industrial development where the manufacturing sector is skewed towards one industrial subsector. As a consequence, Malaysia's economy is vulnerable to the global demand for its E&E and IT products (which tend to be volatile due to their short product life-cycles).

Best and Rasiah[13] found that Malaysia's electronics industry is still mainly operating in lower value-added production activities and lacks the technological capabilities to move up the value chain. It is still an industry that is dominated by MNCs while local industries are engaged in component manufacturing or assembly of imported components.

This would be fine if there is a little competition in global manufacturing. But Malaysia is currently facing stiff competition from other Southeast Asian countries like Thailand as well as China and India

Table 11.3
Performance of Malaysia's Electronics Industry, 1996–2000

Year	Output (RM Billions)	Employment (Number)	Exports (RM Billions)	Imports (RM Billions)
1996	76.0	329,100	64.6	68.0
1997	85.6	343,300	80.8	75.7
1998	103.5	320,600	114.2	96.6
1999	129.8	381,000	144.9	108.3
2000	167.1	416,976	166.8	141.0

Source: World Trade Organization (2001).

which are creating similar production facilities and are catching up fast especially in the production of semiconductors.

Protected Industries

Malaysia also continues to protect domestics industries, such as national carmakers Proton and Perodua, at a time when global consolidation of the automobile industry makes it extremely difficult for small independent carmakers to survive. It is a numbers game and Proton and Perodua clearly do not have the production volume to be commercially viable.

In recent years, competitive pricing, low interest rate payments, and the entry of aggressive new players (particularly Korean cars viz. Hyundai, Kia, and Ssangyong) have resulted in an erosion of Proton's market share. Proton's share of the local market has fallen from 48.5 per cent in 2003 to 30.7 per cent last year. Furthermore, current trends towards global consolidation of car manufacturing will make it extremely difficult for a small carmaker such as Proton to be commercially viable without national protection. Proton's technical cooperation agreement with Germany's Volkswagen in October 2004 has been viewed by some auto analysts as crucial for the national carmaker's longer term survival.[14]

It does not look like the playing field is going to be levelled anytime soon. To comply with AFTA rules this year, the Malaysian government has reduced import duties on made-in-ASEAN cars from as high as 190 per cent down to 20 per cent but at the same time excise duties on cars have gone up sharply (Malaysian carmakers enjoy a 50 per cent rebate on excise duties).

Malaysia's Trade Strategy

In ASEAN, Malaysia is a member of the AFTA which was launched in 1992. The Common Effective Preferential Tariff (CEPT) Scheme under AFTA was fully implemented in 2003 by the original six members of ASEAN i.e. ASEAN-6 (Malaysia, Singapore, Indonesia, the Philippines, Thailand, and Brunei) and requires that tariff rates on a wide range of products traded within the region be reduced to between 0 and 5 per cent. Meanwhile, for the newer members of ASEAN, Vietnam is expected to reach its target for tariff reduction to between the 0 and 5 per cent range for its items in the inclusion list by 2006, Laos and Myanmar are expected to do so by 2008 and Cambodia by 2010.[15]

However, there has been rising concerns that Singapore's moves towards bilateral free trade agreements (FTAs) since 2001 would not only undermine AFTA specifically but also ASEAN economic integration in general. Also, such FTAs could create discriminatory effects for member ASEAN countries such as Malaysia which are just as dependent on trade for economic growth and share many of the same trading partners as Singapore.[16] In other words, Malaysian exports could end up being less competitive in markets where preferential treatment had been given to its competitors via FTAs.

While the jury is still out as to whether there are net benefits from being a member of an FTA, it does appear that non-member countries could lose out either due to trade diversion, reduced exports, or worsened terms of trade.[17]

As a defensive move, it has led Malaysia to pursue bilateral FTAs to avoid discriminatory treatment by its trading partners. Malaysia has finalised a Comprehensive Economic Partnership with Japan (expected to be signed in December 2005) and has recently signed a Trade and Investment Framework Agreement with the US (a first step towards an FTA between the two countries). Malaysia is also in FTA talks with China and South Korea. Abidin[18] argues that Malaysia's FTA strategy must take into account its economic structure (i.e. that it is a small, open economy with a reasonable-sized domestic market) and could be used as a tool to enhance its competitiveness and economic growth.

However, due to its preferential nature, an FTA is essentially the second-best option compared to the multilateral trading system which is non-discriminatory. At the negotiating table, small trade-dependent economies such as Malaysia and Singapore are at a disadvantage when dealing with large economies such as the US, China, and Japan; it is a classic case of "you need us more than we need you".

Furthermore, Malaysia should take a cautious approach to FTAs and not duplicate Singapore's FTA strategy. This is because unlike Singapore, Malaysia is still a developing economy with sensitive socio-economic issues to consider. If Malaysia agrees too quickly or makes too many compromises, it may destabilise the country, creating social and economic unrest. Hence, there may be a need for greater public consultation before embarking on a bilateral FTA, particularly with a developed country.

Developing countries like Malaysia also lack the institutional and technical capacity to negotiate multiple bilateral FTAs. This trade strategy could strain valuable resources as the time and effort on undertaking these FTAs could have been better utilised on multilateral negotiations at the WTO.

The Dismantling of the Ringgit Peg

Over six years have past and almost all the capital controls imposed on 1 September 1998 have been removed except for the exchange rate peg which was fixed at RM3.80 to US$1. On 21 July 2005, Bank Negara Malaysia (BNM) scrapped the Ringgit peg and allowed the currency to operate under a managed float exchange rate system. Under a managed float, the value of the Ringgit is maintained against a trade-weighted basket of currencies of its major trading partners.

BNM's hand was forced to some extent as the Chinese authorities de-pegged their currency from the US dollar that same day and moved towards a managed float. The Ringgit peg was scrapped within an hour after the People's Bank of China's announcement to float the Yuan. The Yuan peg was no longer sustainable as China's monetary authorities struggled in recent years to sterilise the excess liquidity (as a result of substantial capital inflows) which was overheating the domestic economy.

The near synchronised de-pegging of the two currencies was to ensure that the Ringgit was not misaligned with the Yuan. Over the past decade, China has become so economically integrated with Northeast and Southeast Asia that a misalignment of exchange rates would have serious negative implications on regional economies like Malaysia. China's rapid industrialisation has led to international production networks linking the country with the newly-industrialised economies of Korea, Taiwan, and Hong Kong and with the more industrialised ASEAN countries viz. Singapore, Malaysia, and Thailand.

For Malaysia, there are economic benefits in dismantling the Ringgit peg. For example, some economists have argued that the benefits from export competitiveness were phasing out and that an undervalued

Ringgit was actually penalising domestic industries as imported parts and machinery become increasingly expensive. (Input costs from some manufacturing products could be as much as half of total costs.) The weak Ringgit has also led to a significant rise in imported inflation over the past year. However, until the recent Ringgit de-pegging, there was some reluctance among Malaysian policy makers to undo an exchange rate system that has hitherto worked reasonably well.

Given that Malaysia is a very open economy in terms of trade and investments, a more flexible exchange rate system is clearly the best option. In many ways, the floating of the Ringgit marks the return of Malaysia into the international financial system. Given Malaysia's war chest of foreign reserves (US$78.7 billion in end July 2005) and healthy economic fundamentals, the country is more than capable of withstanding any external shocks. In fact, a managed float would be more desirable as it offers policy flexibility and avoids the kind of excessive exchange rate volatility that often haunts a pure free-floating regime. Many economists expect BNM to manage a gradual appreciation of the Ringgit with the currency likely to appreciate between 2 to 8 per cent against the US dollar in the short term.

Revisiting Poverty Issues

Malaysia's track record in eradicating poverty over the past three decades has been impressive. Overall incidence of poverty declined from 52.4 per cent in 1970 to 6.8 per cent in 1997.

However, Malaysia's poverty reduction efforts suffered a setback during the Asian financial crisis. Between 1997 and 1998, overall incidence of poverty increased from 6.8 per cent to 7.6 per cent while incidence of hardcore poverty increased from 1.4 per cent to 1.5 per cent over the same period. Nevertheless, Malaysia's economic recovery over the past few years has resulted in incidence of poverty decreasing from 7.5 per cent in 1999 to 5.1 per cent in 2002. Meanwhile, incidence of hardcore poverty also declined from 1.4 per cent to 1 per cent over the same period (see Table 11.4).

Notwithstanding these improvements in poverty levels, Malaysia faces numerous challenges in the areas of poverty eradication and income distribution. Poverty eradication also plays an important part in Abdullah

Table 11.4
Incidence of Poverty among Malaysians and Number of Households

	1999			2002		
	Total	Urban	Rural	Total	Urban	Rural
Incidence of poverty (%)	7.5	3.4	12.4	5.1	2.0	11.4
No. of households ('000)	360.1	89.1	271.0	267.9	69.6	198.3
Incidence of hardcore poverty (%)	1.4	0.5	2.4	1.0	0.4	2.3
No. of households living in hardcore poverty ('000)	66.0	13.9	52.1	52.9	12.6	40.3

Note: The poverty line used in 2002 was at the income level of RM529 for
Semenanjung Malaysia, RM690 for Sabah, and RM600 for Sarawak.
Source: Eighth Malaysia Plan Mid-Term Review.

Badawi's economic policy agenda since he took over as Malaysia's prime minister last November.

Income inequality in Malaysia is one of the highest in the region. The World Bank estimates Malaysia's Gini coefficient at 0.49 in 1995. Part of the reason for this inequality is that the poor are concentrated in the east coast of Malaysia (viz. Kelantan and Terengganu) and East Malaysia (viz. Sabah and Sarawak). Also, the income disparity ratio between rural and urban households appear to be widening from 1:1.81 in 1999 to 1:2.11 in 2002.

One of the major challenges for Malaysia is the changing dimensions of poverty as a result of economic development.[19] Rapid urbanisation and rural-urban migration in the country would imply that urban poverty has become more critical than rural poverty. Furthermore, new forms of poverty have also emerged among the most vulnerable such as the single female-headed households, aboriginies (*orang asli*) and the indigenous people of East Malaysia, migrant workers, unskilled workers, and the elderly. Hence, there should be more emphasis on tackling urban poverty and other forms of poverty. Poverty eradication policies in Malaysia tend to focus on the rural sector.

Where is Malaysia's Future Growth Coming From?

The Multimedia Super Corridor (MSC) was set up in 1996 with the aim of creating a home-grown ICT cluster that would leapfrog Malaysia into the information age. The Malaysian government has invested billions of dollars on the necessary physical infrastructure to attract world-class ICT companies to the MSC.

However, the MSC has not quite turned out the way the authorities intended. Rather than a dynamic cluster of high-tech companies involved in R&D activities, the MSC is fast becoming a regional centre for business process outsourcing. The outsourcing business is great for creating jobs but it is not going to transfer the kind of high technology to domestic industries to catch up with the West and Japan.

The Malaysian government also launched an ambitious biotechnology project called BioValley about two years ago. By 2006, the government plans to spend RM100 million to build the necessary infrastructure and facilities to support biotechnology research activities. Similar to Singapore's Biopolis, BioValley is essentially a biotechnology cluster consisting of biotechnology research institutions, universities, and biotechnology companies.

Like the MSC, the Malaysian government aims to use BioValley to move up the technology ladder. But biotechnology is a very risky and expensive business. Since the 1970s, for example, more than half the biotech companies in the US have either merged or closed down. Biotechnology research also demands substantial financial support and a long gestation period before biotech products can be commercialised.

The Malaysian government is also pursuing other potential sources of economic growth such as agriculture, healthcare, tourism, and SME development. In particular, Prime Minister Abdullah Badawi has taken a keen interest in reviving the agriculture sector. Nevertheless, it would be a tall order to expect these sectors — some of which have been neglected for decades — to pick up the slack of declining FDIs in the near term.

In the financial services sector, the government's plans to promote Malaysia as a regional centre for Islamic banking and finance seems incongruous with its inconvertible, hard-pegged domestic currency and coddled banking sector. If such a project is to be successfully realised, Malaysia would need to reintegrate itself back into the global financial system. As was discussed earlier, the government has now taken the appropriate step in dismantling the Ringgit peg.

Conclusion

In light of the challenges Malaysia is facing, the country's economy is clearly at the crossroads. The Malaysian government recognises that the economy urgently needs to move up the value-added chain. Hence, the government has been investing heavily in such high-tech projects as the MSC and BioValley. However, the severe shortage of skilled manpower and limited technological capabilities will surely be a major stumbling block to their development. Perhaps a rethink of the economic strategy is needed to determine if this is the right direction to take.

In this regard, sustainable economic growth and development would depend on Malaysian policy makers being far-sighted enough to make the right strategic choices. In particular, one hopes that policy makers would take a critical hard look at the kind of potential sources of economic growth that would keep Malaysia competitive in the years to come.

NOTES

1. See UNCTAD (2004, p. 14).

2. Asian Development Bank, *Asian Development Outlook 2004* (Manila: Asian Development Bank, 2004).

3. M. Okabe, "Rapid Recovery of Foreign Direct Investment into Malaysia", *Tsusho Koho* no. 15523 (August 2004).

4. Y. Okamoto, "Agglomeration and International Competitiveness: Can Malaysia Growth be Sustainable?", in *Industrial Clusters in Asia: Analyses of Their Compeition and Cooperation*, edited by Akifumi Kuchiki and Masatsuga Tsuji, IDE Development Perspectives Series no. 6 (Chiba: Institute of Developing Economies, 2004).

5. H.C. Ong and D. Hew, "Malaysia: Productivity Growth and Industrial Structure, 1970–1997", in: *PECC Pacific Economic Outlook — Structure Project: Productivity Growth and Industrial Structure in the Pacific Region*, edited by Akira Kohsaka (Osaka: Japan Committee for Pacific Economic Outlook, June 2000).

6. D. Hew, "Entrepreneurship and SMEs in Southeast Asia's Economic Development", in *Entrepreneurship and SMEs in Southeast Asia*, edited by D. Hew and W.N. Loi (Singapore: Institute of Southeast Asian Studies, 2004).

7. V. Kanapathy, "Industrial Restructuring in Malaysia: Policy Shifts and the Promotion

of New Sources of Growth", in *Industrial Restructuring in East Asia: Towards the 21ˢᵗ Century*, edited by Seiichi Masuyama, Donna Vandenbrink, and Chia Siow (Tokyo: Tokyo Club Foundation for Global Studies, 2001).

8. World Bank, *Malaysia, Meeting Labor Needs: More Workers and Better Skills* (Washington, DC: World Bank, 1995).

9. Ibid.

10. The HRDF was launched by the Malaysian government in 1993 to encourage private sector participation in skills development programmes. The HRDF operates on the basis of a levy or grant system where employers who contribute will be eligible for grants from the fund to defray or subsidise costs incurred in training their Malaysian employees.

11. Y. Okamoto, *Industrial Clusters in Asia: Analyses of Their Compeition and Cooperation*; S.-Y. Tham, "The Future of Industrialisation in Malaysia under the WTO", *Asia-Pacific Development Journal* 11, no. 1 (June 2004).

12. Malaysia Government, *Eighth Malaysian Plan* (Kuala Lumpur: Government Printers 2001).

13. M.H. Best and R. Rasiah, *Malaysian Electronics: At the Crossroads* (Vienna: United Nations Development Organization, 2003).

14. "No Stir from Proton's Price Hike", *The Star*, 22 January 2005.

15. At the multilateral level, Malaysia has been a member of the WTO since its independence in 1957 (then called GATT).

16. To date, Singapore has concluded six FTAs with New Zealand, Japan, Australia, the European Free Trade Association (EFTA), the US, and Jordan. Meanwhile, Singapore has on-going FTAs (under study or negotiations) with Mexico, Canada, India, Sri Lanka, Korea, Panama, Egypt, and Bahrain.

17. Asian Development Bank, *Asian Development Outlook 2002* (Manila: Asian Development Bank, 2002).

18. M.Z. Abidin, "Malaysia's Approach Towards FTAs" (paper presented at the International Conference on FTAs in the Asia-Paific Region: Implications for Australia, University of Western Australia, 4–6 July 2004).

19. N. Sulochana, "Poverty in Malaysia: A New Look at an Old Problem" (paper present at the Annual Conference of the International Sociological Association Research Committee on Poverty Social Welfare and Social Policy RC 19, Oveido, Spain, 2001).

12

Promising Start to Malaysia-Singapore Relations

K. KESAVAPANY

Introduction

The period stretching from 1997 to 2002 was one of the most stressful in the short history of relations between Malaysia and Singapore. A number of confrontational issues came to a boil in the mean time, making it all the more difficult for them to be resolved. Some older issues were resurrected, such as the return of CPF contributions to Malaysian workers and railway land and the Tanjong Pagar railway terminus, on which a Points of Agreement (POA) had been signed in 1990. The legality of the POA was subsequently questioned by the Malaysians, making it an issue within an issue. Among the new issues that emerged were the pricing of raw water supplies from Malaysia to Singapore, Singapore military access to Malaysian airspace, a proposal for a new bridge to replace the Causeway, and land reclamation by Singapore in what Malaysia alleged was its territory.

Several attempts to find solutions through negotiations were made at various official levels, including two visits to Kuala Lumpur in 2000 and 2001 by then Senior Minister Lee Kuan Yew. In fact, if Malaysia had stood by its offer of 60 sen per thousand gallons (as stated in then Malaysian Prime Minister Dr Mahathir's letter to SM Lee dated 21 February 2001) a solution could have been reached in the second round of negotiations. Malaysia inexplicably asked for RM3 per thousand gallons. This meant an increase of 100 times more than the existing price of raw water, or in percentage terms a 10,000 per cent increase. Such a demand made it difficult for any common ground to be reached and led to a stalemate in the negotiations.

At about this time, Singapore achieved a strategic breakthrough in its capacity to be self-sufficient in its water requirements. Significant advances in water technologies, together with increase in reservoir capacity, were the contributory factors for this breakthrough. Hereafter, the water issue with Malaysia would be on the basis of "willing seller, willing buyer".

The only agreement arrived at was on Pedra Branca, a small islet that both countries claimed as theirs. The two parties agreed on submitting the matter to the International Court of Justice in the Hague, promising at the same time that they would abide by its ruling. This move defused tensions that were building up, which could have led to armed confrontation.

Governments near and far had, since the late 1990s, been confused and concerned about the bitter exchanges between the leaderships of both countries. Foreign investors began to question the wisdom of investing in an area that increasingly appeared volatile. What was of even greater concern was that the acrimony had generated unhealthy trends emerging at the people-to-people level, e.g. the Singapore team to the SEA Games in Kuala Lumpur in 2001 was booed during the march-past at the opening ceremony. Taking the cue from the leadership, officials began to cut down contact including the Civil Service and Foreign Ministers' games. Among the few that survived was the University of Malaya-National University of Singapore (UM-NUS) golf tournament. Held over many years, the games had succeeded in building a sense of camaraderie among the academics of both countries. UM's chancellor Sultan Azlan Shah, the true sportsman that he is, insisted that the annual tournament should not be held hostage to the vagaries of political fortune.

With the level of acrimonious exchanges growing day by day, and realising that the resolution of these issues of contention would not be forthcoming as long as Mahathir remained in office, it was felt that the best option was to sit things out.

The impasse ended with Datuk Seri Abdullah Badawi becoming the prime minister of Malaysia in October 2003. Earlier, in February 2001, then DPM Abdullah Badawi had visited Singapore and held talks with Singaporean leaders on some outstanding issues —"just trying to move forward and trying to resolve whatever remains to be resolved", as he then put it. This helped to break the spiral of bad relations between the two countries.

The Singaporean leadership under then PM Goh Chok Tong and his successor-to-be, DPM Lee Hsien Loong, responded positively. These friendly gestures helped to remove some of the animus that had crept into the relationship and a state of normalcy returned. Never again should the peoples of both countries be put in a position where they are made to feel like enemies.

The rapprochement between the two countries should also be seen against the backdrop of the changing climate of international and local developments, including the rise of religious extremism, the spread of international terrorism, and the threat of epidemics such as Severe Acute Respiratory Syndrome (SARS) and the avian influenza. These cross-border human security issues brought home to the leadership on both sides of the Causeway that a fresh start should be made to "rebuild relations".

The impact of the fast-growing economies of China and India and a slowdown in the flow of FDI to the region was another factor that argued for amicable relations. Together with the rest of the ASEAN member countries, Malaysia and Singapore moved towards the creation of an integrated economic community.

Plucking Low-hanging Fruits

On his courtesy visit to Singapore in October 2003, Malaysian Prime Minister Abdullah Badawi made known his view on how bilateral ties can be improved. He said, "We can make things move forward by getting some things resolved rather than [putting] everything ... in that one package and nothing [gets] resolved … so we have to pluck some low-hanging fruits before the 'musang' (civet cat) comes and takes them away."[1]

Both PM Goh and DPM Lee went along with Abdullah Badawi's approach and the negotiation process was back on track. The marked improvement in relations led PM Lee to say, during his own courtesy visit to Malaysia in early October in 2004, that relations between Singapore and Malaysia were "very good" and that steady improvements had been made over the last year.

Visits exchanged at the prime ministerial level were soon followed by a series of calls made at the ministerial and official levels. A significant development was the reinstatement of exchanges between the two civil services and the foreign ministries.

On 13 December 2004, the education ministers of both countries, Malaysia's Hishamuddin Hussein Onn and Singapore's Tharman Shanmugaratnam, met in Singapore at the Singapore-Malaysia Forum and decided on a programme to bring students from the secondary school level and above to hold joint activities. Schools on both sides of the Causeway were to pair themselves and initiate joint projects outside the classroom in areas ranging from adventure camps to information technology.

The following day, Malaysia's information minister Datuk Seri Abdul Kadir Sheikh Fadzir and Singapore's minister for information, communications and the arts, Dr Lee Boon Keng, met in Kuala Lumpur. One immediate outcome of the meeting was the restarting of joint TV productions after a hiatus of seven years. In April 2005, Singapore's MediaCorp and Radio Televisyen Malaysia held a Muzika Ekstravageza in Singapore. Speaking on the occasion, Datuk Abdul Kadir Sheikh Fadzir said that the event "truly showed that we are one country and one people, even though we are ruled by two governments". To his credit, Abdul Kadir had expressed this view even when he was minister for culture and tourism in the Mahathir administration. Speaking about future collaboration, Dr Lee Boon Yang said, "We share a lot with Malaysians, and it makes for much better regional understanding if we have a deeper understanding of each other." Such a move went far beyond the mere thawing of ties at the diplomatic and political levels, and in fact sought to satisfy a general wish to bring the populations of the two countries together.

Defence and Security

It is noteworthy that even in the worst of times, ties between the two countries in the fields of defence and security remained intact. Common threats such as terrorism, religious extremism, and piracy led to intensified cooperation between the defence and security forces. Both countries also maintained their links through the multilateral Five Power Defence Arrangements (FPDA), which includes Australia, New Zealand, Britain, Malaysia, and Singapore.

Despite their quarrels, both have common enemies that are best fought and common interests that are best protected through institutionalised cooperation.

Outstanding and Long-lasting Issues

The improved climate in bilateral relations had an immediate impact on at least one of the contentious issues: land reclamation. In 2001 and 2002, Malaysia had alleged that Singapore had encroached into its waters and had undertaken reclamation work. Disputing this, Singapore maintained that it was within its right to undertake such work in its own territorial waters. As in the case of Pedra Branca, to defuse the build-up of tensions, both sides agreed to refer the issue to the International Law of the Sea Tribunal in Hamburg.

In January 2005, it was announced that the independent group of experts formed on the orders of the Tribunal had reached a final agreement. The wording of the joint statement that was issued on that occasion revealed a decided consciousness to resolve problems in an atmosphere of goodwill.

> The positive outcome of the meeting between the Malaysia and Singapore delegations reflects the goodwill and cooperation which exist between them and their respective Governments. This augurs well for the further strengthening of good relations between these two friendly and close neighbours.[2]

An agreement on the land reclamation issue was subsequently signed on 26 April 2005, with the foreign ministers of both countries, George

Yeo and Syed Hamid Albar, present. Both were optimistic about the future. George Yeo said that "the civil and civilised manner in which we have been able to settle this dispute gives us confidence that our other bilateral disputes can be settled the same way", while Syed Hamid was "very delighted that our two countries have been able to reach an amicable solution".[3]

Commenting on the outcome, a *New Straits Times* editorial[4] stated "the level-headed manner in which officials of the two countries had [sealed] the deal suggested the value of doing the hard bargaining out of the harsh glare of publicity". The editorial added, "such discussions were held without feelings running high and as such it was easier to mend fences and reach acceptable compromises".

With a positive outcome reached on the land reclamation issue, naturally, there is hope that settlement can be reached on the other outstanding issues. However, these are complex issues that would require a display of even greater goodwill and negotiating skills. In some of the issues, domestic political considerations, particularly in Malaysia, have begun to come into the picture. For instance, on the proposal to replace the Causeway with a bridge, doubts have been expressed whether the bridge (with its high cost) is really necessary. Johore MP and chairman of the Backbenchers Club, Shahrir Samad, had suggested that Malaysia shelf the plans for a replacement bridge for the Causeway and terminate Malaysian Railway's rail service in Johore Bharu instead of Tanjong Pagar in southern Singapore. Shahrir Samad said that such a move would contribute towards maintaining an atmosphere conducive to negotiations, strengthen Malaysia's bargaining position on other issues, and free resources for improving Johore Bharu's infrastructure.

However, Shahrir Samad found his suggestion shot down immediately. Malaysia's Foreign Minister Hamid Alkbar (also a Johorean) said that the issue of the new bridge must be resolved quickly because a customs, immigration, and quarantine complex will be ready in 2005 and a delay in the bridge construction would increase the cost of the project.[5]

Yet another issue that had a local (Johorean) overtone was the issue of Singapore's military access to Malaysian airspace. Although the federal government appeared to be positive on this issue, Johore politicians, particularly from UMNO, insisted on being consulted on this and other matters that concerned Johore. As the state of Johore is generally considered as the bastion of UMNO and delivers a large share of parliamentary and state seats, the Abdullah Badawi government had to pay heed to these concerns. As far as Singapore is concerned, the outcome on this issue would show whether or not Malaysia regards its southern neighbour as a friend.

On issues such as water, CPF, and railway land, the main drawback to finding solutions is the absence of any *quid pro quo*. Until October 2002, all these issues were negotiated as a package and there was the possibility of "give and take". However, in October of that year, the Mahathir government asked for the package to be unravelled and for the issues to be negotiated separately, starting with the pricing of water. Although this ran contrary to the spirit of the 1990 understanding reached in Hanoi, Singapore went along with this approach. However, this meant that all the concessions that Singapore had made in 2002 on the other issues were no longer on the table. It remains to be seen how progress can be made in finding solutions to these issues. One recourse would be to refer the issues such as water pricing and railway land to third-party arbitration.

Happily, however, both sides have not allowed failure to make progress on the issues to affect bilateral relations. On the contrary, agreement has been reached on the general principles to govern the negotiations on the outstanding issues. Among these is the acknowledgement that whatever proposal is tabled or whatever solution is proposed, "it must bring about mutually beneficial results and certainly, [no] proposal or solution to an issue should disadvantage the other party".

Strengthening of Economic Ties

Encouraged by the new and positive political atmosphere, the private sectors of both countries, constrained for so long by political tensions, have moved quickly in areas such as strategic investments, corporate purchases, and joint business ventures.

In 2004, there was a surge in investments across the Causeway, with Singapore's Temasek Holdings and the Government of Singapore

Investment Corporation (GIC) accounting for about two-thirds of this investment flow. These two Government-linked entities alone were responsible for investing over US$800 million in Malaysia. Their investments included the following:

- In March 2004, Temasek acquired 5 per cent of Malaysia's Telekom for US$421 million. This was its first major direct investment in Malaysia.
- In June 2004, GIC Real Estate Pte Ltd (GIC RE), which is part of GIC, bought a 70 per cent stake in Johor Baru City Square. This deal totalled US$123 million. Earlier, GIC RE had already made investments in Sunway Pyramid Mall, Sunway City Bhd, Menara Standard Chartered, and RB Land Sdn Bhd.
- In July 2004, GIC bought a 5 per cent stake in Gamuda Bhd — one of Malaysia's largest construction companies — for US$53 million. Also in July, GIC purchased another 5 per cent stake in Malaysia's Shell Refining Co. for US$28 million.
- Also in July 2004, Temasek-owned Mapletree Capital Management went into partnership with the Malaysian investment bank, CIMB. This deal involved an initial capital of US$132 million and created what was in fact the first private institutional real estate fund in Malaysia.
- In December 2004, Malaysia's Bank Negara gave permission for a company owned by Temasek to obtain a 15 per cent stake in Malaysian Plantations (MPlant) worth US$124 million. The deal was finally completed on 7 March 2005. Since MPlant owns Alliance Bank — which is Malaysia's smallest national bank, but which nevertheless has assets amounting to S$12.4 billion — the deal was the first major investment by a Singaporean company in a Malaysian financial institution. Analysts saw this move as "a prelude to more mergers in Malaysia's crowded banking sector".[6]

Investments have also been flowing in the other direction as well, and many Malaysian companies have started to search for opportunities in Singapore. For example, Malaysia's government investment arm, Khazanah Nasional, had on several occasions been expressing interest in buying significant stakes in Singapore's government-linked companies

(GLCs). One of Malaysia's largest conglomerates, Sime Darby, acquired a 29.9 per cent stake in shipbuilder Jaya Holdings for S$223 million. A year earlier in April 2003, Malaysian shipping company, MISC, had bought American Eagle Tankers — one of the companies belonging to Singapore's Neptune Orient Lines (NOL) — for US$445 million.

Should a trading link between both countries' stock exchanges, i.e. Bursa Malaysia-SGX into KLSE-SGX, be realised as planned by the end of 2005, business activities, especially cross-border mergers and acquisitions, would be further stimulated. A precursor to this was the acquisition by CIMB, a top Malaysian investment bank, of a significant stake in Singapore's No. 2 stockbroker G. K. Goh. This gave CIMB nothing less than a foothold in the Singapore — and Hong Kong — broking business.

In February 2005, the Scomi Group, Malaysia's fast-growing oil services firm, acquired the marine assets of the Singapore shipping company Chuan Hup Holdings. The S$1.3 billion deal involved joint ownership by Scomi and Chuan Hup in Malaysian jeweller Habib Corporation. Through this purchase, the Malaysians gained access to 155 vessels owned directly or indirectly by Chuan Hup, while the latter finally achieved a long-sought entry into the lucrative oil and gas markets in Malaysia and the Middle East.

In August 2005, Malaysia's state investment arm, Khazanah Nasional, announced their decision to team up with Telekom Malaysia to buy a 12.06 per cent stake in Singapore's MobileOne Ltd for S$260.8 million. The stake was subsequently increased twice to 18.45 per cent, and later to 23.64 per cent worth about S$500 million. The joint venture, known as SunShare Limited, executed the conditional sale and purchase agreement with Great Eastern Telecommunications Ltd.

Another dramatic corporate development was the signing in February 2005 of a "codeshare" agreement between Malaysia Airlines (MAS), Singapore Airlines (SIA), and SilkAir, allowing the cross-selling of their seats to customers wishing to fly to selected Malaysian destinations in Sabah, Sarawak, Penang, and Kedah. Kuantan may be added to this list in the future. This deal paves the way for the Asean Open Skies policy that is to be implemented by 2008, when all Asean national capitals can be openly accessed by any Asean national carrier.[7]

Tourism between the two countries was another area that profited from the steady building of ties between the two economies. In 2004, 9 million Singaporean visitors to Malaysia brought S$15 billion in foreign exchange into the country. Furthermore, a tourism development fund of S$2 billion was set up for promoting both countries as a joint tourist destination.

In July 2004, a Singapore-Malaysia Third Country Business Development Fund worth RM10 million was set up to help Singaporean and Malaysian companies undertake joint feasibility studies for investment or business projects to third countries. The Singapore-Malaysia Business Council had prior to this been formed to foster networking activities between the business communities of both countries.

In April 2005, Malaysia's third largest bank, RHB, decided to build its brand name and increase its market presence in Singapore by becoming title sponsor for the Singapore Cup, promising S$1.5 million annually for three years. At the same time, it will also become product sponsor for the Singapore soccer league.[8]

These developments have shown that the business and investment sectors were major beneficiaries of the improved political climate. Should more uncertainties be removed, greater economic and business cooperation between the two countries can be expected in the years to come.

Presidential Visit

The visit of President S.R. Nathan and Mrs Nathan to Kuala Lumpur in April 2005 brought the level of the bilateral relationship to a higher plane. The second such presidential visit (after Mr Wee Kim Wee's visit between 19–22 November 1991), the occasion called for the red carpet to be rolled out. Remarking on the attention to detail in the programme for the visit, President Nathan said it signified Malaysia's close relationship with Singapore.

On receiving the president, the Yang di-Pertuan Agong depicted the bilateral relationship as "*bagaikan aur dengan tebing*" ("like the bamboo grove and the riverbank") and "neither would survive without the other and neither would gain if the other weakens or perishes". This was in sharp contrast to the imagery used during the

Mahathir era when Singapore was expected to behave like an *adek* to Malaysia's *abang*.

The president, as chancellor of the National University of Singapore, also called on his counterpart, Sultan Azlan Shah, the sultan of Perak. Among other issues, they discussed plans for the joint centennial celebrations of the universities, founded in 1905. The president and Mrs Nathan ended their Malaysian visit with a two-day stay in Sarawak.

Minister Mentor Lee Kuan Yew's four-day visit to Malaysia in end April 2005 was the latest and the strongest indicator of the perceptible upswing in bilateral relations. Staying clear of outstanding bilateral issues, Minister Mentor Lee focussed on the enhancement of bilateral interaction at the public level. His confidence in the direction the two countries were taking and the maturity of the bilateral relations prompted him to propose the limited circulation on both sides of the Causeway, after a 30-year ban, of each country's newspapers. Minister Mentor Lee also called for the pragmatic approach of moving "slowly and comfortably as both sides feel" and to "see each other as we are and not through caricature, not stereotype".

Conclusion

The past two years have shown that given goodwill and tolerance, the two countries and their peoples can cooperate and co-exist.

Devoid of the politicisation of outstanding issues and away from media glare, solutions satisfactory to both countries can be reached. The settlement reached on the reclamation issue is a case in point. Likewise, the decision of the two governments not to publicly or prematurely comment on the on-going discussions on the outstanding bilateral issues is a new phenomenon and a clear indication that both sides are now determined to resolve the problems without the distraction of them being politicised.

Equally important is the realisation and acceptance that even with such issues pending, it is imperative that both sides look at the big picture and work together for mutual benefit in a region and a world that is fast changing. The two countries are small players on the world stage but have the capacity and the wherewithal to contribute meaningfully to regional security and well-being. As President Nathan, during his visit to Kuala Lumpur in April 2005, observed, "As founding members of ASEAN and two of the more developed economies in the region, there is also much scope for Singapore and Malaysia to pool our efforts to strengthen ASEAN".[9]

This is the pragmatic way forward. The scope and the advantage of working together are enormous even as the two countries compete where they must and collaborate where they can. Nevertheless, as with any two close neighbours, the prospects of downturns in bilateral relations cannot and should not be precluded. It is in the interest of both countries and their peoples to guard against such downturns by careful management of the relationship.

NOTES

1. S. Ramesh and Dominique Loh, "Singapore and Malaysia Determined to Put Ties Back on Track", *ChannelNewsAsia*, 12 January 2004 <http://www.channelnewsasia.com/stories/singaporelocalnews/view/65895/1/.html>.

2. "Malaysia and Singapore Settle Reclamation Row", *Dredging News Online* no. 149, 28 January 2005 <http://www.sandandgravel.com/news/news/news_1610.html>.

3. "Settlement Points the Way Forward", *The Straits Times* (Singapore), 27 April 2005.

4. "Reclaiming Warmer Ties", *The New Straits Times* (Malaysia), 26 April 2005.

5. "SM Goh in Talks with Abdullah", *The Straits Times* (Singapore), 1 March 2005.

6. "Temasek Agrees to Buy Stake in MPlant", *The Straits Times* (Singapore), 8 March 2005; "Temasek Likely to Lead S'pore's Investment Charge into Malaysia", *The Straits Times* (Singapore), 11 December 2004.

7. "MAS, SIA, SilkAir Sign Deal to Boost Air Links", *The Straits Times* (Singapore), 25 February 2005.

8. "RHB Banking on S'pore Football", *The Straits Times* (Singapore), 22March 2005.

9. "Closer S'pore-M'sia Ties Crucial: Nathan", *The Business Times* (Singapore), 12 April 2005.

Bibliography

Abdul Majid Ismail. *Report of the Committee Appointed by the National Operations Council to Study Campus Life of Students of the University of Malaya*. Kuala Lumpur: Government Printing Press, 1971.

Abdul Manaf Bin Haji Ahmad. *Negara Islam: Satu Analisa Perbandingan*. Kuala Lumpur: Yayasan Dakwah Islamiah Malaysia, 2004.

Abdul Rahim Abd. Rashid. *Education and Nation Formation in Malaysia: A Structural Analysis*. Kuala Lumpur: University of Malaya Press, 2002.

Abdul Rahman Embong. "The Culture and Practice of Pluralism in Postcolonial Malaysia". In *The Politics of Multiculturalism. Pluralism and Citizenship in Malaysia, Singapore, and Indonesia*, edited by Robert W. Hefner. Honolulu: University of Hawaii, 2001.

Abdul Rahman Embong. *State-led Modernization and the New Middle Class in Malaysia*. New York: Palgrave, 2002.

Abdul Razak Hussain. *Report of the Education Committee 1956*. Kuala Lumpur: Government Printing Press, 1956.

Abdullah Ahmad Badawi. *Managing Success*. Subang Jaya, Malaysia: Pelanduk Publications, 2003.

Abdullah Ahmad Badawi. "Forward Towards Excellence". Presidential speech given at the 55th General Assembly of the United Malays National Organization (UMNO), Putra Jaya, 23 September 2004.

Abdullah Hassan, ed. *Prosiding Persidangan Antarabangsa Melayu Beijing ke-2 Jilid 1: Agama, Budaya, Pendidikan, Ekonomi, Sejarah dan Seni*. Kuala Lumpur: Dewan Bahasa dan Pustaka, 2002.

Abdullah Sanusi Ahmad. "Public Administration Reforms in Malaysia: A Developing Country Perspective". In *Governance. Promoting Sound Development Management.* Manila: Asian Development Bank, 1997.

Abidin M.Z. "Malaysia's Approach Towards FTAs". Paper presented at the International Conference on FTAs in the Asia-Paific Region: Implications for Australia, University of Western Australia, 4–6 July 2004.

Ahmad Sarji, ed. *Malaysia's Vision 2020. Understanding the Concept, Implications & Challenges.* Petaling Jaya: Pelanduk Publications, 1993/1997.

Ahmad Sarji. *The Civil Service of Malaysia: Towards Vision 2020.* Kuala Lumpur: Government of Malaysia, 1995.

Alagasari, Govin. *Mahathir, The Awakening.* Kuala Lumpur: Uni-strength Sdn Bhd, 1994.

Alavi, R. *Industrialisation in Malaysia: Import Substitution and Infant Industry Performance.* London: Routledge, 1996.

Alias Mohamed. *PAS' Platform: Development and Change 1951–1986.* Selangor: Gateway Publishing House, 1994.

Altbach, Philip G. "Globalization and the University: Myths and Realities in Unequal World". *Teritary Education and Management 10*, no. 1 (March 2004): 3–25.

Aminuddin Baki. *The National School of Malaya: Its Problems, Proposed Curriculum and Activities.* Kuala Lumpur: Arkib Negara Malaysia, 1953. Reprinted 1981.

Anual Bakhri Haron. *UMNO Tolak Hudud.* Kota Bharu: Pustaka Qamar, 2002.

Anwar Ibrahim. *The Asian Renaissance.* Kuala Lumpur: Times Books International, 1996.

Asian Development Bank. *Asian Development Outlook 2002.* Manila: Asian Development Bank, 2002.

Asian Development Bank. *Asian Development Outlook 2004.* Manila: Asian Development Bank, 2004.

Asiaweek. "One Nation, One People. Mahathir Lays the Groundwork for Stronger Unity". 6 October 1995 <http://www.asiaweek.com/asiaweek/95/1006/nat4.html>.

Asmah Omar. *Language and Society in Malaysia.* Kuala Lumpur: Dewan Bahasa dan Pustaka, 1982.

Barlow, C. and L.K.Y. Francis, eds. *Malaysian Economics and Politics in the New Century.* Cheltenham: Edward Elgar, 2003.

Bartels, Frank L. "The Future of Intra-regional Foreign Direct Investment Patterns in Southeast Asia". In *The Future of Foreign Direct Investment Patterns in Southeast*

Asia, edited by Nick J. Freeman and Frank L. Bartels. London: Routledge Corzon, 2004.

Bergsten, R. "Back to the Future: APEC Looks at Sub-regional Trade Agreements to Achieve Free Trade Goals". Speech given at the Pacific Basin Economic Council Luncheon, Washington DC, 31 October 2000.

Best, M.H. and R. Rasiah. *Malaysian Electronics: At the Crossroads*. Vienna: United Nations Development Organization (UNIDO), 2003.

Black, Antony. *The History of Islamic Political Thought: From the Prophet to the Present*. Edinburgh: Edinburgh University Press, 2001.

Case, William. *Politics in Southeast Asia*. Richmond: Curzon, 2002.

Chamil Wariya. *Abdullah Ahmad Badawi — Perjalanan Politik PM Ke 5*. Kuala Lumpur: Utusan Publications and Distributors Sdn Bhd, 2004.

Chamil Wariya. *Kesinambungan Dan Perubahan*. Kuala Lumpur: Utusan Publications and Distributors Sdn Bhd, 2004.

Chander, R. *General Report of the Population Census of Malaysia 1970*, vols. 1 and 2. Kuala Lumpur: Department of Statistics, 1977.

Chandra Muzaffar. *Protector?: An Analysis of the Concept and Practice of Loyalty in Leader-led Relationships within Malay Society*. Penang: Aliran, 1979.

Chandra Muzaffar. "Fighting Corruption". 2000 <http://www2.jaring.my/just/fighting-corruption.htm>.

Cheah Boon Kheng. *Malaysia: The Making of a Nation*. Singapore: Institute of Southeast Asian Studies, 2002.

Chee, Stephen. "Administrative Reform and Economic Growth in Malaysia: Restructuring the Role of the Public Sector". In *Administrative Reform Towards Promoting Productivity in Bureaucratic Performance*, edited by Zhang Zhijian, Raul P. De Guzman, and Mila A. Reforma. Manila: Eropa Secretariat General, 1992.

Clad, James. *Behind the Myth. Business, Money, and Power in Southeast Asia*. London: Unwin Hyman, 1989.

Crouch, Harold. "Authoritarian Trends, the UMNO Split and the Limits to State Power". In *Fragmented Vision: Culture and Politics in Contemporary Malaysia*, edited by Francis Loh Kok Wah and Joel Khan. Sydney: Allen & Unwin, 1992.

Crouch, Harold. *Government and Society in Malaysia*. St Leonards: Allen & Unwin, 1996.

Derichs, Claudia. "Looking for Clues: Malaysian Suggestions for Political Change". Project discussion paper no. 10/2001, Discourses on Political Reforms and Democratization in East and Southeast Asia in the Light of New Processes in Regional Community Building, Institut für Ostasienwissenshaften (Institute for East Asian Studies/East Asian Politics) Duisburg, Germany, February 2001 <http://www.uni-duisburg.de/Institute/OAWISS/neu/downloads/pdf/orange/discuss10.pdf>.

Derichs, Claudia. "A Step Forward: Malaysian Ideas for Political Change". *Journal of Asian and African Studies 37*, no. 1 (2002): 43–65.

Dredging News Online, 28 January 2005, no. 149. "Malaysia and Singapore Settle Reclamation Row" <http://www.sandandgravel.com/news/news/news_1610.htm>.

Esman, Milton. *Administration and Development in Malaysia*. Ithaca, NY: Cornell University Press, 1972.

Esman, Milton. "Public Administration, Ethnic Conflict, and Economic Development". *Public Administration Review* (November/December 1997).

Esman, Milton. *Management Dimensions of Development: Perspective and Strategies*. West Hartford, CT: Kumarian Press, 1991.

Faaland, Just et al. *Growth and Ethnic Inequality: Malaysia's New Economic Policy*. Kuala Lumpur: Dewan Bahasa dan Pustaka, 1990.

Farish Noor. "Looking for *Reformasi*: The Discursive Dynamics of the *Reformasi* Movement and its Prospects as a Political Project". *Indonesia and the Malay World 27*, no. 77 (1999): 5–18.

Farish Noor. *The Other Malaysia: Writings on Malaysia's Subaltern History*. Kuala Lumpur: Silverfish Books, 2000.

Farish Noor. "PAS Post-Fadzil Noor: Future Directions and Prospects". Working paper 8, Institute of Southeast Asian Studies, Singapore, August 2002.

Farish Noor. "Malaysia's Islamic Fanaticism". *Daily Times*, 14 October 2004 <http://www.dailytimes.com.pk/default.asp?page=story_12-6-2004_pg3_2>.

Felker, G. "The Politics of Industrial Investment Policy Reform in Malaysia and Thailand". In *Southeast Asia's Industrialisation: Industrial Policy, Capabilities and Sustainability*, edited by K.S. Jomo. Basingstoke: Palgrave, 2001.

Findlay, C., H. Piei, and M. Pangestu. "Trading with Favourites: Free Trade Agreements in the Asia Pacific". In *APEC in the 21ˢᵗ Century*, edited by Riyana Miranti and Denis Hew. Singapore: Institute of Southeast Asian Studies 2004.

Fisk, E.K. "Features of the Rural Economy". In *The Political Economy of Independent Malaya*, edited by T.H. Silcok and E.K. Fisk. Canberra: Eastern Universities Press, 1963.

Funston, John. "Malaysia's Elections: Malay Winds of Change?". In *Trends in Malaysia: Election Assessment*, no. 1, January. Singapore: Institute of Southeast Asian Studies, 2000*a*.

Funston, John. "Malaysia's Tenth Elections: Status Quo, *Reformasi* or Islamization?". *Contemporary Southeast Asia 22*, no. 1 (April 2000*b*).

Funston, John. *Malay Politics in Malaysia: A Study of PAS and UMNO*. Kuala Lumpur: Heinemann, 2000*c*.

Furnivall, J.S. *Colonial Policy and Practice: A Comparative Study of Burma and Netherlands Indies*. Cambridge: University Press, 1948.

Furnivall, J.S. "Plural Societies". In *Sociology of South-East Asia. Readings on Social Change and Development*, edited by Hans-Dieter Evers. Oxford in Asia University Readings. Kuala Lumpur: Oxford University Press, 1980.

Ganesan, N. "Malaysia in 2002: Political Consolidation and Change?". *Asian Survey* XLIII, no. 1 (2003): 147–55.

Goh Beng-Lan. *Modern Dreams. An Inquiry into Power, Cultural Production, and the Cityscape in Contemporary Urban Penang, Malaysia*. Ithaca, NY : Cornell Southeast Asia Program, 2002.

Goh, Winnie and Jomo Sundram. "Privatization in Malaysia: A Social and Economic Paradox". In *Who Benefits from Privatization?*, edited by Moazzem Hossain and Justin Malbon. London: Routledge, 1998.

Gomez, Edmund Terence. *Political Business: Corporate Involvement of Malaysian Political Parties*. Townsville, Australia: James Cook University of North Queensland, 1994.

Gomez, Edmund Terence. *The 1995 Malaysian General Election: A Report and Commentary*. Singapore: Institute of Southeast Asian Studies, 1996.

Gomez, Edmund Terence. *Chinese Business in Malaysia. Accumulation, Accommodation and Ascendance*. Surrey: RoutledgeCurzon Press, 1999*a*.

Gomez, Edmund Terence. *Chinese Business in Malaysia: Accumulation, Ascendance, Accommodation*. Honolulu: University of Hawaii Press, 1999*b*.

Gomez, Edmund Terence. "Tracing the Ethnic Divide: Race, Rights and Redistribution in Malaysia". In *Ethnic Futures: The State and Identity Politics in Asia*, edited by Joanna Pfaff-Czarnecka, Darini Rajasingham-Senanayake, Ashis Nandy, and Edmund Terence Gomez, New Delhi: Sage, 1999*c*.

Gomez, Edmund Terence, ed. *Political Business in East Asia*. London: Routledge, 2002.

Gomez, Edmund Terence, ed. *The State of Malaysia: Ethnicity, Equity and Reform*. London: RoutledgeCurzon, 2004.

Gomez, Edmund Terence and Michael H.H. Hsiao, eds. *Chinese Enterprise, Transnationalism and Identity*. London: RoutledgeCurzon, 2004.

Gomez, Edmund Terence and K.S. Jomo. *Malaysia's Political Economy: Politics, Patronage and Profits*. Cambridge: Cambridge University Press, 1997.

Government of Malaysia. Ministry of Education. *Educational Statistics of Malaysia 1980*. Kuala Lumpur: National Printing Press, 1980.

Government of Malaysia. Ministry of Education. *Educational Statistics of Malaysia 1990*. Kuala Lumpur: National Printing Press, 1990.

Government of Malaysia. Ministry of Education. *Educational Statistics of Malaysia 1995*. Kuala Lumpur: National Printing Press, 1995.

Government of Malaysia. Ministry of Education. *Educational Statistics of Malaysia 1999*. Kuala Lumpur: National Printing Press, 1999.

Government of Malaysia. Ministry of Education. *Educational Statistics of Malaysia 2000*. Kuala Lumpur: National Printing Press, 2000.

Government of Malaysia, Ministry of Finance. *Economic Report 2003/2004*. Kuala Lumpur: National Printing Press, 2003.

Government of Malaysia, Ministry of Trade and Industry. *Second Industrial Master Plan, 1996–2005*. Kuala Lumpur: National Printing Press, 1996.

Government of Malaysia. *Second Malaysia Plan, 1971–1975*. Kuala Lumpur: The Government Press, 1971.

Government of Malaysia. *Fourth Malaysian Plan*. Kuala Lumpur: National Printing Press, 1981.

Government of Malaysia. *Fifth Malaysian Plan*. Kuala Lumpur: National Printing Press, 1986.

Government of Malaysia. *Sixth Malaysian Plan*. Kuala Lumpur: National Printing Press, 1991.

Government of Malaysia. *Seventh Malaysian Plan*. Kuala Lumpur: National Printing Press, 1996.

Government of Malaysia. *Eighth Malaysia Plan*. Kuala Lumpur: National Printing Press, 2001.

Government of Malaysia. *Eighth Malaysian Plan: Mid-Term Review*. Kuala Lumpur: National Printing Press, 2003.

Halimah Awang. "Human Capital and Technology Development in Malaysia". *International Educational Journal 5*, no. 2 (2004): 239–46.

Hall, Stuart. "New Ethnicities". In *'Race', Culture and Difference*, edited by J. Donald and A. Rattansi. London: Sage, 1992.

Hasnul Rahman. *Hudud: Siapa Khianati Hukum Allah, UMNO Atau PAS?*. N.p.: DLSB, 2001.

Hefner, Robert W. and Patricia Horvatich, eds. *Islam in an Era of Nation-States: Politics and Religious Renewal in Muslim Southeast Asia*. Hawaii: University of Hawaii Press, 1997.

Heng Pek Koon and Sieh Lee Mei Ling. "The Chinese Business Community in Peninsular Malaysia, 1957–1999". In *The Chinese in Malaysia*, edited by Lee Kam Hing and Tan Chee-Beng. Selangor: Oxford University Press, 2000.

Heryanto, Ariel and Sumit K. Mandal, eds. *Challenging Authoritarianism in Southeast Asia: Comparing Indonesia and Malaysia.* London: RoutledgeCurzon, 2003.

Hew, D. "Entrepreneurship and SMEs in Southeast Asia's Economic Development". In *Entrepreneurship and SMEs in Southeast Asia,* edited by D. Hew and W.N. Loi. Singapore: Institute of Southeast Asian Studies, 2004.

Hilley, John. *Malaysia: Mahathirism, Hegemony and the New Opposition.* London & New York: Zed Books, 2001.

Hirschman, Albert O. *Journeys Toward Progress. Studies of Economic Policy-making in Latin America.* New York: W.W. Norton & Co., 1963.

Ho Khai Leong. "Indigenizing the State: The New Economic Policy and the Bumiputera State in Peninsular Malaysia". Ph.D. dissertation, Ohio State University, 1988.

Ho Khai Leong. "The Dynamics of Policy-making in Malaysia: The Formulation of the New Economic Policy and the National Development Policy". *The Asian Journal of Public Administration 14,* no. 2 (1992): 204–27.

Ho Khai Leong. "Bureaucratic Accountability in Malaysia: Control Mechanisms and Critical Concerns". In *Handbook of Comparative Public Administration in the Asia-Pacific Basin,* edited by Wong Hoi-kwok and Hon S. Chan. New York: Marcel Dekker, 1999.

Ho Khai Leong. "The Political and Administrative Frames: Challenges and Reforms under Mahathir". In *Mahathir's Administration: Performance and Crisis,* edited by Ho Khai Leong and James Chin. Singapore: Times Academic Press, 2001.

Ho Khai Leong. "Reinventing the Bureaucracy? Malaysia's New Administrative Reforms Initiatives". *Journal of Comparative Asian Development 1,* no. 1 (Spring 2002): 87–104.

Ho Khai Leong and J. Chin, eds. *Mahathir's Administration.* Kuala Lumpur: Times Books International, 2001.

Horowitz, Donald L. "The Quran and the Common Law: Islamic Law Reform and the Theory of Legal Change". *The American Journal of Comparative Law 42* (1994): 233–93.

Hwang In-Won. *Personalized Politics: The Malaysian State under Mahathir.* Singapore: Institute of Southeast Asian Studies, 2003.

Ibrahim Abu Shah. *The Use of Higher Education as an Intervention Strategy in the Economic Development of a Plural Society: A Case Study of MARA Institute of Technology in the Economic Policy of Malaysia.* Ann Arbor, MI: UMI, 1987.

Ibrahim Saad. *Competing Identities in a Plural Society: The Case of Peninsular Malaysia.* Singapore: Institute of Southeast Asian Studies, 1980.

Institute of Strategic and International Studies. Polytechnic Development Study, Technical report for the Ministry of Education, Kuala Lumpur, 1997.

Ismail Noor. *Pak Lah — A Sense of Accountability.* Kuala Lumpur: Utusan Publications and Distributors Sdn Bhd, 2003.

Ismail Noor. *Come Work With Me!.* Batu Cave, Malaysia: Thinker's Library Sdn. Bhd, 2004.

Ismail Salleh and H. Osman Rani. *The Growth of the Public Sector in Malaysia.* Malaysia: Institute of Strategic and International Studies, 1991.

Jomo, K.S. *Mahathir's Economic Policies.* Kuala Lumpur: Institute of Social Analysis (INSAN), 1988.

Jomo, K.S. *Growth and Structural Change in the Malaysian Economy.* Basingstoke: Macmillan, 1990.

Jomo K.S. "Introduction". In *Malaysian Eclipse: Economic Crisis and Recovery,* edited by K.S. Jomo. London: Zed Books, 2001.

Jomo, K.S., ed. *After the Storm: Crisis, Recovery and Sustaining Development in Four Asian Economies.* Singapore: Singapore University Press, 2004.

Jomo, K.S. and Ahmad Shabery Cheek. "Malaysia's Islamic Movements". In *Fragmented Vision: Culture and Politics in Contemporary Malaysia,* edited by Francis Loh Kok Wah and Joel Khan. Sydney: Allen & Unwin, 1992.

Jomo, K.S., G. Felker, and R. Rasiah, eds. *Industrial Technology Development in Malayia: Industry and Firm Studies.* London: Routledge, 1999.

Jomo K.S. and Edmund Terence Gomez. "The Malaysian Development Dilemma". In *Rents, Rent-Seeking and Economic Development: Theory and Evidence in Asia,* edited by Mushtaq H. Khan and K.S. Jomo. Cambridge: Cambridge University Press, 2000.

Jones, L.W. *The Population of Borneo.* London: Athlone Press, 1966.

Kanapathy, V. "Industrial Restructuring in Malaysia: Policy Shifts and the Promotion of New Sources of Growth". In *Industrial Restructuring in East Asia: Towards the 21st Century,* edited by Seiichi Masuyama, Donna Vandenbrink, and Chia Siow. Tokyo: Tokyo Club Foundation for Global Studies, 2001.

Kanapathy, V. and M.S. Ismail. *Malasyian Economy: Selected Issues and Policy Directions.* Kuala Lumpur: Institute of Strategic and International Studies, 1994.

Khan, Joel S. "Growth, Economic Transformation, Culture and the Middle Class". In *The New Rich in Asia: Mobile Phones, McDonald's and Middle Class Revolution,* edited by Richard Robison and David S.G. Goodman. London: Routledge, 1996.

Khong Kim Hoong. *Merdeka: British Rule and the Struggle for Independence in Malaya 1945–1957.* Petaling Jaya, Malaysia: SIRD, 1984.

Khong Kim Hoong. *Malaysia's General Election 1990: Continuity, Change, and Ethnic Politics.* Singapore: Institute of Southeast Asian Studies, 1991.

Khong Kim Hoong. *Merdeka! British Rule and the Struggle for Independence in Malaya 1945–1957.* Petaling Jaya: Strategic Information Research Development, 2003.

Khoo Boo Teik. *Paradoxes of Mahathirism. An Intellectual Biography of Mahathir Mohamad.* Shah Alam: Oxford University Press, 1995.

Khoo Boo Teik. *Beyond Mahathir. Malaysian Politics and its Discontents.* London & New York: Zed Books, 2003.

Khoo Boo Teik. "Malaysian Politics in 2004: Transitions and Elections". In *Political and Security Outlook 2004: Political Change in Southeast Asia.* Trends in Southeast Asia Series 7, February. Singapore: Institute of Southeast Asian Studies, 2004.

Khoo Boo Teik. "Masyarakat Cina, Politik Malaysia dan Dunia Islam". Paper presented at the Seminar Politik Kelantan, Pusat Kajian Strategik, Kota Bharu, 23 May 2004.

Khoo K.-H. *Abdullah Administration.* Selangor, Malaysia: Pelandok Publications, 2004.

Khoo Soo Gim. *General Report of the Population Census of Malaysia 1991*, vols. 1 and 2. Kuala Lumpur: Department of Statistics, 1995.

Khoo Teik Huat. *General Report of the Population Census of Malaysia 1980,* vols. 1 and 2. Kuala Lumpur: Department of Statistics, 1983.

Khuri, R.K. *Freedom, Modernity and Islam: Toward a Creative Synthesis.* Syracuse: Syracuse University Press, 1998.

Kua Kia Soong. *The Chinese Schools in Malaysia: A Protean Saga.* Kuala Lumpur: United Chinese School Committees Association of Malaysia, 1985.

Lee Hock Guan. "Malay Dominance and Opposition Politics in Malaysia". In *Southeast Asian Affairs 2001.* Singapore: Institute of Southeast Asian Studies, 2002.

Lee Hwok Aun. "The NEP, Vision 2020, and Dr. Mahathir: Continuing Dilemmas". In *Reflections. The Mahathir Years,* edited by Bridget Welsh. Washington DC: Southeast Asia Studies Program, Johns Hopkins University SIAS, 2004.

Lee Kam Hing and Heng Pek Koon. "The Chinese in the Malaysian Political System". In *The Chinese in Malaysia,* edited by Lee Kam Hing and Tan Chee-Beng. Selangor: Oxford University Press, 2000.

Lee Kam Hing and Tan Chee-Beng, ed. *The Chinese in Malaysia.* Kuala Lumpur: Oxford University Press, 2000.

Lim Hong Hai. "The Delineation of Peninsular Electoral Constituencies: Amplifying Malay and UMNO Power". In *New Politics in Malaysia,* edited by Francis Loh Kok Wah and Johan Saravanamuttu. Singapore: Institute of Southeast Asian Studies, 2003.

Lim, I. and H. Nesadurai. "Managing the Malaysian Industry Economy: The Policy and Reform Process for Industrialisation". In *Industrial Restructuring in East Asia: Towards the 21ˢᵗ Century,* edited by Seiichi Masuyama, Donna Vandenbrink, and Chia Siow. Tokyo: Tokyo Club Foundation for Global Studies, 1997.

Lim Kit Siang. *IT for All.* Petaling Jaya: Democratic Action Party, 1997.

Lim Kit Siang. "UMNO Exploitation of Suqiu is Going to be Greatest Test as to Whether Vision 2020 and Bangsa Malaysia are Obsolete Barisan Nasional Concepts to be Consigned to the Dustbin of History". DAP press statement, 17 December 2000 <http://www.malaysia.net/dap/lks0597.htm>.

Lim Kit Siang. Press statement, 2001 <http://www.malaysia.net/dap/lks1298.htm>.

Ling Liong Sik. "Address at the 48th Annual General Meeting of the MCA, 4 August 2001". <http://www.mca.org.my/story.asp?file=/articles/speeches/2001/576. html&sec=Speeches>.

Loh Kok Wah, Francis. "Withdraw Decision to Include Religion in Our ICs". Aliran press statement, 13 October 1999 <http://www.malaysia.net/aliran/ms991013. htm>.

Loh Kok Wah, Francis. "Developmentalism and the Limits of Democratic Discourse". In *Democracy in Malaysia. Discourses and Practices*, edited by Francis Loh Kok Wah and Khoo Boo Teik. Richmond, Surrey: Curzon, 2002.

Loh Kok Wah, Francis. "Towards a New Politics of Fragmentation and Contestation". In *New Politics in Malaysia*, edited by Francis Loh Kok Wah and Johan Saravanamuttu. Singapore: Institute of Southeast Asian Studies, 2003.

Loh Kok Wah, Francis and Johan Saravanamuttu, eds. *New Politics in Malaysia*, Singapore: Institute of Southeast Asian Studies, 2003.

Mahathir Mohamad. "New Government Policies". In *Mahathir's Economic Policies*, edited by K.S. Jomo. Kuala Lumpur: Institute of Social Analysis (INSAN), 1988.

Mahathir Mohamad. *The Way Forward (Vision 2020)*. Kuala Lumpur: Institute of Strategic and International Studies (ISIS), 1991*a*.

Mahathir Mohamad. *Wawasan 2020*. Kuala Lumpur: Institute of Strategic and International Studies (ISIS), 1991*b*.

Mahathir Mohamad. *Malaysia: The Way Forward*. Kuala Lumpur: Malaysian Business Council, 1991*c*.

Mahathir Mohamad. *Malaysia: The Way Forward*. Speech presented at the First Conference of the Malaysian Trade Council, 28 February 1991. Kuala Lumpur: Biro Tatanegara Jabatan Perdana Menteri Malaysia, 1991*d*.

Mahathir Mohamad. Speech at the Opening of the International Institute of Islamic Thought and Civilization (ISTAC), Kuala Lumpur, 2 June 1993*a*.

Mahathir Mohamad. Speech at the Opening of the Islam and Industrial Conference, Kuala Lumpur, 21 January 1993*b*.

Mahathir Mohamad. Speech at the 10th Anniversary Celebration of the International Islamic University Malaysia, Selangor, 24 August 1993*c*.

Mahathir Mohamad. *The Way Forward*. London: Weidenfeld & Nicolson, 1998*a*.

Mahathir Mohamad. Speech at the 52ND UMNO General Assembly at the Putra World Trade Centre, Kuala Lumpur, 19 June 1998*b*.

Mahmood bin Taib, Tan Sri Dato, and Johari bin Mat. "Administrative Reforms in Malaysia Toward Enhancing Public Service Performance". *Governance: An International Journal of Policy and Administration 5*, no. 4 (October 1992): 423–37.

Malaysia Department of Statistics. *General Report of the Population Census (1980)*. Kuala Lumpur: National Printing Press, 1980.

Malaysia Department of Statistics. *General Report of the Population Census (1991)*. Kuala Lumpur: National Printing Press, 1991.

Malaysia Department of Statistics. *General Report of the Population Census (2000)*. Kuala Lumpur: National Printing Press, 2002.

Malaysia Department of Statistics. *Education and Social Characteristics of the Population*. Kuala Lumpur: National Printing Press, 2002.

Malaysiakini. "Malaysian Chinese Party Leader Criticizes State TV Station for 'Distortion'". 18 November 2002 <http://www.asu.edu/educ/epsl/LPRU/newsarchive/Art1398.txt>.

Malhi, Amrita. "The PAS-BN Conflict in the 1990s: Islamism and Modernity". In *Malaysia: Islam, Society and Politics*, edited by Virginia Hooker and Norani Othman. Singapore Institute of Southeast Asian Studies, 2003.

Mandal, Sumit. "Transethnic Solidarities, Racialisation and Social Equality". In *The State of Malaysia: Ethnicity, Equity and Reform*, edited by Edmund Terence Gomez. London: RoutledgeCurzon, 2004.

Mansoor Marican, Y. "Combating Corruption: The Malaysian Experience". *Asian Survey 19*, no. 6 (June 1979): 597–610.

Martin-Jones, David. "Badawi to the Bone?: Post-Mahathir Malaysia at the Polls". *The Review 29*, no. 4 (April 2004).

Maznah Mohamad. "The Contest for Malay Votes in 1999: UMNO's Most Historic Challenge?". In *New Politics in Malaysia*, edited by Francis Loh Kok Wah and Johan Saravanamuttu. Singapore: Institute of Southeast Asian Studies, 2003.

Means, Gordon. *Malaysian Politics: The Second Generation*. Singapore: Oxford University Press, 1991.

Milne, R.S. and Diane K. Mauzy. *Malaysia: Tradition, Modernity, and Islam*. Boulder & London: Westview Press, 1986.

Montgomery, John D. and Milton Esman. *Development Administration in Malaysia*. Kuala Lumpur: The Government Printers, 1966.

Muhammad Syukri Salleh. "Establishing an Islamic State: Ideals and Realities in the State of Kelantan, Malaysia". *Southeast Asian Studies 37*, no. 2 (1999): 235–56.

Muhammad Syukri Salleh. "Reformasi, Reradikalisasi dan Kebangkitan Islam di Malaysia". *Pemikir 20* (2000): 35–50.

Mustapa B. Kassim. *Preferential Policy in Higher Education in Malaysia: A Case Study of Malay Graduates at the University of Science, Malaysia*. Ann Arbor, MI: University Microfilms International, 1991.

Nagata, Judith. "How to be Islamic without Being an Islamic State: Contested Models of Development in Malaysia". In *Islam, Globalisation and Post-modenity*, edited by Akbar S. Ahmed and Hastings Donnan. London: Routledge, 1994.

Nair, Sheila. "Colonial 'Others' and Nationalist Politics in Malaysia". *Akademika 54* (January 1999).

Nathan, K.S. "Vision 2020: Implications for Malaysian Foreign Policy. Part 1". *Asian Defence Journal* (January 1992).

Nathan, K.S. "Malaysia: 11 September and the Politics of Incumbency". In *Southeast Asian Affairs 2002*. Singapore: Institute of Southeast Asian Studies, 2003.

New Straits Times, 2 March 1991.

New Straits Times, March 2004. "Election 2004 Results". Supplement.

New Straits Times, 1 August 2004. "A Balanced Approach that is Islam Hadhari".

New Straits Times, 2 October 2004. "Malaysia as a Model Islamic Nation".

New Straits Times, 26 April 2005. "Reclaiming Warmer Ties".

Nidzam Sulaiman. "Anjakan Paradigma Budaya Politik Melayu Dari Feudal Kepada Neo-Feudal". In *Prosiding Persidangan Antarabangsa Pengajian Melayu Beijing ke-2 Jilid 1*, edited by Abdullah Hassan. Kuala Lumpur: Dewan Bahasa dan Pustaka, 2002.

Norhashimah Mohd Yassin. *Islamisation/Malaynisation: A Study on the Role of Islamic Law in the New Economic Development of Malaysia: 1969–1993*. Kuala Lumpur: A.S Noordeen, 1996.

Okabe, M. "Rapid Recovery of Foreign Direct Investment into Malaysia". *Tsusho Koho* no. 15523 (August 2004).

Okamoto, Y. "Agglomeration and International Competitiveness: Can Malaysia Growth be Sustainable?". In *Industrial Clusters in Asia: Analyses of their Competition and Cooperation*, edited by Akifumi Kuchiki and Masatsuga Tsuji. IDE Development Perspectives Series 6. Chiba: Institute of Developing Economies, 2004.

Ong, H.C. and D. Hew. "Malaysia Productivity Growth and Industrial Structure, 1970–1997". In *PECC Pacific Economic Outlook — Structure Project: Productivity Growth and Industrial Structure in the Pacific Region*, edited by Akira Kohsaka. Osaka: Japan Committee for Pacific Economic Outlook, 2000.

Ooi Kee Beng. "Three-Tiered Social Darwinism in Malaysian Ethnographic History". *Tonan Ajia Kenkyu* [Southeast Asian Studies] *41*, no. 2 (September 2003): 162–79.

Organisation for Economic Co-operation and Development. *Public Management and Administrative Reform in Western Europe*. Paris: Organisation for Economic Co-operation and Development (OECD), 1997.

Parti Islam SeMalaysia. *Isu Memali: Hakikat dan Realiti*. Kuala Lumpur: Jabatan Penerangan PAS Pusat, 2002*a*.

Parti Islam SeMalaysia, *Almarhum Dato' Haji Fadzil Noor Dalam Kenangan 1937–2002*. n.p.: 2002*b*.

Parti Islam SeMalaysia. *Ulasan Terkini ... Tuan Guru Ab. Hadi Restui Pengganas?*. Tanjong Karang: Dewan Pemuda PAS, 2003.

Pelaksanaan Hukum Hudud di Kelantan. Kota Bharu: Telda Corporation, 1994.

Phar Kim Beng. "Islam Hadhari vs Islam Madani". *Malaysiakini*, 8 September 2004 <http://www.malaysiakini.com/columns/29830>.

Radio Singapore International. "What Lies Ahead for Anwar's Political Future?". 3 September 2004 <http://rsi.mediacorpradio.com/english/newsline/view/20040903155034/1/.html>.

Raja Petra Kamarudin. "An Uneven Playing Field, the Putrajaya Experience". *Harakah*, 17 March 2004.

Ramesh, S. and Dominique Loh. "Singapore and Malaysia Determined to Put Ties Back on Track". *Channel NewsAsia*, 12 January 2004 <http://www.channelnewsasia.com/stories/singaporelocalnews/view/65895/1/.html>.

Rasiah, R. "Industrial technology transition in Malaysia". In *Competition, FDI and Technological Activity in East Asia*, edited by Sanjay Lall and Shujiro Urata. Cheltenhan, England: Edward Elgar, 2003.

Roald, Anne S. *Tarbiya: Education and Politics in Islamic Movements in Jordan and Malaysia*. Lund, Sweden: Almqvist & Wiksell International, 1994.

Roslan Abdul Hamid. *Abjad Kemuliaan — 100 Hari Pertama*. Kuala Lumpur: Indah Abjad, 2004.

Rosnani Hashim. *Educational Dualism in Malaysia: Implications for Theory and Practice*. Kuala Lumpur: Oxford University Press, 1996.

Saliha Hassan. "Islamic Revivalism and State Response to Islamic-Oriented Non-Governmental Organisations in Malaysia". Paper presented at the Islamic Revivalism and State Response: The Experiences of Malaysia, Indonesia and Brunei Workshop, Singapore, 2–3 June 1997.

Saravanamuttu, Johan. "The Look East Policy and Japanese Economic Penetration in Malaysia". In *Mahathir's Economic Policies*, edited by K.S. Jomo. Kuala Lumpur: Institute of Social Analysis (INSAN), 1988.

Saw Swee Hock. *The Population of Peninsular Malaysia*. Singapore: Singapore University Press, 1988.

Scott, James C. *The Moral Economy of the Peasant: Rebellion and Subsistence in Southeast Asia*. New Haven: Yale University Press, 1976.

Seidentopf, Heinrich. "Introduction: Government Performance and Administrative Reform". In *Strategies for Administrative Reform*, edited by Gerald Caiden and Heinrich Siedentopf. Lexington, MA: D.C. Heath and Company, 1982.

Shaari Bin Abdul Rahman. *Education and Social Characteristics of the Population 2000*. Kuala Lumpur: Department of Statistics, 2001*a*.

Shaari Bin Abdul Rahman. *Population Distribution and Basic Demographic Characteristics 2000*. Kuala Lumpur: Department of Statistics, 2001*b*.

Shaari Bin Abdul Rahman. *Population Distribution by Local Authority Areas and Mukims 2000*. Kuala Lumpur: Department of Statistics, 2001*c*.

Shaari Bin Abdul Rahman. *Preliminary Count Report for Urban and Rural Areas 2000*. Kuala Lumpur: Department of Statistics, 2001*d*.

Shamsul, A.B. "The Battle Royal: The UMNO Elections of 1987". In *Southeast Asian Affairs 1987*. Singapore: Institute of Southeast Asian Studies, 1988.

Shamsul, A.B. "The Economic Dimension of Malay Nationalism. The Socio-Historical Roots of the New Economic Policy and its Contemporary Implications". *Developing Economies XXXV* (September 1997*a*): 240–61.

Shamsul, A.B. "Identity Construction, Nation Formation and Islamic Revivalism in Malaysia". In *Islam in an Era of Nation-States: Politics and Religious Renewal in Muslim Southeast Asia*, edited by Robert W. Hefner and Patricia Horvatich. Hawaii: University of Hawaii Press, 1997*b*.

Shamsul, A.B. "Identity Contestation in Malaysia: A Comparative Commentary on 'Malayness' and 'Chineseness'". *Akademika 55* (July 1999).

Shamsul, A.B. "'Malay' and 'Malayness' in Malaysia Reconsidered: a Critical Review". *Communal/Plural 9*, no. 1 (April 2001*a*): 69–80.

Shamsul, A.B. "The Redefinition of Politics and the Transformation of Malaysian Pluralism". In *The Politics of Multiculturalism. Pluralism and Citizenship in Malaysia, Singapore and Indonesia*, edited by Robert W. Hefner. Hawaii: University of Hawaii Press, 2001*b*.

Sharifuddin Zainuddin. "Malaysia". In *The International Encyclopedia of Public Policy and Administration*, edited by Jay M. Shafritz. Boulder: Westview Press, 1998.

Shennan, M. *Out in the Midday Sun — The British in Malaya 1880–1960*. London: John Murray, 2000.

Sivalingam, G. and Yong Siew Peng. "The System of Political and Administrative Corruption in a West Malaysian State". *Philippine Journal of Public Administration XXXV*, no. 3 (July 1991): 264–86.

Sloane, Patricia. *Islam, Modernity and Entrepreneurship Among the Malays.* Basingstoke: Macmillan Press, 1999.

Sulochana, N. "Poverty in Malaysia: A New Look at an Old Problem". Paper presented at the Annual Conference of the International Sociological Association Research Committee on Poverty Social Welfare and Social Policy RC 19, Oveido, Spain, 2001.

Syed Ahmad Hussein. "Muslim Politics and the Discourse on Democracy". In *Democracy in Malaysia: Discourses and Practices*, edited by Francis Loh Kok Wah and Khoo Boo Teik. Surrey: RoutledgeCurzon, 2002.

Syed Husin Ali. "The Role of Malaysian Social Scientists in a Fast Changing Society". In *Reinventing Malaysia. Reflections on its Past and Future*, edited by K.S. Jomo. Bangi: Penerbit Universiti Kebangsaan Malaysia, 2001.

Syed Othman AlHabshi. *An Inspiration for the Future of Islam: A Brief History and Objectives of the Institute of Islamic Understanding Malaysia (IKIM).* Kuala Lumpur: IKIM, 1994.

Tan Ai Mei. *Malaysian Private Higher Education : Globalisation, Privatisation, Transformation and Marketplaces.* London : Asean Academic Press, 2002.

Tan Liok Ee. "The Rhetoric of Bangsa and Minzu: Community and Nation in Tension. the Malay Peninsula, 1900–1955". Working paper 52, Centre of Southeast Asian Studies, Monash University, Victoria, 1988.

Tan Liok Ee. *The Politics of Chinese Education in Malaya, 1945–1961.* Kuala Lumpur: Oxford University Press, 1997.

Tan Liok Ee. "Baggage from the Past, Eyes on the Future: Chinese Education in Malaysia Today". In *Ethnic Chinese in Singapore and Malaysia: A Dialogue between Tradition and Modernity*, edited by Leo Suryadinata. Singapore: Times Academic Press, 2002.

Taylor, R.D. "The Malaysian Experience: The Multimedia Super Corridor". In *Information Technology Parks of the Asia Pacific: Lessons for the Regional Digital Divide*, edited by Makeroo Jusawalla and Richard D. Taylor. New York: M.E. Sharpe, 2003.

Tham, S-Y. "The Future of Industrialisation in Malaysia under the WTO". *Asia-Pacific Development Journal 11*, no. 1 (June 2004).

The Business Times, April 12, 2005. "Closer S'pore-M'sia Ties Crucial: Nathan".

The Star, 24 October 1991.

The Star, 11 September 1995.

The Star, 5 August 2004. "Islam Hadhari Unit for State".

The Straits Times, 9 January 2003. "Facing the Fundamentalist Challenge".

The Straits Times, 9 March 2004. "Abdullah Offers 'Inclusive' Islam".

The Straits Times, 13 March 2004. "PAS and UMNO Beginning to Look Alike".

The Straits Times, 22 March 2004. "Triumph for Progressive Vision of Malaysia".

The Straits Times, 16 September 2004. "Return of a Rebel: Former DPM Poised to Unite Opposition".

The Straits Times, 29 September 2004. "Other Muslim States Show Interest in Islam Hadhari".

The Straits Times, 15 October 2004. "Malaysia to Send Islamic Scholars to Thai South".

The Straits Times, 11 December 2004. "Temasek Likely to Lead S'pore's Investment Charge into Malaysia".

The Straits Times, 15 December 2004. "S'pore, KL to Co-produce Quality TV Drama Programmes".

The Straits Times, 25 February 2005. "'KL will Seek Johor's Views on Singapore Talks': Abdullah".

The Straits Times, 25 February 2005. "MAS, SIA, SilkAir Sign Deal to Boost Air Links".

The Straits Times, 1 March 2005. "SM Goh in Talks with Abdullah".

The Straits Times, 8 March 2005. "Temasek Agrees to Buy Stake in MPlant".

The Straits Times, 22 March 2005. "RHB Banking on S'pore Football".

The Straits Times, 12 April 2005. "President Describes Links with Malaysia as Unique".

The Straits Times, 27 April 2005. "Settlement Points the Way Forward".

The Straits Times, 28 April 2005. "MM Lee and Mahathir Exchange Views".

The Sunday Times, 26 August 1951.

Van Rijckeghem, Caroline and Beatrice Weder. "Bureaucratic Corruption and the Rate of Temptation: Do Wages in the Civil Service Affect Corruption, and by How Much?". *Journal of Development Economics 65*, no. 2 (August 2001): 307–31.

Verma, V. *Malaysia — State and Civil Society in Transition*. Petaling Jaya, Malaysia: SIRD, 2004.

Wang Gungwu. "Local and National: A Dialogue between Tradition and Modernity". In *Ethnic Chinese in Singapore and Malaysia. A Dialogue between Tradition and Modernity*, edited by Leo Suryadinata. Singapore: Times Academic Press, 2002.

Wee Chong Hui. "Issues in the Evolution of the Malaysian Federal Systems: The Changing Role of the State and Local Governments". In *Malaysia's Public Sector in the Twenty-First Century: Planning for 2020 and Beyond*, edited by Sulaiman

Mahbob et. al. Kuala Lumpur: Malaysian Institute of Economic Research, 1997.

Weiss, Meredith L. "The 1999 Malaysian General Elections: Issues, Insults, and Irregularities". *Asian Survey XL*, no. 3 (2000): 413–35.

Weiss, Meredith L. "The Changing Shape of Islamic Politics in Malaysia". *Journal of East Asian Studies 4* (2004): 139–73.

Weiss, Meredith L. and Saliha Hassan, eds. *Social Movements in Malaysia*. London: Routledge, 2002.

Welsh, Bridget. "Real Change? Elections in the *Reformasi* Era". In *The State of Malaysia: Ethnicity, Equity and Reform*, edited by Edmund Terence Gomez. London: RoutledgeCurzon, 2004*a*.

Welsh, Bridget, ed. *Reflection — The Mahathir Years*. Washington DC: Johns Hopkins University, 2004*b*.

Wong, C.S. "Time to Remove the Ringgit Peg". *The Edge*, 15 November 2004.

World Bank. *Malaysia, Meeting Labor Needs: More Workers and Better Skills*. Washington, DC: World Bank, 1995.

Yahaya Ismail, *Pak Lah dari Kepala Batas ke Putrajaya*. Petaling Jaya: Usaha Teguh Sdn Bhd, 2004.

Ye Lin-Shen. *The Chinese Dilemma*. Kingsford, Australia: East West Publishing Pty Ltd, 2003.

<http://www.groups.yahoo.com/group/kini-malaysia/>

<http://www.malaysiakini.com>

<http://www.malaysia-today.net>

<http://www.parti-pas.org>

<http://www2.hawaii.edu/~fredr/glocon.htm>

<http://www.thestar.com.my/umno/story.asp?file=/2004/9/24/umno/8966474& sec=umno>

Index

1999 Elections
  aftermath, 138–39
2000 Census, 7, 10
2004 Elections
  campaign, 145–46
  candidates, 145–46
  Code of Ethics for candidates, 141
  contest and voting statistics,
    135–37
  electoral politics, 148–49
  implications, 153–55
  issues, 146–48
  Malay electorate, 132–56
  mandate for Barisan Nasional,
    101–05
  monitoring standards of Election
    Committee, 117–19
  Reformasi, decline in, 101–05
  results, 133–34, 152–53

A
Abdullah Ahmad
  dismissal of, 113
Abdullah Badawi, 26, 39, 158, 195
  administrative reforms, 202–207

change in emphasis of policies,
    114–15
  corruption, zero tolerance, 143
  dismissal of Abdullah Ahmad,
    113
  improving relations with Singapore,
    277
  Islamic background, 143
  Malaysia under, 78–80
  personal appeal of, 159
  reform agenda, 78–80
  stress on agricultural sector, 114–15
  suspending large infrastructure
    programmes, 114
Abdul Hadi Awang, 28, 39, 107
Abdullah Md Zin, 38
Abdul Razak Ahmand, 91
Abu Bakar Basyir, 112
administrative reforms, 196
agama schools
  three kinds, 251, 252
agricultural sector
  emphasis on, 114, 115
Agus Dwikarna, 112
Angkatan Belia Islam (ABIM), 27, 251

Keadilan's leadership, attempt to take over, 102
political agendum, 29
Angkatan Perpaduan Ummah (APU), 110
Anti-Corruption Academy, 176
Anti-Corruption Agency (ACA), 79, 144, 218
Anwar Ibrahim, 28, 31
  sacking, 29, 202
  injustice against, 148
  The Asian Renaissance, 36
Arab-Israeli war
  ideological impact, 30
ASEAN-China ISEAS Forum, 213
Asian financial crisis, *see* financial crisis period
avian influenza, 277
Azman Mokhtar, 221

B
bangsa
  definition, 51
Bangsa Malaysia, 49, 53
  acceptance and disagreement, 60, 61
  "buying time interpretation, 55
  hegemony interpretation, 54
  "hot air" interpretation, 53
  inadvertence interpretation, 53
  multiculturalist concept, 57
  national maturity interpretation, 55
  opportunity interpretation, 54
  pluralism interpretation, 54
Barisan Alternatif (BA), 77, 104
Barisan Nasional (BN), 60
  2004 elections, performance at, 132–56, 157–94, 186
  institutional reforms, discussions on, 96
  media, control of, 111
  popular vote, increase in, 158
  strategic positions, 170–71
  support in Bumiputera majority constituencies, 81, 82

support in Chinese-majority constituencies, 86–88
Bio Valley, 272
Black, Antony, 39
British Military Administration (BMA), 162
Buddhism, 19
Bumiputera
  definition of, 13
  other, *see also* Other Bumiputera
  rural, 75
Bumiputera Commercial and Industrial Community (BCIC), 63
bureaucratic inefficiency, 206–07
Bursa Malaysia, 212
business process outsourcing, 272–73

C
Celcom, 77
Chia, Eric, 78, 218
Chinese
  definition of, 12
Chinese electorate
  ambivalence, 92
Chinese immigrant settlers, 6
Christianity, 19
Christian Science Monitor
  2004 election results, comments on, 134
citizenship pattern, 9–12
  urban-rural classification, 14
civil service
  reforms, 195–209
Client Charter, 199
code of ethics
  for ministers, 203
Code on Takeovers and Mergers, 213
Commonwealth Association for Public Administration and Management (CAPAM), 200
Communists, 162
Companies Act, 212, 214
Comprehensive Economic Partnership with Japan, 268

Confucianism, 20
Constitution of Malaysia
  Article 160(2), 13
corporate governance, 212
  before financial crisis, 223
corporate Malaysia
  definition, 211, 212
  governance, 210–29
corruption
  eradication, 203–205

D
Daim Zainuddin, 79
dakwah movement, 27–31, 178
Darul Arqam, 178
Datuk Onn Jaafar, 63, 164
Democratic Action Party (DAP), 77,
  201
  2004 elections, 101
  losing stronghold in Kota Melaka, 89
"developmentalism", 103
diploma holders
  distribution, 241
DRB-HICOM, 76, 77

E
Eastern Industrial Corridor (EIC), 79,
  80
economy
  challenges facing, 260–74
  upswing, 140
education
  equality of opportunity, 243–47
  ethnic integration, 230–59
  ethnic minorities, 247–52
  Malay participation, 240
educational development, 232–37
  expenditure, 233
Education Ordinance, 249
Elections Act
  amendments, 118
Elections Committee (EC)
  poor monitoring standards, 117–19
  oversight, 149–51

Elections Offences Act, 141
electoral changes, 141, 145
electoral trends, 80–92
  2004, in, 92–96
electronic government training
  programme, 200
electronics industry, 266–67
enrolment
  college education, 235
  higher education, 233–34
ethnic composition, 12–18
  rate of increase, 14
ethnic integration in education, 220–59
ethnic minorities
  education, 247–52
ethnic preferential policies, 243–47
Eurocentrism
  Mahathir's disapproval, 49

F
Fadzil Noor, 28, 33
  death of, 109
Federal Territory of Kuala Lumpur, *see*
  Kuala Lumpur
Federation of Peninsular Malay Students
  Association (GPMS), 60
Fernandez, Joe
  assassination of, 112
financial crisis period, 59, 202
Five Power Defence Arrangements,
  279
foreign direct investment (FDI), 260
  inflows, 263
  quality important, 262
  rising competition, 262

G
gerrymandering, 141, 183–84
Global Corporate Governance Forum,
  226
globalisation, 230–59, 260–74
"good governance", 115
government-linked corporations,
  214–15

ex-CEOs tried for breach of trust,
   176
management, 224–26
significant role to play, 217
target of clean up, 221
gross domestic product
real growth, 261
Guidelines on the Regulation of
   Acquisition of Assets, Mergers
   and Takeovers of Companies and
   Businesses, 213

H
Harakah
   restricted circulation, 108, 139, 171
Harun Din, 94
Hassan Shukri, 110
higher education
   enrolment, 246
   ethnic participation, 237–42
High Level Finance Committee on
   Corporate Governance, 215, 219
Hinduism, 20
Hishamuddin Hussein Onn, 278
historical consciousness
   role in 2004 Elections, 161–65
hudud laws, 105
Human Rights Commission of
   Malaysia, 117

I
Ibn Khaldun, 39
Ibrahim Libya, 112
Independent Chinese Secondary
   Schools (ICSS), 249
Indians
   definition of, 12
Indonesia
   migration from, 4, 10
industries
   protected, 267
information technology, 200, 201
Institut Kajian Dasar (Institute of Policy
   Development), 31

Institute of Islamic Understanding
   Malaysia (IKIM), 32
An Inspiration for the Future of Islam,
   booklet entitled, 34
Internal Security Act (ISA), 102, 140
International Islamic University, 31
international migration
   inflow, 4
Iranian revolution
   alteration of Malaysia's political
   landscape, 30
Islam
   dominance of, 22
   progressive, *see* Islam *Hadhari*
Islam *Hadhari*, 26–43, 66, 102, 172,
   179, 180
   institutionalization, 40
   principles, 66, 67, 116
   theme of Abdullah Badawi's
   administration, 115
   values for globalization era, 40
Islamic challenges, 177–82
Islamic Development Foundation, 31
Islamic Insurance Company, 31
Islamic religious education, 250
   madrasah system, 251
   pondok system, 250
Islamic revivalism, 178
Islamic State Document (ISD), 107
   interpretation by non-Muslims, 109
Islamic Teachers College, 252
Islam *Madani*, 37, 39
ISO 9000 quality standard, 200

J
Jemaah Islamiah, 112

K
Kalimullah Hassan, 113
Kasitah Gadam, 218
Kelantan
   inability to enforce Syariah Criminal
   Code, 106
   PAS stronghold, 84

Kesler, C., 165, 166
Khazanah Nasional, 221
Khoo Boo Teik, 57
Kota Melaka, 89, 98
Kubang Pasu, 83
Kuala Lumpur, 8
  1969 riot, 164
Kuala Lumpur Composite Index, 225
Kuala Lumpur Stock Exchange, *see*
  Bursa Malaysia

L
Lee Hwok Aun, 62
Lim Kit Siang, 53, 95, 154, 201, 228
Ling Liong Sik, 61
Look East Policy, 49

M
Mahathir Mohamad, 73
  abandoning rural Malays, 168
  advisor to Proton and Petronas, 204
  bailing out companies, 76
  big businesses, rapid rise of, 76
  champion of *Melayu Baru*, 58
  declaration that Malaysia an Islamic
    state, 107
  favouritism, allegations of, 76
  legacy, 165–75
  Malay supporters, 166
  nationalistic, 47, 48
  period of rule, 74–78
  policies, 48
  progressive Islam, 35
  reforming bureaucracy, 207
Majlis Amanah Rakyat (MARA), 243
Malacca, 8
Malay
  medium of instruction, as, 231
Malay professional class
  sizeable number, 240
Malay society, 13
  bohsia culture, 75
  divorce rates, rise in, 75
  dominance, 24

global economy, impact of, 41
  lepak culture, 75
  restructuring, 50
Malayan Union, 161, 163
Malay nationalism
  challenge for ruling coalition, 64
Malay political culture
  over-honouring leaders, 114
Malaysiakini, 148
Malaysian Administrative,
    Modernization and Management
    Planning Unit (MAMPU), 201
Malaysian Airlines (MAS), 77
Malaysian Chinese Association (MCA),
    14, 159
  attempt to merge with Gerakan, 187
Malaysia Inc
  propaganda of, 48
Malaysian Indian Congress (MIC), 95
Malaysian Institute for Integrity, 176
Malaysian Institute of Corporate
    Governance, 213
Malaysian problem
  international significance, 64
manufacturing sector
  challenges, 263–67
  poor industrial linkages, 263
  productivity, low, 265, 266
  skilled labour, lack of, 265
  technological capabilities, poor, 265,
    266
MARA Institute of Technology, 243,
    244
MARA Junior Science Colleges, 244
Maznah Mohamad, 109
Melayu Baru
  central to concept of Bangsa
    Malaysia, 65
Memali incident, 112
Merdeka University, 168
minzu
  definition, 51
Mohamed Dzaiddin Abdullah, 205
Mujahidin Group of Malaysia, 111, 112

Muhammad Iqbal, 37
Multimedia Super Corridor (MSC), 58,
    200, 271–73
Muslims, 18
    Sunni, 20
Mustafa Ali, 110
migration, *see also* international
    migration

N
National Development Policy (NDP),
    25, 103
National Integrity Plan, 176, 218, 219,
    228
New Economic Policy (NEP), 25, 34,
    48, 62, 74
National Education Act, 237
National Institute Of Public
    Administration (INTAN), 200
National Justice Party (Keadilan), 36,
    see also Parti Keadilan Nasional
national primary schools, 247
National Registration Department,
    117
new public management paradigm, 195,
    197–98
Nik Aziz, 179
Nik Ramlah Nik Mahmood, 227
Nilam Puri Islamic Higher Education
    Foundation, 252
Non-Aligned Movement (NAM), 167,
    176
non-Bumiputera persons
    migration to Singapore, 2
non-Citizens
    highest concentration in Selangor, 10

O
opposition
    1990 to 2004, 80
    decline, 74
    disarray, 139–40
    support for, 84
orang asli, 13

Organization of Islamic Conferences
    (OIC), 167, 176
Other Bumiputera, 13

P
Pangkor Treaty, 161
Pan-Malaysia Islamic Party (PAS), 22,
    27, 75
    defeat in 2004 elections, 100–31
    emergence, 24
    fundamentalism-secularism binary,
        41
    inability to communicate to
        non-Muslim allies, 106, 107
    Islam *Hadhari*, opposition of, 181
    lawsuit against Petronas, 117
    legitimacy from *ummah*, 33
    maintaining share of Malay votes,
        154
    political agendum, 29
    reasons for defeat, 105–17
    response to election defeat, 117–19
    ulama leadership, rise in, 30
    violence and terrorism, linkage with,
        112
    Youth wing, *see* PAS Youth
pan-Malaysian Census
    first, 4, 9, 10
    second, 2
    third, 1
Parti Bangsa Dayak Sarawak (PBDS),
    159
Parti Islam SeMalaysia (PAS), *see* Pan
    Malaysia Islamic Party
Parti Keadilan Nasional (Keadilan), 75,
    77, 169
    2004 elections, defeat in, 100–31
    factional conflicts, 140
    leadership, 202
    leaders resigning, 120
    maintaining share of Malay votes,
        154
    members' reentry to UMNO, 102
    result of elections, 89, 91

Parti Rakyat Malaysia, 77
PAS Youth
    criticism of leadership, 111, 181
Pedra Branca, 276
Penang
    Chinese majority, 16
People's Action Party (PAP), 164
petroleum royalty payments
    withdrawal, 140
Petronas
    distribution of royalty blocked, 173
Philippines,
    migration from, 4, 10
police brutality
    eradiction, 205, 206
police force
    royal commission to review, 79
political change, 201, 202
political culture, 157–94
politicians
    sensitiveness to mention of ethnicity,
        63
politics
    race and religion, linked to, 24
polytechnics
    increasing numbers, 232
population
    causes, 2
    distribution, 6–9
    distribution by citizenship, 11, 15,
        21, 23
    distribution by ethnic group, 14, 15
    distribution by religion, 23
    growth, 1–6
    growth by region, 3
    growth caused by migration, 2
    natural increase, 2
    pattern of growth, 4
poverty
    issues concerning, 270–71
private colleges
    non-Malay enrolment, 253
Private Higher Education Institutions
    Act, 233

private tertiary institution, 233
privatisation, 198–200
professionals
    registered, membership of, 242
Pusat Islam, 31

R
Ratnam Committee, 247
Razak Report, 230, 248
reformasi movement, 36, 38
    decline in, 101–05
reinventing governance
    definition, 211, 212
religions pattern, 18–24
Renong Group, 76
Residential Secondary School system, 244
Ringgit peg
    dismantling, 269–70
Royal Commission for the Improvement
    of the Police Force, 79, 177, 205
rubber
    introduction as plantation crop, 6
rural areas
    growth of population, 5, 6
    marginalisation, 75
rural Bumiputera
    marginalization, 93
Rural and Industrial Development
    Authority (RIDA), 243

S
Sabah
    indigenous people, 16
    Kadazan Dusuns, 16
    minority tribes, 18
    Muruts, 17
Sarawak, 8
    Bidayahs, 17
    Melanaus, 17
    minority tribes, 18
    Ibans, 17, see also sea dayaks
    indigenous people, 16
    population, 3
Sarawak National party (SNAP), 159

sea dayaks, 17
Second Outline Perspective Plan
    (OPP2), 58
Securities Commission, 214, 219
Securities Commission Act, 212
Securities Commission's Policies and
    Guidelines on Issue/Offer of
    Securities, 213
Sedition Act, 190
Selangor, 10
September 11, 139
Seventh Malaysia Plan, 200
Severe Acute respiratory Syndrome
    (SARS), 277
short term capital withdrawal, 227
Singapore
    economic ties, 281–84
    land reclamation issue, 280
    military access to airspace, 280
    Minister Mentor's visit, 285
    outstanding issues with, 279–81
    Points of Agreement (POA), 275
    Presidential visit, 284–85
    relations with, 275–86
    self sufficiency in water, 276
Sisters in Islam, 42
Sixth Malaysia Plan (6MP), 58, 200
small and medium enterprises (SMEs)
    promotion, 78
social contract
    enshrined in
sovereignty
    Malay perception, 162
Suqui episode, 59, 60, 61, 190
Syariah Criminal Code
    inability of Kelantan government to
        enforce, 106
Syariah Criminal Offences Enactment
    Terengganu, passed by, 106

T

Tabligh movement, 178
Tan Sri Dr Mazlan Ahmad, 197
Taoism, 20

Telekom Malaysia, 77, 221
Tenaga Nasional Berhad, 221, 222
Tengku Razaleigh Hamzah, 57, 78
tertiary education
    distribution of enrolment by ethnic
        group, 239
    Malay participation, 252
    number of persons completing, 236
The Australian
    commenting on 2004 election results,
        134
trade strategy, 267–69
Trengganu
    diminished Malay support, 84
    farming, promotion of, 79
    passing Syariah Criminal Offences
        Enactment, 106
    petroleum royalty payments,
        withdrawal by government, 140
Tun Abdul Razak, 160
Tunku Abdul Rahman, 164
Tunku Abdul Rahman College, 59, 244

U

UMNO Team B, 78
United Malays' National Organization
    (UMNO), 22
    2004 election, 157–94
    Bumiputera support , loss of, 92
    developments favouring, 139–44
    dominant role in BN, 160
    Islamization, 31–33
    legitimacy from *ummah*, 33
    media, control of, 111
    managing a coalition, 182–87
    non-Malay support, 172
    performance in 2004 elections, 85,
        86
    Puteri wing, 188
    regaining lost ground, 85
    response to PAS's Islamic synthesis,
        29
    role in Malay consciousness, 163
    women candidates, fielding more, 94

universities
  increasing number, 232
University Tunku Abdul Rahman, 173
University of Malaya
  establishment of ABIM, 28
urban areas
  definition, 5
  growth of population, 5, 6
Vision 2020, 33–38, 50, 166, 198, 232
  abstract from speech, 68, 69, 232
Vision Islam, 33–38
  progressiveness in, 35, 36

W
Wan Azizah, 91, 97, 202
West Malaysia
  Malays, domination by, 16
women candidates in elections
  UMNO fielding more, 94
Wong Kok Keong
  study of mainstream media coverage
    of elections, 119

Y
Yuan
  floating, 269